THE OFFICIAL® PRICE GUIDE TO

SCIENCE FICTION AND FANTASY COLLECTIBLES

DON and MAGGIE THOMPSON

Third Edition

House of Collectibles • New York

Important Notice. All of the information, including valuations, in this book has been compiled from the most reliable sources, and every effort has been made to eliminate errors and questionable data. Nevertheless, the possibility of error, in a work of such immense scope, always exists. The publisher will not be held responsible for losses which may occur in the purchase, sale, or other transaction of items because of information contained herein. Readers who feel they have discovered errors are invited to *write* and inform us, so they may be corrected in subsequent editions. Those seeking further information on the topics covered in this book are advised to refer to the complete line of *Official Price Guides* published by the House of Collectibles.

© 1989 Random House, Inc.

All rights reserved under International and Pan-American Copyright Conventions.

Published by: The House of Collectibles
201 East 50th Street
New York, New York 10022

Distributed by Ballantine Books, a division of Random House, Inc., New York and simultaneously in Canada by Random House of Canada Limited, Toronto.

Manufactured in the United States of America

Library of Congress Catalog Card Number: 84-647218

ISBN: 0-876-37754-1

Third edition: June 1989

10 9 8 7 6 5 4 3 2 1

To Densie Emerson, Betsy Curtis, Valerie Thompson, and Steve Thompson, because

> our mothers *didn't* throw ours away
> and

our children have lived among our clutter without being intolerant of it,

> and because
> we love you all.

And to Basil and Margaret Wells, who brought us together and made everything else possible.

Table of Contents

Acknowledgments   *viii*

Introduction   *3*
   An Overview of This Guide   *3*
   Using This Guide   *5*

Getting to Know Science Fiction and Fantasy   *7*
   Types of Stories   *7*
   Factual Magazines   *10*
   Fiction Magazines and Books   *11*

Collecting Science Fiction and Fantasy   *12*
   What You Can Collect   *12*
   Where You Can Collect   *15*
   Collecting Artwork   *17*
   Make a Want List   *19*
   Storing Your Collection   *20*
   Selling What You Own   *21*

Evaluating Science-Fiction and Fantasy Collectibles   *23*
   Grading   *23*
   Dust Jackets   *25*
   Defects   *26*
   Bonuses   *29*

History of the Field   *32*

The Market   *40*

Building and Identifying a Collection   42

    Collecting by Magazine   *42*
    Collecting by Author   *43*
    Collecting by Artist   *43*
    Building a Collection for Investment   *43*
    Building a Collection for Pleasure   *44*
    However You Build a Collection   *45*
    Identifying Collectibles   *45*

Fantasy and Science-Fiction Names   46

List of Color Plates   *(following p. 246)*

American Fiction Magazines   273

British Fiction Magazines   374

Science Fiction and Fantasy in Comic Books   390

Science-Fiction and Fantasy Drama   394

    Doctor Who   *395*
    Doctor Who Magazine   *404*
    Star Trek   *404*
    Star Trek Books   *409*
    Star Wars   *413*
    U.N.C.L.E.   *414*

Filksongs and Other Recordings   417

    Singers on Videotape   *418*
    Singers on Records   *419*
    Singers on Audio Tape   *419*
    Convention and Anthology Recordings on Tape   *425*
    Spoken Word   *428*

Collecting the Best   432

    Hugo Awards   *432*
    Nebula Awards   *445*
    World Fantasy Awards   *450*
    Collections of the Best   *454*

You Can't Have It All 462

Science-Fiction and Fantasy Glossary 464

Non-Fiction/Reference Material 467

Afterword 470

Index 473

Acknowledgments

We appreciate the help many, many people offered us in the formation of this book, of whom there are too many to list. We thank everyone who offered help and support, and single out: Robert Coulson, who provided detailed information every time we asked; Debra Daemmrich, who came through; Gene DeWeese, who did the same; Larry Frank, our favorite skilled photographer; Frank Kelly Freas, whose cooperation and support was spontaneous and immediate; Joe Bell of Soft Books who supplied information gleaned from years of experience; Hank Luttrell of 20th Century Books, an old friend whose advice is invaluable; John Koenig, who is a joy to work with; Robert Madle, whose catalog has acted as more than one retailer's price guide and who willingly shared his thoughts with us; Jon Warren, whose ACEX gives a picture of the field; and Robert Weinberg, who has been selfless in his friendly sharing of information and guidance.

We appreciate and welcome, in advance, input from the legion of fans and collectors who make up the science fiction and fantasy collecting and creative world. It's a community dedicated to sharing information and to nit-picking any published research in the field. We hope they'll make the *next* edition of this work an even more helpful identification and pricing guide.

Of course, we especially appreciate the constant input, guidance, and aid of Dorothy Harris, who nagged us into doing the book we needed to help our own collecting. We tried to talk her into hiring someone *else* to do the job, since we have never needed more pastimes to fill our empty hours, but she talked us into doing it instead. Thank you for your confidence, Dottie—and your faith.

SCIENCE FICTION AND FANTASY COLLECTIBLES

Introduction

The science-fiction or fantasy collector usually begins on a small scale, often in response to an event. He is delighted by a *Star Trek* production. She buys a comic book with an adaptation of a Harlan Ellison story. He reads a Ray Bradbury story in a high-school class and wants to read more. She has a friend who attends a science fiction convention and takes her along. He sees a science-fiction movie and decides to read the book.

Fascination with fantasy and science fiction grows out of a love of extrapolation. What if? What if you could stop time? What if you could read minds? What if you could eat whatever you wanted and never gain weight? What if you could fly, or walk through walls, or never grow old, or play baseball in space, or. . . ?

However fantasy or science-fiction fans began to enjoy thinking "what if?", they became enchanted by the world of the possible and wanted to get more of it. In so doing, they became science-fiction or fantasy fans.

This volume is designed to guide the novice in the field and to be a handbook for the more experienced collector. If you've just discovered Theodore Sturgeon and want to know what else he has written— or if you have picked up five issues of *Planet Stories* and want to know exactly how many more you'll have to locate to complete your collection—this guide offers tips and information. In this respect, the book serves primarily as an identification guide. Where possible, of course, we have also provided a guide to prices collectors can expect to pay. The focus of this edition, however, is to provide a list of what collectors are hunting for in science fiction and fantasy.

AN OVERVIEW OF THIS GUIDE

- This is *primarily* an identification guide to American fantasy and science-fiction collectibles designed for adults. The listing for a book which had its first edition in Britain will probably only indicate American editions. The marvelous, award-winning Prydain series by Lloyd Alexander is delightful; Lewis Carroll's Alice and Sylvie and Bruno volumes have caught the fancies of generations of readers. This guide will not devote copious space to such material.

- There will be some coverage of amateur and self-published material; decades of limited-edition publications by fans are traditional in the field. Again, there is so much (and much of what there is would be impossible for many people to come by, thanks to print runs of fewer than 100 copies in many cases) that this guide's coverage will do little more than touch on the existence of this aspect of the field.

- The prices suggested in this guide are those you can expect to *pay* a retailer in the field. They are *not* the prices you can expect to get if you attempt to sell items to that same retailer. Remember, a science-fiction shop has to cover such expenses as maintenance, employee payments, storage, and other overhead—and still needs to make a profit to survive. Unless you are selling an item of high quality, in perfect condition, and in high intense demand, you may be offered only 20%–30% of the prices in this guide.

- The prices in this guide are, *unless otherwise noted*, those prices that retailers are likely to charge for an item in "good" condition. Better condition will mean a higher price. Worse condition will mean a lower price. See the section on "Grading" for more information.

- You will note the use of the specific term "science fiction" in this guide; collectors who entered the field through an affection for science fiction in films and television often refer to the field as "sci-fi," a term coined by Forrest J. Ackerman, a long-time fan and long-time editor of the magazine *Famous Monsters of Filmland*. Many science-fiction fans—especially those devoted to book and magazine science fiction—avoid use of the word or limit its use to poorly made, sensationalistic science fiction movies and TV shows. Others use the term SF. For clarity's sake, we opt for "science fiction."

- There are affiliated fields in which items associated with science fiction and fantasy are produced: sound recordings, comic books, toys, videotapes, and the like. Many of these fields have their own collecting traditions, rules, and prices. In some cases, we have identified a *nonexhaustive* sampling of the material available and in some cases we have recommended other reference materials. For example, there are many science-fiction comic books; *Superman* has a science-fictional premise and was created by science-fiction fans Jerry Siegel and Joe Shuster. We recommend Robert M. Overstreet's *Official Overstreet Comic Book Price Guide* (from House of Collectibles) for science-fiction fans who want exhaustive coverage of the comic-book world. Our guide will tend to focus on the cases in which known, identifiable science-fiction writers produced comic-book material.

We consider robot toys, for example, to be more importantly *toys* and not even necessarily of interest to the hard-core science-fiction collector. Collectors who want more information on that field can begin by checking the "Battery-Operated Toys" section in *The Official Price Guide to Collectible Toys*.

Collectors seeking listings of *Star Trek* and *Star Wars* memorabilia will find that House of Collectibles devoted an entire volume to that subject, too.

• Collections of fiction will probably develop according to the collector's taste. We have tried to give an impression of the field's overall standards and interests, but that impression is necessarily filtered through our own. For an indication of tastes of the times, see the chapter "Collecting the Best."

USING THIS GUIDE

We suggest the following alternative methods of using this guide:

• If you have read and enjoyed the work of a particular author, you can use the "Names" chapter to find what other material may be available.

• If you have scattered issues of an assortment of science-fiction or fantasy magazines, you can use the "Magazines" chapters to find out how many issues will be required to complete your collection.

• If you enjoy folk music and science fiction or fantasy, you can use the "Filksongs and Other Recordings" chapter to find so-called "filksongs"—songs composed and performed by fans who enjoy linking music and the worlds of "what if." Performances vary from amateur to professional; lyrics are often outstanding.

• If you're interested in the field but want to know more about its scope, use the "Best" chapter to begin a core collection. Books that win national awards for their quality are almost invariably kept in print, have had many thousands of copies produced over the years, and offer a rewarding place to start in the field.

• Another way to learn about the field quickly is to read the magazines currently in bookshops and newsstands. Check our chapters on "Magazines."

• You'll also find information on the field in our "Getting to Know Science Fiction and Fantasy."

• You can even use this book as a checklist. As collectors, we grieve every time a book is defaced—but we're going to use a copy for our own checklist of what we have. We'll cross out items as we acquire them (and circle items we have but intend to replace with better-condition copies). The book itself will serve as our want list; we may even highlight entries we most want to buy.

You'll quickly develop your own system of collecting; we hope this volume helps you to do it.

Getting to Know
Science Fiction and Fantasy

Chances are more than excellent that anyone picking up this guide is doing so because he or she is interested in collecting fantasy or science fiction. Chances are good that many people looking at such a volume, however, know science fiction or fantasy from a relatively limited viewpoint.

Some science-fiction and fantasy fans know little more than what they have learned from following *Star Trek* or *Doctor Who* or *The Lord of the Rings*. That is not to say that each is not an admirable example of its type of material; it is simply to say that science fiction and fantasy are fields so broad that each example is only a tiny fraction of the overall body of work that the collector may enjoy.

TYPES OF STORIES

One of the reasons for the length of the title of this book is that our work—and much of the work created in the field—is devoted to *both* science fiction and fantasy. Neither takes place in "the real world." But science fiction deals with things that, given particular evolution of invention or sociology (or developments elsewhere in the universe), *could happen*. Fantasy does not necessarily limit itself to what *could* happen; it can postulate the impossible, ask "what if?", and resolve the question.

In some cases, what is considered "science fiction" and "fantasy" are simply what people agree to call "science fiction" and "fantasy" when they point to them. Stories of talking dogs and cats can be considered fables by someone discussing Aesop but fantasy when they appear in a novel by George Orwell. Another person might say stories in which dogs communicate as equals with humans are *always* fantasy—but Harlan Ellison's "A Boy and His Dog" offers a view of the concept most readers would consider science fictional.

In alphabetical order—and with no attempt to be exhaustive—we suggest the following as among the types of stories deemed typical of science fiction and fantasy. They're old hat and easily accepted as basic postulates by fans, who may easily slip into a concept as familiar as a pair of Levis. The concepts may confuse new readers to the point at which a story becomes incomprehensible for them.

Alternate Universes

What if Hitler had won World War II? What if the South had won the war between the states? Many stories have been set in alternate worlds, and Philip K. Dick and Keith Laumer are among writers who have used the concept extensively.

Elves, Gnomes, Fairies, and Assorted Other Little People

These come to us from folklore and appear in everything from children's stories to swashbuckling adventure tales, up to and including Mr. O'Malley, the fairy godfather in Crockett Johnson's comic strip *Barnaby*.

Holocaust

Nuclear annihilation—or near-annihilation—of humanity is a common theme in today's science fiction, as is fiction devoted to survivors of near-annihilation. Sometimes the disaster comes from other causes, like the plague in Stephen King's *The Stand*. Entire bodies of work use a post-holocaust world as the environment for their extrapolation. Such movies as the *Mad Max* series, such comics as the *Judge Dredd* stories, and such books as Andre Norton's *Starman's Son* explore these postulated worlds.

Invisibility

The desire to see unseen is common and has produced a number of stories, most famous of which is H. G. Wells' *The Invisible Man*.

Lost Civilizations

This genre is not often seen in stories today, but it was popular earlier in the century. Whether the civilization is lost in the jungle, hidden in the center of the earth, or submerged in the ocean, the discovery of a society cut off from the rest of the world was grist for the mill of such writers as H. G. Wells and Edgar Rice Burroughs.

Myth

There are fantasies involving Greek gods, a la Thorne Smith's *Night Life of the Gods*. Many writers have written books explaining the ancient myths in science-fictional terms—the "gods" were extraterrestrials, sorcerers actually had extra-sensory powers, and the like.

Space Exploration

This is the basic fabric of what the public today thinks of as science fiction. It has furnished the concepts for everything from Isaac Asimov's *Foundation* series to the black comedy film *Dark Star*.

Telepathy

Sometimes redundantly referred to as "mental telepathy"—what other kind of telepathy could there be?—the ability to read minds or communicate mentally has produced some thought-provoking stories. One of the classics of this literature is A. E. van Vogt's *Slan*. Another is Alfred Bester's *The Demolished Man,* which involves an ingenious method of getting away with murder in a society of telepaths.

Time Travel

So far as science knows, time travel is, flatly, impossible. Stories of people from the future who visit the present and stories of people from the present who visit the future at any speed faster than one second per second (the speed at which we all live)—these are time-travel stories. Properly speaking, they are fantasies; by all the rules of science, they cannot happen. But usage has made them science fiction, and one of the earliest usages (strictly in a fantasy context) is in Charles Dickens' *A Christmas Carol*. Later prominent works are H. G. Wells' *The Time Machine* and Robert Silverberg's *Up the Line,* but there are many excellent, thought-provoking works of fiction on the topic.

Vampires

The most famous vampire is Bram Stoker's *Dracula*. Do we have to say more about the undead who survive by drinking the blood of their victims?

Werewolves

People who turn into wolves are called "werewolves." People who turn into other animals also fall into this fantasy category. One of the best stories in the field is Anthony Boucher's "The Compleat Werewolf," but we're also fond of Ron Goulart's "Please Stand By," in which a character turns into an elephant on national holidays. The classic in the field is probably Guy Endore's *Werewolf of Paris,* which, unlike the other examples cited, is *not* a humorous treatment.

You get the idea. Reading one of any of the "best of the year" anthologies in either science fiction or fantasy will demonstrate many more.

FACTUAL MAGAZINES

There are three publications which you should check when you decide to collect science fiction and fantasy.

• The first is *Locus*. Subtitled "the newspaper of the science fiction field," that is exactly what it is. Published monthly, *Locus* has won a dozen Hugos as "best of the year." It has grown from an amateur newsletter to a slick, professional publication which keeps the science-fiction world in touch with itself (no mean feat). It is a must for the serious science fiction—*and* fantasy—collector.

Its December 1987 issue was #323, and its coverage of the field includes listings of virtually every science-fiction and fantasy book and magazine as they are published. The letters column is filled with communications from professionals in the field; feature articles on professionals are filled with fascinating information; analyses of the field abound. It carries news, reviews, and commentary, as well as advertisements for upcoming publications. Its annual industry survey and its annual readers' poll provide valuable views of the field; more fans vote in its awards poll than vote on the Hugo awards. It carries some ads—mostly classified ads—for mail-order suppliers of current and back-issue books and magazines, as well as for specialty science fiction and fantasy shops.

If you collect fantasy or science fiction, you should consider a subscription. Send a self-addressed, stamped envelope to Locus Publications, 34 Ridgewood Lane, Oakland, California 94611, and ask for information.

- The second is *Science Fiction Chronicle*. Subtitled "the monthly science fiction and fantasy newsmagazine," that is exactly what it is. Slimmer than *Locus,* it provides a valuable additional view of the field. Its December 1987 issue was #99. It also carries news, reviews, and commentary—and, yes, advertisements for upcoming publications.

 It will round out your view of the field, and we make a point of getting it as well as *Locus* each month. For information, send a self-addressed, stamped envelope to Science Fiction Chronicle, Algol Press, P.O. Box 2730, Brooklyn, New York 11202.

- The third is (and here we cough with some embarrassment) *Comics Buyer's Guide*. The reason for our slight hesitation is that we edit this weekly newspaper, and are, therefore, biased.

 Make no mistake—*Comics Buyer's Guide* is aimed at people in the comic-book field. Our audience is composed of comic-book professionals and collectors, and the bulk of our content is oriented along those lines. But there is a heavy science-fictional content to many comics, and more than 40% of our readers said, when polled, that they considered themselves science-fiction collectors.

 As a result, we try to carry some news, reviews, and commentary on the science fiction field, including a monthly column in which Robert Coulson reviews the month's science-fiction magazines. There are often a number of advertisements for science-fiction and fantasy items in *Comics Buyer's Guide*. For information, send a self-addressed, stamped envelope to *Comics Buyer's Guide,* Dept. BEF, 700 East State Street, Iola, Wisconsin 54990.

FICTION MAGAZINES AND BOOKS

The other way to get to know the field is to begin by collecting current books and magazines and working back from them. You'll find more suggestions along these lines later in this volume, in the chapter on "American Fiction Magazines."

Collecting Science Fiction and Fantasy

You can collect something just by acquiring a stack of it. But there are those who would say that that would be an accumulation, not a collection—that a collection would involve more systematic acquisition and storage. Assuming you would prefer some method in your collecting mania, we offer some suggestions.

WHAT YOU CAN COLLECT

You can pick your field of interest by limiting your purchases in some way: "I only buy magazines." "I'm not interested in science fiction written before men landed on the moon." "I like books written by people connected with *Star Trek*." "I only want to spend money on original art."

Of course, our enthusiams lead us to suggest that collectors who limit themselves *too* severely are missing a lot of wonderful possibilities. Given that caution, you can, of course, collect in any of the following ways:

• Everything associated with a favorite work. If you collect *Doctor Who* memorabilia, you can even go so far as to collect jelly babies, a candy especially favored by the fourth incarnation of The Doctor. That's not to mention Avon earrings shaped like question marks, dolls and role-playing-game models, toy talking Daleks (cyborg monsters on the BBC-TV serial), pre-recorded videotapes and records—and, of course, the novelizations and associated books. You can even learn to knit and prepare a fourteen-foot scarf (another trademark of the fourth Doctor).

• Everything by a favorite creator. You can collect all the paperbacks with Frank Frazetta covers, buy original Frank Frazetta art, and pay big bucks for old comics with Frazetta artwork. This will even lead you out of the realm of science fiction and into such areas as motion-picture poster collecting.

* Everything on a similar theme. If alternate-worlds stories strike your fancy, there are enough of them to keep you reading for some time. You'd be well advised in this case to find a reference work on the field (the out-of-print but excellent *The Science Fiction Encyclopedia,* edited by Peter Nicholls [1979], is one such) and compose a want list based on the entries for "alternate worlds" and "parallel worlds." Keep an eye, too, on the details of current books as listed in *Locus* and *Science Fiction Chronicle.*

* All issues of a favorite magazine. That's simple enough; just look at the magazine listings in this book. Every issue published through December 1987 should be there—we *really* tried to make this list complete and comprehensive. If you want a complete collection of *Cosmos* (either one), it shouldn't be too expensive, or even too complicated, to purchase. If, on the other hand, you've got your heart set on a complete collection of *Amazing Stories* or *Weird Tales,*

Cosmos Science Fiction and Fantasy, September 1953, about 5¼″ × 7¼″; cover not credited. This was the first issue. Copyright 1953 by Star Publications, Inc.

Cosmos Science Fiction and Fantasy, November 1953, about 5¼″ × 7¼″; cover by B. Safran. Copyright 1953 by Star Publications, Inc.

Cosmos Science Fiction and Fantasy, March 1954, about 5¼″ × 7¼″; cover by B. Safran. Copyright 1954 by Star Publications, Inc.

Cosmos Science Fiction and Fantasy, July 1954, about 5¼″ × 7¼″; cover by B. Safran. This was the last issue. Copyright 1954 by Star Publications, Inc.

it's going to take you a while and get pretty pricey, even at the relatively low prices for magazines in today's market.

WHERE YOU CAN COLLECT

Look in the yellow pages of telephone books of your own community and those of nearby metropolitan areas. Listings for bookstores and similar specialty shops will be under "bookstores," "used bookstores," and "periodicals." Be sure to check all three—and visit all the shops on the list. Comics shops, for example, often carry science fiction as a sideline or maintain a second-hand paperback rack as an adjunct to their main product line.

If you are really devoted to chasing down every last avenue of used books, you may even find yourself visiting garage sales and thrift shops in the quest. This will not usually be time-effective if you are *only* interested in science-fiction and fantasy collectibles. In a decade and a half of scavenging garage sales, for example, Maggie has struck science fiction and fantasy in quantity only a couple of times. On the other hand, college communities are usually more promising hunting grounds for such searches. (You might even post an offer to buy on appropriate collegiate bulletin boards.) We've had much better luck in used bookstores.

The dream of most science-fiction and fantasy collectors is having a science-fiction specialty shop in a nearby location. There are some outstanding shops around America, staffed by experts in the field. They offer current material and back stock, they can recommend other items you might like, and they're all too rare, even in this age of specialization. If you have one nearby, treasure it, patronize it, and keep it going by being a good customer.

You may find that even a less specialized bookshop—especially one that also carries used books—will be willing to help you maintain your collection if you express continuing interest in a particular type of material. Even the Waldenbooks chain offers a newsletter devoted to science fiction, with discounts on specified science-fiction material. If you get to know the staff of your area bookstores and buy certain sorts of items regularly, you may lead them to increase the volume of that sort of material they stock.

In fact, wherever you bought this book would almost certainly be a good starting place for building your collection.

As you begin your search for books, don't forget *Books in Print*. This multi-volume set is a standard in most libraries; it simply lists all the books technically in print and available for ordering, along with their prices. If you want every book Anthony Boucher ever wrote, you won't find many in *Books in Print*. If you want every *Dune* novel by Frank Herbert, you can just place your order at your local bookstore—assuming it doesn't have all of them in stock. You'll be able to buy every one quite easily. Availability really varies sharply from author to author (and artist to artist). Some books remain constantly in print; others have the life expectancy of mayflies.

The books listed in *Books in Print* will, you understand, be the most recent editions of books; *BiP* will not be much help in tracking down first editions or out-of-print books. The book also is *not* a reliable guide to a book's first appearance in book form—it lists the date of the most recent edition.

You can also collect at science-fiction conventions, large and small. At most, you will have to pay a membership fee to get into a science-fiction convention, but once in you'll get a chance to mingle with celebrities and/or experts in the field—and to buy collectibles in what often is (fondly) referred to as ''The Hucksters' Room.''

While many conventions in collectibles fields grew out of the desire to provide a location for buying and selling, science-fiction conventions began with the desire of fans and professionals to get together and exchange ideas. Many fantasy and science-fiction conventions are attended by old friends whose chief aim is to get together with other old friends for the equivalent of a weekend party. "Vile hucksters" at early conventions were jovially sneered at and needled. The definition under "Huckster" in the fanzine dictionary *Fancyclopedia II* (copyright 1959 by Richard H. Eney) was "A person sufficiently . . . degraded to try and make money from stf." ("Stf" is an archaic abbreviation for "science fiction"; it is a condensation of Hugo Gernsback's early term "scientifiction.")

Actually, prices are usually relatively low at convention tables, and most people selling there are fans who have known and loved the field for decades. *Locus, Science Fiction Chronicle,* and *Comics Buyer's Guide* carry convention information.

Finally, a way to shop throughout America is to deal with mail-order firms. Many of these, too, are run by long-time fans and specialists. Of special help in the preparation of this volume were such specialists as: Robert A. Madle, 4406 Bestoy Drive, Rockville, Maryland 20853; Joe Bell, Soft Books, 89 Marion Street, Toronto, Ontario M6R 1E6 Canada; and Robert and Phyllis Weinberg, Weinberg Books, P.O. Box 423, Oak Forest, Illinois 60452. You will find listings of other mail-order firms in *Locus, Science Fiction Chronicle,* and *Comics Buyer's Guide.*

One other source of collectibles is auction houses. Two which carry a noticeable percentage of science-fiction and fantasy collectibles are American Collectibles Exchange, 4 Shingle Road, Chattanooga, Tennessee 37409 and Hake's Americana & Collectibles, P.O. Box 1444, York, Pennsylvania 17405. Send a self-addressed, stamped envelope to both and ask for information on receiving their auction catalogs.

COLLECTING ARTWORK

One of the most attractive areas of science-fiction and fantasy collecting is artwork. Your collection can function simultaneously as interior decorating, because much of what you collect can be mounted for display.

You can collect original art and limited-edition prints and cheaper, large-run posters. You can also collect science-fiction and fantasy movie posters (although framing and hanging movie posters is an expensive prospect, because of the size of what you will frame). You may opt to measure your largest poster and purchase a frame designed to display it, then rotate movie posters in the frame from month to month.

Original artwork can be as simple as a quick sketch done with a felt-tip marker (be aware that these may not last—the ink may fade or bleed in a few years) or as complex as a full, detailed oil painting. In the mid-range come finished black-and-white works (often used as interior illustrations in magazines and books), color roughs (preliminary, unfinished paintings often used as indications of cover possibilities for editors to pick from), and simple finished paintings.

There has been a great volume of professional artwork produced over the years in the field; if it had all survived, there would be enough originals of published artwork to provide each fan with a sample. However, a tragic number of paintings and drawings from the twenties through the fifties were destroyed. In at least one case, a publisher called in an art appraiser to evaluate the stock of paintings and black-and-white art that was ''worth retaining''—and threw out the rest.

At world science-fiction conventions up through the fifties, many black-and-white magazine illustrations, donated by publishers, were simply jumbled on ''sketch tables'' and sold for less than $10.00 each. (In those cases, at least, most purchasers were collectors; much of the artwork was saved from destruction and placed in the hands of people almost certain to preserve the material.) Today, you can find displays of original art (including fine work by amateurs who display in ''fan art shows'') at conventions. Studying such work is one of the best ways to learn what *you* are interested in collecting and what prices go with what items.

If your interests lie in purchasing original art from earlier eras (or in choosing from the widest possible variety of available work), you'll want to contact specialists in original art. Robert Weinberg, Weinberg Books, P.O. Box 423, Oak Forest, Illinois 60452, is one of the foremost professionals who buys and sells original science-fiction and fantasy art. Russ Cochran, P.O. Box 469, West Plains, Missouri 65775, also specializes in art, especially comic-book and comic-strip art. You can send each a self-addressed, stamped envelope and ask how to get copies of their listings of available material.

These are *not* the only dealers in the art field. There are a few art galleries which specialize in fantasy and science-fiction work; some specialty bookstores also offer associated art.

Paintings and drawings are not the only forms of art you can collect; there are sculptors in the field, and science-fiction and fantasy jewelry is available. (Anne McCaffrey once showed us a beautiful silver dragon ring so elaborate she could only wear it on occasions when she was not working with her hands.)

Advertisements from retailers who handle such material can be found in collector publications, and professional artists who display work at conventions often have additional work available for private sale. Many artists will accept commissions for work designed for the customer.

MAKE A WANT LIST

You may already have a want list; you almost certainly do if you've been buying books and magazines for any length of time. Whatever the case, make a want list. That is, simply, a list of items you want to buy.

Making a want list is not hard; what *is* hard is not having one and trying to remember every book and magazine you want to buy (and what ones you already have) when you're at a convention four hundred miles away from home.

And make a duplicate want list. That's not hard, either; what *is* hard is trying to *re*create a want list when your only copy gets lost at that convention four hundred miles away from home. And, yes, both things have happened to us. Of course, we learn the hard way—but we *do* learn.

As we've already noted, we plan to use a copy of this book as a want list, but we will also maintain a more general want list because we collect a lot more than science fiction and fantasy. You'll probably want to do the same.

You may also want to buy items cheaply in good condition (or even poorer) and replace them by buying better copies as you find them. In that case, you should work out a code (underlining or circling or marking in some other form) that indicates when you have a copy but need a replacement.

STORING YOUR COLLECTION

After moving a number of times and storing boxes of stuff a number of times, we have the following suggestions:

However you store your collection—whether on shelves like books or in boxes or filing cabinets—plastic-bag everything that you consider a collectible book or magazine.

You *can* use plastic food storage bags on a temporary basis (but keep an eye on them to be sure the bags do not begin to age, discolor, or otherwise change; if they do, replace them).

You'll be better off ordering special collectibles storage bags. These have been standard collecting equipment in the comic-book field for some time, and we are absolutely sold on their usefulness. We have had unprotected books and magazines wrinkle and scuff and even mildew or stick together. We have had *no* such problems with material we have bagged.

We have known more than one friend to suffer losses from severe water damage—from a broken pipe or from actual flooding. One who had such severe flooding that she had to be evacuated from her town by helicopter commented about her collectibles, "Plastic bags were more help than insurance." In case of flooding like that, there may be some damage; but there will be less than there would have been without bags. Bag those books!

You'll find a number of excellent sources for collectibles bags. We suggest the following:

Bags Unlimited, 53 Canal Street, Dept. C, Rochester, New York 14608

Bill Cole Enterprises, Inc., P.O. Box 60, Dept. 778, Randolph, Massachusetts 02368

Lee Tennant Enterprises, Inc., 6963 West 111th Street, P.O. Box 296, Worth, Illinois 60482

Moondog's, 301 Lively Boulevard, Elk Grove Village, Illinois 60007

Nevada Bags, 563 North Pine Street, Nevada City, California 95959

All of these carry bags in sizes appropriate for comic books; that size will also hold many sizes of books. Some companies, including Bags Unlimited, carry a wide variety of bag sizes, some designed to hold pulp magazines, some for digest magazines, and some for paperback books. Measure the cover dimensions of what you want to bag, be sure to allow space for the thickness of the books or magazines, and figure how many bags you'll need.

Send a self-addressed, stamped envelope with a request for information on the cost of the supplies you are interested in buying.

You may also find convenient the magazine holders called "Magafiles." They are so designed as to hold a number of magazines or books in convenient small cardboard boxes; the boxes are designed to hold one or several items upright, without spine damage from bending. They come in about a dozen sizes. Write to The Magafile Company, P.O. Box 66, 606 South Maple, Vandalia, Missouri 63382, for explanatory information and a measuring graph you'll need when you order.

If your collection includes a number of pieces of original art, you can handle, store, and display them as you would any other piece of original art. Avoid long-term exposure of artwork to strong light, including sunlight.

SELLING WHAT YOU OWN

You will almost certainly *not* get the prices we have listed in this guide when you sell items from your collection—not unless you go into business for yourself, selling as a retailer to customers.

If you want to dispose of many items at once, the fastest, most simple way to do it probably is to locate a nearby science-fiction specialty store and offer your collection as a lot to the owner, if you're lucky enough to have such a shop nearby. The owner will *not* offer you the prices he will put on the items, of course; he couldn't survive as a businessman if he did.

An alternative is to sell the collection by mail to a mail-order retailer. In this case, be sure to "grade conservatively" when you describe each item. You'll need to prepare a list like the one the dealer uses to describe what he sells:

"*Astounding* 1959 Jan cover loose otherwise good"
"*F&SF* 1963 Aug tape on spine"
"Roger Zelazny *Eye of Cat* Book Club mint with mint dj"

And so on. (Practically, when you have a number of recent digest magazines, you can probably lump most of them together and say something like, "45 digest magazines in at least good condition from

1975–1983.'' Be sure to specify if you have any high-demand items; see our magazine list.)

Once you've got such a list, you may decide to sell the items yourself. You could set prices, photocopy the list, and take small ads in collector publications offering to send the list to anyone sending the postage. (Don't forget to weigh the list in an envelope; you may find your list is so long that it costs more than a dollar to mail; you'll want to specify how much postage is needed.) You could offer to sell the collection as a lot the same way.

If you live in an area with many mall shows and conventions—and one with enough readers to support a number of bookstores—you might rent a table at a mall show or convention and sell your stock there. We paid our way to many small science-fiction conventions by setting up a table with our unwanted items and duplicates and selling them at half cover price (minimum 25¢ per item). Sometimes, at the convention's end we sold the remainder of our ''stock'' for a lump sum to one of the other dealers; sometimes, we took it home and saved it for the next convention.

If you have exceptional items for sale—limited-edition books, original art, and the like—you should consider a display advertisement in one of the collector publications. (One pulp dealer took a full-page ad in *Comics Buyer's Guide* some years ago and listed a large number of hard-to-find pulps at excellent prices; he sold out the entire stock in less than two weeks.)

Another possibility is to turn the entire collection, or the premium items, over to an auction house. Such an organization will keep a percentage of the final amount realized from the sale as its fee for getting the best possible price on each item.

Information on the Hake's Americana & Collectibles and ACEX auction houses appears earlier in this chapter. To see whether you would benefit from such an arrangement, send a self-addressed, stamped envelope and request information from either, or both.

Evaluating Science-Fiction and Fantasy Collectibles

GRADING

Grading in such fields as comic-book collecting has reached an established point of agreed-upon standards. A missing chunk of paper from a comic book automatically means it cannot be in better than "fair" condition, as far as most comic-book collectors are concerned.

Science-fiction collecting has not yet become so cut-and-dried in its assessment of condition. Pulp magazines virtually shed bits of themselves over the years, due to untrimmed pages and covers, the effects that reading the magazine have on the spine, and the unstable nature of the pulp paper itself. There is bound, for example, to be some bending of the edges of pulp magazine covers; irregular edges of the underlying pages were bound to deform the cover stock.

Grading is absolutely dependent on the total item being graded; "mint except for chunks missing from cover" is *not* mint. If restored, the item must be noted as such and priced at a lower price than if in that condition unrestored.

In most of the pricing information in our identification guide, you will find we have chosen to list the price you can expect to pay for the item in "good" condition. That is the *minimum* condition considered to be of "collectible" quality. Every grade above that will increase the usual asking price of the item.

The following are general guidelines to condition and an indication of the percentage of the "good" condition price each may bring in the market:

Mint

This condition is as good as it gets. The publication should look as good as you would find it if you bought it new today. It is entirely undamaged, though covers and untrimmed pages of pulps may be slightly bent at the edges. Books have their dust jackets complete and undamaged. There is no tape. There can be no more than the slightest damage of the spine. Magazines may have pencilled arrival dates on the cover and slight color fading. A "mint" copy will go for 400% of the prices in this guide.

Fine

This is a very nice looking item. It may have been read more than once, but there are no creases or writing (other than arrival date) on the cover. There may be flaking of the spine and/or around the cover or dust jacket of a book, but the cover is tight. There is no tape. There may be some page darkening. It would ordinarily bring 300% of the prices in this guide.

Very Good

This looks as though it has been read repeatedly, but by a careful handler. There may be cover creases on the cover of a pulp magazine, slight scuffing, and some very minor tears, but no tape is present. There is no staining and the issue is complete. A book is still in nice shape, also with no stains or writing; a dust jacket may be slightly worn or have its edges frayed. It is obviously used but not obviously mishandled. It will be priced at about 200% of the prices in this guide.

Good

This is an average used copy, but nothing is missing. The item may be slightly dirtied and there may be minor tears. Covers may be defaced by creasing. Small pieces of the spine may be missing on pulp magazines. On paperback books, the glue may be brittle. There may be *minor* tape repairs on magazines—though not something as extreme as the entire front cover being taped on—and the repair is a definite defect. It will probably list for 100% of the prices given in most areas of this guide.

Fair

This copy has been handled extensively and may be soiled but is missing no more than, for example, a large portion of the spine paper or a small chunk of the cover. There may be multiple tapings, tears,

Planet Stories, Spring 1955, about 7″ × 10″; cover by (Frank) Kelly Freas (1922–). Defects include cover creasing, missing chunk, tear, and discoloration. Copyright 1955 by Love Romances Publishing Co., Inc.

markings of cover or interior, folds, and the like, but it is still a complete copy. A portion of the jacket may have torn loose on a book. It is worth 50%–75% of the prices listed in this guide.

Poor

This copy might range from good enough to read to so bad it is not worth collecting. There would probably be no monetary value to the item, unless it is of incredible collector interest and rarity.

DUST JACKETS

Some retailers consider dust jackets separately from the basic book itself; presence or absence of the dust jacket should be noted on a book that was originally released with one. Prices in this guide assume the presence of the dust jacket as being part of the book in question. The notation "wraps" on a book in a price list does not refer to a dust wrapper; it indicates a paperback edition. Note carefully the mail-order catalog listings of abbreviations; if the retailer lists two copies of a first edition, one just marked "good" at a low price and one marked "good" *and* "fine DJ" at a much higher price, chances are the "good" copy does not have a dust jacket at all. Most catalogs list the *presence* of a dust jacket rather than its absence.

Soft Books' Joe Bell said, "In the case of most collectible books, the dust jacket is worth up to 85% of the value. I feel it is easier to consider the book and dust jacket as one and books which have lost their dust jackets are, to a great extent, without value." (He commented that this changes with the age of the book: "No one, for example, expects a first-edition H. G. Wells to be in a dust jacket.")

Robert Weinberg said, "A. Merritt first editions without dust jackets routinely sell for $25.00–$50.00 per copy. In jacket, books like *Face in the Abyss* and *The Moon Pool* go for $400–$500 each. Ray Cummings first editions from the late twenties go for $25.00–$35.00 each without jackets and ten times that price in nice jackets; the jackets are the rare part."

He also commented on the way book-club editions have increased the importance of dust jackets: "In the sixties, Doubleday stopped publishing separate editions for many of their science-fiction books. They just did one printing and used different jackets for a trade edition and a book-club edition. So the jacket alone made the difference and could change the value of a book from $1.00 a copy to $50.00 or more."

DEFECTS

A general commentary on defects has been given in the "Grading" section. A rule of thumb is: *Avoid repairs.* In decades past, tape companies encouraged amateurs to use their tape to repair torn pages; some pulp collectors even fancied that they'd avoid damage to their magazines if they'd simply reinforce covers by running tape around the edges of all their covers. Those issues have been permanently damaged by the "precaution" taken in the forties. That is an extreme example, but we encourage collectors to take a lesson from it: Leave bad enough alone. Bag your collectible; don't try to erase pencil marks, bleach stains, or attempt other "repairs" that may in the long run damage it even more.

Planet Stories, March–May 1947, about 7″ × 10″; cover uncredited. Defects include a frayed right edge and tape on the left edge. Copyright 1947 by Love Romances Publishing Co., Inc.

Defect: This issue of *Weird Tales* has a frayed spine which has separated from the body of the magazine.

Defect: The fraying of this book jacket is a typical defect of such jackets and diminishes the value. (The book shown is Ray Bradbury's *Dark Carnival*, copyright 1947 by Ray Bradbury and published by Arkham House.)

Chipping. This indicates tiny pieces missing, usually from jacket or cover edges.

Dog-Eared Pages. Some people mark their places in books by turning down the corner of a page. This would move a book to no better than "fine" condition.

Fading. This damage is just what it says and happens most frequently when a book or piece of art is overexposed to bright light, especially sunlight.

Foxing. The brownish spotting referred to as "foxing" is not often found in science-fiction and fantasy collectibles of this century, but it can occur. It is especially frequent in Victorian-era books and is promoted by damp storage. It would probably make an item no better than "good."

Library Copy. It would seem obvious that a book taken from a library is stolen property; however, many libraries discard books no longer desired for their collections and sell such volumes to raise money. In this case, the book is *usually* stamped "discard" or "withdrawn." In any case, library processing involved applications of call numbers, copy identifications, glued dust jacket protectors, and pockets which hold book cards. All of these are defects and reduce the value of the book. If the book has no additional defects, it could be considered "good." Ordinarily, however, it would probably be only "fair."

Loose Bindings. The cover has separated from the interior pages. It may be held on by the endpapers; it may have separated completely. If the former, it could still be "good"; if damage is severe, it may be only "fair."

Markings. They may be in pencil or ink, as minor as a name written on a flyleaf or as annoying as defacement of a cover picture with ink additions or entire passages highlighted with a marker. If marks are minor, the item may still be considered "good." Of course, an autograph from the author is *not* considered a defect.

Famous Fantastic Mysteries, June 1949, about 7″ × 9¼″; cover by Lawrence (Stern Stevens) (1886–1960). Defects include frayed right edge, cover separating from spine, and bookstore stamp and pencil marks on cover. Listed as copyright 1949 by All-Fiction Field, Inc. Copyright 1949 by Popular Publications. Reprinted by permission of Blazing Publications, The Argosy Co.

Water Damage. This can be slight and only involve minor page warping or so bad that pages have stained and deformed and covers have faded. Slight water damage could be found in a "good" copy.

Bell said, "Be very clear about the fact that in many cases an item is almost valueless when damaged. Stephen King items, for example, have to be *perfect* to demand the prices asked."

BONUSES

Some things increase the value of even a mint collectible.

Autograph

The signature of the creator of the collectible will probably increase its value as a collectible, but one problem with autographs is authenticating them. There have been entire books written on the subject of

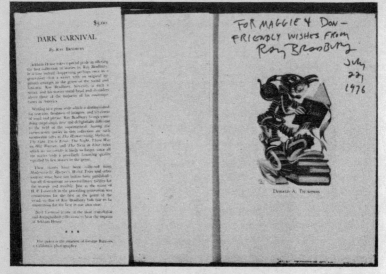

This flyleaf (about 5″ × 7½″) shows a 1951 bookplate by Hannes Bok (1914–1964) and an autograph by Ray Bradbury on a Bradbury hardcover from 1947. Note that the autograph is dated—and that the date is 29 years after the release of the book. An autograph dated 1947 on this book would be worth more.

autographs. We will simply note that the best autograph is usually the most complete autograph—signed and dated by the creator. Working out the value of a particular creator's signature is a tricky matter and depends on the availability of the signature, what the signature is on, etc. The date of an autograph can be important; a book signed immediately after publication is more valuable than a copy autographed years after it was printed.

In the case of an autographed copy of the Arkham House hardcover *Dark Carnival*, for example, Weinberg said, "Ray Bradbury's signature increases the value. It is a major book, his first, and his signature—while not impossible to get—is not that easy. I would think it would raise the value of the book by $100." Bell said he'd increase the price of a signed *Dark Carnival* by 25%, because few are signed.

But the value is not a fixed amount; it varies not only by date of signing but from creator to creator. Weinberg continued, "Heinlein's autograph is quite desirable and quite scarce. On an extremely important book, like *Stranger in a Strange Land*, I feel the price would increase significantly, probably from $400 to around $750. (I suspect Heinlein's signature *at least* doubles the value of a book—sometimes more than that.)''

Bell commented, ''The fact that an author is dead does not drastically increase the value; this depends more on scarcity. Lord Dunsany, for example, wrote dozens of books that were all published several times in his lifetime, yet his signature is quite scarce and would likely double the value. On the other hand, certain August Derleth titles are hard to locate *without* his name on someplace.''

Review Editions

These are preliminary editions, sometimes bound galleys, sometimes preliminary bindings of a later stage in production. *Sometimes* they have more value than the first edition; they are a collecting oddity and one more example of the problems in constructing a complete identification guide of each possible variation of a creator's work. Signed, numbered editions of books aimed at the hard-core collector may have ''artist's proof'' copies in which a notation such as ''A/P'' replaces the numbering but the signature of the creator is still on the edition. Such copies may have been sent to friends, reviewers, and the like. These editions also *may* command a premium price.

Review Slip

The addition of a review slip to a book can increase its value, usually by $1.00 to $5.00. It indicates that the volume was sent early to professional reviewers. The slip may be an extensive press release or a small notice that the item is à review copy.

History of the Field

Entire books have been devoted to the respective histories of science fiction and fantasy. We will cover the topic more briefly.

Fantasy stories are as old as storytelling; storytellers made up fantastic yarns about what prowled about just outside the light of the campfire, what powers for good or ill danced or lurked in the woods, and just what lay in wait for those who failed to heed the tribal elders. Science fiction came later, since it had to be based on reason, not just superstition. Still, it has been around a while.

Prior to the twentieth century, there were a few indisputable science-fiction stories, such as Mary Shelley's *Frankenstein*. Some science-fiction historians trace science fiction back to legends of Gilgamesh the immortal, to stories of Lucian of Samothrace or to the writings of Cyrano de Bergerac. Edgar Allan Poe, who created the detective story, also wrote a number of fantasies and some stories which are arguably science fiction. But the first who could really be called professional science-fiction writers are Jules Verne and H. G. Wells.

But today's science-fiction and fantasy collectors are less concerned with first American editions of the works of Verne and Wells (or of fantasists such as Poe or Lewis Carroll) than they are with the writings of Philip K. Dick, Jack Vance, Ray Bradbury, and Stephen King. If science-fiction fans want to read Poe, most are quite happy with a modern omnibus edition of the complete stories and poems of Poe— which is just as well, since first editions of Poe's stories and poems can run into the hundreds of thousands of dollars. We're not talking collectibles here. We're talking *rare* books, the kind which are auctioned at galleries to crowds made up of super-wealthy collectors.

Modern science fiction hasn't been around all that long. Wells, Verne, Edgar Rice Burroughs, Sir Arthur Conan Doyle, and a few others wrote novels which are today regarded as science fiction. The people who wrote them didn't call them that, because Hugo

Gernsback had yet to invent the term. They were usually called something like "scientific romances" or just "books."

Gernsback published some science-fiction stories in his magazines for experimenters with electricity and/or radio. The early part of this century was a great time for tinkerers, from the ordinary guy in his basement with a homemade crystal set all the way up to Thomas Alva Edison. Gernsback ran some science-fiction stories for his readers, who liked them, and eventually (April 1926) he published an entire magazine devoted to these stories, *Amazing Stories*.

Eventually, Gernsback lost control of *Amazing Stories* and his other magazines in the Great Depression and went on to found a bunch of other publications, including some devoted to science-fiction. Other publishers entered the field as well. After World War II, with paper shortages over and TV still not more than a cloud the size of the proverbial man's hand, the magazine business blossomed. At one point, in 1953, there were 39 science-fiction and fantasy magazines crowding each other off the newsstands. This boom was followed by a bust, unsurprisingly. There simply weren't enough science-fiction readers to support that many magazines—yet; or that many stories worth printing—yet.

To that point, comparatively few science-fiction books had appeared. It was a rare year that saw a dozen science-fiction novels in hardcover and there were even fewer in paperback. (Those of you who discovered science fiction during the last decade may consider the foregoing sentence to be fantasy, but it's not.) This started to change in the early fifties.

A pioneer in the field of paperback science-fiction publishing was Ballantine Books, which was launched in 1953 with a series of original books, not reprints as most previous paperbacks had been, published (in most cases) simultaneously with a hardcover book from an allied publisher. The sixteenth Ballantine Book was *Star Science Fiction Stories,* an anthology of original science-fiction stories, edited by Frederik Pohl. This was followed by other science-fiction books, and Ballantine soon was publishing such acknowledged classics as Theodore Sturgeon's *More Than Human,* Ray Bradbury's *Fahrenheit 451,* and Frederik Pohl and C. M. Kornbluth's *The Space Merchants.* Other publishers took note of how well Ballantine's science-fiction publishing program was going and decided to take a flyer themselves.

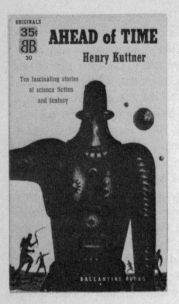

Ahead of Time by Henry Kuttner, about 4¼" × 7"; cover by (Richard M.) Powers (1921–). This is the 30th book Ballantine Books released, and it was issued simultaneously in hardcover. Copyright 1953 by Henry Kuttner.

In the early days, publishers rarely put out more than one science-fiction book every month; that was considered a very ambitious program in the fifties. Gradually, through the fifties and sixties, paperbacks supplanted magazines as the source for science-fiction novels.

That was a major change. During the forties, any science-fiction writer who wrote a novel did so with the goal of having it serialized in *Astounding Science Fiction*. No other science-fiction magazine ran serials except on a *very* occasional basis. The shocking mathematics (shocking to today's fans, at least) is that *ASF* could accommodate only about four serials a year; each serial ran three parts, and the magazine was monthly. Four novels a year—and you were competing for those four slots with the likes of Isaac Asimov, Hal Clement, L. Ron Hubbard, and Robert A. Heinlein. If your novel missed selling to *ASF,* you *might* be able to sell an abridged version to *Startling Stories*—or you could forget about it or rewrite it as a novelette for *Thrilling Wonder Stories* instead.

In 1950, *Galaxy* made its debut and became the second science-fiction magazine to feature serials regularly, immediately doubling the magazine market for novels. Eight a year.

Star Science Fiction Stories edited by Frederik Pohl, about 4¼″ × 7¼″; cover by (Richard M.) Powers (1921–). This is the first science-fiction book published by Ballantine Books, the 16th book issued by the company. Among other items, it contains the first publication of Arthur C. Clarke's classic short story "The Nine Billion Names of God." A hardcover edition priced at $1.50 was issued simultaneously. Copyright 1953 by Ballantine Books, Inc.

By about the mid-fifties, there were enough book publishers to change the way novels were written. From the late forties until then, a novel was written for serialization in *Astounding* (or, later, *Galaxy*) with the hope that it could be resold to a book publisher. In the mid-fifties, however, the book publishers began commissioning novels, and authors began writing specifically for book publication, hoping that maybe they could pick up a few hundred bucks extra by having it serialized in *ASF* or *Galaxy,* if there was time to schedule it in the magazine before the book publication date.

Today, we are back to having *Analog* (as *Astounding* is now called) as the only magazine regularly publishing serials. Most science-fiction novelists write for book publication with no thought of prior magazine serialization. Written science-fiction is dominated by book publishers—primarily paperback publishers (and Ballantine Books is still in

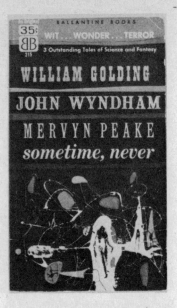

Sometime, Never by William Golding, John Wyndham, and Mervyn Peake, about 4¼″ × 7″; cover by (Richard M.) Powers (1921–). The original edition from Ballantine Books is copyright 1956 by William Golding, John Benyon Harris, and Mervyn Laurence Peake.

the forefront, with its science-fiction and fantasy line now known as Del Rey Books).

The other major change in science-fiction over the last three decades came in movies and television. Science-fiction movies existed from the beginning of movies as an entertainment medium. Georges Melies made a special-effects film based on Jules Verne's *From the Earth to the Moon* in 1905. There were classic science-fiction films scattered among the output of Hollywood through the thirties and forties. The fifties saw an explosion of science-fiction movies, mostly cheap shockers about giant insects (thanks to inferior special effects and sloppy double exposures, many were giant *transparent* insects) with an occasional good movie. Televised science-fiction was even worse— *Space Cadet* and *Captain Video* and similar primitive material.

Slowly, sophistication came to both media. *Twilight Zone,* for example, offered thought-provoking dramatizations, sometimes of stories the fans had already read in their magazines. Some episodes of *Outer Limits* also achieved a high level of quality. *Star Trek* on TV and *Star Wars* on movie screens did the rest. Science fiction became very big, very profitable. And science fiction suddenly changed its demographics, attracting more women.

Magazine science-fiction has been around just over sixty years. For the first half of that time, the field grew slowly but stubbornly and achieved a level of modest success. Science-fiction novels sold pretty well, though not as well as westerns. Science-fiction movies did fairly well, though not as well as westerns. On TV, science fiction didn't even *begin* to compete with westerns.

The truly rapid growth of science-fiction has come in the last thirty years. The notion that science-fiction writers like Isaac Asimov and Robert A. Heinlein would regularly have their novels on the bestseller lists would have been too fantastic even for a science-fiction story.

For the collector, things have changed just as drastically. In 1952, Donald Day remarked in the introduction to his *Index to the Science-Fiction Magazines 1926–1950* that he had decided against including *Weird Tales* in his index because "to do so would mean a delay of at least two years and a considerable outlay of money to accumulate a complete set of the back issues." We know people who have been trying for decades to do what Day could have done in two years. And, while we can only guess at what Day considered a considerable outlay of money, we are acquainted with a fan who bought a complete set of *Weird Tales* five years after Day wrote those words—he paid one thousand dollars for the set. If you can find someone willing to sell a complete set of *Weird Tales* today for one thousand dollars, please feel free to put him in touch with us.

While the field has not been widely collected until relatively recently, one aspect has been constant almost since the days of the earliest issues of *Amazing Stories*: fan involvement with publishing.

Many early fans published their own material, usually amateur fiction or their reviews of the magazines. These "fanzines" (coined from the obvious combination of the words "fan" and "magazine") were hectographed, spirit duplicated, or mimeographed magazines of small circulation which the amateur editor sent to his friends and fellow editors. Some fans began lengthy discussions with fellow fans in the pages of these magazines—and in the letter columns of the professional magazines. The surviving fans of this era call themselves "First Fandom," fans who were active in the field before 1938.

While much of this material was not of professional quality, many of the amateurs went on to become professionals in the field. Jerry Siegel and Joe Shuster published a story about a "Superman" character in a science-fiction fanzine, then went on to create a comic-book hero of that name. Stephen King's first published story appeared in a fanzine. Some fan writers went on to careers in other fields; Pulitzer Prize-winning film critic Roger Ebert had material published in many science-fiction fanzines in the early sixties.

Some fans devoted themselves to publishing on a professional level in a different way—they formed publishing houses devoted to producing high-quality, science-fiction books. August Derleth's Arkham House imprint survived its author/editor/publisher and is still known as a publisher of outre fantasy and science fiction. Arkham House published some of the most highly collectible editions in the field, including H. P. Lovecraft's *The Outsider and Others* and Robert E. Howard's *Skullface,* as well as the first books of Ray Bradbury, Fritz Leiber, and Robert Bloch.

In the early fifties, Gnome Press (founded by David Kyle and Martin Greenberg—no relation to today's anthologist Martin Harry Greenberg) was the pre-eminent science-fiction hardcover publisher, giving first book publication to Isaac Asimov's *Foundation, Foundation and Empire,* and *Second Foundation.*

Today, there are a number of firms specializing in quality bookmaking. Such companies as Charles L. Grant, Underwood/Miller, and Graphitti produce books which are masterpieces of the bookbinder's art and are designed to be collectibles from the moment of publication. Some of the volumes produced by such companies have limited, signed-and-numbered editions which sell out before publication. In our listing of names, such volumes are sometimes indicated by prices in higher categories. A volume published in, say, 1986 with a price indicated as $30.00 in "good" condition is probably such a volume and may already be going for even more than that amount, assuming you could find it. The chances are you will never see a copy in "good" condition because all copies were purchased upon publication by collectors and maintained in "mint" condition.

The beginning collector may decide to enter the field with slightly more timidity, beginning his purchases with mass-market paperbacks before trying for, say, a first edition of Stephen King's *Eyes of the Dragon*—one of the books designed from the outset to have a print run far smaller than the demand.

There are a lot of different editions available of major books by major authors, which is why this edition serves more as an identification guide than a price guide. It is difficult to give a price range (at least in a reasonable amount of space) for a book which may have had:

- A limited-edition, signed-and-numbered first edition from a specialty house.
- A first edition from a major hardcover publisher.
- Subsequent printings from the major publisher.
- A hardcover book club edition.
- A trade paperback first edition.
- Subsequent printings of the trade paperback edition.
- A mass-market paperback edition.
- Subsequent reprintings—perhaps dozens of them—of the mass-market paperback edition.

Such a book could well have a price range of from 50¢ for a used paperback to hundreds, maybe thousands, of dollars for the limited, signed-and-numbered edition. Such a detailed listing of each book from a prolific author would quickly eat up all the space in this book. In fact, there are entire books devoted to a listing of all the editions of all the books of such writers as Jack Vance, L. Sprague de Camp, Philip K. Dick, Ray Bradbury, Harlan Ellison, and Roger Zelazny.

Of the price listings we *do* give for books, you'll note that many consist of no more than a starting, bottom price. In all cases of book listings, you'll also note that those prices we give are for items in "good" condition. If you're after a mint-condition copy of the lowest-priced edition, it will still probably cost you *four times as much* as the "good" price we list. Prices depend on rarity, demand, *and condition* today.

The Market

As we talked to retailers about our plans for this guide, we were repeatedly told that science-fiction magazines just don't sell well right now. And the prices we've seen in catalogs and in "prices realized" in auction seem to bear this out.

Think of it: Pulp magazines with stories or art which would be hotly collected if they had appeared in comic books, cost less than $100 in today's market. The first issue of the *Buck Rogers* comic book from 1940, which consisted of reprints of the Rick Yager comic strip, costs $100 in good condition. You can expect to pay less than $70 for a good-condition copy of the first appearance *ever* of the character—because it was in a pulp magazine (the August 1928 *Amazing*).

Why should this be? We offer some suggestions:

- Pulps haven't been sold for decades; modern readers may find the "girlie" covers downright quaint.

- Science-fiction and fantasy collecting seems to have become increasingly focused on the book market, as the book market has increased the quantity of science fiction and fantasy it provides.

- Magazines are often hard to find on newsstands.

- Anthologies (which is what magazines are, when you come right down to it) do not seem to sell as well in today's market as novels. We think the following is a major reason. There has not been a convenient, widely available listing of just what there is that can be collected in the magazine field. If you pick up a current copy of *Isaac Asimov's Science Fiction Magazine* (which won the 1988 *Locus* Award as best magazine and whose editor won a Hugo award as best editor of 1987—both for the same time period), you may feel the urge to begin to collect the magazine. But how far back was the magazine published and how much will it cost?

New readers have few guidelines when it comes to collecting recent magazines, not to mention older ones. It is hardly amazing that collectors have chosen to pay more attention to books. (In case you wondered, *Isaac Asimov's Science Fiction Magazine* began in 1977, and a complete collection of the prize winner in "good" condition should cost less than $75.00.)

What *is* being collected are the limited-edition, signed-and-numbered collectors' edition books of "hot" writers. Many are selling out before the editions have come off the press. While we list prices for some in "good" condition, it is unlikely you will find any copies of these premeditated collectors' items in that condition, since every copy went into the hands of collectors who maintain them in "mint" condition. Fortunately for the reader who focuses on building a collection in order to read enjoyable material, most such volumes have other, mass-market editions sooner or later.

Building and Identifying a Collection

Librarians and scholars have come to expect that a "proper" bibliographic reference will invariably include a detailed listing of all works by city of publication, name of publisher, and year of initial copyright—possibly with the addition of information on the year of printing of the particular edition referred to.

In our history of the field, we have shown why such a listing for every form taken by every book in the field would not fit in a single volume. We have indicated in a few cases the number of editions a particular work has had as a general indication of availability, but this sort of information is not vital to the collector; it does not, after all, indicate how many copies were printed in each edition—though it may indicate an item which has been kept in print.

How, then, *can* the collector find a way through the field using this guide, retailers' stock, and a want list?

It should relieve new collectors to find that few genre collectors collect by publisher. (This is, we should note, as opposed to paperback collectors, who may well collect only, say, map-back and dime paperbacks.) Virtually all retailer lists, convention displays, and store displays are organized—like library fiction shelves—in alphabetical order by author.

COLLECTING BY MAGAZINE

American magazines are listed in the chapter devoted to them with complete identification of the number of issues published of each and the price you can expect to pay for each in "good" condition.

Current issues can be found in specialty shops, some bookstores, and by subscription from the publications, as indicated. Back issues are carried by specialty retailers, including many mail-order dealers. You'll also find back issues at many science-fiction conventions.

COLLECTING BY AUTHOR

Authors are listed in alphabetical order in our guide with as complete a list as we were able to make of the books published under their names. If there is a year listed, *it is the year of first publication*. Stephen King collectors will know that a paperback copy of Stephen King's *Salem's Lot* with a painted face on a flat front cover and King's name printed with the book's title on that cover is *not* the first paperback edition. (The first paperback edition had a black cover with the face in a three-dimensional relief with no type on the front and only a red drop of blood showing to relieve the black.) But simply by checking the entry on "Stephen King" in this guide, you will see that the first edition of *Salem's Lot* appeared in 1975. If you pick up a volume with a printing date of 1984, you know that it is a later edition. The year an edition is published is customarily identified on the copyright page, often with a detailed publishing history.

Retailers selling science fiction and fantasy will usually list books by author names but specify editions on their sales lists. Retailers with shops will usually shelve according to author name.

COLLECTING BY ARTIST

If you intend to build an extensive library of the works of science-fiction and fantasy artists, an excellent way to begin is with Robert A. Weinberg's *A Biographical Dictionary of Science Fiction and Fantasy Artists,* discussed in our chapter on "Non-Fiction/Reference Material." He offers checklists of much work by artists in the field. With the exception of the work of such highly collectible artists as Frank Frazetta, books will be offered for sale by most shops, mail-order houses, etc., by a book's author, rather than the artist, so his checklists are especially valuable to collectors of printed art. Original art by science-fiction and fantasy artists is handled by a few dealers, and there are often art shows showcasing new work held in conjunction with science-fiction conventions.

BUILDING A COLLECTION FOR INVESTMENT

If your primary purpose in building a science-fiction collection is to build yourself the equivalent of an investment portfolio, look for the following:

- Signed, numbered limited editions.
- First editions, both hardcover and paperback.
- Mint condition.

You will need to maintain the items, once purchased, in the same condition in which you bought them. Aside from flipping through a copy to be sure a book is complete and undamaged, you may even decide to file the book or magazine unread. This is, admittedly, an extreme measure, but there are few people who handle a book or magazine with enough care to maintain mint condition. *If* your *sole* purpose in collecting is to accumulate a high-value collection, meticulous handling and storage is essential.

At this point, pulp magazines from the thirties, forties, and fifties are available at comparatively low prices (compared, for example, with prices on comic books of similar ages). However, you will want to limit purchases to "fine" to "mint" condition and expect to pay at least three times the prices listed in our magazine guide, in which prices given are for items in "good" condition.

BUILDING A COLLECTION FOR PLEASURE

If your primary purpose in building a science-fiction collection is to build yourself the equivalent of a personal library of reading material to your tastes, look for the following:

- Material by your favorites—and award-winners.
- Guidance by critics whose comments have led you dependably.
- Economy.

This does not mean you *have* to avoid signed, numbered limited editions—nor does it mean that you should abuse the books you collect. But, if you intend to buy to read, you will do well to begin by filling the holes in your collection with whatever edition you locate at the best price—and then, if you enjoy the material, you may work your way up to more expensive versions. In that fashion, you'll be able to use the cheap copy to read—and maintain the expensive item in pristine condition.

HOWEVER YOU BUILD A COLLECTION

Keep track of new releases by maintaining subscriptions to *Locus* and *Science Fiction Chronicle,* which carry news and reviews every month.

Build good relations with shops and mail-order firms which offer the material you want to buy. When you deal by mail, be sure your name and address are on your letter as well as on your envelope; if possible, type your letter; at least print clearly. Enclose a self-addressed, stamped envelope, so that the dealer can respond to your letter.

IDENTIFYING COLLECTIBLES

What edition do I have?

If you buy a magazine, matters are simple enough. Each issue can be identified by using our magazine guide. Simply note the month and year of publication (or, in a few cases, the number of the magazine), and you will know what the item is, when it was published, and how many other issues you will need to build a complete collection.

When you buy a book, matters are more complex. If you are building a collection of a writer's work, you can identify what you *don't* have from our list. But which edition do you have, once you've bought it? Look at the copyright page, usually following the title page.

Old or new, it probably contains the following information:

- The copyright year and who owns the copyright. (This can often offer clues to pen names, incidentally. If the name on the copyright is different from the author, it may indicate a pseudonym.)
- The name and address of the publisher.
- The name of other publishers of the work to that point, if any. This comes most often when a paperback publisher has arranged to publish a mass edition of a hardcover book, but it also occurs when a specialty publisher has arranged a limited, signed, and numbered edition.
- The number of the edition—and sometimes a publishing history.

What it may *not* reveal is earlier, magazine publication of a work, especially if the earlier work is heavily revised for book publication.

Fantasy and Science-Fiction Names

We should establish some ground rules from the beginning, some of which have already been indicated in our general "Introduction."

We can't list every writer or artist who has ever written a science-fiction or fantasy short story—or illustrated one. We don't have room to list every writer who has ever written a science-fiction or fantasy book—or series. In future editions there are sure to be additions, and we welcome suggestions for such additions. We have also recommended throughout this book other information sources to supplement our material.

This chapter lists *only* books, not individual short stories, in its formal listings; it also lists *only* science-fiction and fantasy work, not associated material, be it detective fiction, westerns, or horror. The emphasis is on providing a listing of material by creator, not even (at least in this edition) on providing a complete guide to the pricing in the field. For a more elaborate discussion of this aspect, see the "Introduction."

Due to space constraints, we are also forced to give short shrift to most anthologies. Works of such anthologists as Martin Harry Greenberg and Groff Conklin are not fully represented, although anthologies can provide good introductions to aspects of the field.

For details on book publication in the field, please see the introductory passages.

When the time comes for another edition of this volume, there will probably be so many "shared universe" series that they will call for a separate chapter. A "shared universe" is one in which a so-called "bible" has been established; it contains all the basic background of a fictional universe. Then, a number of different writers produce their own, individual stories or novels fitting into that basic concept. The worlds of comic books, television series, and animated cartoons have operated on that basis for years. But at this point there aren't quite enough such series in book form to lead us into setting aside a chapter for them. Where possible, we've listed novels in currently running shared universes under the author of the volume in question.

As you'll note in the chapter devoted to science-fiction and fantasy magazines, this book is a guide primarily to material published in America. Many classic works of science fiction and fantasy were first published in England. The emphasis in this guide is necessarily on American releases, though some British creators are included.

We are *severely* limited as regards space in this guide. It is possible to devote entire volumes to listing variant editions of work by single authors—authors far less prolific than Isaac Asimov; in fact, where possible, we have noted some such volumes. (Among others, there have been book-length bibliographies published for Jack Vance, Roger Zelazny, L. Sprague de Camp, Philip K. Dick, and Harlan Ellison.) Obviously, we have neither space nor information to list all editions of, say, Robert A. Heinlein's *Stranger in a Strange Land* with all their variant prices. We are forced to adopt what we hope will function as a guideline to pricing—a price *range* on a particular title. For example, Ray Bradbury's *Fahrenheit 451* has appeared in mass-market paperback in several editions, had several hardcover—including book-club—editions, had variant contents (after the earliest printings, the two short stories in the volume were dropped), and had one of the earliest special collectors' editions in the field: Ballantine's 200-copy run of an asbestos-bound, signed, numbered volume. You might expect to find a "good" condition recent paperback copy of *Fahrenheit 451* for 50¢—but you'd have to pay *considerably* more for the asbestos-bound copy in "near mint" condition.

Our intention in the "Names" portion of this guide is to provide the beginning of an identification guide to material in the field. We know that, despite the number of volumes you'll find in this section, we have missed more than one book. Many previous price guides have provided listings for only volumes which had been listed for sale in the preceding year. We have tried to provide far, far more information on what the collector can hunt for—but that has meant less input on book pricing, especially taking the variant editions into account.

We cannot express fervently enough our request for more information for future editions. What we want to offer is a listing of all science-fiction and fantasy books by the authors listed—listed in order of the year of first publication *as a book*. In those listings which do *not* carry an indication of first publication date, it means we have not located the information at this point. We felt it more important to run the information we had than to omit reference to a work simply because we lacked a detail.

We also welcome input on the subject of authors who should be included in future editions.

In this chapter, we have given a price *range*, instead of a specific average price, for a specific condition of collectible wherever possible. The beginning collector can try to grab a copy in "good" shape at the lowest price; if the item proves interesting, the collector can go after the most highly collectible version—or something in-between. Where a single price is listed, the book is recent and has not had a variety of editions.

The price range is for the cheapest edition in "good" condition to the most expensive edition in "good" condition. Note, however, that a "good" condition copy of a signed, numbered edition may be almost impossible to find. If it was intended to be marketed only to the most demanding collectors, it is unlikely that the purchaser treated it so shabbily that it is now only in "good" condition (although accidents do happen and every collector has his horror stories of burst water pipes and young relatives with crayons or scissors). It's very likely that a high-ticket item will only be available at a price three or four times the price listed here. But for that money you'll be getting an item in fine or mint condition.

All prices are the averages of the price ranges of different editions *asked for the editions by retailers selling them in "good" condition.* This means the book is an average used copy, but nothing is missing; if it came with a dust jacket, the jacket is present. The book may be slightly dirtied and there may be minor tears. Glue used in binding may be brittle. There is no tape on any paperback edition and only the most minor of tape repairs on a hardcover edition—and the repair is a definite defect; tape is *always* counted against the book in determining its condition, never for it. A book with an unrepaired tear will be rated higher than one with a tear which has been taped.

If the book in question is in "very good" condition, retailers would ask about twice the price listed here. A "very good" copy will have no tape repairs and it will be clean. The cover may be loose and there may be fraying of the dust jacket. Pages may have darkened, it may have minor marking, and it is a read copy.

If the book is in "fine" condition, retailers would ask about three times the price listed here. A "fine" issue is a very nice looking item. It may have been read more than once, but there are no creases or writing (other than arrival date with some paperbacks) on the cover. There may be slight fraying of the dust jacket, but the book is tight. There may be slight page darkening.

If the book is in "mint" condition, retailers would ask about four times the price listed here. This condition is about as good as it gets. The hardcover or paperback should look as good as you would find it if you bought it new today. It is entirely undamaged.

While there is a back-issue market for collectible paperbacks, *in general* you would pay about as much for a near-mint copy of a 25¢ paperback as you would pay for a new edition of the same book—around $3.50 to $5.00. Except for a comparatively few hardcore paperback book collectors, the market is filled with people who just want to read the book and don't care what edition it is. For this reason, prices can fall suddenly on an old collectible paperback if a new edition is released.

Beware of book-club editions, which can mislead you into thinking you have stumbled across a valuable book. With rare exceptions, book-club editions are worth a couple of dollars, sometimes less. Exceptions include omnibus volumes and cases where the book-club edition is the first hardcover edition of a novel which originally appeared in paperback. Generally, though, book-club editions are good reading editions, but not valuable or highly collectible.

Beware, too, of the very few unscrupulous dealers who try to pass off book-club editions as trade editions. Check the dust jacket: If the bottom corner of the flap on the inside front cover of the book has been clipped off, it may have been done to remove the words "Book Club Edition." This is not done by professional science-fiction and fantasy back-copy dealers, but some general used-book stores follow this practice.

EDWIN A. ABBOTT (1838–1926)

Abbott wrote only one notable fantasy, but it is a delightful story of life in two dimensions. There have been many trade paperback editions and copies are easily found.

1884   *Flatland: A Romance of Many Dimensions* (psd. A. Square)

FORREST J(AMES) ACKERMAN (1916–)

Probably the best known science-fiction fan for decades, Ackerman was awarded one of the first Hugos in 1953 for being the "#1 Fan Personality." He later became editor of *Famous Monsters of Filmland,* with which publication he influenced a generation of filmmakers. Ackerman coined the term "sci-fi," which he popularized with many so-called "media fans." He has been an agent, an editor, and a writer, though most of his writing has been in the form of articles about fantasy and science-fiction movies and their stars (see his book about Boris Karloff, *The Frankenscience Monster,* for an example of this). He also edited the *Perry Rhodan* series of paperback books/magazines (see the "Magazines" listing).

1953   Hugo (#1 Fan Personality)

1969   *Science Fiction Worlds of Forrest J Ackerman & Friends*   pb*50¢*

DOUGLAS ADAMS (1952–)

First known to most fans for his work on the *Doctor Who* television show and as scripter for the radio series *Hitchhiker's Guide to the Galaxy,* he became more widely known when he transferred the latter work into book form. The books became bestsellers in America.

1979   *The Hitchhiker's Guide to the Galaxy*   hc*$2.00*   pb*50¢*
1981   *The Restaurant at the End of the Universe*   hc*$2.00*   pb*50¢*
1982   *Life, the Universe and Everything*   hc*$2.00*   pb*50¢*
1985   *So Long and Thanks for the Fish*   hc*$2.00*   pb*50¢*
1985   *The Original Hitchhiker Radio Scripts*   trade pb*$2.50*
1986   *The Hitchhiker's Quartet* (omnibus, 1st 4 books)   *$2.00*
1987   *Dirk Gently's Holistic Detective Agency*   hc*$5.00*   pb*$1.00*

ROBERT AICKMAN

Aickman was a British writer noted for his short fantasy fiction.

1975   WFA (Short Fiction): "Pages from a Young Girl's Diary"

1976   *Cold Hand in Mine*   ss
1977   *Tales of Love and Death*   ss
1979   *Painted Devils: Strange Stories*   ss

BRIAN W(ILSON) ALDISS (1925-)

Aldiss is a British author who has been a major force in the field, as author and as critic, since the 1950s. He won the short-fiction Hugo Award for a series of stories which have been collected in book form as *The Long Afternoon of Earth*. He is the author of *Billion Year Spree* and co-author with David Wingrove of *The Trillion Year Spree*, both notable books about science fiction.

Books about Aldiss include *Item Eighty-Three: Brian W. Aldiss, a Bibliography* (1972) by Margaret Aldiss, and *Aldiss Unbound: The Science Fiction of Brian W. Aldiss* (1977) by Richard Mathews.

1962   Hugo (Short Fiction): The Hothouse Series (aka *The Long Afternoon of Earth*)

1987   Hugo (Non-Fiction): *Trillion Year Spree* (with David Wingrove)

1958   *Equator*
1958   *Starship*
1959   *Vanguard from Alpha*
1959   *No Time Like Tomorrow*   ss
1959   *Galaxies Like Grains of Sand*   ss
1960   *Bow Down to Nul*
1961   *The Primal Urge*
1962   *The Long Afternoon of Earth*
1963   *Starswarm*   ss
1964   *The Dark Light Years*
1964   *Greybeard*
1965   *Earthworks*
1965   *Who Can Replace a Man?*   ss
1966   *The Saliva Tree and Other Strange Growths*   ss
1967   *Cryptozoic!*   pb50¢
1968   *Report on Probability A*   pb50¢
1969   *Barefoot in the Head*   ss
1969   *Neanderthal Planet*   ss
1970   *The Moment of Eclipse*   ss
1972   *The Book of Brian Aldiss*   ss
1973   *Frankenstein Unbound*
1974   *The Eighty-Minute Hour: A Space Opera*
1976   *The Malacia Tapestry*   pb75¢

1977 *Brothers of the Head*
1979 *New Arrivals, Old Encounters* ss **hc$2.50 pb50¢**
1981 *An Island Called Moreau* **pb50¢**
1987 *The Year Before Yesterday* (including *Equator*) **hc$4.25**
1987 *Seasons in Flight*
Last Orders ss
Enemies of the System
Helliconia series
  1982 *Helliconia Spring* **hc$4.00**
  1983 *Helliconia Summer*
  1985 *Helliconia Winter* **$1.00–**

POUL ANDERSON (1926–)

Poul Anderson has been a major writer of science fiction since the
late 1940s. He is equally adept with heroic fantasy, adventure science
fiction, and hard-science science fiction. He has written several series,
including the ''Hoka'' stories (in collaboration with Gordon R. Dickson), about a planet of teddy-bear-like aliens who base various civilizations on Earth fiction, from Sherlock Holmes to westerns. The

*Two Complete Science-Adventure
Books,* Winter 1953 (October–
December), about 7″ × 10″; cover
by (Frank) Kelly Freas (1922–). De-
fect: creasing of lower right cover.
Copyright 1953 by Wings Publishing
Co., Inc.

first collection of "Hoka" stories (*Earthman's Burden*) has illustrations by Edd Cartier; the 1970 paperback edition of that book from Avon Camelot has the Cartier illustrations and a cover by Vaughn Bode, making it a doubly desirable collectible for art fans.

Much of Anderson's fiction, particularly in recent years, has been in collaboration with his wife, Karen.

A book about him is David Stever and Andrew Adams Whyte's *The Collector's Poul Anderson* (1976).

1961 Hugo (Short Fiction): "The Longest Voyage"

1964 Hugo (Short Fiction): "No Truce with Kings"

1969 Hugo (Novelette): "The Sharing of Flesh"

1971 Nebula (Novelette): "The Queen of Air and Darkness"

1972 Hugo (Novella): "The Queen of Air and Darkness"

1972 Nebula (Novelette): "Goat Song"

1973 Hugo (Novelette): "Goat Song"

1979 Hugo (Novelette): "Hunter's Moon"

1981 Nebula (Novella): "The Saturn Game"

1982 Hugo (Novella): "The Saturn Game"

1952 *Vault of the Ages*

1954 *Brain Wave*

1954 *Three Hearts and Three Lions*

1954 *The Broken Sword*

1955 *No World of Their Own*

1956 *Planet of No Return*

1958 *War of the Wing-Men*

1959 *The Enemy Stars* (reissued with "The Ways of Love" in 1987) **pb***50¢*–

1959 *War of Two Worlds* (Ace Double) **pb$***1.00*

1959 *We Claim These Stars*

1960 *Earthman, Go Home!* ss (Ace Double) **pb$***1.00*

1960 *The High Crusade*

1960 *Guardians of Time* ss ("Time Patrol" series)

1961 *Twilight World* ss

1961 *Strangers from Earth* ss *50¢*–

1961 *Orbit Unlimited* ss ("Rustum" series)

1961   *Flandry of Terra*   ss
1962   *Un-Man and Other Novellas*   ss
1962   *After Doomsday*
1962   *The Makeshift Rocket*
1963   *Shield*
1963   *Let the Spacemen Beware* (later as *The Night Face*)
1964   *Three Worlds to Conquer*
1964   *Time and Stars*   ss
1964   *Trader to the Stars*   ss
1965   *Agent of the Terran Empire*   ss
1965   *The Corriders of Time*
1965   *The Star Fox*
1966   *The Fox, the Dog, and the Griffin*
1966   *The Trouble Twisters*   ss
1966   *Ensign Flandry*
1967   *World Without Stars*
1968   *The Horn of Time*   ss   pb50¢
1969   *Seven Conquests*   ss
1969   *Beyond the Beyond*   ss
1969   *Satan's World*
1969   *The Rebel Worlds*
1970   *A Circus of Hells*
1970   *Tau Zero*
1970   *Tales of the Flying Mountains*   ss (as Winston P. Sanders)
1970   *The Byworlder*
1971   *Operation Chaos*   ss
1971   *The Dancer From Atlantis*
1972   *There Will Be Time*
1973   *The People of the Wind*
1973   *The Day of Their Return*
1973   *Hrolf Kraki's Saga*
1973   *The Queen of Air and Darkness and Other Stories*   ss
1974   *Fire Time*
1974   *Inheritors of Earth* (with Gordon Eklund)
1974   *Midsummer Tempest* (sequel to *Three Hearts and Three Lions*)
1974   *A Knight of Ghosts and Shadow*
1974   *The Many Worlds of Poul Anderson* (**pb** as *The Book of Poul Anderson*)
1975   *Homeward and Beyond*   ss

1975 *The Winter of the World*
1976 *Homebrew* ss
1976 *The Best of Poul Anderson* ss pb50¢
1977 *Mirkheim*
1978 *The Avatar*
1978 *The Earth Book of Stormgate* ss pb$1.00
1979 *The Demon of Scattery* (with Mildred Downey Broxon) pb60¢
1979 *The Merman's Children*
1980 *The Devil's Game* pb75¢
1981 *Fantasy* ss pb75¢
1981 *Winners* ss (all Hugo Award winners) pb75¢
1981 *Explorations* ss pb75¢
1981 *The Dark Between the Stars* hc$1.25 pb50¢
1984 *The Unicorn Trade* ss (with Karen Anderson) pb90¢
1984 *Past Times* ss pb90¢
Conan series
  1980 *Conan the Rebel* pb$1.00
Hoka series (with Gordon R. Dickson)
  1957 *Earthman's Burden* ss hc$8.00 pb$1.00
  1975 *Star Prince Charlie*
  1983 *Hoka!* ss trade pb$2.00
King of Ys series (with Karen Anderson)
  1986 *The King of Ys 1* pb$1.25
  1987 *The King of Ys 2: Gallicenae* pb$1.25
Psychotechnic series
  1956 *Star Ways*
  1958 *The Snows of Ganymede*
  1959 *Virgin Planet*
  1981 *The Psychotechnic League* ss pb75¢

PIERS ANTHONY (*psd. of Piers Anthony Dillingham Jacob*) (1934–)

In recent years, Anthony has joined the handful of science-fiction writers whose novels invariably appear on the *New York Times* and *Publishers Weekly* bestseller lists. Consequently, his later books are generally easy to find because of their large printings. Most of his earlier works are available in later reprintings.

Anthony has written his autobiography, *Bio of an Ogre*.

1967   *Chthon*   pb50¢–
1968   *The Ring* (with Robert E. Margroff)
1969   *Macroscope* (18 printings by 1986)   pb50¢–
1970   *The E.S.P. Worm* (with Robert E. Margroff)   pb50¢–
1971   *Prostho Plus*
1973   *Race Against Time*
1974   *Triple Detente*
1975   *Phthor* (sequel to *Chthon*)
1976   *But What of Earth?* (revised by Robert Coulson)
1976   *Steppe*
1977   *Hasan*
1981   *Mute*   pb (7th printing by 1986)   pb75¢–
1982   *Viscous Circle*   pb75¢–
1985   *Anthonology*   ss
1986   *Ghost*   pb$1.00–
1986   *Shade of the Tree*   pb$1.00
1987   *Dragon's Gold* (with Robert E. Margroff)   pb$1.00–
Balook
Rings of Ice
Apprentice Adept series
  Split Infinity
    1981   *Blue Adept*   hc$2.75   pb90¢
  Juxtaposition
    1987   *Out of Phaze*   hc$4.50   pb$1.00
    1988   *Robot Adept*
Battle Circle trilogy
    1968   *Sos the Rope*   pb75¢
    1973   *Var the Stick*   pb90¢
    1975   *Neq the Sword*   pb90¢
    1977   *Battle Circle* (trilogy in one volume)   pb$1.00
Bio of a Space Tyrant series
  Refugee
  Mercenary
  Politician
  Executive
  Statesman
Cluster trilogy
    1977   *Cluster*
    1978   *Chaining the Lady*

1978   *Kirlian Quest*
Incarnations of Immortality series
1983   *On a Pale Horse* (10 printings by 1987)   hc$2.00   pb90¢–
1984   *Bearing an Hourglass*   pb$1.00–
1985   *With a Tangled Skein*   pb$1.00–
1986   *Wielding a Red Sword*   hc$4.25   pb$1.00
1987   *Being a Green Mother*   hc$4.50
1988   *For Love of Evil*
Magic of Xanth series
1977   *A Spell for Chameleon*
1979   *The Source of Magic*   pb50¢–
1979   *Castle Roogna*   pb50¢
1982   *Centaur Aisle*   pb75¢
Ogre, Ogre
Night Mare
Dragon on a Pedestal
Crewel Lye: A Caustic Yarn
Golem in the Gears
Vale of the Vole
Of Man and Manta series
1968   *Omnivore*
1971   *Orn*
1976   *Ox*   pb50¢
Tarot series
1979   *God of Tarot*   pb75¢
Vision of Tarot
Faith of Tarot

CHRISTOPHER ANVIL *(psd. of Harry C. Crosby, Jr.)*

"Anvil" is primarily known for his stories in *Astounding/Analog*. Under his own name, he had a story in *Imagination* which was reprinted in *Playboy;* no other writer can make that statement.

1964   *The Day the Machines Stopped*
1969   *Strangers in Paradise*   ss
1972   *Pandora's Planet*
1975   *Warlord's World*

EDWIN LESTER ARNOLD (1857–1935)

Arnold wrote the kind of adventuresome fantasies that made H. Rider Haggard and Edgar Rice Burroughs famous. The most notable of Arnold's books is the unpromisingly titled *Lt. Gullivar Jones: His Vacation*. This novel was reprinted by Ace Books with the argument by Richard A. Lupoff that it was the inspiration for Burroughs' John Carter stories. Ace used a more dramatic title—*Gulliver of Mars*—and Marvel Comics adapted it into a short-lived comic-book series in *Creatures on the Loose* under the title "Warrior of Mars." Yes, Arnold spelled the name "Gullivar" and Ace spelled it "Gulliver."

1890   *The Wonderful Adventures of Phra the Phoenician*
1895   *The Story of Ulla, and Other Tales*   ss
1901   *Lepidus the Centurion: A Roman of Today*
1905   *Gulliver of Mars* (*Lt. Gullivar Jones: His Vacation*)

ISAAC ASIMOV (1920–)

While others have written more books, no one has written as many books on as many different subjects as Isaac Asimov. However, although he has written mystery stories, histories, science books—hundreds of books on dozens of topics—he is best known as a science-fiction writer. And, as a science-fiction writer, he is best known for his "Foundation" series. Originally a series of short stories, novelettes, and serials in *Astounding Science Fiction*, these were collected into three novels (*Foundation, Foundation and Empire, Second Foundation*) which have remained in print for decades in many editions. The first editions of these books were published by Gnome Press, one of the first science-fiction specialist publishers. These three books won Asimov his first Hugo, the only one ever given in the category of Best Series. In recent years, Asimov has gone back to the "Foundation" series and has written novels tying it to his robot series, particularly the adventures of robot detective R. Daneel Olivaw.

Asimov wrote a novelization of the movie *Fantastic Voyage* and has written another book based on that premise. He also wrote science-fiction juveniles as "Paul French"; currently he is writing a juvenile series about Norby the robot with his wife, psychiatrist Janet O. Jeppson.

Books about him include *Asimov Analyzed* (1972) by Neil Goble; *The Science Fiction of Isaac Asimov* (1974) by Joseph F. Patrouch,

Jr.; and *Isaac Asimov* (1977), edited by Martin Harry Greenberg and Joseph D. Olander. Autobiographical information can be found in his two-volume autobiography, *In Memory Yet Green* and *In Joy Still Felt*, as well as in the books celebrating each 100 books he has written, *Opus 100, Opus 200,* and *Opus 300*. The *Opus* books also serve as samplers of his various writing and each contains a bibliography listing the 100 books represented in that volume.

The list here includes only Asimov's science fiction.

Asimov has edited five volumes of *The Hugo Winners,* collecting all the short-fiction award winners. He has edited many other anthologies, most frequently in collaboration with Martin Harry Greenberg. Due to space limitations, those are not included in this book. Of particular note to collectors is Asimov's 1974 anthology, *Before the Golden Age,* which reprints his favorite science-fiction stories from the magazines Asimov read as a boy. Those stories are seldom anthologized and generally are available only in the original magazines.

1963	Hugo (Special): "Adding Science to Science Fiction"	
1966	Hugo (All-Time Series): *Foundation* series	
1972	Nebula (Novel): *The Gods Themselves*	
1973	Hugo (Novel): *The Gods Themselves*	
1976	Nebula (Novelette): "The Bicentennial Man"	
1977	Hugo (Novelette): "The Bicentennial Man"	
1983	Hugo (Novel): *Foundation's Edge*	
1986	SFWA Grand Master	

1950	*Pebble in the Sky*	
1951	*The Stars Like Dust*	
1952	*The Currents of Space*	
1955	*The Martian Way and Other Stories*	ss pb50¢–
1955	*The End of Eternity*	
1957	*Earth is Room Enough*	ss pb50¢–
1959	*Nine Tomorrows*	ss pb50¢–
1961	*Triangle* (omnibus of *Pebble, Stars, Currents*)	
1966	*Fantastic Voyage* (movie novelization)	pb50¢–
1969	*Through a Glass, Clearly*	ss
1969	*Nightfall and Other Stories*	ss

1969   *Opus 100*   ss
1972   *The Gods Themselves*   **pb**50¢–
1972   *The Early Asimov*   ss
1973   *The Best of Isaac Asimov*   ss
1974   *Have You Seen These?*   ss
1975   *The Heavenly Host* (juvenile)
1975   *Buy Jupiter and Other Stories*   ss   **pb**50¢–
1976   *Good Taste*
1976   *The Bicentennial Man and Other Stories*   ss   **pb**50¢–
1979   *Opus 200*
1983   *The Winds of Change and Other Stories*   ss
1984   *Opus 300*
1985   *The Edge of Tomorrow*   ss
1986   *The Best Science Fiction of Isaac Asimov*   ss   **hc/pb**
1986   *The Alternate Asimovs*   ss   **hc/pb**
1987   *Fantastic Voyage II: Destination Brain*   **hc**$6.00
Foundation series
   1951   *Foundation*
   1952   *Foundation and Empire*
   1953   *Second Foundation*
   1964   *The Foundation Trilogy* (omnibus of first three books)
   1982   *Foundation's Edge*
   1986   *Foundation and Earth*   **hc**$4.25
Lucky Starr series (juveniles, originally as by "Paul French")
   1952   *David Starr: Space Ranger*   **pb**50¢–
   1953   *Lucky Starr and the Pirates of the Asteroids*   **pb**50¢–
   1954   *Lucky Starr and the Oceans of Venus*   **pb**50¢–
   1956   *Lucky Starr and the Big Sun of Mercury*   **pb**50¢–
   1957   *Lucky Starr and the Moons of Jupiter*   **pb**50¢–
   1958   *Lucky Starr and the Rings of Saturn*   **pb**50¢–
Norby series (with Janet Asimov)
   1983   *Norby, the Mixed-Up Robot*
   1984   *Norby's Other Secret*
   1986   *The Norby Chronicles* (omnibus of first two books)
Robot series
   1950   *I, Robot*   ss
   1954   *The Caves of Steel*   **pb**50¢–
   1957   *The Naked Sun*   **pb**50¢–
   1964   *The Rest of the Robots*   ss

1982   *The Complete Robot*   ss
1983   *The Robots of Dawn*
1985   *Robots and Empire*   pb$1.00–
1986   *Robot Dreams*   ss   pb$2.00–   hc$12.50

ROBERT LYNN ASPRIN

Asprin's primary claims to fame are the "Myth" series of novels (light-hearted fantasy in the *Unknown Worlds* vein) and the "Thieves' World" shared-universe anthologies and novels. Because of the significance of these anthologies—they basically started the trend toward shared universes—we are including them despite our general prohibition against listing anthologies. The novels in this series to date are *Beyond Sanctuary, Beyond the Veil,* and *Beyond Wizardwall,* all by Janet Morris, *Shadowspawn* by Andrew J. Offutt, and *Dagger* by David Drake.

The "Myth" novels involve an apprentice wizard and his mentor, a demon who has lost the ability to do magic himself. The stories are curently appearing in black-and-white comic-book form, and the earlier comics (done with Phil Foglio) have been collected as full-color graphic albums by Donning Press/Starblaze, which also is publishing graphic-album versions of *Thieves' World* and *Duncan and Mallory,* an Asprin series about a dull-witted knight who travels with a swindling dragon.

The "Thieves' World" series began as a series of anthologies and has recently been expanded to include novels by various writers.

Many of Asprin's books, including the later "Thieves' World" anthologies and the Donning/Starblaze graphic novels set in that world, are produced in collaboration with his wife, Lynn Abbey.

1977   *The Cold Cash War*   hc$5.00   pb50¢
1979   *Tambu*   pb50¢
1979   *The Bug Wars*   hc$5.00   pb50¢
Mirror Friend, Mirror Foe (with George Takei)   pb$1.00
Myth series
    1978   *Another Fine Myth . . .*   trade pb$2.50   pb75¢
    1980   *Myth Conceptions*   trade pb$2.50   pb75¢
    1982   *Myth Directions*   trade pb$2.50   pb75¢
    1983   *Hit or Myth*   trade pb$2.50   pb75¢
    1984   *Myth-ing Persons*   trade pb$2.50   pb75¢–

1985   *Little Myth Marker*   **trade pb$2.50   pb75¢–**
1986   *M.Y.T.H. Inc. Link*   **trade pb$2.50   pb75¢–**
1987   *Myth Alliances* (book club: 1st 3 books)   **hc$2.50**
1987   *Myth-Nomers and Im-Pervections*   **trade pb$2.50   pb75¢–**
Thieves' World series
1979 (ed.)   *Thieves' World*   **pb$1.00**
1980 (ed.)   *Tales From the Vulgar Unicorn*   **pb50¢**
1981 (ed.)   *Shadows of Sanctuary*   **pb$1.00**
1982 (ed.)   *Sanctuary* (book club, 1st 3 books)   **hc$2.50**
1982 (ed.)   *Storm Season*   **pb$1.00**
1983 (ed. with Lynn Abbey)   *The Face of Chaos*   **pb$1.00**
1984 (ed. with Lynn Abbey)   *Wings of Omen*   **pb$1.00**
1985 (ed. with Lynn Abbey)   *The Dead of Winter*   **pb$1.00**
1986 (ed. with Lynn Abbey)   *Soul of the City*   **pb$1.00**
1986 (ed. with Lynn Abbey)   *Blood Ties*   **pb$1.00**
1987 (ed. with Lynn Abbey)   *Aftermath*   **pb$1.00**

ALICIA AUSTIN (1942–)

Alicia Austin won a Hugo as best fan artist before turning professional. Value of her original black-and-white work ranges from $100 to $250. The range on her paintings is $400–$700, and publication or non-publication has little effect on the pricing.

1979   WFA (Artist)

J(AMES) G(RAHAM) BALLARD (1930–)

J. G. Ballard has achieved a reputation for literary excellence both within and outside the science-fiction field. His earliest stories appeared in the British magazine *New Worlds*. His semi-autobiographical novel became the basis for the recent movie, *Empire of the Sun*.

A collection of articles on him can be found in *J.G. Ballard: the First Twenty Years* (1976), edited by James Goddard and David Pringle. Many American short-story collections contain different stories than the same-titled British editions.

1962   *The Wind From Nowhere*
1962   *The Voices of Time*   **ss**
1962   *Billenium*   **ss**
1963   *The Drowned World*   **hc$3.75**

1963   *The Four-Dimensional Nightmare*
1963   *Passport to Eternity*   ss
1964   *The Terminal Beach*
1964   *The Burning World*
1966   *The Crystal World*   pb75¢
1966   *The Impossible Man*
1967   *The Disaster Area*   ss
1967   *The Day of Forever*   ss
1967   *The Overloaded Man*   ss
1970   *Love and Napalm: Export USA*   ss
1971   *Vermillion Sands*   ss
1971   *Chronopolis*   ss
1973   *Crash*
1974   *Concrete Island*
1975   *High-Rise*
1976   *Low-Flying Aircraft*   ss
1977   *The Best of J.G. Ballard*   ss

EDWIN BALMER (1883–1959)

Balmer is best known in science-fiction circles for his collaboration with Philip Wylie on *When Worlds Collide* (made into a George Pal movie and a short-lived comic strip, *Speed Spaulding,* the only comic strip to date to end with the destruction of Earth). They also collaborated on a sequel, *After Worlds Collide.*

1910   *The Achievements of Luther Trant*   ss (with William MacHarg)
1927   *The Flying Death*
1933   *When Worlds Collide* (with Philip Wylie)
1934   *After Worlds Collide* (with Philip Wylie)

JOHN KENDRICK BANGS (1862–1922)

A friend of Mark Twain and Theodore Roosevelt, Bangs was a famous writer whose work appeared in all the top-paying magazines through the 1890s. He is still highly regarded and his books are eagerly sought by collectors. His most notable fantasies are the short story "The Water Ghost of Harrowby Hall" and the book *The Houseboat on the Styx,* in which the shades of famous men swap stories aboard their floating clubhouse. In addition to his fantasies, he also wrote stories linking two famous literary figures of his day: Sherlock Holmes the detective and Raffles the gentleman burglar.

John Kendrick Bangs: Humorist of the Nineties (1941) was a biography written by his son, Francis Hyde Bangs.

1893 *Toppleton's Client, or A Spirit in Exile*
1894 *The Water Ghost and Others* ss
1895 *Mr. Bonaparte of Corsica*
1896 *A House-Boat on the Styx* (later *The Houseboat on the Styx*)
1897 *The Pursuit of the House-Boat*
1898 *Ghosts I Have Met, and Some Others* ss
1899 *The Enchanted Typewriter*
1901 *Mr. Munchausen*
1902 *Olympian Nights*
1907 *Alice in Blunderland*

CLIVE BARKER

No other writer has had such an immediate success in the horror field as Clive Barker, who burst on the scene with a series of six books of short stories, collectively known as *The Books of Blood*. Since then, his sales helped by praise from Stephen King, he has written novels, more short stories, and movies. Some of his stories are being adapted into comic-book form and published by Eclipse Comics under the title *Tapping the Vein*.

1985 WFA (Collection): *Clive Barker's Books of Blood, I-III*

1984 *Clive Barker's Books of Blood,* Vols. I–III (omnibus)
1985 *The Damnation Game* hc$5.00 pb$1.00
1986 *The Inhuman Condition* (*Books of Blood, Vol. IV, 1985*) hc$1.50
1986 *In the Flesh* (*Books of Blood, Vol. V, 1985*) hc$1.50
1987 *Weaveworld* hc$5.00 pb$1.00

GEORGE BARR (1937–)

Barr's art is seen on book covers, movie posters, and in magazines. The Spring 1988 *Weird Tales,* first issue of that magazine's latest incarnation, is entirely illustrated by Barr, using the styles of various artists known for their *Weird Tales* work. A collection of his art was published in a limited-edition hardcover by Donald M. Grant.

Value of his original black-and-white work ranges from $100 to $200. The range on his color work is $700–$1,100, and publication or non-publication has little effect on pricing.

1976   *Upon the Winds of Yesterday*   *$20.00*

J(AMES) M(ATTHEW) BARRIE (1860–1937)

Sir James M. Barrie is best known for his play and book version of the story of the boy who never grew up, *Peter Pan,* which has been performed by Mary Martin and others on stage and was made into an animated feature by Walt Disney. Barrie donated all royalties from *Peter Pan* in perpetuity to a children's hospital.

1904   *Peter Pan*   pb50¢–hc
1906   *Peter Pan in Kensington Gardens*   pb/hc
1928   *Peter Pan* (the play)   pb75¢–hc

JOHN BARTH (1930–)

Barth is a noted mainstream author who frequently uses fantasy in his novels.

1960   *The Sot-Weed Factor*
1966   *Giles Goat-Boy, or The Revised New Syllabus*
1968   *Lost in the Funhouse: Fiction for Print, Tape, Live Voice*   ss
1972   *Chimera*   ss

L(YMAN) FRANK BAUM (1856–1919)

Noted for his Oz Books, this American fantasist has a devoted legion of fans who collect his work. All of his Oz books and many of the sequels written after Baum's death by Ruth Plumly Thompson are available in paperbacks from Del Rey Books. Most went through several hardcover printings over the years.

Those interested in collecting all the fantasies of Baum in hardcover, some of which àre extremely difficult to locate and quite expensive, can learn about them by joining The International Wizard of Oz Club, Box 95, Kinderhook, Illinois.

The Wizard of Oz, about 4″ × 7″; cover
by Michael Herring (1947–). The Ballantine Fantasy Classic edition was released
in 1979. Copyright 1956 by Contemporary
Books, Inc.

1901   *The Master Key*
Oz series
   1900   *The Wonderful Wizard of Oz*   **pb$1.00**
   1904   *The Land of Oz*   **pb$1.00**
   1907   *Ozma of Oz*   **pb$1.00**
   1908   *Dorothy and the Wizard in Oz*   **pb$1.00**
   1909   *The Road to Oz*   **pb$1.00**
   1910   *The Emerald City of Oz*   **pb$1.00**
   1913   *The Patchwork Girl of Oz*   **pb$1.00**
   1914   *Tik-Tok of Oz*   **pb$1.00**
   1915   *The Scarecrow of Oz*   **pb$1.00**
   1916   *Rinkitink in Oz*   **pb$1.00**
   1917   *The Lost Princess of Oz*   **pb$1.00**
   1918   *The Tin Woodman of Oz*   **pb$1.00**
   1919   *The Magic of Oz*   **pb$1.00**
   1920   *Glinda of Oz*   **pb$1.00**

PETER S(OYER) BEAGLE (1939–)

Beagle's output is small but much admired. He has written an auto-biographical book, *I See by My Outfit*.

1960   *A Fine and Private Place*
1968   *The Last Unicorn*
1976   *The Fantasy Worlds of Peter Beagle* (*A Fine and Private Place, Last Unicorn,* and two short stories)   hc$5.00   pb$1.00
1986   *The Folk of the Air*   hc$5.00   pb50¢

GREG BEAR

Bear has achieved a notable success as a novelist. He illustrated some of his early magazine stories and even painted covers for them, since he is an artist as well as a writer.

1983   Nebula (Novella): "Hardfought"
1983   Nebula (Novelette): "Blood Music"
1984   Hugo (Novelette): "Blood Music"
1986   Nebula (Short Story): "Tangents"
1987   Hugo (Short Story): "Tangents"

1979   *Hegira*   pb50¢–
1981   *Strength of Stones*   pb75¢
1984   *The Wind from a Burning Woman*   ss
1984   *Corona* ("*Star Trek*" novel)
1984   *The Infinity Concerto*   pb75¢
1984   *Eon*   hc$5.00   pb$1.00
1985   *Blood Music*   hc$5.00   pb75¢
1986   *The Serpent Mage* (seq to *Concerto*)   pb90¢
1987   *The Forge of God*   hc$6.00

CHARLES BEAUMONT *(psd. of Charles Nutt)* (1929–1967)

Beaumont burst onto the scene with a series of sharp, well-written fantasies, many in *The Magazine of Fantasy and Science Fiction*, whose editor, Anthony Boucher, presciently remarked that he felt it his duty to buy everything he could from Beaumont before the slick magazines discovered him. Soon after, the slick magazines did discover Beaumont, particularly *Playboy,* which published many of his stories and articles.

Hollywood also discovered Beaumont, and he wrote episodes for *Twilight Zone* and screenplays for movies (including *The Seven Faces of Dr. Lao*) before his early death. He wrote only one novel, *The Stranger,* a non-fantasy.

1957 *The Hunger* ss
1957 *Shadow Play* ss
1958 *Yonder* ss   pb*50¢*
1960 *Night Ride and Other Journeys* ss   pb*50¢–*
1962 (editor) *The Fiend in You*   pb*50¢–*
1965 *The Magic Man* ss (collects stories from earlier books)
1966 *The Edge* ss
1982 *Best of Beaumont*   ss (collects stories from earlier books)

EDWARD BELLAMY (1850–1898)

Looking Backward is one of the seminal science-fiction novels, written last century and looking at the end of this one. It set the pattern for much early magazine science fiction, with someone from our civilization visiting another and being lectured on the differences.

1888 *Looking Backward, 2000–1887*
1897 *Equality* (sequel to *Backward*)
1898 *The Blindman's World and Other Stories* ss

STEPHEN VINCENT BENET (1898–1943)

The most popular fantasy writer of his time, Benet wrote stories and poems for all of the top mainstream magazines. Despite his one-time popularity and the fact that his stories still hold up, little of his work remains in print.

The movie *All That Money Can Buy,* starring Walter Huston as Old Scratch, is based on Benet's most famous story, ''The Devil and Daniel Webster.'' The movie is sometimes shown under Benet's original title.

1937 *Thirteen O'Clock* ss
1938 *Johnny Pye and the Fool Killer* ss
1939 *Before Midnight* ss

1943   *Twenty-Five Short Stories*   ss
1946   *The Stephen Vincent Benet Pocket Book*   ss

GREGORY BENFORD (1941–)

Benford, a professional scientist, is noted for the scientific accuracy of his novels.

> 1974   Nebula (Novelette): "If the Stars Are Gods" (with Gordon Eklund)

> 1980   Nebula (Novel): *Timescape*

1970   *Deeper Than the Darkness*
1975   *Jupiter Project*
1977   *If the Stars Are Gods* (with Gordon Eklund)   pb50¢
1977   *In the Ocean of Night*   pb75¢–
1978   *The Stars in Shroud* (revision of *Deeper Than the Darkness*) hc$5.00   pb75¢
1980   *Shiva Descending* (with William Rotsler)   pb75¢–
1980   *Timescape* (5th printing by 1987)   pb75¢–
1980   *Find the Changeling* (with Gordon Eklund)   pb50¢
1983   *Across the Sea of Suns* (revised for 1987 edition)   pb75¢–
1986   *Heart of the Comet* (with David Brin)   hc$5.00   pb$1.00–
1986   *In Alien Flesh*   ss   hc$5.00   pb$1.00
1987   *Great Sky River*   hc$4.50

ALFRED BESTER (1913–1987)

Bester was a writer for DC comic books (on the Golden Age "Green Lantern" stories, among others) and a columnist for *Holiday* magazine for many years. He wrote for television and wrote a novel about the TV and advertising world, *Who He?* (published in paperback as *Rat Race*).

But it is in the field of science fiction that he is best known. He began writing for *Unknown Worlds* but turned out little science fiction or fantasy over the next decade. He burst forth in 1953 with *The Demolished Man,* a serial in *Galaxy* which instantly became famous because of the literary tricks he used, such as naming a character "T8" (for "Tate"), and for its theme of how to commit a perfect crime in a world of telepaths.

He followed this with several short stories and novelettes and another novel, *The Stars My Destination*. Praise for that novel, the plot of which was unabashedly taken from Alexandre Dumas' *The Count of Monte Cristo*, was even higher than for *The Demolished Man*. Either of those novels—or any of several shorter works such as "Fondly Fahrenheit" or "5,271,009"—would be sufficient to establish a literary reputation.

1953   Hugo (Novel): *The Demolished Man*

1953   *The Demolished Man*
1957   *The Stars My Destination*   pb50¢–
1958   *Starburst*   ss
1964   *The Dark Side of the Earth*   ss
1974   *The Computer Connection*
1976   *The Light Fantastic*   ss
1976   *Star Light, Star Bright*   ss
1976   *Starlight: The Great Short Fiction of Alfred Bester* (book-club omnibus of *Light Fantastic* and *Star Light, Star Bright*)   hc$2.50
1980   *Golem*[100]   hc$5.00   pb50¢
1981   *The Deceivers*   pb75¢–$1.25

AMBROSE BIERCE (1842–1914?)

This cynical newspaperman and Civil War veteran was known as "Bitter Bierce" for his satires (many of them fantasies) of the things so many held dear. His best-known work, often quoted today, is *The Devil's Dictionary*, a collection of caustic comments on marriage and other institutions, which is pretty reliably kept in print. Collections of his stories are readily obtainable. In particular, Citadel published *The Collected Writings of Ambrose Bierce*, containing most of his better-known stories, in 1946. Trade paperback editions of that book were still in print in the 1960s.

Bierce disappeared in Mexico in 1914, where he had gone to join Pancho Villa. The date and circumstances of Bierce's death are unknown—which has resulted in Bierce himself becoming a character in many fantasy or science-fiction stories about what happened to him, stories which have Bierce, Judge Crater, and Amelia Earhart in some fantastic world, still adventuring to this day. Bierce recently appeared as a character in *The Lost Planet,* a comic-book mini-series from Eclipse Comics.

1864   *Ghost and Horror Stories of Ambrose Bierce*   ss
1970   *The Collected Short Stories of Ambrose Bierce*   ss

LLOYD BIGGLE, JR. (1923–)

A musicologist, Biggle frequently uses music to great effect in his science-fiction writing.

1961   *The Angry Espers*
1963   *All the Colors of Darkness*
1965   *The Fury Out of Time*   pb50¢–
1966   *Watchers of the Dark*
1967   *The Rule of the Door and Other Fanciful Regulations*   ss
1968   *The Still, Small Voice of Trumpets*
1971   *The World Menders*
1972   *The Light That Never Was*
1972   *The Metallic Muse*   ss
1974   *Monument*
1975   *The Darkening Universe*
1976   *A Galaxy of Strangers*   ss
1977   *Silence Is Deadly*
1985   *Alien Main* (with T. L. Sherred)

EANDO BINDER *(psd. of Earl and Otto Binder)*

This pseudonym was widely used in early science-fiction magazines, originally by the brothers Earl Andrew Binder and Otto Oscar Binder ("Eando" is from their initials, E and O). Otto (1911–1975) later used the name solo, after Earl (1904–?) left the field. Otto largely dropped out of science fiction during the 1940s, when he wrote prolifically for comic books—he wrote most of the adventures of Captain Marvel, Captain Marvel, Jr., and Mary Marvel, among scores of other comic books. (Mary Marvel usually was drawn by another Binder brother, Jack.) In the early 1950s, when Captain Marvel was sued off the newsstands by Superman, Binder resumed writing some science fiction but comic books remained his primary outlet. He simply switched from writing about Captain Marvel, Captain Marvel, Jr., and Mary Marvel to writing about Superman, Superboy, and Supergirl.

His robot series about Adam Link was adapted into comic-book form by the EC line of comics, a cult collectible today. The series was re-adapted into comic-book form for the Warren Magazine line of horror comics (*Creepy, Eerie, Vampirella*), which adapted the stories EC had done and several more.

1949   *Lords of Creation*
1965   *Adam Link—Robot* ss
1965   *Anton York, Immortal*
1965   *Enslaved Brains*
1967   *The Avengers Battle the Earth Wrecker*
1967   *The Impossible World*
1968   *Five Steps to Tomorrow*
1969   *Menace of the Saucers*
1971   *Night of the Saucers*
1971   *Puzzle of the Space Pyramids*
1971   *The Double Man*
1971   *Get Off My World*
1971   *Secret of the Red Spot*
1972   *The Mind From Outer Space*
1972   *The Forgotten Colony*

MICHAEL BISHOP (1945–)

Many of Bishop's novels are set in a future Atlanta, GA. As a result, used-book stores in the Atlanta area have reported difficulty in keeping any Bishop book in stock.

1981   Nebula (Novelette): "The Quickening"
1982   Nebula (Novel): *No Enemy but Time*

1975   *A Funeral for the Eyes of Fire*
1976   *And Strange at Ecbatan the Trees*
1977   *Stolen Faces*
1977   *A Little Knowledge*
1979   *Catacomb Years*
1982   *Blooded on Arachne*   hc$3.50
1982   *No Enemy But Time*

(DREXEL) JEROME (LEWIS) BIXBY (1923–)

Jerome Bixby was an editor of *Planet Stories* and *Two Complete Science-Adventure Books;* an assistant editor on *Startling Stories, Thrilling Wonder Stories,* and *Galaxy;* and the co-author (with Otto Clement) of the story for the movie *Fantastic Voyage.* He also wrote many short stories, including "It's a *Good* Life," which was dramatized on the original *Twilight Zone* series and again in *Twilight Zone: The Movie.* (It's the one about the little boy who could make anything happen just by wishing for it.)

Bixby wrote a number of other short fantasy and science-fiction stories (no novels) before departing for Hollywood. He had two short-story collections, both long out of print and hard to find, particularly the second, which was packaged and marketed as an occult book.

1964 *Space by the Tale* ss
1964 *The Devil's Scrapbook* ss

JAMES BLISH (1921–1975)

Blish was a Hugo-winning author, a critic of considerable renown (under the pseudonym of William Atheling, Jr.), the editor of the one-issue *Vanguard Science Fiction* magazine, and the adaptor of the original *Star Trek* series into novelettes which were published as *Star Trek* through *Star Trek 11* by Bantam Books. He also wrote the first original *Star Trek* novel, *Spock Must Die!* (*Star Trek* books are dealt with in a separate section of this book.)

One of Blish's great concepts was the notion that, with antigravity, the size and shape of a spaceship made no difference. He took this idea and came up with galaxy-traveling cities—the cities of Earth, flying through space in quest of work. These became known as the "Okie" stories and were collected into four books.

Another Blish-produced book was *Thirteen O'Clock and Other Zero Hours,* a collection of stories by C. M. Kornbluth. That book is listed under Kornbluth.

1959 Hugo (Novel): *A Case of Conscience*

1952 *Jack of Eagles*
1953 *The Warriors of Day*

1957 *The Frozen Year* (Blish argued this was not science fiction; few agreed)
1957 *The Seedling Stars*
1958 *VOR* (with Damon Knight)
1958 *A Case of Conscience* pb50¢–
1959 *Galactic Cluster* ss pb50¢
1959 *The Duplicated Man* (with Robert Lowndes) pb50¢
1961 *Star Dwellers* pb50¢
1961 *So Close to Home* ss
1961 *Titan's Daughter*
1962 *The Night Shapes*
1964 *Doctor Mirabilis*
1965 *Best Science Fiction Stories of James Blish* ss
1965 *Mission to the Heart Stars*
1967 *A Torrent of Faces* (with Norman L. Knight) pb50¢
1968 *Black Easter* pb50¢
1968 *The Vanished Jet*
1968 *Welcome to Mars!*
1970 *Anywhen* ss
1970 *The Day After Judgment* pb50¢
1971 *. . . And All the Stars a Stage*
1972 *Midsummer Century* ss pb50¢
1973 *The Quincunx of Time*
1979 *The Best of James Blish* pb50¢
1982 *The Star Dwellers* pb50¢
Okies series
   1955 *Earthman, Come Home*
   1956 *They Shall Have Stars* (pb as *Year 2018!*)
   1958 *The Triumph of Time* pb50¢
   1962 *A Life for the Stars*
   1970 *Cities in Flight* (omnibus of all four "Okies" books)

ROBERT BLOCH (1917–)

Bloch's most famous novel is *Psycho* (1959), a non-fantasy novel which became a highly successful Alfred Hitchcock movie. His most famous short story is "Yours Truly, Jack the Ripper" (written in 1943). In addition to those, he has written more than 50 books, and a recent collection of his short stories filled three volumes without beginning to exhaust the supply.

Because of the enduring popularity of *Psycho*, Bloch had numerous paperback collections of his fantasy and science-fiction and crime stories published during the sixties and seventies. While none of those collections is currently in print, copies are relatively easy to find in used-book stores.

1959   Hugo (Short Story): "That Hell-Bound Train"

1975   WFA Life Achievement Award

1945   *The Opener of the Way* ss (Arkham House) hc$20.00
1960   *Pleasant Dreams* ss (Arkham House) hc$20.00
1961   *Nightmares* ss (from *Pleasant Dreams*) pb50¢
1961   *Blood Runs Cold* ss pb50¢
1962   *Atoms and Evil* ss pb50¢
1962   *Yours Truly, Jack the Ripper* ss pb50¢
1962   *More Nightmares* ss pb50¢
1963   *Horror-7* ss pb50¢
1963   *Bogey Men* ss pb50¢
1965   *Tales in a Jugular Vein* ss pb50¢
1965   *The Skull of the Marquis de Sade* ss pb50¢
1966   *Chamber of Horrors* ss pb50¢
1967   *The Living Demons* ss pb50¢
1967   *Torture Garden* ss pb50¢
1967   *The Night Walker* (novelization by Sidney Stuart of Bloch screenplay)
1968   *Ladies' Day/This Crowded Earth* (two stories) pb50¢
1969   *Dragons and Nightmares* ss hc$10.00
2969   *Bloch and Bradbury* ss (stories by Bloch and stories by Ray Bradbury) pb50¢
1971   *Fear Today, Gone Tomorrow* ss pb50¢
1971   *It's All in Your Mind* pb50¢
1971   *Sneak Preview* pb50¢
1977   *The King of Terrors* ss hc$5.00
1977   *Cold Chills* ss hc$5.00
1977   *The Best of Robert Bloch* pb50¢
1979   *Such Stuff as Screams Are Made Of* ss pb50¢
1979   *Strange Eons* pb50¢

1979   *There Is a Serpent in Eden* (also as *The Cunning*)   pb50¢
1981   *Mysteries of the Worm*   pb75¢
1983   *Twilight Zone: The Movie* (novelization)   pb$1.00
1987   *Lost in Time and Space with Lefty Feep*   hc$3.25–$10.00
1987   *Midnight Pleasures*   ss   hc$3.25
1987   *Selected Stories of Robert Bloch* (3 volumes,   hc$25.00)
Volume 1: *Final Reckonings*   ss
Volume 2: *Bitter Ends*   ss
Volume 3: *Last Rites*   ss

HANNES BOK (1914–1964)

Although best known as an artist, particularly for *Weird Tales,* Bok also was a writer, completing A. Merritt's *The Black Wheel* and *The Fox Woman* and writing a couple of novels on his own.

A book about Bok is *And Flights of Angels: The Life and Legend of Hannes Bok* by Emil Petaja (1968).

Value of his original black-and-white work ranges from $800 to $1,300. The range on his paintings is $3,500–$5,000.

Stirring Science Stories, April 1941, about 7″ × 10″; cover by Hannes Bok (1914–1964). Copyright 1941 by Albing Publications.

1953   Hugo (Cover Artist)

1946   *The Fox Woman and The Blue Pagoda* (with A. Merritt) hc*$20.00*

1947   *The Black Wheel* (with A. Merritt)   hc*$20.00*   pb*$1.00*

1969   *The Sorcerer's Ship*   pb*50¢*

1970   *Beyond the Golden Stair*   pb*50¢*

JORGE LUIS BORGES (1899–1986)

This blind Argentine was a writer of short stories—many of them fantasies—and essays.

1979   WFA Life Achievement Award

1962   *Labyrinths* ss

1970   *The Aleph and Other Stories 1933–1969*   ss

1981   *Borges: A Reader*   pb/hc*$2.50–$4.50*

ANTHONY BOUCHER *(psd. of William Anthony Parker White)* (1911–1968)

Boucher was better known under his pseudonym than by his real name and, in fact, White had a joint bank account with Boucher in order to make it easier to cash royalty checks. He also wrote under the names "H. H. Holmes" and "Herman W. Mudgett." (Boucher was an avid fan of true-crime stories and took both those pseudonyms from a mass murderer, Herman W. Mudgett, who operated under the alias of H. H. Holmes.)

With J. Francis McComas, Boucher created and edited *The Magazine of Fantasy and Science Fiction*. He continued editing it for several years after McComas left.

Although he wrote several mystery novels, Boucher wrote no fantasy or science-fiction novels, though he produced a number of excellent short stories. He did write one mystery novel of particular interest to science-fiction fans. *Rocket to the Morgue* (originally published as by H. H. Holmes but since reprinted as by Boucher) is about a murder involving a science-fiction writers' organization; real writers are concealed behind fake names, but Robert Heinlein, Otto Binder, Julius Schwartz, and Edmond Hamilton are among the more recognizable ones.

In addition to editing *F&SF* and several collections of stories from that magazine, Boucher edited *A Treasury of Great Science Fiction*, a two-volume anthology. A two-volume memorial anthology was edited by J. Francis McComas in which various authors dedicated stories to Boucher and told what he had meant to them. One of the volumes, *Special Wonder*, was made up of science-fiction and fantasy stories; the other, *Crimes and Misfortunes*, contained crime and mystery stories.

1955 *Far and Away* ss   pb$1.00
1969 *The Compleat Werewolf and Other Stories* ss

BEN(JAMIN WILLIAM) BOVA (1932–)

Ben Bova became editor of *Analog* after John W. Campbell died and was the first fiction editor of *Omni*. Since leaving that magazine, he has concentrated on writing. He is noted both for his novels and for his non-fiction.

In collaboration with Harlan Ellison, he wrote a story called "Brillo," about a robot policeman. Again in collaboration with Ellison, he successfully sued ABC-TV for plagiarism when that network broadcast a series about a robot policeman. Bova also wrote a novel called *The Starcrossed* which is based on Ellison's misfortunes with another TV series called *The Starlost*.

1973   Hugo (Professional Editor)
1974   Hugo (Professional Editor)
1975   Hugo (Professional Editor)
1976   Hugo (Professional Editor)
1977   Hugo (Professional Editor)
1979   Hugo (Professional Editor)

1959 *The Star Conquerors* juv
1964 *Star Watchmen*
1967 *The Weathermakers*
1968 *Out of the Sun*
1969 *The Dueling Machine*
1970 *Escape!*
1971 *THX 1138* (movie novelization) pb50¢

1972 *As on a Darkling Plain*
1973 *The Winds of Altair*
1973 *When the Sky Burned*
1973 *Forward in Time* ss
1974 *Gremlins, Go Home!* (with Gordon R. Dickson)
1975 *The Starcrossed* pb50¢
1976 *The Multiple Man* pb50¢–
1976 *Millennium*
1976 *City of Darkness* juv pb75¢–
1978 *Maxwell's Demons* ss pb50¢
1979 *Kinsman* (prequel to *Millennium*) hc$4.00 pb$1.00
1981 *Voyagers* hc$3.75
Exiles series
  1971 *Exiled From Earth*
  1972 *Flight of Exiles*
  1975 *End of Exile*
  1980 *The Exiles Trilogy* (omnibus of all three books) pb$1.00

LEIGH BRACKETT (1915–1978)

Leigh Brackett was the wife of Edmond Hamilton (married 1946) and they divided their time between their farm in Kinsman, Ohio, and Los Angeles. While in Los Angeles, Brackett wrote for the movies, including such films as *The Big Sleep* (she wrote the screenplay in collaboration with William Faulkner), *Rio Bravo*, and *The Empire Strikes Back* (she turned in the screenplay the day before she went into the hospital, where she died of cancer). Her other writing was usually adventurous science fiction; she wrote for *Planet Stories* and *Thrilling Wonder Stories*, but she also had stories in *Astounding* and *F&SF*. In addition, she wrote mystery novels and at least one western. In 1974, she edited *The Best of Planet Stories, No. 1;* there never was a second volume.

1951 *Shadow Over Mars*
1951 *The Nemesis From Terra* (Ace Double) pb$2.00
1952 *The Starmen* (also as *The Galactic Breed, The Starmen of Llyrdis)* pb50¢
1953 *The Sword of Rhiannon* (Ace Double) pb$3.00
1955 *The Big Jump* (Ace Double) pb$3.00
1955 *The Long Tomorrow* hc$5.00 pb50¢

1963   *Alpha Centauri—or Die!* **pb**; as Ace Double   *$2.00,* as
       single   *50¢*
1964   *The Secret of Sinharat* (Ace Double)   **pb$1.00**
1964   *People of the Talisman* (Ace Double)   **pb$1.00**
1967   *The Coming of the Terrans*   **ss**
1973   *The Halfling and Other Stories*   **ss**   **pb50¢**
1977   *The Best of Leigh Brackett* (ed. by Edmond Hamilton)
Eric John Stark series
   1974   *The Ginger Star*
   1974   *The Hounds of Skaith*
   1976   *The Reavers of Skaith*
   1976   *The Book of Skaith* (book club, three novels)   **hc$2.50**

RAY (DOUGLAS) BRADBURY (1920–)

Bradbury has lived in California for 50 years, but much of his fiction
continues to be based on his Midwestern childhood; he was born in
Waukegan, Illinois. He was helped in his early years by such established professionals in science fiction as Henry Hasse and Leigh
Brackett.

Most of Bradbury's early short stories appeared in pulp magazines,
such as *Weird Tales* and *Planet Stories*. Those same stories went on
to form collections including *The Martian Chronicles, The Illustrated
Man,* and *The October Country,* each of which has gone through multiple printings. Today, when Bradbury writes a story—much of his
recent output has been in the form of poems, novels, or adaptations
of his earlier works to movies, television, or the stage—it generally
appears in one of the slick mainstream magazines.

Bradbury has edited two anthologies, both paperback originals, both
fantasy. One of them, *Timeless Stories for Today and Tomorrow,* has
gone through multiple editions and is readily available. The other,
The Circus of Dr. Lao and Other Improbable Stories, apparently was
too successful for its own good. Bradbury brought Charles Finney's
The Circus of Dr. Lao back into public awareness, and that story was
snatched from Bradbury's anthology and published independently. The
Bradbury collection went out of print.

Other paperback originals of Bradbury stories which may be hard
to locate are the comic-book adaptations done by EC Comics in the

early 1950s. Sixteen of the twenty-four Bradbury adaptations have been collected in *Tomorrow Midnight* and *The Autumn People*.

Not all of Bradbury's books are included in this list because not all are fantasy or science fiction.

1977 WFA Life Achievement Award

1947 *Dark Carnival* ss
1950 *The Martian Chronicles* ss
1951 *The Illustrated Man* ss
1952 (editor) *Timeless Stories for Today and Tomorrow*
1953 *The Golden Apples of the Sun* ss
1953 *Fahrenheit 451* (some early editions contain two stories in addition to the novel; later editions have an afterword by Bradbury; 70th printing in 1987; Ballantine issued 200 copies in asbestos binding, signed and numbered, in 1953—simultaneously with a hardcover and a paperback edition, all three being first editions) *50¢-*
1955 *Switch on the Night* juv
1955 *The October Country* (has many stories from *Dark Carnival*) ss
1956 (ed.) *The Circus of Dr. Lao and Other Improbable Stories*
1959 *A Medicine for Melancholy* ss
1962 *R Is for Rocket* ss
1962 *Something Wicked This Way Comes*
1964 *The Machineries of Joy*
1965 *The Vintage Bradbury*
1965 *The Autumn People* (adapted by Albert B. Feldstein)
1966 *S Is for Space* ss
1966 *Tomorrow Midnight* (adapted by Albert B. Feldstein)
1966 *Twice Twenty-Two* (omnibus of *Melancholy, Golden Apples*)
1969 *I Sing the Body Electric* ss pb50¢
1969 *Bloch and Bradbury* (stories by Robert Bloch and stories by Bradbury) pb50¢
1972 *The Halloween Tree* juv
1976 *Long After Midnight*
1980 *The Stories of Ray Bradbury* ss
1983 *Dinosaur Tales* ss

MARION ZIMMER BRADLEY (1930–)

Marion Zimmer Bradley has frequently cited C. L. Moore as one of the primary influences on her writing. Her novels are action-filled and are set in colorful, fully realized worlds, chief among them the planet Darkover. In addition to her novels and comparatively few shorter stories, she has edited anthologies of sword and sorcery, of fantasy, and of stories by others which are set in her worlds.

Most of her science-fiction novels have been paperback originals, published by Donald A. Wollheim, first at Ace, later at his own publishing company, DAW Books. In recent years, her fantasy novels have become national bestsellers, particularly *The Mists of Avalon.*

1960   *The Door Through Space*
1962   *Seven From the Stars*
1963   *The Colors of Space*
1964   *The Dark Intruder and Others*   ss   pb$1.00
1964   *The Falcons of Narabedla* (Ace Double, with *Dark Intruder*)   pb$1.00
1969   *The Brass Dragon*
1973   *Hunters of the Red Moon*
1974   *The Jewel of Arwen*
1975   *Endless Voyage*
1978   *The Ruins of Isis*   pb50¢
1980   *Two to Conquer*
1982   *The Mists of Avalon*   hc$5.00   trade pb$3.00   pb$1.00
1983   *Web of Light*   pb75¢–
1984   *Web of Darkness*   pb75¢–
1985   *The Best of Marion Zimmer Bradley*   ss   trade pb$2.00   pb$1.00
1987   *The Fall of Atlantis (Web of Light, Web of Darkness)*   pb$1.00
1987   *The Firebrand*   hc$5.00

Darkover series (this is the order of publication, not the order in which events within the novels occur)

1962   *The Planet Savers*
1962   *The Sword of Aldones*
1964   *The Bloody Sun*
1965   *Star of Danger*
1970   *Winds of Darkover*
1971   *The World Wreckers*

1972   *Darkover Landfall*
1974   *The Spell Sword* (11th printing in 1987)   **pb50¢–**
1975   *The Heritage of Hastur* (13th printing in 1987)   **pb50¢–**
1976   *The Shattered Chain*   **pb50¢**
1977   *The Forbidden Tower*
1980   *Two to Conquer* (7th printing in 1987)   **50¢–**
1981   *Sharra's Exile*   **pb75¢**
1982   (ed.) *Sword of Chaos*
1987   (ed.) *Red Sun of Darkover*

DAVID BRIN

David Brin is a Hugo-winning writer who seemingly rose to top-of-the-field popularity almost instantly.

1983   Nebula (Novel): *Startide Rising*

1984   Hugo (Novel): *Startide Rising*

1985   Hugo (Short Story): "The Crystal Spheres"

1988   Hugo (Novel): *The Uplift War*

1980   *Sundiver* (9th printing in 1987)   **75¢–**
1983   *Startide Rising*
1984   *The Practice Effect* (6th printing in 1987)   **75¢–**
1985   *The Postman*   **hc$5.00 pb$1.00–**
1986   *The River of Time*   **pb95¢–**
1986   *Heart of the Comet* (with Gregory Benford)
1987   *The Uplift War*   **$1.50–$15.00**

TERRY BROOKS

Terry Brooks was a lawyer until his fantasy novel *The Sword of Shannara* catapulted him onto the bestseller lists—as a matter of fact, it was the first work of fiction to land on the *New York Times* trade paperback bestseller list (it remained there for six months). He continued his law practice for a few years but eventually gave it up to be a full-time writer. He specializes in writing trilogies.

Magic Kingdom series
1986   *Magic Kingdom for Sale—Sold!*   **pb$1.00–**
1987   *The Black Unicorn*

1988   *Wizard at Large*   hc$4.50
Shannara series
  1977   *The Sword of Shannara*
  19—   *The Elfstones of Shannara*
  1985   *The Wishsong of Shannara*

FREDRIC BROWN (1906–1972)

Collectors of the work of Fredric Brown find themselves in a strange position: There aren't enough Brown fans to make it profitable for publishers to reprint his work in mass-market editions but there are enough of them to raise the price on his books to uncomfortable levels.

Brown wrote mysteries as well as science fiction and fantasy, and he has avid fans in both fields. Currently, his mystery stories—some of them, at least—are more available than his science-fiction/fantasy works.

Brown usually wrote with a light touch (his first science-fiction novel poked fun at science-fiction fans and conventions) and he became known as an extremely adept writer of short-short stories. Challenged by editors, he kept making stories shorter and shorter, culminating in a series of short-shorts so brief that most of them were no more than plot summaries.

Brown is primarily known to today's science-fiction audience as the author of "Arena," a story on which the plot of one of the *Star Trek* television episodes was based.

1949   *What Mad Universe*
1951   *Space on My Hands*   ss
1953   *The Lights in the Sky Are Stars*
1954   *Angels and Spaceships* (also published as *Star Shine*)
1955   *Martians, Go Home*   75¢–
1957   *Rogue in Space*
1958   *Honeymoon in Hell*   ss
1961   *The Mind Thing*
1961   *Nightmares and Geezenstacks*   ss   pb$2.00
1968   *Daymares*   ss   pb50¢
1971   *Mickey Astromouse*   juv
1973   *Paradox Lost*

1977   *The Best of Fredric Brown*   pb*50¢*
1987   *And the Gods Laughed*   ss   hc*$5.00*

MARGARET BRUNDAGE (1900–1976)

Margaret Brundage was an artist whose covers for *Weird Tales*—sexy for their time—make those issues more desired by collectors and hence more expensive and hard to find.

Her black-and-white work, if any, is not on the market; her published paintings go for prices as high as $25,000, when they can be found. Her published works only appeared in *Weird Tales* and *Golden Fleece* pulp magazines, and it is that material which commands the high prices. Her unpublished works bring only a fifth or sixth of her published material.

> *NOTE:* Listed prices are for items in *GOOD* condition.
> *Very Good = two times listed price.*
> *Fine = three times listed price.*
> *Mint = four times listed price.*

JOHN (KILIAN HOUSTON) BRUNNER (1934–)

Before he was 20, Brunner had sold a cover story to *Astounding* ("Thou Good and Faithful," March 1953, under the pseudonym of John Loxmith), a short novel to *Two Complete Science-Adventure Books* (under the name Kilian Houston Brunner), and a novel to a British publisher which was published under a house name and which Brunner declines to identify. He was off to a flying start and has never really slowed down, turning out a shelf full of science fiction, some mainstream novels and suspense novels, and even some poetry. His two best-known novels are *Stand on Zanzibar* and *The Sheep Look Up; Zanzibar* is a Hugo-winning novel about overpopulation and *Sheep* deals with pollution.

He wrote several novels which were published in Ace Double books under the pseudonym of Keith Woodcott.

1969   Hugo (Novel): *Stand on Zanzibar*

1959   *Echo in the Skull* (Ace Double)   pb*$1.00*
1959   *The Hundredth Millennium* (expanded as *Catch a Falling Star*)

1959   *The Brink*
1959   *Threshold of Eternity* (Ace Double)   **pb$1.00**
1959   *The World Swappers* (Ace Double)   **pb$1.00**
1960   *The Atlantic Abomination*
1960   *Slavers of Space* (Ace Double)   **pb$2.00**
1960   *The Skynappers* (Ace Double)   **pb$2.00**
1960   *Sanctuary in the Sky* (Ace Double)   **pb$1.00**
1961   *Meeting at Infinity*   **pb50¢**
1961   *I Speak for Earth* (as by Keith Woodcott; Ace Double)
1962   *The Ladder in the Sky* (as by Keith Woodcott; Ace Double)
1962   *The Super Barbarians*
1962   *Times Without Number*
1962   *No Future in It*   ss
1963   *The Astronauts Must Not Land* (Ace Double)   **pb50¢–**
1963   *The Rites of Ohe* (Ace Double)
1963   *The Dreaming Earth*
1963   *Listen! The Stars!* (revised as *The Stardroppers*)
1963   *The Psionic Menace* (as by Keith Woodcott; Ace Double)   **pb$1.00**
1964   *Endless Shadow* (Ace Double)   **pb50¢**
1964   *The Whole Man*
1964   *To Conquer Chaos*
1965   *The Martian Sphinx* (as by Keith Woodcott)   **pb50¢**
1965   *Enigma from Tantalus* (Ace Double)   **pb50¢**
1965   *The Squares of the City*
1965   *Now Then!*   ss
1965   *The Repairmen of Cyclops*   **pb50¢**
1965   *Day of the Star Cities* (expanded as *Age of Miracles*)
1965   *The Long Result*   **pb50¢**
1966   *No Other Gods But Me*   ss
1966   *A Planet of Your Own* (Ace Double)   **pb50¢**
1967   *Out of My Mind*   ss
1967   *Born Under Mars*
1967   *The Productions of Time*   **pb50¢**
1967   *Quicksand*
1968   *Bedlam Planet*
1968   *Father of Lies*
1968   *Not Before Time*   ss
1968   *Into the Slave Nebula* (revision of *Slavers*)

1968   *Stand on Zanzibar*
1969   *The Jagged Orbit* pb50¢
1969   *Double, Double*
1969   *Times Without Number* pb50¢
1969   *Timescoop*
1969   *The Evil That Men Do*
1971   *The Gaudy Shadows*
1971   *The Dramaturges of Yan*
1971   *The Wrong End of Time*
1971   *The Traveler in Black* ss (later pb *The Compleat Traveler in Black* pb$2.25) pb75¢–
1972   *Entry to Elsewhen* ss
1972   *From This Day Forward* ss
1972   *The Sheep Look Up* hc/pb75¢–
1973   *Time-Jump* ss
1973   *More Things in Heaven* (rev *Astronauts*) pb50¢–
1973   *The Stone That Never Came Down*
1974   *Give Warning to the World* pb50¢
1974   *Total Eclipse*
1974   *Polymath* pb50¢
1974   *Web of Everywhere*
1975   *The Evil That Men Do* (with *The Purloined Planet* by Lin Carter) pb50¢–
1975   *The Shockwave Rider*
1976   *The Book of John Brunner* ss
1980   *Foreign Constellations* ss
1980   *The Infinitive of Go* pb50¢
1980   *Players at the Game of People* pb55¢
1983   *The Crucible of Time* hc/pb$1.00–
1986   *The Compleat Traveler in Black* ss trade pb$2.50

Galactic Empire series
  1963   *The Space-Time Juggler* (Ace Double) pb50¢
  1965   *The Altar on Asconel*
  1976   *Interstellar Empire* (contains both books)

Zarathustra Refugee Planets series
  1962   *Secret Agent of Terra* (revised as *The Avengers of Carrig*) pb50¢
  1963   *Castaway's World* (Ace Double)
  1965   *The Repairmen of Cyclops* (Ace Double) pb50¢

EDWARD BRYANT (1945–)

In a field where literary reputations are almost always made with novels, Bryant persists in writing short stories. He did write a novel *(Phoenix Without Ashes)* based on Harlan Ellison's original teleplay for an aborted TV series, *The Starlost,* but the bulk of his output remains short fiction. Several of his stories have received Hugo and Nebula nominations. *Particle Theory* contains his Nebula winners, "Stone" and "giANTS."

    1978   Nebula (Short Story): "Stone"
    1979   Nebula (Short Story): "giANTS"

1973   *Among the Dead* ss
1975   *Phoenix Without Ashes* (with Harlan Ellison)
1976   *Cinnabar* ss
1981   *Particle Theory* ss   **pb75¢**

ALGIS BUDRYS *(Algirdas Jonas Budrys)* (1931–)

Despite his several acclaimed novels, Budrys is best known today as a critic. He had a long run as book critic for *Galaxy* and has for years written about books and authors (it would be inaccurate and incomplete to say he reviews books) for *The Magazine of Fantasy and Science Fiction.* He also edits an annual anthology featuring stories by new writers, *Writers of the Future,* sponsored by L. Ron Hubbard's publishing operations.

1954   *False Night* (revised as *Some Will Not Die*)
1958   *Who?* **pb50¢–**
1958   *Man of Earth*
1959   *The Falling Torch*
1960   *The Unexpected Dimension* ss
1960   *Rogue Moon*
1961   *Some Will Not Die* (revised version of *False Night*)
1963   *Budrys' Inferno* ss   **pb50¢–**
1967   *The Amsirs and the Iron Thorn*
1977   *Michaelmas*
1978   *Blood & Burning* ss   **pb50¢–**

H. KENNETH BULMER (1921–)

Bulmer, a prolific British writer of science fiction, also is noted for continuing the *New Writings in SF* series of original-story anthologies after the death of E. J. Carnell.

Somewhere along the line while he was writing the "Dray Prescott" series, he stopped using the pseudonym of Alan Burt Akers and started writing the novels under the hero's name: by "Dray Prescott as told to Alan Burt Akers."

1952 *Encounter in Space*
1952 *Space Treason*
1953 *Empire of Chaos*
1953 *Galactic Intrigue*
1953 *Mission to the Stars* (as Philip Kent)
1953 *Zhorani* (as Karl Maras)
1953 *Vassals of Venus* (as Philip Kent)
1953 *Space Salvage*
1953 *The Stars Are Ours*
1954 *World Aflame*
1954 *Home Is the Martian* (as Philip Kent)
1954 *Peril From Space* (as Karl Maras)
1954 *Challenge*
1954 *Slaves of the Spectrum* (as Philip Kent)
1957 *The City Under the Sea*
1958 *The Secret of ZI*
1959 *The Changeling Worlds*
1960 *The Earth Gods Are Coming*
1961 *Beyond the Silver Sky*
1961 *No Man's World*
1962 *Fatal Fire*
1962 *The Wind of Liberty* (novel and short story)
1963 *Defiance*
1963 *The Wizard of Starship Poseidon*
1964 *Demons' World*
1964 *The Million Year Hunt* (Ace Double)
1965 *Behold the Stars*
1966 *Worlds for the Taking*
1967 *Cycle of Nemesis*
1967 *To Outrun Doomsday*

1968   *The Doomsday Men*
1969   *Kandar*
1969   *The Star Venturers*
1969   *The Ulcer Culture*
1970   *Quench the Burning Stars*
1970   *Star Trove*
1970   *Swords of the Barbarians*
1971   *The Electric Sword-Swallowers*
1971   *The Insane City*
1972   *On the Symb-Socket Circuit*
1972   *Roller Coaster*

Dray Prescott series (as by Alan Burt Akers)

Delian Cycle
  1972   *Transit to Scorpio*
  1973   *The Suns of Scorpio*
  1973   *Warrior of Scorpio*
  1973   *Swordships of Scorpio*
  1974   *Prince of Scorpio*

Havilfar Cycle
  1974   *Manhounds of Antares*
  1975   *Arena of Antares*
  1975   *Fliers of Antares*
  1975   *Bladesmen of Antares*
  1975   *Avenger of Antares*
  1976   *Armada of Antares*

Krozair Cycle
  1976   *The Tides of Kregan*
  1976   *Renegade of Kregan*
  1977   *Krozair of Kregan*

Vallian Cycle
  1977   *Secret Scorpio*
  1977   *Savage Scorpio*
  1978   *Golden Scorpio*

Kregan Cycle
  1978   *A Life for Kregan*
  1979   *A Sword for Kregan*
  1979   *A Fortune for Kregan*
  1980   *A Victory for Kregan*

Antarean Cycle
 1980 *Allies of Antares*
 1980 *Beasts of Antares*
 1981 *Rebel of Antares*
Hook series (as by Tully Zetford)
 1974 *Whirlpool of Stars*
 1974 *The Boosted Man*
 1975 *Star City*
 1975 *The Virility Gene*
Keys to the Dimensions series
 1965 *Land Beyond the Map*
 1967 *The Key to Irunium*
 1968 *The Key to Venudine*
 1969 *The Wizards of Senchuria*
 1970 *The Ships of Durostorum*
 1971 *The Hunters of Jundagai*
 1972 *The Chariots of Ra*

JIM BURNS (1948–)

The British artist's paintings bring $2,000–$3,000.

 1987 Hugo (Professional Artist)

EDGAR RICE BURROUGHS (1875–1950)

In addition to creating Tarzan (with Sherlock Holmes, Superman, and Mickey Mouse, one of the world's best-known fictional creations), Burroughs created John Carter of Mars, Carson of Venus, and David Innes of Pellucidar (the world within the hollow Earth). His stories are fast-moving and, thanks to the simple but effective trick of separating his hero and heroine early in the book and getting each in a perilous situation at the end of a chapter, difficult to put down.

In the 1960s, Burroughs' stories were issued in paperback form, manuscripts were discovered and given first publication, and Burroughs achieved a greater popularity than ever before.

Special note: There were five unauthorized Tarzan novels by "Barton Werper," published by Gold Star Books. The Burroughs estate had the novels withdrawn from sale. Copies of these books are difficult to locate and of indifferent quality but, as Tarzan-related items, they are much sought after by collectors. They are *Tarzan and the Silver Globe, Tarzan and the Cave City, Tarzan and the Snake People, Tarzan and the Abominable Snowmen,* and *Tarzan and the Winged Invaders.*

There has, to date, been only one authorized Tarzan novel by anyone other than Edgar Rice Burroughs: *Tarzan and the Valley of Gold,* a movie novelization by Fritz Leiber. However, there exists in typescript (and, allegedly, innumerable photocopies) a novel by "John Bloodstone" (Stuart J. Byrne) called *Tarzan on Mars,* which stars both Tarzan and John Carter.

Prices on Burroughs books run a gamut that really *is* a gamut. Some used paperbacks can be picked up cheaply (50¢ or thereabouts) but the original editions and many of the later editions can be *extremely* expensive—and very hard to find. Even the paperbacks from the sixties can be expensive because the Burroughs collector must compete with the art collector; the Burroughs paperbacks have had cover art by Frank Frazetta, Roy Krenkel, and other sought-after artists.

For guidance on collecting Burroughs, try to find a copy of Richard A. Lupoff's book, *Edgar Rice Burroughs: Master of Adventure* (1965). The hardcover is as hard to find as many ERB books, but the paperback edition is more attainable. Another excellent book on Burroughs is Henry Hardy Heinz's *A Golden Anniversary Bibliography of Edgar Rice Burroughs,* but virtually all copies of that book are in the hands of devout collectors of Burroughs and the book has been a rarity since it was published in 1962.

1924   *The Land That Time Forgot*   ss   *pb50¢–*
1925   *The Eternal Lover*
1925   *The Cave Girl*   *pb50¢–*
1926   *The Moon Maid*   ss   *pb50¢–*
1929   *The Monster Men*   *pb50¢–*
1932   *Jungle Girl*   *pb50¢–*
1957   *Beyond Thirty*   *pb50¢–*
1965   *Beyond the Farthest Star*   ss   (from *Tales of Three Planets*)   *pb$1.00*
Carson of Venus series
   1934   *Pirates of Venus*   *pb50¢–*
   1935   *Lost on Venus*   *pb50¢–*
   1939   *Carson of Venus*   *pb50¢–*

1946   *Escape on Venus*   pb50¢–
1964   *Tales of Three Planets*   ss   pb50¢–
1970   *The Wizard of Venus*   ss   pb50¢–
John Carter series
1917   *A Princess of Mars*   pb50¢–
1918   *The Gods of Mars*   pb50¢–
1919   *The Warlord of Mars*   pb50¢–
1920   *Thuvia, Maid of Mars*   pb50¢–
1922   *The Chessmen of Mars*   pb50¢–
1928   *The Master Mind of Mars*   pb50¢–
1931   *A Fighting Man of Mars*   pb50¢–
1936   *Swords of Mars*   pb50¢–
1940   *Synthetic Men of Mars*   pb50¢–
1948   *Llana of Gathol*   pb50¢–
1964   *John Carter of Mars*   pb50¢–
Pellucidar series
1922   *At the Earth's Core*   pb50¢–
1923   *Pellucidar*   pb50¢–
1929   *Tanar of Pellucidar*   pb50¢–
1930   *Tarzan at the Earth's Core*   pb50¢–
1937   *Back to the Stone Age*   pb50¢–
1944   *Land of Terror*   pb50¢–
1963   *Savage Pellucidar*   pb50¢–
Tarzan series
1914   *Tarzan of the Apes*   pb50¢–
1915   *The Return of Tarzan*   pb50¢–
1916   *The Beasts of Tarzan*   pb50¢–
1917   *The Son of Tarzan*   pb50¢–
1918   *Tarzan and the Jewels of Opar*   pb50¢–
1919   *Jungle Tales of Tarzan*   ss   pb50¢–
1920   *Tarzan the Untamed*   pb50¢–
1921   *Tarzan the Terrible*   pb50¢–
1923   *Tarzan and the Golden Lion*   pb50¢–
1924   *Tarzan and the Ant Men*   pb50¢–
1927   *The Tarzan Twins*   pb50¢–
1928   *Tarzan, Lord of the Jungle*   pb50¢–
1929   *Tarzan and the Lost Empire*   pb50¢–
1930   *Tarzan at the Earth's Core*   pb50¢–
1931   *Tarzan the Invincible*   pb50¢–

1932   *Tarzan Triumphant*   pb50¢–
1933   *Tarzan and the City of Gold*   pb50¢–
1934   *Tarzan and the Lion Man*   pb50¢–
1935   *Tarzan and the Leopard Man*   pb50¢–
1936   *Tarzan and the Tarzan Twins with Jad-bal-ja the Golden Lion*
1936   *Tarzan's Quest*   pb50¢–
1938   *Tarzan and the Forbidden City*   pb50¢–
1939   *Tarzan the Magnificent*   pb50¢–
1947   *Tarzan and "The Foreign Legion"*
1964   *Tarzan and the Madman*
1965   *Tarzan and the Castaways*   ss

F. M. BUSBY

Most science-fiction writers seem to start writing professionally while they are still in their teens. F. M. ("Buz") Busby is an exception. While he wrote a few earlier magazine stories and helped produce a Hugo-winning fan magazine, *Cry of the Nameless,* it was only after he had retired from his engineering career that he began producing novels.

1980   *Zelde M'tana*   50¢
1987   *Getting Home*   ss   *$1.00*
The Demu Trilogy
  1973   *Cage a Man*   50¢–
  1975   *The Proud Enemy*   50¢–
  1980   *End of the Line*   50¢–
  1980   *The Demu Trilogy* (omnibus)   pb50¢–
Hulzein Dynasty series
  1984   *Star Rebel*   50¢–
  1984   *Rebel's Quest*   50¢–
  1987   *The Rebel Dynasty, Volume I* (omnibus of both books)
Rissa Kerguelen series
  1976   *Rissa Kerguelen*
  1976   *The Long View*
  1977   *Rissa Kerguelen* (omnibus)   pb50¢

OCTAVIA E. BUTLER

Octavia E. Butler is a Hugo and Nebula award-winning writer who lives in Los Angeles.

    1984   Hugo (Short Story): "Speech Sounds"

    1984   Nebula (Novelette): "Bloodchild"

    1985   Hugo (Novelette): "Bloodchild"

Mind of My Mind
Survivor
1977   *The Patternmaster*
1979   *Kindred*
1980   *Wild Seed*   70¢
Clay's Ark
1987   *Dawn*   hc$4.00

JAMES BRANCH CABELL (1879–1958)

Cabell's witty fantasy novels are all set in the imaginary kingdom of Poictesme. A number of his fantasy novels were reprinted by Ballantine Books in recent years, including *Jurgen,* his best-known work.

1905   *The Line of Love*
1907   *Gallantry*
1909   *Chivalry*
1913   *The Soul of Melicent* (revised as *Domnei*)
1917   *The Cream of the Jest*   pb75¢–
1919   *Jurgen*   pb75¢–
1921   *Figures of Earth*   pb75¢–
1925   *The High Place*   pb75¢–
1926   *The Silver Stallion*   pb75¢–
1927   *Something About Eve*   pb75¢–

JOHN W(OODS) CAMPBELL, JR. (1910–1971)

Campbell held degrees in physics from Massachusetts Institute of Technology and Duke University. He used this background in science to produce science-fiction stories, starting while he was still in his teens. His early role model was E. E. Smith, who produced galaxy-sweeping adventure stories involving wars where suns were used as weapons. Under the name Don A. Stuart (a pseudonym taken from Dona Stuart, Campbell's first wife), he wrote more character-oriented stories, more concerned with the effects of scientific advancement than with the spectacle of the gadgets in operation.

Best-known of the "Stuart" stories is "Who Goes There?" That horror story about a shape-changing alien in Antarctica has twice been filmed (as *The Thing From Another World* in 1951 and as *The Thing* in 1982), although neither movie followed the story closely.

By the time "Who Goes There?" was published, Campbell had embarked on his real career, as the most influential science-fiction magazine editor of all time. He became editor of *Astounding Stories* in 1937, changed the title to *Astounding Science Fiction,* and proceeded to reshape science fiction, aided immeasurably by his "discovery" of Isaac Asimov, Lester del Rey, Theodore Sturgeon, A. E. van Vogt, L. Sprague de Camp, L. Ron Hubbard, Clifford D. Simak, and Robert A. Heinlein. Some of these—de Camp, Hubbard, Simak—were already writers, but they came to full flower as science-fiction writers under Campbell's nurturing editorship.

Campbell continued as editor of the magazine (he changed the name again, to *Analog,* in 1960) until his death in 1971. He also edited what many continue to consider the ultimate fantasy magazine, *Unknown* (later called *Unknown Worlds*), from 1939 to 1943. He devoted his full time to editing and wrote very little fiction after becoming editor of *Astounding*; most of his novels and stories first saw book publication years after they were written.

He championed L. Ron Hubbard's "Dianetics" theories (which later evolved into Scientology) and published the first two articles by Hubbard on the topic.

For more by and about Campbell, see *Collected Editorials from Analog* (1966), selected by Harry Harrison, and *The John W. Campbell Letters, Volume 1* (1985), edited by Perry A. Chapdelaine, Sr., Tony Chapdelaine, and George Hay.

1947   *The Mightiest Machine*
1948   *Who Goes There?*   ss (**pb** as *Who Goes There? and Other Stories*)
1949   *The Incredible Planet*
1950   *The Moon Is Hell*   ss
1952   *The Cloak of Aesir*   ss

1953   *The Black Star Passes*
1957   *Islands of Space*
1961   *Invaders from the Infinite*
1966   *The Ultimate Weapon*
1966   *The Planeteers*
1973   *John W. Campbell Anthology (Black Star, Islands, Invaders)*
1973   *The Best of John W. Campbell*   **pb50¢**
1976   *The Space Beyond*

RAMSEY CAMPBELL

Ramsey Campbell is a British writer and editor of dark fantasy. Under the pseudonym of "Carl Dreadstone," he wrote novelizations of several classic horror films. In an odd sort of self-collaboration, each of Dreadstone's books had an introduction by Ramsey Campbell.

   1978   WFA (Short Fiction): "The Chimney"

   1980   WFA (Short Fiction): "Mackintosh Willy"

The Inhabitants of the Lake   ss
1973   *Demons by Daylight*   ss   **pb50¢**
1976   *The Height of the Scream*   ss
1976   *The Doll Who Ate His Mother*
1977   *The Mummy* (novelization by Carl Dreadstone)
1977   *The Bride of Frankenstein* (novelization by Carl Dreadstone)
1977   *Creature from the Black Lagoon* (novelization by Carl Dreadstone)
1977   *The Werewolf of London* (novelization by Carl Dreadstone)
1977   *The Wolfman* (novelization by Carl Dreadstone)
1977   *Dracula's Daughter* (novelization by Carl Dreadstone)
1980   *The Parasite* (won British Fantasy Society Award)   **pb75¢**
1981   *The Nameless*   **hc$3.25**
1982   *Dark Companions*   ss   **hc$3.50   pb90¢**
1983   *Incarnate*
1983   *The Face That Must Die*
The Hungry Moon
Obsession
1987   *Scared Stiff: Tales of Sex and Death*   ss   **hc$5.00**
1987   *Cold Print*   ss   **pb$1.00**

THOMAS CANTY

The artist does not put much of his material on the market. His black-and-white work sells for $300–$500; his color work sells for $1,000–$2,000.

1986 WFA (Artist)

KAREL CAPEK (1890–1938)

Karel Capek was a Czechoslovakian writer whose fame today rests primarily on two works of science fiction: the play *R.U.R.* (Rossum's Universal Robots), which introduced the word "robot," and a satirical novel, *War with the Newts*. Both are available in English translations.

1921 *R.U.R.*
1936 *War with the Newts*

ORSON SCOTT CARD

Card won the John W. Campbell Award in 1988. The sequel to *Ender's Game* won the 1986 Nebula and 1987 Hugo. "Hatrack River" is a part of *Seventh Son*.

Card also reviews books for *The Magazine of Fantasy and Science Fiction*.

1985 Nebula (Novel): *Ender's Game*

1986 Hugo (Novel): *Ender's Game*

1986 Nebula (Novel): *Speaker for the Dead*

1987 Hugo (Novel): *Speaker for the Dead*

1987 WFA (Novella): "Hatrack River"

1988 Hugo (Novella): "Eye for Eye"

1979 *Hot Sleep: The Worthing Chronicle* **pb75¢**
1979 *Capitol* **pb50¢**
1979 *A Planet Called Treason*
1980 *Songmaster* **pb75¢**
1981 *Unaccompanied Sonata and Other Stories* ss **hc$4.00**
       pb75¢

1983   *The Worthing Chronicle* (incorporates *Hot Sleep, Capitol*)   pb75¢
1986   *Speaker for the Dead*   pb$1.00
1987   *Wyrms*   hc$3.75
Tales of the Mormon Sea series
The Tales of Alvin Maker series
   1987   *Seventh Son*   hc$6.00

JOHN DICKSON CARR (1906–1977)

Primarily known for his mystery novels, Carr occasionally dabbled in fantasy. A modern-day detective would find himself inexplicably transported into a previous century where he would have to solve a crime without benefit of modern technology, or a series of murders would be the result of witchcraft—in both cases, Carr wrote mysteries which had strong fantasy elements.

1937   *The Burning Court*
1957   *The Devil in Velvet*   50¢–

TERRY CARR (1937–1987)

Although he won considerable praise for his short stories (in particular "The Dance of the Changer and the Three"), Terry Carr was best known as an editor. A later breed of editor, he never edited a magazine but specialized in anthologies, some reprint and some original-story anthologies.

He won his first Hugo in 1959 for the fanzine he co-edited with the late Ron Ellik, *Fanac*.

He began as an assistant editor at Ace Books in 1964 and created the original Ace Specials series. His best-of-the-year anthologies and his *Universe* original anthologies are excellent. He later worked as a freelance editor and was the first to win the Hugo—his third—as best editor for books only, not magazines.

A memorial anthology, *Terry's Universe,* was edited by Beth Meacham and published by Tor Books in 1988.

   1959   Hugo (Fanzine): *Fanac* (co-edited with Ron Ellik)
   1973   Hugo (Fan Writer)

1985   Hugo (Professional Editor)

1987   Hugo (Professional Editor)

1963   *Warlord of Kor*
1976   *The Light at the End of the Universe*   ss
1979   *Cirque*

LEWIS CARROLL *(psd. of Charles Lutwidge Dodgson)* (1832–1898)

The Rev. Dodgson, a noted mathematician who also wrote extensively on symbolic logic, is best known under his pseudonym for his two "Alice" books and for his long poem, "The Hunting of the Snark." First editions of any Carroll book are difficult to find and prohibitively expensive, the province of collectors of truly rare books of literary significance.

The reader who wants to enjoy these fantasies to their fullest would do well to track down *The Annotated Alice* and *The Annotated Snark,* both of which contain extensive commentary and analysis by Martin Gardner. Modern Library published a *Complete Works of Lewis Carroll* which contains virtually all of his fiction, including the "Alice" books, the almost-forgotten fantasies *Sylvie and Bruno* and *Sylvie and Bruno Concluded,* and "The Hunting of the Snark."

LIN(WOOD VROOMAN) CARTER (1930–1988)

As a writer, Carter is known primarily for his pastiches of Edgar Rice Burroughs, Clark Ashton Smith, Otis Adelbert Kline, and Robert E. Howard. He achieved considerable financial success as a novelist during the late sixties and the seventies. With L. Sprague de Camp, he wrote a number of new adventures of Robert E. Howard's "Conan the Barbarian."

He did not receive much critical acclaim for his writing, but his editing—particularly of the Ballantine Adult Fantasy series of books—was another matter. Carter rediscovered and presented to modern audiences books by Lord Dunsany, Ernest Bramah, E. R. Eddison, Evangeline Walton, James Branch Cabell, and others, and assembled new collections of work by H. P. Lovecraft and Clark Ashton Smith. He also compiled several excellent collections of fantasy stories and of sword-and-sorcery stories.

Carter edited four volumes of a paperback magazine, continuing the classic pulp fantasy publication *Weird Tales*. He also wrote non-fiction books about fantasy, including *Imaginary Worlds, Lovecraft: A Look Behind the Cthulhu Mythos*, and *Tolkien: A Look Behind "The Lord of the Rings."*

1966 *The Man Without a Planet* pb50¢–
1966 *The Star Magicians* (Ace Double) pb50¢
1967 *Destination Saturn* (with David Grinnell) pb50¢–
1967 *The Flame of Iridar* pb50¢–
1967 *King Kull* ss (with Robert E. Howard) pb$1.00
1968 *The Thief of Thoth* pb50¢–
1968 *Tower at the Edge of Time* pb50¢–
1969 *The Purloined Planet* pb50¢–
1969 *Beyond the Gates of Dream* ss pb50¢–
1969 *Tower of the Medusa* pb50¢–
1969 *Lost World of Time* pb50¢–
1970 *Star Rogue* pb50¢–
1971 *The Quest of Kadji* pb50¢–
1971 *Outworlder* pb50¢–
1973 *The Black Star* pb50¢–
1973 *The Man Who Loved Mars* pb50¢–
1973 *The Valley Where Time Stood Still* pb50¢–
1974 *Time War* pb50¢–
1975 *The Purloined Planet* (with *The Evil That Men Do* by John Brunner) pb50¢
1977 *The City Outside the World* pb50¢–
1981 *Darya of the Bronze Age* pb50¢
1982 *Eric Of Zanthodon* pb50¢
1987 *Callipygia* pb50¢–
Callisto series
   1972 *Jandar of Callisto* pb50¢–
   1972 *Black Legion of Callisto* pb50¢–
   1973 *Sky Pirates of Callisto* pb50¢–
   1975 *Mad Empress of Callisto* pb50¢–
   1975 *Mind Wizards of Callisto* pb50¢–
   1975 *Lankar of Callisto* pb50¢–
   1977 *Ylana of Callisto* pb50¢–

Conan series

    1967 *Conan* ss (with Robert E. Howard and L. Sprague de Camp) **pb$1.00**

    1968 *Conan the Wanderer* ss (with Robert E. Howard and L. Sprague de Camp) **pb$1.00**

    1968 *Conan of the Isles* (with L. Sprague de Camp) **pb$1.00**

    1969 *Conan of Cimmeria* (with Robert E. Howard and L. Sprague de Camp) ss **pb$1.00**

    1971 *Conan the Buccaneer* (with L. Sprague de Camp) **pb$1.00**

    1977 *Conan of Aquilonia* ss (with L. Sprague de Camp) **pb$1.00**

    1978 *Conan the Swordsman* ss (with L. Sprague de Camp and Bjorn Nyberg) **pb$1.00**

    1979 *Conan the Liberator* (with L. Sprague de Camp) **pb$1.00**

    1982 *Conan the Barbarian* (movie novelization, with L. Sprague de Camp) **pb60¢**

Green Star series

    1972 *Under the Green Star* **pb50¢**

    1973 *When the Green Star Calls* **pb50¢–**

    1974 *By the Light of the Green Star* **pb50¢–**

    1975 *As the Green Star Rises* **pb50¢–**

    1976 *In the Green Star's Glow* **pb50¢–**

Thongor series

    1965 *The Wizard of Lemuria* **pb50¢–**

    1966 *Thongor of Lemuria* **pb50¢–**

    1967 *Thongor Against the Gods* **pb50¢–**

    1968 *Thongor in the City of Magicians* **pb50¢–**

    1968 *Thongor at the End of Time* **pb50¢–**

    1970 *Thongor Fights the Pirates of Tarakus* **pb50¢–**

World's End series

    1969 *Giant of World's End* **pb50¢–**

    1974 *The Warrior of World's End* **pb50¢–**

    1975 *The Enchantress of World's End* **pb50¢–**

    1976 *The Immortal of World's End* **pb50¢–**

    1977 *The Barbarian of World's End* **pb50¢–**

Zarkon series

    1975 *Zarkon, Lord of the Unknown, in The Nemesis of Evil* **pb50¢–**

1975   *Zarkon, Lord of the Unknown, in Invisible Death*   **pb50¢–**
1976   *Zarkon, Lord of the Unknown, in The Volcano Ogre*   **pb50¢–**

EDD CARTIER *(Edward Daniel Cartier)* (1914–)

Edd Cartier brought to life the fantastic characters of *Unknown Worlds,* L. Ron Hubbard's "Ole Doc Methuselah," and Poul Anderson and Gordon R. Dickson's "Hokas." He was one of the best-known science-fiction magazine artists of the forties and illustrated some Gnome Press books. Action and humorous approaches dominated his work, and his clean style attracted readers. He had left the field almost completely by 1956. A collection of his art was published by Gerry de la Ree.

His black-and-white work brings $600–$1,000. He did not do much color work, and it almost never comes on the market. One which did is being offered at $7,000.

1977   *Edd Cartier: The Known and the Unknown*   **$10.00**

HUGH B. CAVE

Cave was a quintessential pulp writer, writing for a variety of genres. In the fantasy field, he is best known for his work in *Weird Tales.*

    1978   WFA (Collection/Anthology): *Murgunstrumm and Others*

1978   *Murgunstrumm and Others*   ss   **hc$5.00**
1980   *The Nebulon Horror*   **pb50¢**
1981   *The Evil*   **pb$1.00**

JACK L(AURENCE) CHALKER (1944–)

A long-time science-fiction fan, Chalker began writing fiction in 1976 and rapidly rose to prominence as the author of a number of novels and series of novels, primarily for Ballantine/Del Rey Books.

Prior to his debut as a fiction writer, he had produced several nonfiction works, including a bibliography of H. P. Lovecraft and a "biography" of Scrooge McDuck (Donald Duck's wealthy uncle, the creation of Carl Barks).

1976   *A Jungle of Stars* (6th printing by 1987)   **pb75¢–**
1978   *Dancers in the Afterglow*   **pb50¢**

1978 *The Web of the Chozen* (5th printing by 1987) **pb75¢–**
1979 *And the Devil Will Drag You Under* **pb50¢**
1987 *Dance Band on the Titanic* ss **pb$1.00**
The Saga of the Well World series
  Midnight at the Well of Souls
  Exiles at the Well of Souls
  Quest for the Well of Souls
  The Return of Nathan Brazil
  Twilight at the Well of Souls: The Legacy of Nathan Brazil
Four Lords of the Diamond series
  1981 *Lilith: A Snake in the Grass* **pb75¢**
  1982 *Cerberus: A Wolf in the Fold* **pb75¢**
  1983 *Charon: A Dragon at the Gate* **pb75¢**
  1984 *Medusa: A Tiger by the Tail* **pb75¢**
The Dancing Gods series
  The River of Dancing Gods
  Demons of the Dancing Gods
  Vengeance of the Dancing Gods
The Rings of the Master series
  1986 *Lords of the Middle Dark*
  1987 *Pirates of the Thunder* **90¢**
  1987 *Warriors of the Storm* **90¢**
G.O.D. Inc. series
  1987 *The Labyrinth of Dreams* **90¢**
  1987 *The Shadow Dancers* **90¢**
Changewinds series
  1987 *When the Changewinds Blow* **90¢**
Soul Rider series
  Children of Flux and Anchor **pb90¢**

ROBERT W(ILLIAM) CHAMBERS (1865–1933)

A popular writer of historical and other novels, Chambers is today largely forgotten. He is remembered only for his fantasies, most notably a short story, "The King in Yellow." This story, which is about a book called *The King in Yellow* which drives its readers to madness or suicide, has frequently been reprinted. The Chambers collection in which it appears has been reprinted in trade paperback by Dover Books; Ace published a mass-market paperback in the sixties.

Chambers' other well-remembered story, "The Maker of Moons," has also served as the title story for a collection and has also been anthologized.

The famed radio program, *Mr. Keene, Tracer of Lost Persons,* was based on a Chambers book, *Tracer of Lost Persons.*

1895 *The King in Yellow* ss
1896 *The Maker of Moons* ss
1904 *In Search of the Unknown* ss
1913 *The Gay Rebellion* ss
1915 *Police!!!* ss
1920 *The Slayer of Souls*

A(RTHUR) BERTRAM CHANDLER (1912–1984)

Chandler, an Australian Merchant Navy officer, was also a prolific science-fiction author. His best-known series of novels was set in the Rim Worlds, the planets at the edge of the galaxy. Not all of these novels are related other than by location, but many of them involve John Grimes as the protagonist.

1961 *Bring Back Yesterday* pb50¢–
1963 *The Hamelin Plague* pb50¢–
1964 *The Cults of Time* pb50¢–
1964 *Glory Planet* pb50¢–
1964 *The Deep Reaches of Space* pb50¢–
1965 *The Alternate Martian* pb50¢–
1969 *Catch the Star Winds* ss pb50¢–
1971 *The Sea Beasts* pb50¢–
1974 *The Bitter Pill* pb50¢–
Empress series
  1965 *Empress of Outer Space* pb50¢–
  1965 *Space Mercenaries* pb50¢–
  1967 *Nebula Alert* pb50¢–
John Grimes/Rim Worlds series
  1961 *The Rim of Space* hc$3.25
  1961 *Rendezvous on a Lost World* (reprinted as *When the Dream Dies*) hc$3.25
  1963 *The Ship from Outside* pb50¢–
  1963 *Beyond the Galactic Rim* ss pb50¢–

1964   *Into the Alternate Universe*   pb50¢–
1964   *Contraband From Outer Space*   pb50¢–
1967   *The Road to the Rim*   pb50¢–
1968   *Spartan Planet*   pb50¢–
1969   *The Rim Gods*   pb50¢–
1971   *To Prime the Pump*   pb50¢–
1971   *The Dark Dimensions*   pb50¢–
1971   *Alternate Orbits*   ss   pb50¢–
1972   *The Hard Way Up*   ss   pb50¢–
1972   *The Inheritors* (Ace Double with *Gateway*)   pb50¢
1972   *The Gateway to Never* (Ace Double with *Inheritors*)   pb50¢
1975   *The Broken Cycle*   pb50¢–
1975   *The Big Black Mark*   pb50¢–
1977   *Star Courier*   pb50¢–
1978   *The Way Back*   pb50¢–
The Commodore at Sea
1981   *The Anarch Lords*   pb50¢–

SUZY McKEE CHARNAS (1939–)

Charnas is an American writer who spent a year with the Peace Corps in Nigeria.

1980   Nebula (Novelette): "Unicorn Tapestry"

1974   *Walk to the End of the World*
1978   *Motherlines*
1980   *The Vampire Tapestry*   pb75¢

C. J. CHERRYH *(Caroline Janice Cherry)* (1942–)

An American writer and teacher with degrees in Latin and in classical literature, Cherryh has primarily written for DAW Books. Her first novel, *The Gate of Ivrel,* is currently being published as a series of graphic novels by Donning/Starblaze.

1979   Hugo (Short Story): "Cassandra"

1982   Hugo (Novel): *Downbelow Station*

1976   *Brothers of Earth*
1977   *Hunter of Worlds*   50¢–

1979   *Hestia*   50¢–
The Green Gods (with N. C. Henneberg)
Serpent's Reach
Downbelow Station
Merchanter's Luck
1981   *Sunfall*   ss   pb50¢
1981   *Wave Without a Shore*   pb50¢
1982   *Port Eternity*   75¢–
Voyager in Night
Forty Thousand in Gehenna
Cuckoo's Egg
1985   *Angel with the Sword*   75¢
The Dreamstone
The Tree of Swords and Jewels
1986   *Visible Light*   ss   90¢
1987   *Glass and Amber*   ss
Chanur series
  1982   *The Pride of Chanur*   pb75¢–   hc$10.00
  Chanur's Venture
  The Kif Strike Back (Chanur's Revenge)
  1987   *Chanur's Homecoming*
The Faded Sun Trilogy
  The Faded Sun: Kesrith
  1978   *The Faded Sun: Shon'jir*   50¢
  The Faded Sun: Kutath
The Morgaine Trilogy
  1976   *The Gate of Ivrel*
  1978   *Well of Shiuan*   50¢
  Fires of Azeroth

G(ILBERT) K(EITH) CHESTERTON (1874–1936)

The creator of the famous detective Father Brown, Chesterton also wrote some science fiction. His most famous novel, *The Man Who Was Thursday,* is a fantasy.

1904   *The Napoleon of Notting Hill*
1908   *The Man Who Was Thursday*   50¢–

JOHN CHRISTOPHER *(Christopher S. Youd)* (1922–)

Christopher achieved fame with his disaster novel, *No Blade of Grass*, which became a movie. He wrote a number of other novels in which humanity struggles to survive after some calamity. Since the late sixties, he has been concentrating on juvenile novels, many of them science fiction.

1954   *The Twenty-Second Century* ss
1955   *Planet in Peril*
1956   *No Blade of Grass*
1958   *The Caves of Night*
1960   *The Long Voyage*
1962   *The Long Winter*
1964   *Sweeney's Island*
1965   *The Possessors*
1965   *The Ragged Edge*
1967   *The Little People*
1968   *Pendulum*
1969   *The Lotus Caves* juv
1970   *The Guardians* juv
1973   *Dom and Va* juv
1974   *Wild Jack* juv
1977   *Empty World* juv
1981   *Fireball* juv
White Mountains series juv
   1967   *The White Mountains*
   1967   *The City of Gold and Lead*
   1968   *The Pool of Fire*
Prince in Waiting series juv
   1970   *The Prince in Waiting*
   1971   *Beyond the Burning Lands*
   1972   *The Sword of the Spirits*

CHRIS(TOPHER S.) CLAREMONT

Because of his writing of Marvel's *The Uncanny X-Men* (best-selling comic book published in the United States) and its companion publications about mutant heroes, Claremont has a large following, which helped make his first novel a success.

1987 *FirstFlight* **pb$1.00**

ARTHUR C(HARLES) CLARKE (1917-)

The three most famous living writers of science fiction are A, B, and C—Asimov, Bradbury, and Clarke. Clarke, who is diligent about having all the science in his fiction as correct as possible, has attempted to retire on several occasions but has been lured back into writing. His most famous work, which had as its starting point a short-short story called "Sentinel of Eternity" (also published as "The Sentinel"), is the movie he wrote with Stanley Kubrick, *2001: A Space Odyssey*. Clarke has written two sequels to the book on which he based the film. He lives in Sri Lanka.

1956 Hugo (Short Story): "The Star"

1972 Nebula (Novella): "A Meeting with Medusa"

1973 Nebula (Novel): *Rendezvous with Rama*

1974 Hugo (Novel): *Rendezvous with Rama*

1979 Nebula (Novel): *The Fountains of Paradise*

1980 Hugo (Novel): *The Fountains of Paradise*

1985 SFWA Grand Master

1951 *The Sands of Mars* **50¢–**
1951 *Prelude to Space*
1952 *Islands in the Sky* **50¢–**
1953 *Childhood's End*
1953 *Expedition to Earth* **ss**
1955 *Earthlight*
1956 *Reach for Tomorrow* **ss 50¢**
1956 *The City and the Stars* **50¢–**
1957 *Tales From the White Hart* **ss**
1957 *The Deep Range* (11 printings by 1987) **50¢–**
1958 *The Other Side of the Sky* **ss 50¢–**

1961   *A Fall of Moondust*   *50¢–*
1962   *Tales of Ten Worlds*   ss   *pb50¢–*
1963   *Dolphin Island*   *50¢–*
1968   *The Lion of Comarre and Against the Fall of Night* (2 stories)   *50¢*
1972   *The Wind From the Sun*   ss   *50¢*
1973   *Rendezvous with Rama*
1986   *The Songs of Distant Earth*   *90¢*
2001 series
   1968   *2001: A Space Odyssey*
   1982   *2010: Odyssey Two*
   1987   *2061: Odyssey Three*   *hc$6.00*

HAL CLEMENT *(psd. of Harry Clement Stubbs)* (1922–)

A high-school science teacher, Clement is the author most often cited as the one who gets all his science right. His novel *Mission of Gravity* is the one most often cited for having one of the most solid bases in science. Clement also is noted for his ability to portray convincing alien beings, from their biology through their civilizations.

Needle is one of the earliest science-fiction mystery novels.

1950   *Needle*   *pb50¢–*
1953   *Iceworld*   *pb50¢–*
1954   *Mission of Gravity*   *pb50¢–*
1956   *Ranger Boys in Space*   juv
1957   *Cycle of Fire*   *pb50¢*
1964   *Close to Critical*   *pb50¢–*
1965   *Natives of Space*   ss   *pb50¢–*
1967   *Ocean on Top*   *pb50¢–*
1969   *Small Changes* (also as *Space Lash*)   ss   *pb50¢–*
1971   *Star Light*   *pb50¢–*
1978   *Through the Eye of a Needle*   *pb50¢–*
1979   *The Best of Hal Clement*   *pb$1.00*
1980   *The Nitrogen Fix*   *pb75¢*
1987   *Still River*   *hc$4.00*

THEODORE R(OSE) COGSWELL (1918–1987)

Though his published work is not hotly collected today and he may be almost unknown to many current science-fiction readers, Cogswell was of pivotal importance to the professional science-fiction world. Through his fanzine for science-fiction professionals, *The Proceedings of the Institute for Twenty-First Century Studies* (abbreviated *PITFCS*), professionals in the field found a focal point in the fifties which led to formation of the Science Fiction Writers of America. For that group he edited the *SFWA Forum* in the early seventies.

His short stories are frequently anthologized, especially "The Specter General" and "The Wall Around the World." His only novel was a *Star Trek* novel, written in collaboration (see the *Star Trek* section of this book).

1962   *The Wall Around the World*   ss   **pb50¢–**
1968   *The Third Eye*   ss   **pb50¢–**

JOHN COLLIER (1901–1979)

John Collier wrote marvelously crafted fantasy short stories—he re-wrote the ending of "Thus I Refute Beelzy" *twice* after the story had been published. The best of his stories, 50 of them, can be found in *Fancies and Goodnights*. That book and *The John Collier Reader* are largely made up of stories from earlier collections. The best place to start collecting John Collier is with *Fancies and Goodnights,* which has had many paperback editions.

1930   *His Monkey Wife*
1931   *No Traveller Returns*
1932   *Green Thoughts*   ss
1933   *Full Circle*
1935   *Variations on a Theme*   ss
1935   *The Devil and All*   ss
1941   *Presenting Moonshine*   ss
1943   *The Touch of Nutmeg*   ss
1951   *Fancies and Goodnights*   ss   **pb50¢–**
1958   *Pictures in the Fire*   ss
1972   *The John Collier Reader*   ss

GROFF CONKLIN (1904–1968)

Conklin was the first book reviewer in *Galaxy Science Fiction* and was a prolific anthologist (more than 40). His anthologies, particularly his earliest ones, are well worth seeking out because they represent the handiest source of the best magazine science fiction of the twenties, thirties, and forties. Conklin also is credited with inventing the "theme" anthology, made up of stories on a single theme, beginning with *Invaders of Earth*. His massive early anthologies and his first "theme" anthologies are, unfortunately, the only ones we have space to list.

Few of his anthologies have been kept in print. Due to the problems of obtaining reprint rights on every story, it is easier and more profitable for a modern editor to create a new anthology drawing on the same sources. Unfortunately, this leaves some good stories languishing only in the pages of Conklin's hard-to-find collections and the original magazines.

Warning: Many of the paperback editions of these anthologies reprint only a few stories. For example, the hardcover edition of *A Treasury of Science Fiction* contains 30 stories, the paperback only eight. The paperback version of *Science Fiction Thinking Machines* also is severely abridged.

1946   (ed.)   *The Best of Science Fiction*
1948   (ed.)   *A Treasury of Science Fiction*
1950   (ed.)   *The Big Book of Science Fiction*
1952   (ed.)   *The Omnibus of Science Fiction*
1952   (ed.)   *Invaders of Earth*
1953   (ed.)   *Science Fiction Adventures in Dimension*
1954   (ed.)   *Science Fiction Thinking Machines*
1955   (ed.)   *Science Fiction Adventures in Mutation*

RICHARD COWPER *(psd. of John Middleton Murry, Jr.)* (1926–)

Murry, the son of a famous British critic, has also written under the names Colin Murry and Colin Middleton Murry. Those writings have not been science fiction.

1967   *Breakthrough*
1968   *Phoenix*

1971 *Domino*
1972 *Clone* 50¢
1972 *Kuldesak*
1973 *Time Out of Mind* 50¢
1974 *The Twilight of Briareus* 50¢
1974 *Worlds Apart*
1976 *The Custodians* ss
1979 *Profundis* 75¢
1980 *Out There Where the Big Ships Go* ss 75¢
1984 *The Tithonium Factor* ss hc$4.00
Bird of Kinship series
  1975 *The Road to Corlay* 50¢
  1981 *A Dream of Kinship* 75¢
  1982 *A Tapestry of Time* 75¢

LEE BROWN COYE (1907–1981)

Coye was a stylized horror artist who did most of his best work for *Weird Tales*.

There is considerable interest in the work of this pioneer horror illustrator, but the prices on that work have remained moderate. Much of his work from the forties and fifties has been lost; what remains brings $300 to $500. His work from the sixties tends to fall into the range of $100 to $350. There may not be any available Coye in color; almost all his work was in black-and-white. If any Coye paintings were offered for sale, they would probably bring double the black-and-white prices.

  1975 WFA (Artist)
  1978 WFA (Artist)

JOHN CROWLEY (1942–)

  1982 WFA (Novel): *Little, Big*

1975 *The Deep*
1976 *Beasts*
1979 *Engine Summer* pb50¢
1981 *Little, Big* pb75¢–$2.25
1987 *Aegypt* hc$4.50

ROALD DAHL (1916–)

Not all of Roald Dahl's stories are fantasies, but a great many of them are. There was a TV series, *Roald Dahl's Tales of The Unexpected,* adapting his stories, many of which have surprise endings. In addition to his short stories, Dahl writes children's books and adult novels, again often on a fantasy theme.

Dahl wrote the screenplay for the James Bond movie *You Only Live Twice.* His *Charlie and the Chocolate Factory* became the movie *Willy Wonka and the Chocolate Factory.*

1983 WFA Life Achievement

1943 *The Gremlins* juv
1948 *Sometime Never*
1953 *Someone Like You* ss
1960 *Kiss Kiss* ss
1964 *Charlie and the Chocolate Factory* juv
1974 *Switch Bitch* ss
1979 *Tales of the Unexpected* ss pb75¢

PETER (ALLEN) DAVID

Peter David is primarily a comic-book writer—one with a large following, thanks to his work on *The Incredible Hulk, Star Trek* (the DC comic book), and various *Spider-Man* comics. He has written some novels based on game-playing devices. His first fantasy novel, about King Arthur returning and running for mayor of New York City, was well received.

1987 *Knight Life* pb$1.00

AVRAM DAVIDSON (1923–)

Most of Davidson's early stories appeared in *The Magazine of Fantasy and Science Fiction* (he edited *F&SF* from 1962 to 1964).

1958 Hugo (Short Story): "Or All the Seas with Oysters"
1976 WFA (Single-Author Collection): *The Enquiries of Dr. Eszterhazy*
1979 WFA (Short Fiction): "Naples"

1986   WFA Life Achievement

1962   *Or All the Seas with Oysters*   ss
1962   *Joyleg* (with Ward Moore)   pb*50¢*
1964   *Mutiny in Space*   pb*50¢*
1965   *Rogue Dragon*   pb*50¢*
1965   *What Strange Stars and Skies*   ss
1965   *Masters of the Maze*   pb*50¢*
1965   *Rork!*   pb*50¢*
1966   *Clash of Star-Kings* (Ace Double)   pb*$1.00*
1966   *The Kar-Chee Reign* (Ace Double)   pb*$1.00*
1966   *The Enemy of My Enemy*   pb*50¢*
1969   *The Island Under the Earth*   pb*50¢*
1969   *The Phoenix and the Mirror*   pb*50¢*
1971   *Peregrine: Primus*
1971   *Strange Seas and Shores*   hc/pb*50¢*
1973   *Ursus of Ultima Thule*   pb*50¢*
1975   *The Enquiries of Dr. Eszterhazy*   ss   pb*50¢*
1979   *The Kar-Chee Reign/Rogue Dragon*   pb*50¢*
1981   *Peregrine: Secundus* (seq to *Primus*)   pb*70¢*
1982   *Collected Fantasies*   pb*60¢*
1987   *Vergil in Averno*   hc*$3.00*

ROGER DEAN (1944–)

Dean has done science-fiction magazine covers and record album covers.

1977   WFA (Artist)

1984   *Magnetic Storm*

L(YON) SPRAGUE DE CAMP (1907–)

L. Sprague de Camp is equally at home with light fantasy, heroic fantasy, science fiction, science fact, and historical and biographical writing. He wrote biographies of H. P. Lovecraft and Robert E. Howard, as well as *Literary Swordsmen and Sorcerers,* about several major heroic-fantasy authors. He also edited books of articles, essays, and poems about Conan and Howard taken from the fan magazine *Amra.*

Super Science Novels Magazine, March 1941, about 7″ × 9½″; cover uncredited. Listed as copyright 1941 by Fictioneers, Inc. Copyright 1941 by Popular Publications. Reprinted by permission of Blazing Publications, The Argosy Co.

Those can be found in such books as *The Spell of Conan* and *The Blade of Conan.*

With Fletcher Pratt, he wrote several humorous novels and many humorous short stories. Alone and in collaboration with Lin Carter, he has written books featuring Robert E. Howard's "Conan the Barbarian." It was de Camp who initially edited Howard's Conan stories for book form and he posthumously collaborated with Howard by turning story fragments and non-Conan stories into adventures of the popular barbarian.

De Camp also wrote several historical novels which have titles that make them sound like fantasy novels: *The Dragon of the Ishtar Gate, The Arrows of Hercules, The Bronze God of Rhodes.* Some paperback publishers have packaged these novels to look like fantasy, and readers interested only in fantasy should be aware of this. The novels are excellent but they are not fantasy.

1978   SFWA Grand Master

1984   WFA Life Achievement Award

1941 *Lest Darkness Fall*   pb*50¢*
1942 *The Land of Unreason* (with Fletcher Pratt)   pb*50¢*
1948 *The Carnelian Cube* (with Fletcher Pratt)   pb*50¢*
1948 *Divide and Rule*   ss
1949 *The Wheels of If*   ss
1950 *Genus Homo* (with P. Schuyler Miller)
1951 *The Undesired Princess*   ss
1953 *Tales from Gavagan's Bar*   ss (with Fletcher Pratt)
1953 *The Tritonian Ring*   ss
1956 *Solomon's Stone*
1960 *The Glory That Was*
1963 *A Gun for Dinosaur*   ss
1964 *The Clocks of Iraz*   pb*50¢*
1968 *The Goblin Tower* (seq to *Iraz*)   pb*50¢*
1970 *The Reluctant Shaman and Other Fantastic Tales*   ss   pb*50¢*
1971 *The Clocks of Iraz*
1972 *Scribblings*   ss
1972 *The Fallible Fiend* (seq to *Tower*)   pb*50¢*
1976 *The Virgin & The Wheels (The Virgin of Zesh* and *The Wheels of If)*
1978 *The Great Fetish*
1978 *The Best of L. Sprague de Camp*   ss   pb*75¢*
1979 *The Purple Pterodactyls* (Willy Newbury stories)   pb*75¢*
1981 *Footprints on Sand*   ss (with Catherine Crook de Camp)
1983 *The Unbeheaded King*
1987 *The Incorporated Knight* (with Catherine Crook de Camp)   hc*$5.50–$13.00*

Conan series

   1955 *Tales of Conan*   ss (with Robert E. Howard)
   1957 *The Return of Conan* (also as *Conan the Avenger,* with Bjorn Nyberg)
   1966 *Conan the Adventurer*   ss (with Robert E. Howard)   pb*$1.00*
   1967 *Conan*   ss (with Robert E. Howard and Lin Carter)   pb*$1.00*
   1967 *Conan the Usurper*   ss (with Robert E. Howard)   pb*$1.00*
   1968 *Conan the Wanderer*   ss (with Robert E. Howard and Lin Carter)   pb*$1.00*

1968   *Conan the Freebooter* ss (with Robert E. Howard) **pb$1.00**

1968   *Conan of the Isles* (with Lin Carter) **pb50¢**

1969   *Conan of Cimmeria* (with Robert E. Howard and Lin Carter) ss **pb$1.00**

1969   *Conan the Avenger* (with Bjorn Nyberg) **pb$2.00**

1971   *Conan the Buccaneer* (with Lin Carter) **pb$1.00**

1977   *Conan of Aquilonia* ss (with Lin Carter) **pb50¢**

1978   *Conan the Swordsman* ss (with Lin Carter and Bjorn Nyberg) **pb$1.00**

1979   *Conan the Liberator* (with Lin Carter) **pb$1.00**

1980   *Conan and the Spider God* **pb60¢**

1980   *The Treasure of Tranicos* ss (with Robert E. Howard) **pb$1.00**

1981   *The Flame Knife* (with Robert E. Howard) **pb$1.00**

1982   *Conan the Barbarian* (movie novelization, with Lin Carter) **pb60¢**

Harold Shea series (with Fletcher Pratt)

1941   *The Incomplete Enchanter* **pb50¢**

1950   *The Castle of Iron*

1960   *Wall of Serpents*

Krishna series

1951   *Rogue Queen* **pb50¢**

1953   *The Continent Makers and Other Tales of the Viagens* ss

1954   *Cosmic Manhunt* (also as *The Queen of Zamba*) **pb50¢–**

1958   *Tower of Zanid*

1963   *The Search for Zei* (Ace Double) **pb$1.00**

1963   *The Hand of Zei* (Ace Double) **pb$1.00**

1976   *The Virgin of Zesh*

1977   *The Hostage of Zir* **pb50¢**

1982   *The Prisoner of Zhamanak*

1983   *The Bones of Zora* (with Catherine Crook de Camp)

SAMUEL R(AY) DELANY (1942–)

Delany has an unusual dual background: He was raised in Harlem but his well-to-do father had him educated at private schools. Delany edited four volumes of a paperback quarterly which published speculative fiction; see *Quark* in the "Magazines" listing. He has also written some comic-book stories.

1966   Nebula (Novel): *Babel-17*

1967   Nebula (Novel): *The Einstein Intersection*

1967   Nebula (Short Story): "Aye, and Gomorrah"

1969   Nebula (Novelette): "Time Considered as a Helix of Semi-Precious Stones"

1970   Hugo (Short Story): "Time Considered as a Helix of Semi-Precious Stones"

1962   *The Jewels of Aptor* (Ace Double)   pb*$1.00*

1963   *Captives of the Flame* (Ace Double)   pb*$1.00*

1964   *The Towers of Toron* (Ace Double)   pb*$1.00*

1965   *The Ballad of Beta 2*

1966   *City of a Thousand Suns*

1966   *Empire Star*

1966   *Babel-17*   pb75¢

1967   *The Einstein Intersection*   pb*$1.00–*

1968   *Nova*   pb*$1.00–*

1970   *The Fall of the Towers* (*Captives of the Flame, Towers of Toron, City of a Thousand Suns*)

1971   *Driftglass*   ss

1975   *Dhalgren*   pb*$1.00–*

1976   *Triton*

1979   *Tales of Neveryon*   ss   pb*$1.00–*

1981   *Distant Star*   pb*$2.25*

1982   *The Jewels of Aptor*   pb75¢

1986   *The Complete Nebula Award-Winning Fiction* (includes *Babel-17* and *The Einstein Intersection*)   pb*$2.00*

JUDY-LYNN DEL REY (1944–1986)

Judy-Lynn Benjamin read her first science-fiction magazine on the way to a job interview with *Galaxy Science Fiction* magazine. She got the job, read a lot more science fiction, and became the most influential editor the field had seen since John W. Campbell, Jr. While at *Galaxy,* she met and married Lester del Rey. She later left magazine editing for book editing, at Ballantine, which had been pioneering in science-fiction publishing since 1953.

Her efforts as editor of Ballantine Books' science-fiction line were so fruitful—among other things, she sewed up all publishing rights to a movie called *Star Wars* and its sequels before the film opened—that she was made a publisher and the science-fiction line was named Del Rey Books.

In addition to editing the entire line of Del Rey novels, she produced seven volumes of an anthology series called *Stellar* between 1974 and 1981 and a companion volume of *Stellar Short Novels* (1976).

1986   Hugo (Professional Editor) refused by Lester del Rey

LESTER DEL REY *(Ramon Felipe San Juan Mario Silvio Enrico Smith Heathcourt-Brace Sierra y Alvarez del Rey y de los Uerdes—or Ramon Felipe Alvarez-del Rey)* (1915–)

Lester del Rey (the first of the above names is his full given name; the second is his choice) began writing science fiction in 1938, for John W. Campbell's *Astounding*. He became a magazine editor in the fifties and currently is the editor of Del Rey Books' fantasy line. (Del Rey Books was named for his wife, the late Judy-Lynn del Rey.)

When del Rey was editing *Science Fiction Adventures* in 1953, he wrote a serial for the magazine under the pseudonym of Erik van Lhin (taken from the name of his then-wife, Evelyn). This serial was later published in book form as by van Lhin. Still later, it was expanded and published as by Erik van Lhin and Lester del Rey. Subsequent editions have credited it solely to del Rey. The novel is *Police Your Planet,* and it has been listed under all three variations.

He edited five volumes of *The Best Science Fiction Stories of the Year* (Gardner Dozois succeeded him and edited four more) and compiled *Fantastic Science Fiction Art.*

1948   *. . . And Some Were Human* ss
1952   *Marooned on Mars* juv
1952   *Rocket Jockey* juv (as by Philip St. John)
1953   *Attack from Atlantis* juv
1953   *Battle on Mercury* (as by Erik van Lhin)
1953   *The Mysterious Planet* pb50¢
1954   *Step to the Stars* juv

1954   *Rockets to Nowhere* **juv** (as by Philip St. John)
1956   *Nerves* **pb50¢**
1956   *Mission to the Moon* **juv**
1956   *Police Your Planet* (as by Erik van Lhin) **pb50¢**
1957   *Robots and Changelings* **ss**
1959   *Day of the Giants*
1961   *Moon of Mutiny* **juv**
1962   *The Eleventh Commandment*
1963   *Outpost of Jupiter* **pb50¢**
1965   *The Runaway Robot* (with Paul Fairman)
1965   *Mortals and Monsters* **ss**   **pb50¢**
1966   *Tunnel Through Time* (with Paul Fairman) **pb50¢–**
1966   *The Man Without a Planet* (with Paul Fairman)
1966   *Rocket from Infinity* **juv**
1966   *The Scheme of Things*
1968   *Prisoners of Space* (with Paul Fairman)
1969   *The Man Without a Planet* **pb50¢**
1970   *The Eleventh Commandment* (revised) **pb75¢**
1971   *Pstalemate* **pb50¢–**
1973   *Gods and Golems* **ss**
1974   *The Sky is Falling* (with Frederik Pohl)
1975   *Police Your Planet* (expanded, as with Erik van Lhin) **pb50¢**
1975   *The Early del Rey* **ss**
1976   *Badge of Infamy* **pb50¢–**
1978   *The Best of Lester del Rey* **ss**   **pb50¢–**
1978   *Weeping May Tarry* (with Raymond F. Jones) **pb50¢**
1981   *Police Your Planet* (as by Lester del Rey) **pb60¢**

NOTE: Listed prices are for items in *GOOD* condition.
Very Good = two times listed price.
Fine = three times listed price.
Mint = four times listed price.

AUGUST W(ILLIAM) DERLETH (1909–1971)

Derleth, a remarkably prolific writer (he once fulfilled a contract to increase *Weird Tales'* inventory by writing a story a day for a month, in addition to his several other writing assignments), is best known for championing the cause of the late H. P. Lovecraft. In order to assure that Lovecraft's work would not be forgotten, Derleth formed Arkham House to publish Lovecraft's work. Arkham House continues, long after the death of Derleth himself, and the books published by Arkham are among the most collectible fantasy books in the world.

In addition to his fantasy writing, Derleth edited many anthologies of fantasy and wrote regional fiction about southern Wisconsin. He "collaborated" on many stories with H. P. Lovecraft (that is, he completed stories from notes and fragments left by Lovecraft) and wrote a series of mystery stories about Solar Pons, a thinly disguised Sherlock Holmes, utilizing references Sir Arthur Conan Doyle made to Holmes cases which had not been recorded.

1941 *Someone in the Dark* ss
1945 *The Lurker at the Threshold* ss (with H. P. Lovecraft)
1945 *Something Near* ss
1948 *Not Long for This World* ss pb$1.00
1957 *The Survivor and Others* ss   (with H. P. Lovecraft)
1962 *Lonesome Places* ss
1962 *The Mask of Cthulhu* ss pb75¢
1962 *The Trail of Cthulhu* pb75¢
1963 *Mr. George and Other Odd Persons* pb50¢
1966 *Colonel Markesan and Less Pleasant People* ss   (with Mark Schorer)
1968 *The Beast in Holger's Woods*
1974 *The Watcher Out of Time and Other Stories* ss   (with H. P. Lovecraft)
1975 *Harrigan's File* ss
1976 *Dwellers in Darkness* ss

GENE DeWEESE (1934–)

His first published professional science-fiction writing was done in conjunction with Robert Coulson under the joint pseudonym of Thomas Stratton: two new adventures in the *Man from U.N.C.L.E.* paperback book series. His *Adventures of a Two-Minute Werewolf* was broadcast by ABC-TV. Some of his work, including *Adventures,* is for juvenile lines; some novels are Gothics and not listed here, under the pseudonym Jean DeWeese.

1967 *The Invisibility Affair* (U.N.C.L.E., Stratton) **pb50¢–**
1967 *The Mind-Twisters Affair* (U.N.C.L.E., Stratton) **pb50¢–**
1975 *Gates of the Universe* (with Coulson) **pb50¢–**
1976 *Now You See It/Him/Them . . .* (with Coulson)
1976 *Jeremy Case*
1977 *Charles Fort Never Mentioned Wombats* (with Coulson)
1979 *Major Corby and the Unidentified Flapping Object* **juv**
1980 *The Wanting Factor* **pb75¢**
1981 *Nightmares from Space*
1982 *A Different Darkness* **pb75¢–**
1983 *Adventures of a Two-Minute Werewolf* **juv**
1983 *Something Answered* **pb75¢–**
1985 *Black Suits from Outer Space*
1985 *Nightmare Universe* (with Coulson, revision of *Gates of the Universe*) **pb$1.00**
1986 *The Dandelion Caper* **hc$3.50**
1987 *Chain of Attack* (Star Trek) **90¢**
1987 *The Calvin Nullifier*

PHILIP K(ENDRED) DICK (1928–1982)

A number of books by Philip K. Dick—books he apparently was unable to sell during his lifetime—have appeared since his death. Many of these are not science fiction. He remains a popular writer (he is one of the few writers to affect the price of magazines in which his stories appear) and finds new fans every day.

His novel *Do Androids Dream of Electric Sheep?* was made into the movie *Blade Runner*, which was released shortly after his death.

Daniel J. H. Levack wrote *PKD: A Philip K. Dick Bibliography* (Underwood/Miller, 1981).

1963 Hugo (Novel): *The Man in the High Castle*

1955 *A Handful of Darkness* **ss**
1955 *Solar Lottery* (Ace Double) **pb$2.00**
1956 *The World Jones Made* (Ace Double) **pb$2.00**
1956 *The Man Who Japed* (Ace Double) **pb$2.00**
1957 *The Cosmic Puppets*
1957 *The Variable Man and Other Stories* **ss**
1957 *Eye in the Sky* **pb$2.00**

1959   *Time Out of Joint*

1960   *Dr. Futurity* (Ace Double)   pb$2.00

1960   *Vulcan's Hammer* (Ace Double)   pb$2.00

1962   *The Man in the High Castle*

1963   *The Game-Players of Titan*

1964   *The Simulacra*   pb$2.00

1964   *The Penultimate Truth*

1964   *Clans of the Alphane Moon*   pb$2.00

1964   *The Three Stigmata of Palmer Eldritch*

1964   *Martian Time-Slip*   pb50¢

1965   *Dr. Bloodmoney or, How We Got Along After the Bomb*   pb$2.00

1966   *Now Wait for Last Year*   pb50¢

1966   *The Unteleported Man*

1966   *The Crack in Space*   pb$2.00

1967   *The Zap Gun*

1967   *The Counter-Clock World*

1967   *The Ganymede Takeover* (with Ray Nelson)

1968   *Do Androids Dream of Electric Sheep?*

1969   *Ubik*

1969   *Galactic Pot-Healer*

1969   *The Preserving Machine*   ss $1.00

1970   *A Maze of Death*

1970   *Our Friends from Frolix-8*

1972   *We Can Build You*   pb$1.00

1973   *The Book of Philip K. Dick*   pb$1.00

1974   *Flow My Tears, the Policeman Said*   hc/pb50¢–

1976   *Deus Irae* (with Roger Zelazny)

1977   *A Scanner Darkly*   pb50¢–

1977   *The Best of Philip K. Dick*   pb$2.00–

1980   *The Golden Man*   ss

1980   *Dr. Bloodmoney or, How We Got Along After the Bomb* (with new afterword by Dick)   pb$2.00–

1981   *Valis*   pb50¢–

1981   *The Divine Invasion* (sequel to *Valis*)   hc$3.25   pb$1.50

1985   *I Hope I Shall Arrive Soon* $1.00

1985   *Radio Free Albemuth* (a different version of *Valis*) $1.00

1987   *The Collected Stories of Philip K. Dick*   (A collection of Dick's stories published chronologically for a total of $125.00 consists of five volumes from Underwood/Miller. There is also a slipcased deluxe edition with signatures from checks at a higher price.)

1987 *Beyond Lies the Wub* (1947–1952)
1987 *Second Variety* (1952–1953)
1987 *The Father Thing* (1953–1954)
1987 *The Days of Perky Pat* (1954–1964)
1987 *The Little Black Box* (1964–1981)

PETER DICKINSON (1927–)

Though better known both as a mystery writer and as a writer of children's books, Dickinson has also written some fantasy and science-fiction novels for adults.

1968 *The Weathermonger*
1970 *Heartsease*
1971 *The Devil's Children*
1971 *Emma Tupper's Diary*
1972 *The Dancing Bear*
1973 *The Green Gene*
1973 *The Gift*
1975 *The Changes* ss
1975 *Chance, Luck, and Destiny* ss
1976 *The Blue Hawk*
1976 *King and Joker*
1979 *Tulku* pb75¢
1983 *Healer* pb$1.00

GORDON R(UPERT) DICKSON (1923–)

Gordon R. Dickson is best known for his "Childe Cycle" series about the warrior-bred Dorsai, but he has written light fantasy, humorous science fiction, serious science fiction, and everything in-between.

With Poul Anderson, he has written the charming "Hoka" series; see the entry for Poul Anderson for that series.

1965 Hugo (Short Story): "Soldier, Ask Not"
1966 Nebula (Novelette): "Call Him Lord"
1981 Hugo (Novella): "Lost Dorsai"

1981   Hugo (Novelette): "The Cloak and the Staff"

1956   *Alien from Arcturus* (reprinted as *Arcturus Landing*)
1956   *Mankind on the Run*
1960   *Time to Teleport*
1961   *Delusion World*   **pb50¢**
1961   *Spacial Delivery*   **pb50¢**
1961   *Naked to the Stars*
1963   *Alien Art*   **juv**
1965   *Space Winners*   **juv**
1965   *The Alien Way*
1965   *Mission to Universe*
1967   *Planet Run* (with Keith Laumer)
1967   *The Space Swimmers*
1969   *None But Man*   **pb50¢**
1969   *Spacepaw*   **pb50¢**
1969   *Wolfling*
1970   *Hour of the Horde*
1970   *Mutants*   **ss**
1970   *Danger—Human*   **ss**
1970   *The Book of Gordon Dickson*   **ss**   **pb50¢**
1971   *Sleepwalker's World*
1972   *The Pritcher Mass*
1972   *The Outposter*
1973   *The R-Master*
1973   *The Star Road*   **ss**
1974   *Ancient, My Enemy*   **ss**   **pb50¢**
1974   *Gremlins, Go Home* (with Ben Bova)
1976   *The Dragon and the George*   **pb50¢**
1976   *Lifeship* (with Harry Harrison)   **pb75¢**
1977   *Time Storm*   **pb75¢**
1978   *Pro*   **pb50¢**
1978   *Gordon R. Dickson's SF Best*   **ss** (adds two stories as *In the Bone*)   **pb75¢**
1981   *Alien Art & Arcturus Landing*
1981   *Time to Teleport/Delusion World*
The Far Call
Home from the Shore
In Iron Years

Jamie the Red (with Roland Green)
Masters of Everon
1983   *The Man From Earth*   pb75¢
1987   *Way of the Pilgrim*   pb/hc$1.00–$4.25
The Forever Man
Steel Brothers
On the Run
The Man the Worlds Rejected
Beyond the Dar al-Harb
1987   *In the Bone: The Best Science Fiction of Gordon R. Dickson*   pb50¢
Childe Cycle series
   1960   *The Genetic General* (expanded as *Dorsai!*)   **pb$1.00**
   1962   *Necromancer*   pb50¢
   1967   *Soldier, Ask Not*   pb50¢
   1971   *Tactics of Mistake*   pb50¢
   1976   *Dorsai!* (expanded from *The Genetic General*)   **pb$1.00**
   1976   *Three to Dorsai!* (book-club omnibus: *Dorsai!, Necromancer, Tactics*)   hc$2.00
   The Spirit of Dorsai
   The Final Encyclopedia
   1980   *Lost Dorsai*   ss   pb75¢
   1986   *The Dorsai Companion*   ss   **trade pb$2.00**
Secret series   juv
   1960   *Secret Under the Sea*
   1963   *Secret Under Antarctica*
   1964   *Secret Under the Caribbean*

VINCENT DI FATE (1945–)

An illustrator and cover artist for magazines and paperback books, Di Fate is best known for his paintings of machinery. He has been repeatedly nominated for the Hugo award.

His paintings bring $750–$1,000.

1980   *Di Fate's Catalog of Science Fiction Hardware* (with Ian Summers)   **trade pb$2.50**

LEO (1933–) AND DIANE (1933–) DILLON

Leo and Diane Dillon are the only team—and the only husband-and-wife artists—to win a Hugo. They did the covers for the original series of Ace Specials and have done covers for several of Harlan Ellison's books.

Their black-and-white originals sell for $300–$500; their paintings sell for $600–$1,000. Those are the prices typical for the market in the science-fiction and fantasy fields; their children's book illustrations may command different prices in that field.

1972   Hugo (Professional Artist)

1981   *The Art of Leo and Diane Dillon*   *$3.75–$19.00*

THOMAS M(ICHAEL) DISCH (1940–)

Disch is probably even better known as a critic than as a writer. He has also edited anthologies and written Gothic novels.

1965   *The Genocides*   **pb50¢–**
1966   *One Hundred and Two H Bombs*   ss   **pb50¢–**
1966   *Mankind Under the Leash*   **pb50¢–**
1967   *Echo Round His Bones*   **pb50¢–**
1968   *Camp Concentration*   **pb50¢–**
1968   *Fun with Your New Head*   ss   **pb50¢–**
1969   *The Prisoner* (from TV series)   **pb50¢–**
1972   *334*   ss   **pb50¢–**
1976   *Getting into Death and Other Stories*   ss   **pb50¢**
1977   *The Early Science Fiction Stories of Thomas M. Disch*   ss
1979   *On Wings of Song*   **pb50¢–**
1980   *Fundamental Disch*   ss   **pb50¢–**
1982   *The Man Who Had No Idea*   ss
1984   *The Brave Little Toaster*   juv

STEPHEN R. DONALDSON (1947–)

He won the John W. Campbell Award as the best new writer of 1977.

1981   *Gilden-Fire*   *$3.00–$7.50*
Daughter of Regals and Other Tales   ss   **pb$1.00**
The Chronicles of Thomas Covenant the Unbeliever series

1977 *Lord Foul's Bane* (29 pb printings by November 1987)
1977 *The Illearth War* (22 pb printings by November 1987)
1977 *The Power That Preserves* (21 pb printings by November 1987)
The Second Chronicles of Thomas Covenant series
1980 *The Wounded Land* (16 pb printings by November 1987) pb75¢
1982 *The One Tree* (11 pb printings by November 1987) pb75¢
1983 *White Gold Wielder* (9 pb printings by November 1987) pb75¢
Mordant's Need series
1986 *The Mirror of Her Dreams* hc/pb$1.00–$6.50
1987 *A Man Rides Through* hc$6.50

SIR ARTHUR CONAN DOYLE (1859–1930)

In addition to creating Sherlock Holmes, Doyle created a scientific adventurer along the lines of Indiana Jones—Professor George Edward Challenger. Challenger was an intrepid explorer who took in his stride such projects as nipping off to the Amazon to bring back a live dinosaur.

There have been paperback editions of *The Lost World* and of *The Poison Belt*, and diligent searching through used paperbacks may turn them up. The Berkley Medallion paperback of *The Poison Belt* also includes "The Disintegration Machine" and "When the World Screamed."

1912 *The Lost World*
1913 *The Poison Belt* pb50¢
1926 *The Land of Mist*
1929 *The Maracot Deep*
1952 *The Professor Challenger Stories* (omnibus)

GARDNER F. DOZOIS (1947–)

It is not belittling of his fiction to say that Dozois has made more of a mark as an editor than as a writer. In part this is because his editing is so overwhelmingly important. He edits *Isaac Asimov's Science Fiction Magazine*, has produced a series of excellent fantasy anthologies with Jack Dann (*Unicorns!* and *Magicats!* and other titles ending with *!*), and has edited two series of best-of-the-year anthologies, the current one of which is by all odds the best of the "bests," if only because of its massive size—each volume contains a quarter of a million words, making it a virtual certainty that most of the year's best science-fiction short stories, novelettes, or novellas will be in there somewhere.

He also wrote a critical booklet, *The Fiction of James Tiptree, Jr.*, which has been widely praised, despite its embarrassingly dismissing the notion that Tiptree could be a woman. Tiptree revealed herself to be Alice Sheldon at about the time the booklet was published.

    1983   Nebula (Short Story): "The Peacemaker"

    1984   Nebula (Short Story): "Morning Child"

    1988   Hugo (Professional Editor)

1975   *Nightmare Blue* (with George Alec Effinger)
1977   *The Visible Man*

LORD DUNSANY *(Edward John Moreton Drax Plunkett, 18th Baron Dunsany)* (1878–1958)

The Irish writer, who claimed he worked with a quill pen, turned out many volumes of stories, essays, and plays. He was a profound influence on H. P. Lovecraft and other fantasists.

His stories of Jorkens influenced many modern tellers of fantasies told in bars, including the "Gavagan's Bar" stories of L. Sprague de Camp and Fletcher Pratt, the "White Hart" stories of Arthur C. Clarke, the "Brigadier Ffellowes" stories of Sterling E. Lanier, and the "Callahan's Bar" stories of Spider Robinson, among many others.

1905   *The Gods of Pegana* ss
1906   *Time and the Gods* ss
1908   *The Sword of Welleran* ss
1910   *A Dreamer's Tales* ss
1912   *The Book of Wonder* ss
1915   *Fifty-One Tales* ss
1916   *The Last Book of Wonder*
1919   *Tales of Three Hemispheres* ss
1922   *Don Rodriguez: Chronicles of Shadow Valley* pb(1971)*$2.00*
1924   *The King of Elfland's Daughter* pb(1969)*$1.00*

1926   *The Charwoman's Shadow*   pb(1973)*$1.00*
1927   *The Blessing of Pan*
1931   *Travel Tales of Mr. Joseph Jorkens*   ss
1933   *The Curse of the Wise Woman*
1934   *Jorkens Remembers Africa*   ss
1936   *My Talks with Dean Spauley*
1940   *Jorkens Has a Large Whiskey*   ss
1948   *The Fourth Book of Jorkens*   ss
1949   *The Man Who Ate the Phoenix*   ss
1950   *The Strange Journeys of Colonel Polders*
1951   *The Last Revolution*
1952   *The Little Tales of Smethers*   ss
1954   *Jorkens Borrows Another Whiskey*   ss
1970   *At the Edge of the World*   ss   pb*$1.00*
1972   *Beyond the Fields We Know*   ss   pb*$1.00*
1974   *The Food of Death: Fifty-One Tales*   ss
1974   *Over the Hills and Far Away*   ss   pb*$1.00*

E(RIC) R(UCKER) EDDISON (1882–1945)

Eddison was British but drew upon Norse mythology for his heroic fantasies. His books experienced a revival when Lin Carter included them in the Adult Fantasy Series he edited for Ballantine Books.

1922   *The Worm Ouroboros*
Zimiamvian trilogy (books should be read in reverse order of publication dates)
   1935   *Mistress of Mistresses*   pb*$1.00*
   1941   *A Fish Dinner in Memison*   pb*$1.00*
   1958   *The Mezentian Gate*   pb*$1.00*

G. C. EDMONDSON (*Jose Mario Garry Ordonez Edmondson y Cotton*) (1922–)

1965   *Stranger Than You Think*   ss   pb*50¢–*
1965   *The Ship That Sailed the Time Stream*   pb*50¢–*
1971   *Chapayeca* (in pb as *Blue Face*)
1974   *T.H.E.M.*   pb*50¢–*
1975   *The Aluminum Man*
1979   *The Man Who Corrupted Earth*

1981   *To Sail the Century Sea* (seq to *Time Stream*)   **pb50¢–**
1984   *The Takeover* (with C. M. Kotlan)   **pb75¢–**
Cunningham series (with C. M. Kotlan)
  1986   *The Cunningham Equations*   **pb50¢–**
  1986   *The Black Magician*   **pb75¢–**
  1987   *Maximum Effort*   **pb75¢–**

GEORGE ALEC EFFINGER (1947–)

1972   *What Entropy Means to Me*   **hc$2.00–**
1973   *Relatives*   **hc$2.00–**
1974   *Mixed Feelings*   ss   **hc$2.00–**
1975   *Nightmare Blue* (with Gardner Dozois)
1976   *Irrational Numbers*   ss   **hc$2.00–**
1976   *Those Gentle Voices*
1978   *Dirty Tricks*   ss   **hc$2.00–**
1979   *Heroics*   **hc$2.00–**
1981   *The Wolves of Memory*   **hc$3.75**
Planet of the Apes novelizations:
  1974   *Man the Fugitive*   **pb50¢–**
  1975   *Escape to Tomorrow*   **pb50¢–**
  1975   *Journey into Terror*   **pb50¢–**

GORDON EKLUND (1945–)

Eklund and Gregory Benford tied a series of stories, including an award-winning novelette, into a novel, *If the Stars Are Gods*.

   1974   Nebula (Novelette): "If the Stars Are Gods" (with Gregory Benford)

1971   *The Eclipse of Dawn*   **pb50¢–**
1972   *A Trace of Dreams*   **pb50¢–**
1973   *Beyond the Resurrection*
1974   *Inheritors of Earth*
1974   *All Times Possible*
1975   *Falling Toward Forever*
1975   *Serving in Time*
1976   *Dance of the Apocalypse*
1976   *The Grayspace Beast*
1977   *If the Stars Are Gods* (with Gregory Benford)

1979 *The Twilight River* (in *Binary Star #2*) **pb50¢–**
Lord Tedric series
  1981 *Black Knight of the Iron Sphere* **pb50¢**

HARLAN (JAY) ELLISON (1934–)

Harlan Ellison is a prolific writer for many media; among the kinds of stories he writes are a few science-fiction stories. However, he stresses that he is not a science-fiction writer. Most of his stories these days are fantasies, some are crime/suspense, a very few are science fiction. He has won a number of awards within the science-fiction field and has also repeatedly won Writers Guild awards and the Mystery Writers of America's Edgar Allan Poe Award.

In recent years, health problems severely curtailed his output but he is now producing stories, articles, essays, reviews, and books at a prodigious rate—and continuing to win awards.

The Magazine of Fantasy and Science Fiction for July 1977 was a special "Harlan Ellison Issue." It contained three new Ellison stories (including "Jeffty Is Five"), an article by Ellison, and a memoir by his long-time friend Robert Silverberg. That issue provides a great deal of information about Ellison and his feelings.

He has written for movies, for television (including the *Star Trek* episode "City on the Edge of Forever"), and for comic books. His books are difficult to find in used-book stores; people who buy Ellison books tend to keep them.

In addition to his writing, he edited the landmark *Dangerous Visions* anthologies. The first *(Dangerous Visions)* changed the science-fiction field's perception of what could be printed and what could not. The second *(Again, Dangerous Visions)*, since the barriers had already been shattered by the first, had less impact, but both volumes received Special Achievement awards at World Science Fiction Conventions. The third anthology, *The Last Dangerous Visions,* has been delayed for many years, but Ellison has recently attacked the project with renewed vigor and pledges that it will be published. It is to be a three-volume anthology and it will contain the last published stories of several writers, including Leigh Brackett, Edmond Hamilton, and Tom Reamy.

Of particular note among Ellison books is *Partners in Wonder,* in which Ellison collaborates with a number of major science-fiction writers (A. E. van Vogt, Ben Bova, Robert Silverberg, Avram Davidson, and others).

There is considerable overlap of the stories in Ellison collections. Most of the collections contain a mixture of fantasy and non-fantasy stories. Because of the nature of this book, no listing is made of his non-fantasy books, of which there are several, including essays, autobiography, crime and suspense stories, and mainstream stories. All are of great interest to Ellison collectors but space prohibits our listing anything other than the fantasy and science-fiction material.

However, we will note that Pyramid Books in 1975 began issuing an Ellison series which contained Ellison's preferred versions of his stories. These distinctive paperback books are numbered and there are at least 11 of them, including non-fantasy books; they are extremely hard to find and likely to be expensive. Good hunting.

As a public service, we issue this warning: If you find a copy of the book which contains *Doomsman* backed with Lee Hoffman's *Telepower* (Belmont Double Book, 1967), do not ask Harlan Ellison to autograph it. He *hates* that book and has been known to tear copies to shreds when asked to autograph it. True, he then offers the autograph seeker a free copy of one of his other books to replace it, but you're not going to get your *Doomsman* back, autographed or otherwise.

1965 Nebula (Short Story): " 'Repent, Harlequin!' Said the Ticktockman"

1966 Hugo (Short Fiction): " 'Repent, Harlequin!' Said the Ticktockman"

1968 Hugo (Short Story): "I Have No Mouth, and I Must Scream"

1968 Hugo (Special Award)

1969 Hugo (Short Story): "The Beast That Shouted Love at the Heart of the World"

1969 Nebula (Novella): "A Boy and His Dog"

1972 Hugo (Special Award)

1974 Hugo (Novelette): "The Deathbird"

1975 Hugo (Novelette): "Adrift Just Off the Islets of Langerhans: Latitude 38°54′N, Longitude 77°00′13″W"

1977   Nebula (Short Story): "Jeffty Is Five"

1978   Hugo (Short Story): "Jeffty Is Five"

1986   Hugo (Novelette): "Paladin of the Lost Hour"

1960   *The Man with Nine Lives* (Ace Double with *Infinity*)

1960   *A Touch of Infinity* (Ace Double with *Nine Lives*) ss

1962   *Ellison Wonderland* ss

1965   *Paingod and Other Delusions* ss

1967   *I Have No Mouth and I Must Scream* ss

1967   *Doomsman* (bound with *Telepower* by Lee Hoffman; see previous warning) pb

1967   *From the Land of Fear* ss

1968   *Love Ain't Nothing But Sex Misspelled* ss

1969   *The Beast That Shouted Love at the Heart of the World* ss

1970   *Over the Edge: Stories From Somewhere Else* ss

1971   *Alone Against Tomorrow: Stories of Alienation in Speculative Fiction* ss hc$5.00– pb$1.00–

1971   *Partners in Wonder* ss (collaborations) hc$5.00– pb$1.00–

1974   *Approaching Oblivion: Road Signs on the Treadmill Toward Tomorrow* ss hc$5.00– pb$1.00–

1975   *Deathbird Stories: A Pantheon of Modern Gods* ss hc$5.00– pb75¢–

1975   *Phoenix Without Ashes* (with Edward Bryant) pb50¢–

1975   *No Doors, No Windows* ss pb$1.00–

1978   *Strange Wine* ss hc$5.00– pb75¢–

1978   *The Illustrated Harlan Ellison* trade pb$5.00 limited hc$15.00

1979   *The Fantasies of Harlan Ellison* (contains *Paingod, I Have No Mouth*) hc$5.00–

1980   *Shatterday* ss hc$5.00– pb$1.00–

1982   *Stalking the Nightmare* ss hc$5.00– pb$1.00–

1987   *The Essential Ellison* ss $10.00–$20.00

1987   *Night and the Enemy* (graphic novel, with Ken Steacy) $5.00–

ROGER ELWOOD (1933–)

At one point, in the early seventies, Elwood was a major market for new science fiction. After producing a number of reprint anthologies, he suddenly began producing vast numbers of original-story anthologies—somewhere between 75 and 100 of them—in addition to editing the Laser Books line of science-fiction novels, *Odyssey* magazine, and even a four-issue comic book *(Starstream)* which adapted stories by science-fiction writers.

ED(MUND ALEXANDER) EMSHWILLER (1925–)

Under the name "Emsh," he was a prolific cover artist for science-fiction magazines and paperbacks through the fifties and into the sixties. He left science-fiction art to pursue experimental film-making, a field in which he gained wide recognition—so wide that he did not return to the science-fiction field but instead became dean and later provost of the School of Film and Video at California Institute of the Arts.

His black-and-white work sells for $75–$200; his paintings sell for $500–$1,500.

   1953   Hugo (Cover Artist)

   1960   Hugo (Professional Artist)

   1961   Hugo (Profssional Artist)

   1962   Hugo (Professional Artist)

   1964   Hugo (Professional Artist)

GUY ENDORE (1900–1970)

Endore is best known in the fantasy field for his novel *The Werewolf of Paris*. That novel served as the basis for the Hammer film *Curse of the Werewolf*. Endore also worked on screenplays for fantasy films, including *Mad Love*. *The Werewolf of Paris* has had several paperback editions and is relatively easy to find.

1933   *The Werewolf of Paris*
1945   *Methinks the Lady*

DENNIS ETCHISON

1982   WFA (Short Story): "The Dark Country"

1980   *The Fog* (movie novelization)
1981   *Halloween II* (movie novelization as by Jack Martin)
1982   *Halloween III* (movie novelization as by Jack Martin)
1982   *The Dark Country* ss
1982   *Videodrome* (movie novelization as by Jack Martin)
1984   *Red Dreams* ss

PHILIP JOSE FARMER (1918–)

Farmer entered the science-fiction scene dramatically in 1952 with a novella called "The Lovers." It involved sex between human and alien races and was rejected by John Campbell at *Astounding* and by Horace Gold at *Galaxy*. It appeared in *Startling Stories* (August 1952) and caused a major stir among fans. Sex was an uncommon topic in science-fiction magazines to that point. By the time it was expanded and published as a novel, nine years later, sex in science fiction was no longer a novelty, but Farmer kept on breaking new ground.

Farmer has continued to write stories using sex as a theme (some of his novels were originally published by Essex House, a paperback publisher of sex novels), but he is no longer the only writer in the science-fiction field who acknowledges the existence of sex.

Farmer's best-known series is the "Riverworld" series, in which everyone who ever lived on Earth is brought back to life on the shores of an apparently endless river. This series enables Farmer to use any historical figure from Tom Mix to Mark Twain, from Cyrano de Bergerac to Hermann Goering as characters.

Farmer has also written detailed "biographies" of fictional characters in *Tarzan Alive!* and *Doc Savage: His Apocalyptic Life.* These are carefully researched and mix scholarship and spoof, as he ties these characters into the same family tree with Sherlock Holmes and other fictional creations.

Farmer used a number of other authors' creations in his fiction: *The Wind Whales of Ishmael* is a sequel to *Moby Dick*; he wrote three novels starring Doc Caliban and Lord Grandrith, obviously Doc Savage and Tarzan; and he wrote a number of short stories and one novel as if by writers mentioned in other authors' stories. Notable among these is *Venus on the Half Shell,* originally published as by "Kilgore Trout," a character in some of the books of Kurt Vonnegut, Jr. The novel now appears as by Farmer, since Vonnegut withdrew permission to use the Trout name.

1953   Hugo (Best New Author)

1968   Hugo (Novella): "Riders of the Purple Wage"

1972   Hugo (Novel): *To Your Scattered Bodies Go*

1957   *The Green Odyssey*   pb$1.00

1960   *The Day of Timestop* (also published as *A Woman a Day*)   pb50¢–

1960   *Flesh*   pb50¢–

1960   *Strange Relations*   ss   pb50¢–

1961   *The Lovers*   pb50¢–

1962   *The Alley God*   ss   pb50¢–

1962   *The Cache From Outer Space* (Ace Double with *Blueprint*)   *pb$1.00*

1962   *The Celestial Blueprint and Other Stories*   ss (Ace Double with *Cache*)   pb$1.00

1964   *Inside Outside*   pb50¢–

1964   *Tongues of the Moon*   pb50¢–

1965   *Dare*   hc/pb50¢–

1966   *Night of Light*   pb50¢–

1966   *The Gate of Time*   pb50¢–

1970   *The Stone God Awakens*   pb50¢–

1970   *Lord Tyger*   pb75¢–

1971   *The Wind Whales of Ishmael*   pb50¢–

1971   *Down in the Black Gang*

1972   *Time's Last Gift*   pb50¢–

1973   *The Other Log of Phileas Fogg*   pb75¢–

1973   *The Book of Philip Jose Farmer* (revised 1982)   pb50¢–

1973   *Traitor to the Living*   pb50¢

1974   *The Adventure of the Peerless Peer*   hc$4.00

1975   *Venus on the Half Shell* (originally as by Kilgore Trout)   pb50¢–

1976   *Ironcastle* (rewritten from J. H. Rosny aine)   pb50¢–

1979   *Jesus on Mars*   pb50¢

1979   *Dark Is the Sun*   hc$4.00   pb$1.00

1981 *The Cache* ss pb75¢
1981 *Father to the Stars* ss pb75¢
1981 *The Unreasoning Mask* hc$4.00 pb$1.00
1982 *Stations of the Nightmare* pb$1.00
1982 *The Purple Book* ss pb$1.00
1982 *A Barnstormer in Oz* trade pb$2.00
1982 *Greatheart Silver* pb$1.00
1984 *The Classic Philip Jose Farmer 1952-1964* ss hc$2.00
1984 *The Classic Philip Jose Farmer 1964-1973* ss hc$2.00
1984 *The Grand Adventure* trade pb $2.00
1985 *Two Hawks from Earth* pb$1.00
Dayworld series
  1985 *Dayworld* hc$4.00 pb$1.00
  1987 *Dayworld Rebel* $1.50-$4.50
Doc Caliban/Lord Grandrith series
  1969 *A Feast Unknown* pb50¢–
  1970 *Lord of the Trees* (Ace Double) pb50¢–
  1970 *The Mad Goblin* (Ace Double) pb50¢–
Exorcism series
  1968 *The Image of the Beast* pb$1.50-$4.50
  1969 *Blown* pb$1.50-$4.50
  1973 *Traitor to the Living* pb$1.50-$4.50
Opar series
  1974 *Hadon of Ancient Opar* pb75¢–
  1976 *Flight to Opar* pb50¢–
Riverworld series
  1971 *To Your Scattered Bodies Go* hc$4.00– pb75¢–
  1971 *The Fabulous Riverboat* hc$4.00– pb50¢–
  1977 *The Dark Design* hc$4.00– pb$1.00–
  1978 *The Magic Labyrinth* hc$4.00– pb$1.00–
  1979 *Riverworld and Other Stories* ss pb$1.00–
  1980 *Riverworld War: The Suppressed Fiction of Philip Jose Farmer* ss trade pb$4.00
  1983 *The Gods of Riverworld* hc$4.00– pb$1.00–
  1983 *The River of Eternity* hc$5.00
World of Tiers series
  1965 *The Maker of Universes* pb50¢–
  1966 *The Gates of Creation* pb50¢–
  1968 *A Private Cosmos* pb75¢-$4.50

1970 *Behind the Walls of Terra*   **pb50¢–**
1977 *The Lavalite World*   **pb50¢–**
1978 *The World of Tiers* (2-volume omnibus) book club   **hc$3.00**

EDWARD L. FERMAN (1937–)

Ferman has been the editor of *The Magazine of Fantasy and Science Fiction* since January 1966. He has edited several anthologies, including many of stories from *F&SF*.

1981   Hugo (Professional Editor)
1982   Hugo (Professional Editor)
1983   Hugo (Professional Editor)

VIRGIL FINLAY (1914–1971)

Finlay was a noted magazine artist, noted for his fine lines (many of which were lost when printed on pulp paper) and his nude women with artfully placed bubbles. He painted covers and did illustrations for *Weird Tales, Famous Fantastic Mysteries, Galaxy,* and many other magazines from 1935 until his death. There have been collections of his art, but they were produced in limited editions and are long out of print.

"Quality is everything," art dealer Robert Weinberg said, "when you're looking at prices brought by Finlay's work." There is a hot market for it, and black-and-white prices range from $300 to $1,500. His paintings go for $2,500–$8,000.

1953   Hugo (Interior Illustrator)

1971 *Virgil Finlay* (published by Donald M. Grant)
1975 *The Book of Virgil Finlay* (published by Gerry de la Ree)
1981 *Virgil Finlay Remembered* (published by Gerry de la Ree)

CHARLES G(RANDISON) FINNEY

Finney is best known as the author of *The Circus of Dr. Lao* (made into a movie, *The Seven Faces of Dr. Lao*).

1935 *The Circus of Dr. Lao*
1937 *The Unholy City*
1939 *Past the End of the Pavement*

Famous Fantastic Mysteries, April 1942, about 6¾″ × 9¾″; cover by Virgil Finlay (1914–1971). Copyright 1942 by The Frank A. Munsey Company. Reprinted by permission of Blazing Publications, The Argosy Co.

Super Science Stories, May 1943, about 7″ × 9½″; cover by Virgil Finlay (1914–1971). Defects include frayed right cover. Listed as copyright 1943 by Fictioneers, Inc. Copyright 1943 by Popular Publications. Reprinted by permission of Blazing Publications, The Argosy Co.

Famous Fantastic Mysteries, December 1942, about 6½″ × 9¼″; cover by Virgil Finlay (1914–1971). Defect is the inside tape repair (and tear) in the lower left corner. Copyright 1942 by The Frank A. Munsey Company. Reprinted by permission of Blazing Publications, The Argosy Co.

Famous Fantastic Mysteries, February 1947, about 7″ × 9½″; cover by Virgil Finlay (1914–1971). Defects include left-cover crease, tape stain in upper left corner, and frayed bottom cover. Listed as copyright 1946 by All-Fiction Field, Inc. Copyright 1946 by Popular Publications. Reprinted by permission of Blazing Publications, The Argosy Co.

1964   *The Ghosts of Manacle* ss
1968   *The Unholy City* ss *(Unholy City* and *Magician Out of Man-churia)*
1976   *The Magician Out of Manchuria*

JACK FINNEY *(Walter Braden Finney)* (1911–)

Most of Finney's stories have appeared in slick-paper magazines, rather than specialty pulp or digest publications. He writes mysteries and fantasies. His novel *The Body Snatchers* formed the basis for two movies, both called *The Invasion of the Body Snatchers*.

1987   WFA Life Achievement Award

1955   *The Body Snatchers*
1957   *The Third Level* ss
1963   *I Love Galesburg in the Springtime*
1968   *The Woodrow Wilson Dime* pb50¢–
1970   *Time and Again* hc$3.00 pb50¢
1973   *Marion's Wall* pb50¢–
1977   *The Night People* pb50¢–
1987   *3 by Finney* (omnibus of *Dime, Marion's,* and *Night*) hc$3.75

ALAN DEAN FOSTER (1946–)

Foster is primarily known for his novelizations of the *Star Trek* animated cartoon series *(Star Trek Log* 1-9) and of science fiction, fantasy, and horror movies.

1974   *Dark Star* (movie novelization) pb50¢–
1974   *Luana* pb50¢–
1975   *Midworld* pb50¢–
1977   *With Friends Like These . . .* ss pb50¢–
1979   *The Black Hole* (movie novelization) pb50¢–
1979   *Alien* (movie novelization) pb50¢–
1980   *Cachalot* pb75¢–
1981   *Splinter of the Mind's Eye* pb50¢–
1981   *Clash of the Titans* (movie novelization) pb75¢–
1982   *The Thing* (movie novelization) pb75¢–
1982   *Nor Crystal Tears* pb75¢–
1983   *The Man Who Used the Universe* pb75¢–
1983   *Krull* (movie novelization) pb75¢–

1984   *. . . Who Needs Enemies?* ss   pb75¢–
1984   *The I Inside*   pb75¢–
1984   *Shadowkeep*   pb75¢–
1984   *Slipt*   pb75¢–
1984   *Starman* (movie novelization)   pb75¢–
1984   *Voyage to the City of the Dead*   pb75¢–
1985   *Pale Rider* (movie novelization)   pb75¢–
1985   *Sentenced to Prism*   pb75¢–
1986   *Aliens* (movie novelization)   pb75¢–
1986   *The Last Starfighter* (movie novelization)   pb75¢–
1986   *Into the Out of*   hc$4.00   pb75¢–
1987   *Glory Lane* $1.00

The Adventures of Flinx of the Commonwealth series
  1972   *The Tar-Aiym Krang*   pb75¢–
  1973   *Bloodhype*   pb75¢–
  1977   *Orphan Star*   pb75¢–
  1977   *The End of the Matter*   pb75¢–
  1983   *For Love of Mother-Not*   pb75¢–
  1987   *Flinx in Flux*   pb75¢–

Icerigger series
  1974   *Icerigger*   pb50¢–
  1979   *Mission to Moulokin*   pb50¢–
  1980   *The Deluge Drivers*   pb50¢–

Spellsinger series
  1982   *Spellsinger*   pb75¢
  1983   *Spellsinger II: The Hour of the Gate*   pb75¢–
  1984   *Spellsinger III: The Day of the Dissonance*   pb75¢–
  1985   *Spellsinger IV: The Moment of the Magician*   pb75¢–
  1986   *Spellsinger V: The Paths of the Perambulator*   pb75¢–
  1987   *Spellsinger VI: The Time of the Transference*   pb75¢–

FRANK FRAZETTA (1928–)

Frank Frazetta, who began as a comic-book artist, drew the comic
strip *Johnny Comet* (also known as *Ace McCoy*), was a ghost artist on
Li'l Abner, and became a major figure in the art world when he did
covers for paperback books, especially the Tarzan and Conan books.
His covers for Lancer Books' Conan series in particular made him a

top commercial artist; those books command high prices on the collectors' market.

Black-and-white sketches go for $300–$600, but "reasonably nice" finished black-and-white Frazetta material goes for $1,000–$3,000. His *Johnny Comet* comic strips range from $400–$500 for dailies to $1,000 for Sundays. Frazetta paintings bring $7,000—and up. Frazetta has turned down a $44,000 offer for at least one particular painting.

  1966   Hugo (Professional Artist)
  1976   WFA (Artist)

FRANK KELLY FREAS (1922–)

Besides covers for science-fiction paperbacks and magazines, Freas has done covers for *Mad* magazine. He and his wife Polly created the Starblaze line of trade paperback books for Donning. Today, much of his work is in portraiture, but fans can still buy posters of some of his classic paintings.

His sketches go for $10–$100; his finished black-and-white work is priced from $100 to $400. His finished paintings tend to range from $500–$2,500—but there are some at higher prices.

  1955   Hugo (Professional Artist)
  1956   Hugo (Professional Artist)
  1958   Hugo (Professional Artist)
  1959   Hugo (Professional Artist)
  1970   Hugo (Professional Artist)
  1972   Hugo (Professional Artist)
  1973   Hugo (Professional Artist)
  1974   Hugo (Professional Artist)
  1975   Hugo (Professional Artist)
  1976   Hugo (Professional Artist)

RANDALL GARRETT (1927–1988)

Randall Garrett was an exuberant person and a prolific author, collaborating often with Robert Silverberg. Two collections of parodies of science-fiction writers (*Takeoff!* and *Takeoff Too!*) by Garrett were published by Starblaze. Garrett's most popular stories were the "Lord Darcy" series, mystery stories set in an alternate universe where magic works. At least one additional novel in the "Lord Darcy" series, *Ten Little Wizards,* has been written by Michael Kurland.

1959 *Pagan Passions* (with Larry M. Harris) **pb$1.00–**
1962 *Unwise Child* **hc$2.00**
1963 *Anything You Can Do* (as by Darrel T. Langart) **hc$2.00**
1979 *Takeoff* **ss** **trade pb$2.50–**
1980 *Starship Death* **pb75¢–**
1980 *Earth Invader* **pb75¢–**
1982 *The Best of Randall Garrett* **ss** **pb75¢–**
1986 *Takeoff Too!* **trade pb$2.50–**
The Gandalara Cycle (with Vicki Ann Heydron)
   1981 *The Steel of Raithskar* **pb50¢**
   1982 *The Glass of Dyskornis* **pb50¢**
   1983 *The Bronze of Eddarta* **pb50¢**
Lord Darcy series
   1967 *Too Many Magicians* **hc/pb** **pb50¢–**
   1979 *Murder and Magic* **ss** **pb$1.00–**
   1981 *Lord Darcy Investigates* **ss** **pb75¢–**
   1982 *Lord Darcy* (book-club omnibus) **hc$2.00**
Nidorian series (with Robert Silverberg, as by "Robert Randall")
   1957 *The Shrouded Planet* **trade pb$2.00**
   1959 *The Dawning Light* **trade pb$2.00**
Psi series (with Laurence M. Janifer, as by "Mark Phillips")
   1962 *Brain Twister* **pb50¢**
   1962 *The Impossibles* **pb50¢–**
   1963 *Supermind* **pb50¢**

JACK GAUGHAN (1930–1985)

Gaughan, who did most of his magazine work for *Galaxy* and *If,* was the only artist ever to win the Hugo as Fan Artist and Professional Artist in the same year. He came by it fairly, since he remained active doing art for fanzines even while he was in great demand as a paperback cover artist and was art director of *Galaxy*.

His black-and-white work goes for $25–$75; his paintings go for around $200.

    1967   Hugo (Professional Artist)
    1967   Hugo (Fan Artist)
    1968   Hugo (Professional Artist)
    1969   Hugo (Professional Artist)

HUGO GERNSBACK (1884–1967)

Gernsback, who enjoyed putting science fiction stories in his radio and electronics magazines in the early 1900s (he serialized his own slim novel *Ralph 124C41+* in *Modern Electrics* in 1911 and 1912), eventually published the first science-fiction magazine, *Amazing Stories,* in 1926. He lost the magazine in a bankruptcy but bounced back with another group of science-fiction magazines (*Air Wonder Stories, Science Wonder Stories, Wonder Stories Quarterly, Scientific Detective Monthly, Science Wonder Quarterly*), making him the founder of the first six science-fiction magazines. He even tried his hand at a science-fiction comic book; *Superworld Comics,* with covers by Gernsback's regular cover artist, Frank R. Paul, lasted three issues. He merged the *Wonder* group of magazines and eventually sold them, leaving the science-fiction field until 1953, when he published eight issues of *Science Fiction Plus*.

"Plus" apparently had deep meanings for Gernsback, since it was a part of his best-known novel and his last science-fiction magazine. The title of his novel is a sort-of pun, "one to foresee for one-plus."

Although Gernsback published science-fiction magazines only for a few years—he had more success with another magazine, *Sexology*— he is regarded as "The Father of Science Fiction Magazines" and the Science Fiction Achievement Award is named for him: the Hugo.

    1960   Hugo (Special Award): "The Father of Magazine Science
    Fiction"

1925   *Ralph 124C41+*   **hc/pb$1.00–**
1971   *The Ultimate World*

STEVE GERVAIS

His black-and-white work is priced at $150–$300; his color work goes for $500–$1,000.

   1984   WFA (Artist)

WILLIAM GIBSON

   1984   Nebula (Novel): *Neuromancer*

   1985   Hugo (Novel): *Neuromancer*

1984 *Neuromancer* pb only$1.00

1986 *Count Zero* hc$4.00 pb75¢–

1986 *Burning Chrome* ss hc$4.00 pb$1.00

PARKE GODWIN

   1982   WFA (Novella): ''The Fire When It Comes''

1978 *The Masters of Solitude* (with Marvin Kaye) hc2.00 pb50¢–

1982 *Wintermind* (with Marvin Kaye) $1.00–

1983 *A Cold Blue Light* (with Marvin Kaye) $1.00–

1987 *Ghosts of Night and Morning* (with Marvin Kaye) $1.00–

HORACE L. GOLD (1914–)

Before becoming editor of *Galaxy* (and, later, *Beyond, If,* and the *Galaxy Science Fiction Novels*), Gold had been a prolific magazine writer who had written some science fiction for *Astounding* and some fantasy for *Unknown*. He also had been an assistant editor on *Startling Stories, Thrilling Wonder Stories,* and *Captain Future*.

   None of this prepared anyone for the impact *Galaxy* had on a field which had been dominated for more than a decade by *Astounding*. Gold challenged that dominance from the first issue by starting a policy of running serials in virtually every issue, something only *Astounding* had done up to that time. He also took a different approach from Campbell's nuts-and-bolts, engineer-oriented science fiction; Gold encouraged stories involving the social sciences and satires on social trends. Gold's magazine took science fiction bodily into the fifties, with satiric stories about advertising and communications. Gold lured writers who previously had been associated in the science-fiction fans' minds exclusively with *Astounding*—Asimov, Simak, Sturgeon—and fostered such newer writers as Robert Sheckley and F. L. Wallace.

For a decade, he made *Galaxy* one of the field's "Big Three," along with *ASF* and *F&SF,* before ill health forced him to retire.

In addition to the book listed here, he edited several collections of stories from *Galaxy*.

1955   *The Old Die Rich*   ss   hc$5.00–

EDWARD GOREY

Gorey is a set designer and book artist. A great deal of his ghoulish work can be found in three omnibus collections of what look disarmingly like children's books.

   1985   WFA (Artist)

1963   *The Gashlycrumb Tinies*   pb$1.50–
1972   *Amphigorey*   hc$3.00
1975   *Amphigorey Too*   hc$3.00
1983   *Amphigorey Also*   trade pb$3.00
1987   *The Raging Tide* $3.50–

RON(ALD JOSEPH) GOULART (1933–)

Ron Goulart is a prolific, dependable writer who is underrated by many because he "just writes funny stuff"—as if that were an easy thing to do. His early training as an advertising copywriter (he once wrote a series of good-news newspapers for the backs of cereal boxes) made him a remarkably concise novelist; in these days of bloated, 90,000-word books which are only the first part of a trilogy, Goulart's books are slim, trim, and fast-paced, with dialogue carrying the story and with the curtain dropping as soon as the action is over.

Many of his science-fiction stories take place in the Barnum system of planets, a locale he also used for his science-fiction comic strip, *Star Hawks,* which was drawn by Gil Kane. A frequent occurrence in his stories is the breakdown of modern technology, a fact taken for granted by his protagonists.

He writes novels and short stories in both the mystery and science-fiction fields, writes articles about old movies and old comic books, and has written histories of and compiled anthologies from old pulp magazines.

While he has never won a major science-fiction award, he did win the Mystery Writers of America Edgar—for a science-fiction novel, *After Things Fell Apart*.

1968 *The Sword Swallower* pb50¢–
1970 *The Fire-Eater* pb50¢–
1970 *After Things Fell Apart* pb50¢–
1971 *Gadget Man* pb50¢–
1971 *Broke Down Engine and Other Troubles With Machines* ss hc/pb
1971 *Clockwork's Pirates* (Ace Double with *Ghost Breaker*) *pb$1.00*
1971 *Ghost Breaker* ss (Ace Double with *Clockwork's Pirates*) pb$1.00
1971 *Hawkshaw* pb50¢–
1971 *What's Become of Screwloose?* ss
1972 *Wildsmith* pb50¢–
1973 *The Tin Angel* pb50¢–
1973 *Shaggy Planet* pb50¢–
1975 *Spacehawk, Inc.* pb50¢–
1975 *When the Waker Sleeps* pb50¢–
1975 *The Enormous Hourglass* pb50¢–
1975 *Nutzenbolts* ss pb50¢–
1975 *Odd Job No. 101* ss pb50¢–
1975 *The Hellhound Project* pb50¢–
1977 *Challengers of the Unknown* pb50¢–
1977 *Crackpot* pb50¢–
1977 *The Emperor of the Last Days* pb50¢–
1977 *The Island of Dr. Moreau* (movie novelization, as by Joseph Silva) pb50¢–
1977 *The Panchronicon Plot* pb50¢–
1977 *Nemo* pb50¢–
1978 *The Wicked Cyborg* pb50¢–
1978 *Capricorn One* (movie novelization) pb50¢–
1979 *Dr. Scofflaw* (in *Binary Star #3*) pb50¢–
1980 *Skyrocket Steele* pb75¢–
1981 *The Robot in the Closet* pb50¢–

1981 *Brinkman* hc$2.00– pb50¢–
1982 *Upside Downside* pb50¢–
1984 *Hellquad* pb75¢–
1985 *Suicide, Inc.* pb75¢–
1986 *Galaxy Jane* pb75¢–
Battlestar Galactica series (with Glen A. Larson)
  1983 *Greetings from Earth* pb75¢–
  1983 *Experiment in Terra* pb75¢–
  1984 *The Long Patrol* pb75¢–
Chameleon Corps series
  1972 *The Chameleon Corps and Other Shape Changers* ss 50¢–
  1974 *Flux* 50¢–
Exchameleon series
  1987 *Daredevils, Ltd.* pb75¢–
  1987 *Starpirate's Brain* pb75¢–
  1988 *Everybody Comes to Cosmo's* pb75¢–
Harry Challenge series
  1984 *The Prisoner of Blackwood Castle* pb75¢–
  1987 *The Curse of the Obelisk* pb75¢–
Jack Summer series
  1971 *Death Cell* 50¢–
  1972 *Plunder* 50¢–
  1976 *A Whiff of Madness* 50¢–
Jake Conger series
  1973 *A Talent for the Invisible* 50¢–
  1979 *Hello, Lemuria, Hello* 50¢–
Odd Jobs, Inc. series
  1978 *Calling Dr. Patchwork* 50¢–
  1980 *Hail Hibbler* 75¢–
  1982 *Big Bang* 75¢–
  1985 *Brainz, Inc.* 75¢–
Quest of the Gypsy series
  1976 *Quest of the Gypsy* 75¢–
  1977 *Eye of the Vulture* 75¢–
Star Hawks series
  1979 *Star Hawks* (comic strip, with Gil Kane) pb50¢
  1981 *Star Hawks II* (comic strip, with Gil Kane) pb50¢
  1981 *Star Hawks* (novel) pb75¢
  1981 *Star Hawks #2: The Cyborg King* (novel) pb75¢

Vampirella series (based on comic-book stories)
  1975 *Bloodstalk* **pb50¢**
  1975 *On Alien Wings* **pb50¢**
  1976 *Deadwalk* **pb50¢**
  1976 *Blood Wedding* **pb50¢**
  1976 *Deathgame* **pb50¢**
  1976 *Snakegod* **pb50¢**

ROBERT GOULD

Gould is a paperback book cover artist, most noted for his covers for novels by Michael Moorcock.

  1987 WFA (Artist)

CHARLES L. GRANT

Grant is noted for his horror stories and anthologies. He sets many of his horror novels and short stories in the fictitious community of Oxrun Station.

  1976 Nebula (Short Story): "A Crowd of Shadows"

  1978 Nebula (Novelette): "A Glow of Candles, a Unicorn's Eye"

  1983 WFA (Collection): *Nightmare Seasons* ss

1976 *The Shadow of Alpha*
1977 *Ascension*
1977 *The Curse*
1977 *The Hour of the Oxrun Dead*
1981 *A Glow of Candles and Other Stories* ss **pb90¢–**
1981 *The Grave* **pb75¢–**
1981 *Tales From the Nightside* ss **hc$3.00–**
1981 *A Quiet Night of Fear* **pb50¢**
1981 *The Nestling*
1982 *Nightmare Seasons*
1985 *The Dark Cry of the Moon* **$1.00–**

MARTIN GREENBERG (1918–)

Greenberg was co-publisher of Gnome Press, one of the first hard-cover science-fiction book companies. Gnome Press editions are, without exception, desirable collectors' items. Standouts from Gnome are the first editions of Isaac Asimov's *Foundation, Foundation and Empire,* and *Second Foundation,* and the first hardcover editions of Robert E. Howard's Conan stories.

MARTIN HARRY GREENBERG (1941–)

Greenberg (no relation to the Gnome Press publisher) has rapidly eclipsed previous title-holders Groff Conklin and Roger Elwood as the most prolific science-fiction anthologist. Greenberg's specialty is to edit "theme" anthologies with big-name writers (Asimov, Silverberg, Anthony, etc.). He has apparently produced more than 200 anthologies since 1974. Most of his anthologies are reprint, but he is starting to turn out some original-story collections.

Space does not permit a complete listing of his anthologies, but we would recommend his series of retrospective best-of-the-year anthologies, done with Asimov, *Isaac Asimov Presents the Great Science Fiction Stories,* which began with the best stories of 1939 and has continued from that point to, so far, the mid–fifties.

JAMES E(DWIN) GUNN (1923–)

In addition to his science-fiction writing, Gunn is an excellent historian of the field (*Alternate Worlds: The Illustrated History of Science Fiction,* 1975) and has edited an excellent series of anthologies (*The Road to Science Fiction,* four volumes) which traces and gives examples of science fiction from its earliest days to the present. His master's thesis was serialized in *Dynamic Science Fiction.*

His best-known work is *The Immortals,* which was adapted into a TV movie and TV series called *The Immortal.*

1986   Hugo (Special Award)

1955   *This Fortress World*   pb50¢–
1955   *Star Bridge* (with Jack Williamson)   **pb50¢**–
1958   *Station in Space*   ss   **pb50¢**–
1961   *The Joy Makers*   **pb50¢**–

1962 *The Immortals* pb50¢–
1964 *Future Imperfect* ss pb50¢–
1970 *The Witching Hour* ss pb50¢–
1970 *The Immortal* (novelization from TV series) pb50¢–
1972 *The Listeners* pb50¢–
1972 *The Burning* pb50¢–
1972 *Breaking Point* ss pb50¢–
1974 *Some Dreams Are Nightmares* hc/pb$1.00–
1975 *The End of the Dreams* ss
1976 *The Magicians*
1980 *The Dreamers* (in pb as *The Mind Master*) hc$2.00– pb50¢–

(SIR) H(ENRY) RIDER HAGGARD (1856–1925)

Haggard's lost-race and lost-treasure novels, mostly set in Africa, were the epitome of the adventure fantasy emulated by Edgar Rice Burroughs. His two main series, one involving white hunter Allan Quatermain and one involving the immortal Ayesha, She-Who-Must-Be-Obeyed, were brought together in *She and Allan*.

1889 *Cleopatra*
1890 *The World's Desire* (with Andrew Lang) hc/pb$1.00–
1891 *Eric Brighteyes* hc/pb$1.00–
1894 *The People of the Mist* hc/pb$1.00
1895 *Heart of the World*
1906 *The Spirit of Bambatse*
1908 *The Yellow God*
1910 *Sheba's Ring*
1911 *Red Eve*
1919 *When the World Shook* hc/pb$1.00
Allan Quatermain series
  1885 *King Solomon's Mines*
  1887 *Allan Quatermain*
  1888 *Maiwa's Revenge*
  1889 *Allan's Wife and Other Tales* ss
  1912 *Marie*
  1913 *Child of Storm*
  1915 *Allan and the Holy Flower*
  1916 *The Ivory Lake*

1917 *Finished*
1920 *Smith and the Pharaohs and Other Tales* ss
1920 *The Ancient Allan*
1921 *She and Allan*
1924 *Heu-Heu*
1926 *The Treasure of the Lake*
1927 *Allan and the Ice Gods*

Ayesha series

1887 *She*   hc/pb$1.00
1905 *Ayesha: The Return of She*   hc/pb$1.00–
1921 *She and Allan*
1923 *Wisdom's Daughter*   hc/pb$1.00–

PETER HAINING (1940–)

Haining is a British anthologist, primarily of fantasy, who has also written books on the history of the British science-fiction TV series *Doctor Who*.

JOE W(ILLIAM) HALDEMAN (1943–)

Haldeman, who holds degrees in physics and astronomy, served as a combat engineer in Vietnam, where he was wounded. He has written a series of stories about an interstellar war which strongly resembles the Vietnam experience; he combined those stories into a novel, *The Forever War*.

He has also written a *Star Trek* novel, *Planet of Judgment*.

1975 Nebula (Novel): *The Forever War*

1976 Hugo (Novel): *The Forever War*

1977 Hugo (Short Story): "Tricentennial"

1974 *The Forever War*   pb50¢–
1975 *Attar's Revenge* (as by Robert Graham)   pb50¢–
1975 *Nerves* (as by Robert Graham)   pb50¢–
1976 *Mindbridge*   pb50¢–
1977 *All My Sins Remembered*   pb50¢–
1977 *There is No Darkness* (with Jack C. Haldeman II)
1977 *Tool of the Trade*   hc$4.00

1984   *Worlds Apart*   hc$4.00–   pb75¢–
1985   *Dealing in Futures*   ss   pb$1.00

EDMOND (MOORE) HAMILTON (1904–1977)

Hamilton began writing for *Weird Tales* in 1926 and wrote 70 stories for that magazine. However, he is remembered for the space-adventure stories he wrote for the science-fiction magazines and for the creation of Captain Future. He married Leigh Brackett in 1946, but they never collaborated on stories—except for a story in the still-forthcoming (at this writing) *The Last Dangerous Visions* in which Brackett's Eric John Stark meets Hamilton's Star Kings.

1936   *Horror on the Asteroid*   ss   pb50¢–
1949   *The Star Kings*   pb50¢–
1950   *A Yank at Valhalla!*   pb50¢–
1950   *Tharkol, Lord of the Unknown*   pb50¢–
1951   *City at World's End*   pb50¢–
1959   *The Sun Smasher*   pb50¢–
1959   *The Star of Life*   pb50¢–
1960   *The Haunted Stars*   pb50¢–
1961   *Battle for the Stars*   pb50¢–
1964   *Outside the Universe*   pb50¢–
1964   *The Valley of Creation*   pb50¢–
1965   *Crashing Suns*   ss   pb50¢–
1965   *Fugitive of the Stars*   pb50¢–
1966   *Doomstar*   pb50¢–
1974   *What's It Like Out There? and Other Stories*   ss   pb only$1.00
1977   *The Best of Edmond Hamilton*   book club$2.00   pb75¢–
Captain Future series (*The Solar Invasion*, 1969, was by Manly Wade Wellman, not Hamilton)
   1968   *Danger Planet*   pb50¢–
   1969   *Outlaw World*   pb50¢–
   1969   *Quest Beyond the Stars*   pb50¢–
   1969   *Outlaws of the Moon*   pb50¢–
   1969   *The Comet Kings*   pb50¢–
   1969   *Planets in Peril*   pb50¢–
   1969   *Calling Captain Future*   pb50¢–
   1969   *Captain Future's Challenge*   pb50¢–
   1969   *Galaxy Mission*   pb50¢–

1969   *The Tenth Planet*   pb50¢–
1969   *The Magician of Mars*   pb50¢–
1969   *Captain Future and the Space Emperor*   pb50¢–
Starwolf series
1967   *The Weapon From Beyond*   pb50¢–
1968   *The Closed Worlds*   pb50¢–
1968   *World of the Starwolves*   pb50¢–

HARRY HARRISON (1925–)

Harry Harrison began as a comic-book writer and artist (for E. C. Comics, among others) and had his first story in Damon Knight's short-lived *Worlds Beyond* magazine. He has since become an extremely prolific novelist.

His novel about overpopulation, *Make Room! Make Room!*, was the basis for the movie, *Soylent Green*.

He also has edited several anthologies, including the *Nova* series of original stories, the *SF: Author's Choice* series, and the annual *Best SF* series with Brian W. Aldiss.

1962   *Planet of the Damned*   pb50¢–
1962   *War With the Robots*   ss   pb50¢–
1965   *The Plague From Space* (revised as *The Jupiter Plague*)   50¢–
1965   *Bill, the Galactic Hero*   pb50¢–
1965   *Two Tales and Eight Tomorrows*   ss   pb50¢–
1966   *Make Room! Make Room!*   pb50¢–
1967   *The Technicolor Time Machine*   pb50¢–
1968   *The Man from P.I.G.*   pb50¢–
1969   *Captive Universe*   pb50¢–
1970   *The Daleth Effect*
1970   *One Step From Earth*   ss   pb50¢–
1970   *Prime Number*   ss
1970   *Spaceship Medic*
1972   *Tunnel Through the Deeps*   pb75¢–
1973   *Star Smashers of the Galaxy Rangers*
1974   *The Men from P.I.G. and R.O.B.O.T.*   ss   pb50¢–
1975   *The California Iceberg*
1976   *Skyfall*   pb75¢–
1976   *The Lifeship* (with Gordon R. Dickson)   pb75¢–
1976   *The Best of Harry Harrison*   pb50¢–

1981   *Planet of No Return* (seq to *Planet of the Damned*)   pb75¢–
1985   *West of Eden*
1986   *Winter in Eden* (seq to *West of Eden*)   pb/hc$1.00–$4.50
Deathworld series
  1960   *Deathworld*   50¢
  1964   *Deathworld 2*   50¢
  1968   *Deathworld 3*   50¢
  The Deathworld Trilogy (omnibus)
Stainless Steel Rat series
  1961   *The Stainless Steel Rat*
  1970   *The Stainless Steel Rat's Revenge*   pb50¢
  1972   *The Stainless Steel Rat Saves the World*
  1979   *The Stainless Steel Rat Wants You!*
  1987   *The Stainless Steel Rat Gets Drafted* $1.50–
To the Stars series (also published as omnibus)
  1980   *Homeworld*   pb50¢
  1981   *Wheelworld*   pb50¢
  1981   *Starworld*   pb50¢

ROBERT A(NSON) HEINLEIN (1907–1988)

Almost from the time he began writing—in 1939, for John W. Campbell's *Astounding*—Robert Heinlein was at the top of the profession. He had graduated from Annapolis and was a Naval officer when ill health forced him to retire. He tried a variety of things before attempting the writing of science fiction, at which he was an instant success. He also was extremely prolific. In his later years, his novels not only topped the science-fiction bestseller lists, they regularly made the *New York Times* bestseller list.

His first juvenile novel, *Rocket Ship Galileo,* was the basis for the science-fiction movie *Destination Moon.* (Don't let the label "juvenile" fool you; except for Heinlein's first couple of juveniles, all it means is that the heroes are young. They're great reading for all ages; some were serialized in *Astounding* and *F&SF.*) In addition to his novels and short stories, Heinlein edited one anthology, *Tomorrow the Stars,* which remains generally available in paperback.

He was the first recipient of the Science Fiction Writers of America's Grand Master award; Isaac Asimov remarked that it was no surprise to anyone; it was just like choosing George Washington as the first President.

1956 Hugo (Novel): *Double Star*

1960 Hugo (Novel): *Starship Trooper*

1962 Hugo (Novel): *Stranger in a Strange Land*

1967 Hugo (Novel): *The Moon Is a Harsh Mistress*

1974 SFWA Grand Master

1947 *Rocket Ship Galileo* juv hc$4.00– pb50¢–

1948 *Beyond This Horizon* hc$4.00– pb50¢–

1948 *Space Cadet* juv hc$4.00– pb50¢–

1949 *Red Planet* juv hc$4.00– pb50¢–

1949 *The Day After Tomorrow* hc$4.00– pb50¢–

1950 *The Man Who Sold the Moon* hc$4.00– pb50¢–

1950 *Farmer in the Sky* juv hc$4.00– pb50¢–

1950 *Waldo & Magic, Inc.* ss pb/hc50¢–

1951 *The Green Hills of Earth* ss hc$4.00– pb50¢–

1951 *Between Planets* juv hc$4.00– pb50¢–

1951 *The Puppet Masters* hc$4.00– pb50¢–

1951 *Universe* (Dell 10¢ pb) *$4.00*

1952 *The Rolling Stones* juv hc$4.00– pb50¢–

1953 *Assignment in Eternity* ss hc$4.00– pb50¢–

1953 *Starman Jones* juv hc$4.00– pb50¢–

1953 *Revolt in 2100* ss hc$4.00– pb50¢–

1954 *The Star Beast* juv hc$4.00– pb50¢–

1955 *Tunnel in the Sky* juv hc$4.00– pb50¢–

1956 *Time for the Stars* juv hc$4.00– pb50¢–

1956 *Double Star* hc$4.00– pb50¢–

1957 *Citizen of the Galaxy* juv hc$4.00– pb50¢–

1957 *The Door into Summer* hc$4.00– pb50¢–

1958 *Methuselah's Children* hc$4.00– pb50¢–

1958 *Have Space Suit—Will Travel* juv hc$4.00– pb50¢–

1959 *The Menace From Earth* ss hc$4.00– pb50¢–

1959 *Starship Troopers* hc$4.00– pb50¢–

1959 *The Unpleasant Profession of Jonathan Hoag* ss (pb as *6xH*) hc$4.00– pb50¢–

1961 *Stranger in a Strange Land* hc$4.00– pb50¢–

1963 *Orphans of the Sky* ss hc$4.00– pb50¢–

1963 *Podkayne of Mars* hc$4.00– pb50¢–
1963 *Glory Road* hc$4.00– pb50¢–
1964 *Farnham's Freehold* hc$4.00– pb50¢–
1965 *Three by Heinlein (Puppet Masters, Waldo, Magic Inc.)* book club$2.00
1966 *The Worlds of Robert A. Heinlein* ss pb$2.50–
1966 *The Moon Is a Harsh Mistress* pb/hc (37th paperback printing in 1986) hc$5.00 pb75¢–
1967 *The Past Through Tomorrow* ss pb50¢–
1970 *I Will Fear No Evil* hc$5.00 pb75¢–
1973 *Time Enough for Love* hc$5.00 pb75¢–
1980 *The Number of the Beast* hc$4.00 trade pb$2.00 pb$1.00
1982 *Friday* hc$5.00 pb$1.00
1984 *Job: A Comedy of Justice* hc$5.00 pb$1.00
1985 *The Cat Who Walks Through Walls* hc$5.00 pb$1.00–
1987 *To Sail Beyond the Sunset* hc$6.00

NOTE: Listed prices are for items in *GOOD* condition.
Very Good = two times listed price.
Fine = three times listed price.
Mint = four times listed price.

ZENNA HENDERSON (1917–1983)

Zenna Henderson was an elementary school teacher who put her knowledge of children to good work in her fiction, much of which had a school setting. Her most famous stories were the ''People'' series, about a group of gentle aliens with psionic powers trying to blend in on Earth.

1965 *The Anything Box* ss pb50¢–
1971 *Holding Wonder* ss pb50¢–
The People series
  1961 *Pilgrimage: The Book of the People* pb50¢–
  1966 *The People: No Different Flesh* ss (seq to *Pilgrimage*) pb50¢–

FRANK HERBERT (1920–1986)

Herbert is best known for his *Dune* novels which formed the inspiration for the movie *Dune*.

Tim O'Reilly edited a collection of articles and essays by Herbert in 1987, *The Maker of Dune: Insights of a Master of Science Fiction*.

1965 Nebula (Novel): *Dune*

1956 *The Dragon in the Sea* (also as *21st Century Sub, Under Pressure*) hc$5.00 trade pb$2.00 pb50¢–
1966 *The Green Brain* pb50¢–
1966 *The Eyes of Heisenberg* (17th printing by 1986) pb50¢–
1966 *Destination: Void* pb50¢–
1968 *The Heaven Makers* (7th printing in 1987) 50¢–
1968 *The Santaroga Barrier* pb50¢–
1970 *The Worlds of Frank Herbert* ss pb50¢–
1970 *Whipping Star* pb50¢–
1972 *The God Makers* pb50¢–
1973 *Hellstrom's Hive* pb50¢–
1973 *The Book of Frank Herbert* ss pb50¢–
1975 *The Best of Frank Herbert* ss pb50¢–
1977 *The Dosadi Experiment* pb50¢–
1980 *The Direct Descent* hc$4.00– pb$1.00–
1982 *The Soul Catcher* pb50¢–
1982 *The Jesus Incident* (with Bill Ransom) hc$4.00– pb$1.00–
1982 *The Heaven Makers* pb$1.00
1983 *The White Plague* pb$1.00–
1983 *The Lazarus Effect* (with Bill Ransom) hc$4.00– pb$1.00–
1985 *Eye* ss trade pb$2.00–
1986 *Man of Two Worlds* (with Brian Herbert) hc$4.00– pb$1.00–
1988 *The Ascension Factor* (with Bill Ransom) hc$4.00– pb$1.00–

Dune series
1965 *Dune* hc$20.00– pb$1.00–
1969 *Dune Messiah* hc$10.00– pb$1.00–
1976 *Children of Dune* hc$10.00– pb$1.00–
1981 *God Emperor of Dune* hc$4.00– pb$1.50–
1984 *Heretics of Dune* hc$4.00– pb$1.50–
1985 *Chapterhouse: Dune* hc$4.00– pb$1.50–

GREG(ORY) AND TIM(OTHY) HILDEBRANDT (1939–)

Twin brothers, the Hildebrandts worked together on paperback book covers and hardcover book jackets, then went their separate ways after their reputations were established. They did a movie poster for *Star Wars*, and almost all of their work is in the fantasy field.

1979   *The Art of the Brothers Hildebrandt*

WILLIAM HOPE HODGSON (1877–1918)

A British fantasist whose fiction was colored by his early experiences at sea, Hodgson was killed in action in World War I.

1907   *The Boats of the "Glen Carrig"* pb50¢–
1908   *The House on the Borderland* pb50¢–
1909   *The Ghost Pirates* pb50¢–
1912   *The Night Land* pb(2 volumes)50¢–each
1913   *Carnacki the Ghost Finder* ss
1914   *Men of the Deep Water* ss
1916   *The Luck of the Strong* ss
1946   *The House on the Borderland and Other Novels* (Arkham House) hc$25.00–
1967   *Deep Waters* ss
1975   *Out of the Storm* ss

ROBERT E. HOWARD (1906–1936)

Robert E. Howard spent all his life living in his parents' house in Cross Plains, Texas. He wrote stories for *Weird Tales* and other magazines about adventurous, two-fisted heroes living lives of macho glory in exotic places. When he learned that his mother had lapsed into her final coma and would never recover, he committed suicide.

Howard's reputation was revived and he became more popular than ever when first Gnome Press and later Lancer Books published his Conan stories in book format, edited by L. Sprague de Camp. In the wake of this fame, virtually everything he wrote, including westerns and sea stories, were collected into book form. Today, a number of writers are continuing to churn out Conan novels to meet the demand. Conan has even made it into the movies, played by Arnold Schwarzenegger.

Famous Fantastic Mysteries, December 1952, about 7″ × 9¼″; cover by Lawrence (Stern Stevens) (1886–1960). The issue contains not only the classic "Skull-Face" (as it is listed in the magazine) but also Theodore Sturgeon's "Killdozer!" and Ray Bradbury's "The Homecoming." Cover defects include the chipping of the bottom and right edges and minor wrinkling. Copyright 1952 by Popular Publications, Inc. Reprinted by permission of Blazing Publications, The Argosy Co.

Marvel Comics has published more than 200 issues of a monthly color comic book, *Conan the Barbarian*; more than 150 issues of a monthly black-and-white comic magazine, *The Savage Sword of Conan*; and more than 50 issues of a bi-monthly color comic book, *Conan the King*.

Many of the collections of westerns, historical adventure, and pirate stories by Howard have been packaged to look like fantasy collections.

There are a number of continuations of Howard-created characters by other authors; since Howard's name frequently appears larger than the name of the actual author, it is possible to buy a book under the mistaken impression that Howard wrote it. It is also possible to buy a western or pirate story under the impression that it is a Conan story because the name "Conan" is prominently displayed on covers of non-Conan books.

1946   *Skull-Face and Others*   ss   hc (Arkham House)
1963   *The Dark Man and Others*   ss   hc (Arkham House)
1963   *The Dark Man and Others*   ss   pb (Lancer Books)
1964   *Almuric*
1968   *Wolfshead*   ss
1969   *Worms of the Earth*   50¢
1976   *Pigeons From Hell*   ss
1976   *Tigers of the Sea*   ss
1976   *The Book of Robert E. Howard*   ss   pb only$2.00
1976   *The Second Book of Robert E. Howard*   ss   pb only$2.00
1977   *Three-Bladed Doom*   50¢–
1977   *Sword Woman*   ss   pb75¢–
1978   *Black Canaan*   ss   pb$1.00
1978   *Skull-Face*   ss   pb$1.00
1979   *The Gods of Bal-Sagoth*   ss   pb only$2.00
1981   *Lord of the Dead*   ss   pb$3.75
1987   *Cthulhu: The Mythos and Kindred Horrors*   ss   pb75¢
Conan series from Gnome Press (with L. Sprague de Camp)
  1950   *Conan the Conqueror*   hc$15.00
  1952   *The Sword of Conan*   ss   hc$15.00
  1953   *The Coming of Conan*   ss   hc$15.00
  1953   *King Conan*   ss   hc$15.00
  1955   *Conan the Barbarian*   ss   hc$15.00
  1955   *Tales of Conan*   ss   hc$15.00
Conan from Ace Books
  1950   *Conan the Conqueror* (Ace Double)   pb$5.00
Conan series from Lancer Books (this is the order in which events occur, *not* chronological order)
  1968   *Conan*   ss (with L. Sprague de Camp and Lin Carter)
  1969   *Conan of Cimmeria*   ss (with L. Sprague de Camp and Lin Carter)
  1968   *Conan the Freebooter*   ss (with L. Sprague de Camp)
  1968   *Conan the Wanderer*   ss (with L. Sprague de Camp and Lin Carter)
  1966   *Conan the Adventurer*   ss (with L. Sprague de Camp)
  1966   *Conan the Buccaneer* (by L. Sprague de Camp and Lin Carter)
  1967   *Conan the Warrior*   ss (edited by L. Sprague de Camp)
  1967   *Conan the Usurper*   ss (with L. Sprague de Camp)

1967   *Conan the Conqueror* (edited by L. Sprague de Camp)

1969   *Conan the Avenger*   ss (with Bjorn Nyberg and L. Sprague de Camp)   **pb50¢**

1968   *Conan of Aquilonia* (by L. Sprague de Camp and Lin Carter)

1968   *Conan of the Isles* (by L. Sprague de Camp and Lin Carter)

Conan series from Donald M. Grant

1974   *The People of the Black Circle*   **hc$15.00**

1975   *A Witch Shall Be Born*   **hc$15.00**

1975   *Tower of the Elephant*   ss   **hc$15.00**

1975   *Red Nails*   **hc$15.00**

1976   *Rogues in the House*   ss   **hc$15.00**

1976   *The Devil in Iron*   **hc$15.00**

Conan series from Berkley (edited by Karl Edward Wagner)

1977   *The Hour of the Dragon (Conan the Conqueror)*

1977   *The People of the Black Circle*   ss

1977   *Red Nails*   ss

Kull series

1967   *King Kull*   ss (with Lin Carter)

1978   *Kull*   ss

Solomon Kane series

1968   *Red Shadows*   ss hc

1969   *The Moon of Skulls*   ss   pb

1970   *The Hand of Kane*   ss   pb

1971   *Solomon Kane*   ss   pb

L(AFAYETTE) RON(ALD) HUBBARD (1911–1986)

L. Ron Hubbard was a prolific writer of pulp fiction—westerns and other genres as well as fantasy and science fiction. In 1950, he set forth the principles of Dianetics, "a new science of mental health," in the pages of *Astounding*. He later founded Scientology, a religion, and became a millionaire. He returned to writing science fiction in his last years, producing a dekalogy (a 10-novel series) called "Mission Earth," most of which was published posthumously.

1948   *Final Blackout*

1948   *Death's Deputy*

1949   *The Kingslayer*   ss

1949   *Triton & Battle of Wizards*   ss

1951   *Typewriter in the Sky & Fear* (omnibus)

1954   *Return to Tomorrow*
1957   *Fear*
1967   *Slaves of Sleep*
1970   *Ole Doc Methuselah*   ss
1970   *Fear & The Ultimate Adventure* (omnibus)
1982   *Battlefield Earth*   hc$10.00   pb$2.00
Mission Earth series (titles preceded by *Mission Earth:*)
  1985   *The Invaders Plan*   hc$4.75   pb$2.00
  1986   *Black Genesis*   hc$4.75   pb$2.00
  1986   *The Enemy Within*   hc$4.75   pb$2.00
  1986   *An Alien Affair*   hc$4.75   pb$2.00
  1986   *Fortune of Fear*   hc$4.75   pb$2.00
  1987   *Death Quest*   hc$4.75   pb$2.00
  1987   *Voyage of Vengeance*   hc$6.75   pb$2.00
  1987   *Disaster*   hc$6.75   pb$2.00
  1987   *Villainy Victorious*   hc$6.75   pb$2.00
  1987   *The Doomed Planet*   hc$6.75   pb$2.00

ALDOUS HUXLEY (1894–1963)

The English novelist is best remembered in science fiction for his dystopian (anti-utopian) novel, *Brave New World*.

1932   *Brave New World*

SHIRLEY JACKSON (1919–1965)

Jackson, an American writer best remembered for her *New Yorker* short story "The Lottery," was an occasional contributor to *The Magazine of Fantasy and Science Fiction*. None of her work is science fiction; quite a bit of it is fantasy.

1959   *The Haunting of Hill House*   pb50¢–
1949   *The Lottery: The Adventure of the Demon Lover*   ss   hc/pb
1958   *The Sundial*   pb50¢–
1962   *We Have Always Lived in the Castle*   pb50¢–
1968   *Come Along with Me*   ss   hc/pb   pb50¢–

JOHN (WILLIAM) JAKES (1932–)

Like various others who have toiled in the science-fictional vineyards with only moderate success and found fame and (sometimes) fortune in others (Donald E. Westlake, John D. MacDonald, Evan Hunter), John Jakes wrote copious amounts of fantasy and science fiction for little money. It was as the author of the Kent Family Chronicles, a series of historical novels tracing one fictional family through America's history, that Jakes made his reputation—and a great deal of money.

1967   *When the Star Kings Die*
1969   *The Planet Wizard*
1969   *Tonight We Steal the Stars*
1969   *The Last Magicians*
1969   *The Asylum World*
1969   *The Hybrid*
1969   *Secrets of Stardeep*   **juv**
1970   *Mask of Chaos*
1970   *Master of the Dark Gate*
1970   *Monte Cristo No. 99*
1970   *Six-Gun Planet*
1970   *Black in Time*
1972   *Mention My Name in Atlantis*
1972   *Time Gate*   **juv**
1972   *Witch of the Dark Gate*
1973   *On Wheels*
1974   *Conquest of the Planet of the Apes* (movie novelization)   **pb50¢–**
1977   *The Best of John Jakes*   **ss**   **pb50¢–**
Brak the Barbarian series
  1968   *Brak the Barbarian*   **ss**   **pb50¢–**
  1969   *Brak the Barbarian Versus the Sorceress*   **pb50¢–**
  1969   *Brak the Barbarian Versus the Mark of Demons*   **pb50¢–**
  1978   *Brak: When the Idols Walked*   **pb50¢–**

WILL F. JENKINS *(see Murray Leinster)*

JEFF(REY) JONES (1944–)

Jones began his art career doing comic-book work (for the Warren horror magazines, *Creepy* and *Eerie* and for *Heavy Metal,* where he did the strip *Idyl*) and for the science-fiction and fantasy book market. In recent years, he has done little work in the fantasy field, other than some book jackets for Donald Grant. He has been concentrating on fine art painting for galleries.

Of his work within the field, typical prices are $350–$1,000. His paperback-cover paintings go for $700–$2,000.

1986   WFA (Artist)

MARVIN KAYE (1938–)

Kaye is a mystery writer as well as a writer of science fiction and has written several non-fiction books on magic. Some of his books have been written in collaboration with Parke Godwin; see Godwin for a listing of those titles. Kaye has edited several excellent anthologies of fantasy stories.

1979   *The Incredible Umbrella* ss   hc*$1.00–*
1981   *The Amorous Umbrella* ss   hc*$1.00–*
1981   *The Possession of Immanuel Wolf and Other Improbable Tales* ss   hc*$2.50*

DANIEL KEYES (1927–)

Keyes, who was an associate editor of *Marvel Science Fiction* and an occasional writer of magazine science fiction, suddenly blossomed as the author of "Flowers for Algernon," a sensitive story about a man of low intelligence whose IQ is raised to genius level. That story became the basis for the movie *Charly* and was turned into a novel. In recent years, Keyes has concentrated his energies on non-fiction.

1960   Hugo (Short Fiction): "Flowers for Algernon"
1966   Nebula (Novel): *Flowers for Algernon*

1966   *Flowers for Algernon* hc/pb
1968   *The Touch* hc/pb

STEPHEN KING (1947–)

Stephen King sold his first two stories to *Startling Mystery Stories* and had his first novel rejected by Ace Books. That novel later sold to Signet Books under the pseudonym of Richard Bachman, after King had begun hitting the bestseller list under his own name. The first four "Bachman" books were paperback originals from Signet; the fifth was a hardcover from NAL. First editions of these works are at a premium.

King is, clearly, the most successful horror-fantasy writer in the business today. His novels invariably hit the bestseller lists and almost as inevitably are made into movies. Most of his books get special limited-edition release for the collectors' market, since regular first editions of his books are published in the tens of thousands.

Scream/Press, for example, offered a 1,000-copy special edition of *Skeleton Crew* which was to have been a first edition but which was delayed until the regular edition was in release. Even though it was not a first edition, it increased in price rapidly: Advance-priced at $75, the price went to $250 on publication.

Not all of King's books are listed here; *Cujo,* for an example, is not a fantasy. King also wrote a book *about* horror stories, *Danse Macabre.*

1982   WFA (Short Story): "Do the Dead Sing?"

1974   *Carrie* hc$5.00 pb50¢–
1975   *Salem's Lot* hc$5.00 pb50¢–
1977   *Night Shift* ss hc$5.00 pb50¢
1977   *Rage* (as Richard Bachman) pb$5.00–
1978   *The Shining* hc$5.00 pb50¢–
1979   *The Long Walk* (as Richard Bachman) pb$5.00–
1979   *The Dead Zone* hc$5.00 pb$1.00
1980   *Firestarter* hc$5.00 pb$1.00
1981   *Roadwork* (as Richard Bachman) pb$5.00–
1981   *Stephen King* (omnibus) hc$2.00
1982   *Running Man* (as Richard Bachman) pb$5.00–
1982   *Creepshow* (comic-book format, with Berni Wrightson)
1982   *Different Seasons* ss hc$5.00 pb$1.00
1983   *Pet Sematary* hc$5.00 pb$1.00
1983   *Christine* hc$5.00 pb$1.00

1983 *Cycle of the Werewolf* hc$5.00   pb$1.00
1984 *Talisman* (with Peter Straub) hc$5.00   pb$1.00
1985 *Thinner* (as Richard Bachman) hc$5.00   pb$1.00
1985 *Skeleton Crew* ss hc$5.00   pb$1.00
1985 *The Bachman Books* (omnibus: *Rage, Long Walk, Roadwork, Running Man*) hc$5.00   trade pb$3.00   pb$1.00–
1985 *Silver Bullet (Cycle of Werewolf* and screenplay) **trade pb$3.00**
1985 *The Eyes of the Dragon* hc$5.00   pb$1.00
1987 *It* hc$5.00   pb$1.00
1987 *The Tommyknockers* hc$5.00   pb$1.00

Dark Tower series

  1982 *The Dark Tower: The Gunslinger* hc$15.00   trade pb$3.00
  1987 *The Dark Tower II: The Drawing of the Three* hc$8.75–$25.00

RUSSELL KIRK

  1977 WFA (Short Fiction): "There's a Long, Long Tail a-Winding"

1961 *Old House of Fear*
1962 *The Surly Sullen Bell* ss hc/pb
1966 *A Creature of the Twilight: His Memorials*
1979 *The Princess of All Lands* ss (Arkham House)
1979 *Lord of the Hollow Dark*
1984 *Watchers at the Strait Gate* ss (Arkham House)

DAMON KNIGHT (1922–)

Artist, writer, editor, critic—Knight has done it all. He even wrote a biography of Charles Fort (whose work has inspired several science-fiction books and stories) and a history of the Futurians, a fan club, many of whose members went on to write and edit science fiction.

Knight edited 21 books in of the *Orbit* series of original science-fiction stories. He also was editor of *Worlds Beyond* and an editor (briefly) of *If*.

  1956 Hugo (Book Reviewer)

1955 *Hell's Pavement* (also published as *The Analogue Men*)
1959 *The People Maker*
1959 *Masters of Evolution*
1961 *Far Out* ss
1961 *The Sun Saboteurs*
1963 *In Deep* ss
1963 *Beyond the Barrier*
1965 *Off Center* ss (Ace Double with *Mind Switch)*
1965 *Mind Switch* (Ace Double with *Off Center*)
1965 *The Rithian Terror*
1966 *Turning On* ss
1967 *Three Novels* ss
1970 *World Without Children & The Earth Quarter*
1975 *The Best of Damon Knight* ss pb50¢–
1979 *Rule Golden and Other Stories* ss pb$1.00–
1980 *The World and Thorinn* pb50¢–
1984 *The Man in the Tree* pb$1.00–
1985 *CV* pb$1.00–

DEAN R(AY) KOONTZ (1945–)

Koontz is a prolific writer, primarily of horror-fantasy, whose *Demon Seed* was made into a movie.

1968 Star Quest
1969 *Fear That Man*
1969 *The Fall of the Dream Machine*
1970 *Soft Come the Dragons* ss
1970 *The Dark Symphony*
1970 *Dark of the Woods*
1970 *Beastchild*
1970 *Hell's Gate*
1970 *Anti-Man*
1971 *The Crimson Witch*
1972 *A Darkness in My Soul*
1972 *Warlock!*
1972 *Time Thieves*
1972 *The Flesh in the Furnace*
1972 *Starblood*
1973 *Demon Seed* hc/pb

1973   *A Werewolf Among Us*
1973   *The Haunted Earth*
1974   *After the Last Race*
1975   *Nightmare Journey*
1976   *Night Chills*
1977   *The Vision*
1987   *Watchers $2.00–$4.50*

C(YRIL) M. KORNBLUTH (1923–1958)

Kornbluth was a prolific, intense writer who is remembered today primarily for his collaborative novels with Frederik Pohl.

1973   Hugo (Short Story): "The Meeting" (with Frederik Pohl)

1952   *Takeoff*
1953   *The Syndic*
1953   *The Space Merchants* (with Frederik Pohl)
1954   *Search the Sky* (with Frederik Pohl)
1954   *The Explorers* ss
1955   *Not This August* pb/hc50¢–
1955   *Gladiator-at-Law* (with Frederik Pohl)
1957   *Wolfbane* (with Frederik Pohl)
1957   *Gunner Cade* (with Judith Merril as by "Cyril Judd") (Ace Double)
1958   *A Mile Beyond the Moon* ss
1959   *The Marching Morons*
1962   *The Wonder Effect* ss (with Frederik Pohl)
1972   *Thirteen O'Clock and Other Zero Hours* ss (edited by James Blish)
1976   *The Best of C. M. Kornbluth* ss
1977   *Critical Mass* ss (with Frederik Pohl)
1980   *Before the Universe* ss (with Frederik Pohl)
1981   *Not This August* (revised by Frederik Pohl) pb$1.00
1983   *Gunner Cade* (with Judith Merril; plus *Takeoff*) pb$1.00
1986   *Venus, Inc.* (with Frederik Pohl) *(Space Merchants, Merchants' War)*
1987   *Our Best: The Best of Frederik Pohl and C. M. Kornbluth* ss pb$1.00

WILLIAM KOTZWINKLE

Kotzwinkle is a mainstream novelist whose relationship to the science-fiction and fantasy fields is primarily due to his novelization of the movie *E.T.*

1977   WFA (Novel): *Doctor Rat*

1972   *Hermes 3000*
1975   *Swimmer in the Secret Sea*   pb50¢–
1976   *Doctor Rat*   hc$2.00   pb75¢–
1982   *E.T.* (movie novelization)   pb$1.00

ROY (GERALD) KRENKEL (JR.) (1918–1983)

Krenkel drew for E. C. Comics, usually with his friends Frank Frazetta and Al Williamson. He was a constant doodler and scores of his spot illustrations appeared in the Conan fanzine, *Amra*.

Krenkel was one of the highly collectible cover artists on the Edgar Rice Burroughs paperbacks of the sixties.

The Krenkel market is in flux; he drew almost constantly, producing a massive volume of sketches, many of them on both sides of the paper. His black-and-white work brings $25–$600. His monochromatic color paintings bring $1,200–$1,500. His fully finished full-color paintings bring $2,000–$9,000.

1963   Hugo (Professional Artist)

NANCY KRESS

1985   Nebula (Short Story): "Out of All Them Bright Stars"

1981   *The Prince of Morning Bells*   pb90¢
1987   *Trinity and Other Stories* $1.00–

KATHERINE KURTZ (1944–)

Kurtz is best known for her Deryni series.

1986   *The Legacy of Lehr*   hc$4.00
Deryni series
  "Deryni"
    1970   *Deryni Rising* (15th printing in 1987)   pb50¢–

1972   *Deryni Checkmate* (16th printing in 1987) **pb**50¢–
1973   *High Deryni* (15th printing in 1987) **pb**50¢–
"The Legends of Camber of Culdi"
1976   *Camber of Culdi* (16th printing in 1987) **pb**50¢–
1978   *Saint Camber* (10th printing in 1987) **pb**50¢–
1979   *Camber the Heretic* **hc**$4.00 **pb**50¢
"The Histories of King Kelson"
1984   *The Bishop's Heir* **pb**75¢–
1985   *The King's Justice* **pb**75¢–
1986   *The Quest for Saint Camber* **hc/pb**75¢–$4.25

HENRY KUTTNER (1914–1958)

Henry Kuttner was an extremely prolific writer of fantasy and science fiction—all kinds of both. He was equally at home in *Weird Tales*, *Startling Stories*, and (usually in collaboration with his wife, C. L. Moore) in *Astounding* and *F&SF*. Everything he wrote after his marriage to Moore in 1940 should be considered a collaborative story, whether it is bylined as such or not.

1950   *Fury* (also as *Destination: Infinity*)
1950   *A Gnome There Was* ss (as by Lewis Padgett)
1951   *Tomorrow and Tomorrow & The Fairy Chessmen* (as by Lewis Padgett)
1952   *Robots Have No Tails* ss (as by Lewis Padgett)
1953   *Mutant* (as by Lewis Padgett)
1953   *Ahead of Time* ss
1953   *Well of the Worlds* (as by Lewis Padgett)
1954   *Line to Tomorrow* ss (as by Lewis Padgett)
1954   *Beyond Earth's Gates* (as by Lewis Padgett and C. L. Moore)
1955   *No Boundaries* ss (with C. L. Moore)
1961   *Bypass to Otherness* ss (with C. L. Moore)
1964   *Valley of the Flame*
1964   *Earth's Last Citadel* (with C. L. Moore)
1965   *The Dark World*
1965   *The Time Axis*
1968   *The Creature From Beyond Infinity*
1971   *The Mask of Circe*
1975   *The Best of Henry Kuttner* ss

1987   *Prince Raynor* booklet with two stories   *$2.00*
1987   *The Startling Worlds of Henry Kuttner*   ss   pb*$1.00–*

DAVID A. KYLE (1919–)

David Kyle has been an artist, a publisher, and a writer. He was co-owner of Gnome Press in the fifties, wrote two illustrated non-fiction books about science fiction *(A Pictorial History of Science Fiction* and *Science Fiction Inventions and Ideas),* and has continued the "Lensman" series begun by E. E. Smith.

1980   *The Dragon Lensman* (119,000 copies in print by 1981) pb*50¢–*
1981   *Lensman from Rigel*   pb*50¢–*
1983   *Z-Lensman*   pb*50¢–*

R(APHAEL) A(LOYSIUS) LAFFERTY (1914–)

Lafferty is a retired electrical engineer noted for his bizarre characters and his stories, a mixture of erudition and whimsy.

1973   Hugo (Short Story): "Eurema's Dam"

1968   *Past Master*   pb*50¢–*
1968   *Space Chantey* (Ace Double)
1968   *Reefs of Earth*   pb*50¢–*
1969   *Fourth Mansions*   pb*50¢–*
1970   *Nine Hundred Grandmothers*   ss   pb*50¢–*
1971   *The Devil Is Dead*   pb*50¢–*
1971   *Arrive at Easterwine*
1971   *The Fall of Rome*
1971   *The Flame Is Green*
1976   *Not to Mention Camels*
1977   *Archipelago*
1977   *Apocalypses*   ss   pb*50¢–*
1982   *Strange Doings*   ss
1983   *Annals of Klepsis*   pb*75¢–*
1984   *Ringing Changes*   ss   pb*$1.00*
In a Green Tree series
   1987   *My Heart Leaps Up, Chapters 3 & 4*   *75¢–$1.50*

STERLING E. LANIER (1927–)

Lanier is best known for his "Brigadier Ffellowes" stories, a tall-tales-told-in-a-bar series, and the "Hiero" (pronounced "hero") series, set in a post-holocaust world.

1969 *The War for the Lot* juv
1983 *Menace Under Marswood*
Brigadier Ffellowes series
   1972 *The Peculiar Exploits of Brigadier Ffellowes* ss hc$7.50
   1986 *The Curious Quests of Brigadier Ffellowes* ss hc$7.50
Hiero series
   1973 *Hiero's Journey* hc$4.00 pb50¢
   1983 *The Unforsaken Hiero* hc$4.00 pb50¢–

(JOHN) KEITH LAUMER (1925–)

Laumer served in the Army during World War II, studied architecture at the University of Illinois, then served in the Air Force in the fifties and the U.S. foreign service in the sixties. He has used his foreign service experience as background for his most popular series, about an unconventional, damn-the-red-tape-full-speed-ahead interstellar diplomat named Retief. (Spell the name backward and you get "feiter," a phonetic spelling of "fighter.") Retief has starred in many of Laumer's short stories, novelettes, and novels and was, briefly, the star of a black-and-white comic book from Mad Dog Graphics: *Keith Laumer's Retief* (#1–6) and *Retief of the C.D.T.* (#1).

1963 *A Trace of Memory*
1964 *The Great Time Machine Hoax*
1965 *A Plague of Demons* pb50¢–
1966 *The Monitors*
1966 *Catastrophe Planet* (later as *The Breaking Earth*) pb50¢–
1966 *Earthblood* (with Rosel George Brown) pb50¢–
1967 *Nine by Laumer* ss pb50¢–
1967 *Galactic Odyssey*
1967 *The Invaders* (TV adaptation)
1967 *Enemies From Beyond* ss (TV adaptation)
1967 *Planet Run* (with Gordon R. Dickson)
1968 *The Day Before Forever & Thunderhead* ss
1968 *Greylorn* ss pb50¢–

1968   *It's a Mad, Mad, Mad Galaxy*   ss
1968   *The Afrit Affair* (Avengers TV novelization)
1968   *The Drowned Queen* (Avengers TV novelization)
1968   *The Gold Bomb* (Avengers TV novelization)
1969   *The Long Twilight*
1970   *The House in November* (1972 edition adds *The Other Sky*)   pb75¢–
1970   *Time Trap* 75¢–
1971   *Dinosaur Beach*   pb50¢–
1971   *The Star Treasure* (1986 same title has more stories)   pb75¢–
1971   *Once There Was a Giant*   ss
1972   *The Infinite Cage*
1972   *Timetracks*   ss
1972   *The Big Show*   ss
1973   *The Glory Game*
1973   *Night of Delusions*
1974   *The Undefeated*   ss
1976   *Bolo: The Annals of the Dinochrome Brigade*   ss
1977   *The Best of Keith Laumer*   ss
1982   *Star Colony*   hc$4.00   pb$1.00
Imperium series
  1962   *Worlds of the Imperium*
  1965   *The Other Side of Time*
  1968   *Assignment in Nowhere*
  1981   *Beyond the Imperium* (omnibus: *Other Side, Nowhere*)   75¢–
Lafayette O'Leary series
  1966   *The Time Bender*
  1970   *The World Shuffler*
  1972   *The Shape Changer*   pb50¢–
Retief series
  1963   *Envoy to New Worlds*   ss 50¢–
  1965   *Galactic Diplomat*   ss
  1966   *Retief's War*
  1968   *Retief and the Warlords*
  1969   *Retief: Ambassador to Space*   ss
  1971   *Retief of the CDT*   ss 50¢–
  1971   *Retief's Ransom*
  1975   *Retief: Emissary to the Stars*

1979   *Retief Unbound*   75¢–
1986   *Retief in the Ruins*   ss   pb75¢–
1987   *Retief: Envoy to New Worlds*   75¢–

TANITH LEE (1947–)

Tanith Lee is a British writer of fantasy (and occasionally science fiction) for adults and for children.

1984   WFA (Short Fiction): "Elle Est Trois (La Mort)"

1971   *The Dragon Hoard*   juv
1972   *Princess Hynchatti and Some Other Surprises*   ss   juv
1972   *Animal Castle*   juv
1975   *Companions on the Road*   juv
1976   *The Winter Players*   juv
1976   *Don't Bite the Sun*
1977   *Drinking Sapphire Wine*
1977   *Volkhavaar*
1977   *The Storm Lord*
1977   *East of Midnight*   juv
1977   *Companions on the Road*   ss (contains *Companions & Winter Players*)
1980   *Day by Night*   50¢–.
1981   *The Silver Metal Lover*   75¢–
1981   *Unsilent Night*   hc$2.50
1985   *The Gorgon and Other Beastly Tales*   ss   pb75¢
1986   *Dreams of Dark and Light*   ss (Arkham House)   hc$4.00
Birthgrave series
   1975   *The Birthgrave*   pb75¢–
   1978   *Vazkor, Son of Vazkor*   pb75¢–
   1978   *Quest for the White Witch*   pb75¢–
Demon Lords series
   1978   *Night's Master*   pb50¢–
   1979   *Death's Master*   pb50¢–
   1981   *Delusion's Master*   pb50¢–

URSULA K(ROEBER) Le GUIN (1929–)

The daughter of noted anthropologists, Le Guin rapidly rose to prominence in the science-fiction field, starting with stories sold to Cele Goldsmith when Goldsmith was editor of *Amazing* and *Fantastic*.

1969 Nebula (Novel): *The Left Hand of Darkness*

1970 Hugo (Novel): *The Left Hand of Darkness*

1973 Hugo (Novella): "The Word for World Is Forest"

1974 Hugo (Short Story): "The Ones Who Walk Away From Omelas"

1974 Nebula (Novel): *The Dispossessed*

1974 Nebula (Short Story): "The Day before the Revolution"

1975 Hugo (Novel): *The Dispossessed*

1988 Hugo (Novelette): "Buffalo Gals, Won't You Come Out Tonight"

1966 *Rocannon's World* (Ace Double)
1966 *Planet of Exile*
1967 *City of Illusions* pb50¢–
1969 *The Left Hand of Darkness* pb50¢–
1971 *The Lathe of Heaven*
1974 *The Dispossessed*
1975 *The Wind's Twelve Quarters*
1975 *Dreams Must Explain Themselves* ss
1976 *Orsinian Tales* ss pb75¢–
1976 *The Word for World Is Forest* pb50¢–
1980 *The Beginning Piece* 75¢–
1987 *Buffalo Gals and Other Animal Presences* hc$5.00
Earthsea series
  1968 *A Wizard of Earthsea* pb50¢–
  1971 *The Tombs of Atuan* pb50¢–
  1972 *The Farthest Shore*
  1977 *Earthsea* (omnibus)

FRITZ (REUTER) LEIBER (JR.) (1910–)

Leiber, the son of a Shakespearean actor who appeared in many movies (Leiber the younger had a small role in Greta Garbo's *Camille*), is the dean of American fantasy writers. He is equally adept at heroic fantasy set in some dim and timeless past (as with the Fafhrd and Grey Mouser stories) or in modern times (as with the classic *Conjure Wife*). He has written a great deal of powerful, award-winning science fiction as well (he has been chosen a Grand Master by the Science Fiction Writers of America) but has made his mark as a fantasist (where he won the World Fantasy Association Life Achievement Award).

Leiber is the only person other than Edgar Rice Burroughs to write an *authorized* Tarzan novel.

Fantastic Adventures, July 1950, about 7″ × 9¾″; cover by Robert Gibson Jones. Defects include the cover being torn from the spine at top and bottom left, a frayed right edge, and a pencilled name. Copyright 1950 by Ziff-Davis Publishing Company. ''Fantastic'' is a trademark owned by TSR, Inc. Copyright 1989 TSR, Inc. All rights reserved.

1958   Hugo (Novel/Novelette): *The Big Time*
1962   Hugo (Special Committee Award)
1965   Hugo (Novel): *The Wanderer*
1967   Nebula (Novellette): "Gonna Roll the Bones"
1968   Hugo (Novelette): "Gonna Roll the Bones"
1970   Hugo (Novella): "Ship of Shadows"
1970   Nebula (Novella): "Ill Met in Lankhmar"
1971   Hugo (Novella): "Ill Met in Lankhmar"
1975   Nebula (Short Story): "Catch That Zeppelin!"
1976   Hugo (Short Story): "Catch That Zeppelin!"
1976   WFA (Short Fiction): "Belsen Express"
1978   WFA (Novel): *Our Lady of Darkness*
1976   WFA Life Achievement Award
1980   SFWA Grand Master

1947   *Night's Black Agents* ss (Arkham House)
1950   *Gather, Darkness!*
1953   *Conjure Wife* 50¢–
1953   *The Green Millennium*
1953   *The Sinful Ones*
1957   *Destiny Times Three*
1961   *The Big Time* (Ace Double with *Mind Spider*)
1961   *The Mind Spider and Other Stories* ss (Ace Double with *Big Time*)
1961   *The Silver Eggheads* pb50¢–
1962   *Shadows with Eyes* ss   pb50¢–
1964   *The Wanderer* pb50¢–
1964   *Ships to the Stars* ss (Ace Double)
1964   *A Pail of Air* ss
1966   *The Night of the Wolf* ss
1968   *The Secret Songs* ss
1969   *Night Monsters* ss (Ace Double with *Green Millennium*)
1969   *A Specter Is Haunting Texas*
1972   *You're All Alone* ss
1974   *The Best of Fritz Leiber* ss   pb50¢–
1974   *The Best of Fritz Leiber* ss   pb50¢–
1975   *The Second Book of Fritz Leiber* ss   pb50¢

1976   *The Worlds of Fritz Leiber*   **pb50¢–**
1977   *Our Lady of Darkness*
1978   *Destiny Times Three* (in *Binary Star #1*)   **pb$1.00**
1983   *Changewar* ss   **pb$1.00**
1984   *The Ghost Light* ss   **trade pb$2.00**
Fafhrd and Grey Mouser series
  1957   *Two Sought Adventure* ss   **pb50¢–**
  1968   *Swords Against Wizardry* ss   **pb50¢–**
  1968   *Swords in the Mist* ss   **pb50¢–**
  1968   *Swords of Lankhmar*   **pb50¢–**
  1970   *Swords and Deviltry* ss   **pb50¢–**
  1970   *Swords Against Death* ss   **pb50¢–**
  1977   *Swords and Ice Magic* ss   **pb50¢–**
Tarzan series
  1966   *Tarzan and the Valley of Gold* (movie novelization)

MURRAY LEINSTER *(psd. of William Fitzgerald Jenkins)* (1896–1975)

Throughout most of the last two decades of his life, "Leinster" was known as "The Dean of Science Fiction." His first science-fiction story appeared in 1919 in *Argosy* ("The Runaway Skyscraper"), and he was still producing books 50 years later. Under his own name, Will F. Jenkins, he was a prolific writer for the slick magazines such as *The Saturday Evening Post*; he wrote a few science-fiction stories under his own name and as "Will Fitzgerald," but the vast bulk of his science fiction was published under the "Leinster" byline.

  1958 Hugo (Novelette): "Exploration Team" (aka "Combat Team")

1931   *Murder Madness*
1946   *The Murder of the U.S.A.* (as by Will F. Jenkins)
1949   *Fight for Life*
1949   *The Last Space Ship*
1950   *Sidewise in Time* ss
1954   *The Black Galaxy*
1954   *The Brain-Stealers*
1954   *The Forgotten Planet*   **pb50¢–**
1954   *Gateway to Elsewhere*

1954 *Operation Outer Space*
1955 *The Other Side of Here*
1956 *Colonial Survey* also as *The Planet Explorer*)
1958 *War with the Gizmos*   pb50¢–
1959 *Monsters and Such*   ss
1959 *Four From Planet 5*
1959 *The Monster From Earth's End*
1959 *The Pirates of Zan*
1960 *The Aliens*   ss
1960 *Men into Space* (TV series novelization)
1960 *Twists in Time*   ss
1961 *Creatures of the Abyss*
1961 *The Wailing Asteroid*
1962 *Operation Terror*   pb50¢–
1962 *Talents, Incorporated*
1964 *Time Tunnel* (not related to TV series)
1964 *The Duplicators*
1964 *The Greks Bring Gifts*
1964 *Invaders of Space*
1964 *The Other Side of Nowhere*
1966 *Get Off My World!*   ss
1966 *Tunnel Through Time* (not related to TV series)
1966 *Space Captain*
1967 *Time Tunnel* (TV series novelization)
1967 *Checkpoint Lambda*
1967 *Miners in the Sky*
1967 *Space Gypsies*
1967 *Timeslip! (Time Tunnel* TV series novelization)
1968 *Land of the Giants* (TV series novelization)
1969 *Land of the Giants #2: The Hot Spot* (TV series novelization)
1969 *Land of the Giants #3: Unknown Danger* (TV novelization)
1976 *The Best of Murray Leinster*   ss   pb50¢–
Joe Kenmore series   **juv**
  1953 *Space Platform*
  1953 *Space Tug*
  1957 *City on the Moon*
Med Service series
  1959 *The Mutant Weapon*
  1961 *This World Is Taboo*   pb50¢–

1964   *Doctor to the Stars*   ss
1967   *S.O.S. From Three Worlds*   ss   pb50¢–

C(LIVE) S(TAPLES) LEWIS (1898–1963)

Lewis, an associate of J. R. R. Tolkien, wrote both fiction and non-fiction reflective of his strong Christian beliefs. His science-fiction novels, the ''Perelandra'' series, have fallen out of fashion, but his obtensibly juvenile fantasy series about ''Narnia'' remains popular.

1943   *The Screwtape Letters*
1945   *The Great Divorce*
1956   *Till We Have Faces*
1966   *Of Other Worlds*   ss
Narnia series   **juv**
  1950   *The Lion, the Witch, and the Wardrobe*
  1951   *Prince Caspian*
  1952   *The Voyage of the ''Dawn Treader''*
  1953   *The Silver Chair*
  1954   *The Horse and His Boy*
  1955   *The Magician's Nephew*
  1956· *The Last Battle*
Perelandra series
  1938   *Out of the Silent Planet*
  1943   *Perelandra* (also as *Voyage to Venus: Perelandra*)
  1945   *That Hideous Strength* (also as *The Tortured Planet*)

JACK LONDON (1876–1916)

The American writer best known for his stories of the Yukon also produced a respectable body of fantasy.

1906   *Before Adam*
1907   *The Iron Heel*
1915   *The Star Rover*
1915   *The Scarlet Plague*
1975   *The Curious Fragments: Jack London's Tales of Fantasy Fiction*   ss
1975   *The Science Fiction of Jack London*   ss

Famous Fantastic Mysteries, February 1949, about 7″ × 9¼″; cover by Lawrence (Stern Stevens) (1886–1960). Listed as copyright 1948 by All-Fiction Field, Inc. Copyright 1948 by Popular Publications. Reprinted by permission of Blazing Publications, The Argosy Co.

FRANK BELKNAP LONG (1903–)

Long was a friend of H. P. Lovecraft and, like Lovecraft, is best remembered for his stories in *Weird Tales,* although he has written both science fiction and fantasy for many other markets.

1978   WFA Life Achievement Award

1946   *The Hounds of Tindalos*   ss (Arkham House)
1949   *John Carstairs, Space Detective*   ss
1957   *Space Station No. 1*
1960   *Woman From Another Planet*
1961   *The Mating Center*
1962   *Mars Is My Destination*
1963   *The Hounds of Tindalos*   ss   pb (abridged)   pb50¢–
1963   *The Dark Beasts*   ss   pb (from *Hounds of Tindalos*)   pb50¢–
1963   *It Was the Day of the Robot*   pb50¢–

1963   *Three Steps Spaceward*
1963   *Odd Science Fiction* ss pb50¢–
1964   *The Martian Visitors*
1964   *Mission to a Star*
1966   *The Androids*
1966   *This Strange Tomorrow*
1966   *So Dark a Heritage*
1967   *Journey into Darkness*
1968   *. . . And Others Shall Be Born*
1969   *The Three Faces of Time*
1970   *Monster From Out of Time*
1971   *Survival World* pb50¢–
1972   *The Night of the Wolf*
1972   *The Rim of the Unknown* (Arkham House)
1976   *The Early Long*

BARRY B. LONGYEAR

Longyear's double-award-winning "Enemy Mine" was made into the movie of the same name.

1979   Nebula (Novella): "Enemy Mine"

1980   Hugo (Novella): "Enemy Mine"

1980   *Manifest Destiny* ss pb75¢–
1980   *Circus World* pb50¢–
1980   *City of Baraboo* pb50¢–
1987   *Sea of Glass* hc$4.75

H(OWARD) P(HILLIPS) LOVECRAFT (1890–1937)

Generally regarded as the most influential American fantasy writer since Edgar Allan Poe, Lovecraft appeared headed for obscurity when he died. His work, that which had been published at all, had appeared in pulp magazines like *Weird Tales*. August Derleth, a disciple of Lovecraft, determined to ensure his mentor's literary reputation and, with Donald Wandrei, founded Arkham House to publish his works. Derleth also collaborated posthumously with Lovecraft, finishing stories which had existed only as fragments or notes. The purpose of Arkham House was expanded to publish books by other fantasists

The Horror in the Museum and Other Revisions by H. P. Lovecraft (and others), about 4¼″ × 7″; cover by Murray Tinkelman (1933–). A Ballantine SF Horror edition, it is copyright 1970 by August Derleth.

(among others, it published the first books of Fritz Leiber, Ray Bradbury, and Robert Bloch), but it succeeded in its initial goal, keeping Lovecraft's literary reputation alive.

When Lovecraft began appearing in paperback in force in the sixties, his work found an eager audience; Lovecraft, three decades after his death, was more popular than ever.

In recent years, S. T. Joshi has gone over manuscripts and variant editions of Lovecraft and produced new editions of his books for Arkham House which are now regarded as the definitive texts of his stories. For the person who wants all of the stories actually written by Lovecraft—not stories written by others from his notes or stories by others which he revised—these three volumes *(The Dunwich Horror and Others, At the Mountains of Madness and Other Novels,* and *Dagon and Other Tales),* as revised by Joshi and published by Arkham House in the mid–eighties, are the books of choice.

To complete your basic Lovecraft collection, all the Derleth-Lovecraft stories are in *The Watchers Out of Time and Others* and all of Lovecraft's revisions (sometimes complete rewritings, occasionally ghost-writings) are in *The Horror in the Museum and Other Revisions.* The earlier editions are for dedicated collectors with large budgets.

For more on Lovecraft, see L. Sprague de Camp's *Lovecraft: A Biography* and Lin Carter's *Lovecraft: A Look Behind the Cthulhu Mythos.*

1939   *The Outsider and Others*   ss (Arkham House)
1943   *Beyond the Wall of Sleep*   ss (Arkham House)
1944   *Marginalia*   ss
1944   *The Weird Shadow Over Innsmouth*   ss (Bartholomew House   pb)
1945   *The Lurker at the Threshold* (with August Derleth)
1951   *The Case of Charles Dexter Ward*   pb50¢–
1951   *The Dream-Quest of Unknown Kadath*
1957   *The Survivor and Others*   ss (with August Derleth)
1959   *The Shuttered Room and Other Pieces*   ss (with August Derleth)
1963   *The Dunwich Horror and Others*   ss (Arkham House)
1963   *The Dunwich Horror and Others*   ss   pb (abridged)
1964   *At the Mountains of Madness and Other Novels*   ss (Arkham House)
1964   *At the Mountains of Madness and Other Novels*   ss   pb (abridged)
1965   *Dagon and Other Macabre Tales*
1970   *The Horror in the Museum and Other Revisions*   ss
1971   *The Dream Quest of Unknown Sadath*   ss   pb$1.00
1971   *The Doom That Came to Sarnath*   ss   pb$1.00
1971   *The Lurking Fear and Other Stories*   ss   pb50¢–
1974   *The Watchers Out of Time and Others* (with August Derleth)
1985   *The Dunwich Horror and Others*   ss (revised by S. T. Joshi; Arkham House)   hc$4.75
1986   *At the Mountains of Madness and Other Novels*   ss (revised by S. T. Joshi; Arkham House)   hc$4.75
1987   *Dagon and Other Tales* (revised by S. T. Joshi)   hc$4.75

RICHARD A(LLEN) LUPOFF (1935–)

Dick Lupoff and his wife, Pat, won a Hugo for best fanzine (*Xero*, 1963); co-edited (with Don Thompson) two nostalgia-oriented books on comic books, *All in Color for a Dime* (1970) and *The Comic-Book Book* (1973); edited the complete works of Edgar Rice Burroughs for Canaveral Press, giving first publication to some novels; wrote two books about Burroughs and his work, *Edgar Rice Burroughs: Master of Adventure* (1965) and *Barsoom: Edgar Rice Burroughs and the Martian Vision* (1976).

1967   *One Million Centuries*
1971   *Sacred Locomotive Flies*
1974   *Into the Aether*
1976   *The Triune Man*
1976   *The Crack in the Sky*
1976   *Sandworld*
1976   *Lisa Kane*
1976   *Sword of the Demon*
1978   *Space War Blues* ss pb50¢–
1979   *Lisa Kane* hc$2.00–
1979   *The Ova Hamlet Papers* ss trade pb$3.00
1984   *Sun's End*
1984   *Circumpolar!*
1985   *Lovecraft's Book* (Arkham House) hc$4.00
1985   *Countersolar!* hc$4.00
1985   *The Digital Wristwatch of Philip K. Dick* limited hc$6.00 limited pb$2.50

ELIZABETH A. LYNN

1980 WFA (Novel): *Watchtower*

1980 WFA (Short Fiction): "The Woman Who Loved the Moon"

1981   *The Woman Who Loved the Moon and Other Stories* ss pb50¢–
1978   *A Different Light*
1981   *The Sardonyx Net* hc$4.00–
Tornor series
  1979   *Watchtower* 50¢–
  1979   *The Dancers of Arun* 50¢–
  1980   *The Northern Girl*
  1980   *The Chronicles of Tornor* (omnibus) book club hc$2.00–

R. A. MacAVOY

1983   *Tea with the Black Dragon*   50¢–$7.00
1986   *Twisting the Rope* (sequel to *Tea*)   90¢
Damiano series
  1983   *Damiano*
  1984   *Damiano's Lute*
  1984   *Raphael*
  1985   *The Book Of Kells*   pb only$1.00

ANNE (INEZ) McCAFFREY (1926–)

Anne McCaffrey had a short-short story in *Science Fiction Plus* in 1953, but her real career as a writer did not begin for another decade. She is best known for her stories about the dragons and dragon-riders of Pern.

One of her least-known books, but a delight for science-fiction collectors, is *Cooking Out of This World* (1973), a cookbook of favorite recipes by science-fiction writers. It was published only in paperback—if you find it, don't try Larry Niven's recipe: It is potentially lethal.

She also has written suspense novels.

    1968   Hugo (Novella): "Weyr Search"

    1968   Nebula (Novella): "Dragonrider"

1967   *Restoree*
1969   *The Ship Who Sang*   ss
1969   *Decision at Doona*
1973   *To Ride Pegasus*
1975   *A Time When*
1977   *Get Off the Unicorn*   ss
1978   *Dinosaur Planet*
1985   *Killashandra*
Pern series
  1968   *Dragonflight*
  1971   *Dragonquest*
  1976   *Dragonsong*   juv50¢–
  1977   *Dragonsinger*   juv50¢–
  1978   *White Dragon*   hc/pb

1979   *The Dragonriders of Pern* (book-club omnibus: *Dragon-flight, Dragonquest, White Dragon*)   *$2.00*
1979   *Dragondrums*   **juv**
1986   *Nerilka's Story*   **pb/hc***$1.25*

SHAWNA McCARTHY

Shawna McCarthy was the editor of *Isaac Asimov's Science Fiction Magazine* when she won the Hugo. She has since switched to editing science-fiction books.

1984   Hugo (Professional Editor)

JOHN D(ANN) MacDONALD (1916–1986)

Although he is best known for his suspense novels, primarily the "Travis McGee" series, MacDonald wrote for the science-fiction magazines and wrote science-fiction and fantasy novels.

1951   *Wine of the Dreamers* (pb as *Planet of the Dreamers*)
1952   *Ballroom of the Skies*
1962   *The Girl, the Gold Watch & Everything*   **pb only***$1.00*
1978   *Other Times, Other Worlds*   **ss**   **pb only***$1.00*
1980   *Time and Tomorrow* (omnibus: *Wine, Girl, Ballroom*) book club   **hc***$2.00*

VONDA N. McINTYRE

For further listings of books by McIntyre, see the *Star Trek* listing under "Science-Fiction and Fantasy Drama."

1973   Nebula (Novelette): "Of Mist, and Grass, and Sand"
1978   Nebula (Novel): *Dreamsnake*
1979   Hugo (Novel): *Dreamsnake*

1978   *Dreamsnake*
1979   *Fireflood and Other Stories*   **ss**   **hc***$3.00*   **pb***$1.00*
1986   *Barbary*   **juv**   **hc***$3.25*

Super Science Stories, January 1951, about 7″ × 9½″; cover by Lawrence (Stern Stevens) (1886–1960). Listed as copyright 1950 by Fictioneers, Inc. Copyright 1950 by Popular Publications. Reprinted by permission of Blazing Publications, The Argosy Co.

Super Science Stories, July 1950, about 7″ × 9¼″; cover by Lawrence (Stern Stevens) (1886–1960). Listed as copyright 1950 by Fictioneers, Inc. Copyright 1950 by Popular Publications. Reprinted by permission of Blazing Publications, The Argosy Co.

RICHARD M(ILTON) McKENNA (1913–1964)

In his brief writing career (he began in 1958), McKenna produced a small body of science-fiction short stories and a major mainstream novel, *The Sand Pebbles* (which was made into a movie starring Steve McQueen).

1966   Nebula (Short Story): "The Secret Place"

1973   *Casey Agonistes and Other Fantasy and Science Fiction Stories* ss

PATRICIA McKILLIP

1975   WFA (Novel): *The Forgotten Beasts of Eld*

1974   *The Forgotten Beasts of Eld*
1984   *The Throne of the Erril of Sherril*   juv   *$1.00*
1985   *The Moon and the Face*   juv   pb/hc75¢–
1987   *Fool's Run*   hc$4.00
Riddle-Master series
  1977   *The Riddle-Master of Hed*
  1978   *Heir of Sea and Fire*
  1979   *Harpist in the Wind*   pb
  1980   *Riddle of Stars* (omnibus) book club   hc$2.00

KATHERINE (ANNE) MacLEAN (1925–)

Most of her science-fiction output has been in shorter fiction, some-times written as with or by Charles DeVet (her one-time husband). Never a prolific writer (at least by the science-fiction field's standards, where at least a book a year seems to be the norm and authors with more than 100 books to their credit are fairly common), she has not written at all in the field in recent years.

1971   Nebula (Novella): "The Missing Man"

1962   *The Diploids*   ss   pb/hc
1962   *Cosmic Checkmate* (with Charles DeVet) (rev as *Second Game*)   50¢–
1975   *Missing Man*
1980   *The Trouble with You Earth People*   ss   trade pb$2.00

DON MAITZ (1953–)

Maitz is primarily known for his work as a paperback book cover artist, notably on Gene Wolfe's "Book of the New Sun" series and Richard Cowper's *The Road to Corlay*.

His preliminary roughs go for $100–$200; his paintings go for $1,500–$4,000.

    1980 WFA (Artist)

GEORGE R. R. MARTIN (1948–)

In addition to his writing, Martin is the editor of the *New Voices* anthologies featuring new work by newer writers and for his "Wild Cards" shared-universe anthologies which detail the history of the world if it had had real super-heroes since 1945.

    1975 Hugo (Novella): "A Song for Lya"

    1979 Nebula (Novelette): "Sandkings"

    1980 Hugo (Novelette): "Sandkings"

    1980 Hugo (Short Story): "The Way of Cross and Dragon"

    1985 Nebula (Novelette): "Portraits of His Children"

1976 *A Song for Lya* ss
1977 *Dying of the Light*
1977 *Songs of Stars and Shadows* ss
1981 *Windhaven* (with Lisa Tuttle)
1981 *Sandkings* ss
1981 *Nightflyers* (in *Binary Star #5*) pb*$1.00*
1982 *Fevre Dream*
1985 *Nightflyers* *95¢–*
1986 *Tuf Voyaging* *90¢*
1987 *Portraits of His Children* ss *$6.00–$13.00*

RICHARD (BURTON) MATHESON (1926–)

It is unusual for a writer's reputation to be made with his first story, it is unusual for his reputation to be made with a short story, and it is even less common to make a reputation with a short-short story. Richard Matheson's brief but unforgettable first story, "Born of Man and Woman," appeared in *The Magazine of Fantasy and Science Fiction*

(Summer 1950 issue) and made Matheson an important figure in the field at once. He later turned to novels and then to writing for television (notably for *The Twilight Zone*) and for movies (beginning with *The Incredible Shrinking Man*, based on his novel, *The Shrinking Man*). His son, Richard Christian Matheson, is now making his own reputation as a fantasist.

1976 WFA (Novel): *Bid Time Return*

1984 WFA Life Achievement Award

1954 *Born of Man and Woman* ss (abridged pb: *Third From the Sun*)
1954 *I Am Legend*
1956 *The Shrinking Man*
1957 *The Shores of Space* ss
1958 *A Stir of Echoes*
1961 *Shock!* ss
1964 *Shock II* ss
1966 *Shock III* ss
1970 *Shock Waves* ss
1971 *Hell House*
1975 *Bid Time Return*
1978 *What Dreams May Come*

JUDITH MERRIL (1923–)

Although she made a big splash with her first science-fiction story, "That Only a Mother" (*Astounding*, June 1948), and produced some generally well-reviewed novels, it is as an anthologist that Merril is primarily noted. She edited several anthologies, beginning in 1950 with *Shot in the Dark* (blurbed as "A different kind of mystery thrill," it was actually science fiction and fantasy), and went on to edit a best-of-the-year series from 1956 to 1969. She now resides in Toronto and has not published any science fiction or fantasy for several years.

1950 *Shadow on the Hearth*
1957 *Gunner Cade* (with C. M. Kornbluth as by "Cyril Judd"; Ace Double)
1960 *The Tomorrow People*
1960 *Out of Bounds* ss

1960 *Survival Ship and Other Stories* ss
1968 *Daughters of Earth* ss
1976 *The Best of Judith Merril*

A(BRAHAM) MERRITT (1884–1943)

This American fantasy writer was extremely popular during the thirties and forties and retained enough fame seven years after his death that a magazine was named for him (*A. Merritt's Fantasy Magazine*). In recent years, his reputation has faded somewhat, largely because the enormous amounts of newer books are crowding out the old.

Merritt's *Burn, Witch, Burn!* was filmed as *The Devil Doll*. Just to confuse matters a bit, Fritz Leiber's classic *Conjure Wife* was filmed as *Burn, Witch, Burn!*

Sam Moskowitz has written a book-length study of the man and his work, *A. Merritt*.

1919 *The Moon Pool*
1926 *The Ship of Ishtar* (abridged)
1928 *Seven Footprints to Satan*
1932 *Dwellers in the Mirage*
1933 *Burn, Witch, Burn!*
1934 *Creep, Shadow!* (also as *Creep, Shadow, Creep!*)
1946 *The Metal Monster*
1946 *The Fox Woman and the Blue Pagoda* ss (with Hannes Bok)
1947 *The Black Wheel* (completed by Hannes Bok)
1949 *The Ship of Ishtar* (unabridged)
1949 *The Fox Woman* ss
1931 *The Face in the Abyss*

WALTER M(ICHAEL) MILLER, JR. (1922–)

After years of writing for the science-fiction magazines, Miller produced a book which is regarded as a classic in the field, *A Canticle for Leibowitz*. Not long after that, he apparently quit writing altogether.

1955 Hugo (Novelette): "The Darfsteller"
1961 Hugo (Novel): *A Canticle for Leibowitz*

Famous Fantastic Mysteries, August 1942, about 6½″ × 9¼″; cover by Virgil Finlay (1914–1971). Defects include staining and pencilled number. Copyright 1942 by The Frank A. Munsey Company. Reprinted by permission of Blazing Publications, The Argosy Co.

Famous Fantastic Mysteries, June 1942, about 6½″ × 9¼″; cover by Virgil Finlay (1914–1971). Copyright 1942 by The Frank A. Munsey Company. Reprinted by permission of Blazing Publications, The Argosy Co.

Famous Fantastic Mysteries, October 1940, about 7″ × 9½″; cover by Virgil Finlay (1914–1971). Copyright 1940 by The Frank A. Munsey Company. Reprinted by permission of Blazing Publications, The Argosy Co.

1960 *A Canticle for Leibowitz*
1962 *Conditionally Human* ss
1964 *View From the Stars* ss
1980 *The Best of Walter M. Miller, Jr.* ss pb$1.00

MICHAEL MOORCOCK (1939–)

Moorcock is a British writer about equally known for his sword-and-sorcery novels about Elric and Hawkmoon (which have been adapted into comic books and graphic novels) and for his experimental, ''new wave'' science-fiction writing and editing (he edited the final issues of *New Worlds*).

1967 Nebula (Novella): ''Behold the Man''

1979 WFA (Novel): *Gloriana*

1965 *The Sundered Worlds*
1965 *The Winds of Limbo*

1966 *The Shores of Death*
1966 *The Deep Fix* ss (as by James Colvin)
1966 *Somewhere in the Night* (as by Bill Barclay)
1966 *Printer's Devil* (as by Bill Barclay)
1967 *The Wrecks of Time*
1969 *The Ice Schooner* 50¢–
1969 *The Time Dweller* ss
1969 *Behold the Man*
1969 *The Black Corridor*
1971 *The Warlord of the Air*
1971 *The Rituals of Infinity* (revision of *The Wrecks of Time*)
1972 *Breakfast in the Ruins* 90¢–
1974 *The Land Leviathan* (sequel to *Warlord of the Air*)
1976 *Moorcock's Book of Martyrs* ss
1976 *The Time of the Hawklords* (with Michael Butterworth)
1977 *Queens of Deliria* (with Michael Butterworth)
1977 *Sojan* ss
1978 *The Shores of Death*
1978 *The Winds of Limbo*
1978 *The Golden Barge*
1978 *Gloriana*

Cornelius Chronicles series (first 4 in *The Cornelius Chronicles* 1977 pb, 6th printing by 1986 *$1.00)*

  1969 *The Final Programme*
  1971 *A Cure for Cancer*
  1972 *The English Assassin*
  1976 *The Lives and Times of Jerry Cornelius* ss
  1976 *The Adventures of Una Persson and Catherine Cornelius in the Twentieth Century*
  1977 *The Condition of Muzak*

Corum series

  1971 *The Knight of the Swords*
  1971 *The Queen of the Swords*
  1971 *The King of the Swords*
  1973 *The Bull and the Spear*
  1973 *The Oak and the Ram* 75¢–
  1974 *The Sword and the Stallion*
  1977 *The Swords Trilogy* (*Knight, Queen, King*)
  1978 *The Chronicles of Corum* (*Bull, Oak, Sword*) **pb$1.00**

Dancers at the End of Time series

    1972   *An Alien Heat* 75¢–

    1974   *The Hollow Lands*

    1976   *The End of All Songs*

    1976   *Legends from the End of Time* ss

    1977   *A Messiah at the End of Time*

Elric series

    1972   *Elric of Melnibone*

    1976   *The Sailor on the Seas of Fate*

    1977   *The Weird of the White Wolf*

    1977   *The Vanishing Tower* $11.00–

    1977   *The Bane of the Black Sword*

    1977   *Stormbringer*

    1984   *Elric at the End of Time* ss 90¢–

Eternal Champions series

    1970   *The Eternal Champion*

    1970   *The Silver Warriors*

    1986   *The Dragon in the Sword* 90¢–

Hawkmoon series

    1967   *The Jewel in the Skull*

    1968   *The Mad God's Amulet*

    1968   *The Sword of the Dawn*

    1969   *The Runestaff*

    1973   *Count Brass*

    1973   *The Champion of Garathorm*

    1975   *The Quest for Tanelorn*

Michael Kane series (also published as by Edward P. Bradbury)

    1965   *City of the Beast* (also as *Warriors of Mars*) **pb$1.00**

    1965   *Lord of the Spiders* (also as *Blades of Mars*) **pb$1.00**

    1965   *Masters of the Pit* (also as *Barbarians of Mars*) **pb$1.00**

C(ATHERINE) L(UCILLE) MOORE (1911–1988)

A prolific and well-established fantasist before her 1940 marriage to Henry Kuttner, the pair collaborated to varying degrees on everything they wrote—under numerous pseudonyms including Lewis Padgett and Lawrence O'Donnell—until Kuttner's death in 1958. Moore then stopped writing science fiction, instead writing TV scripts for Warner Bros. TV series, such as *Maverick* and *77 Sunset Strip*. She married Thomas Reggie in 1964 and died of Alzheimer's disease in 1988.

It is widely believed that she used initials in her byline to conceal the fact that she was a woman, but Moore denied this. She did it to keep her employers from knowing she was writing for pulp magazines. She has been a strong influence on other writers, particularly on women writers. Marion Zimmer Bradley has frequently acknowledged her debt to C. L. Moore, as have many other women fantasists. Addressing such a group, Moore remarked that they all looked so young. "You could be my daughters," she said. "We are," they replied.

    1981   WFA Life Achievement Award

1952 *Judgment Night* ss hc (pb contains only title story)
1953 *Shambleau and Others* ss
1954 *Northwest of Earth* ss
1954 *Beyond Earth's Gates* (with "Lewis Padgett")
1955 *No Boundaries* ss (with Henry Kuttner)
1957 *Doomsday Morning* 50¢–
1964 *Earth's Last Citadel* (with Henry Kuttner)
1969 *Jirel of Joiry* ss
1975 *The Best of C. L. Moore* ss **hc/pb/book club**
1981 *Northwest Smith* ss **pb$1.00**

NOTE: Listed prices are for items in *GOOD* condition.
Very Good = two times listed price.
Fine = three times listed price.
Mint = four times listed price.

Fantastic Novels Magazine, July 1950, 7″ × 9¼″; cover by Lawrence (Stern Stevens) (1886–1960). Listed as copyright 1950 by New Publications, Inc. Copyright 1950 by Popular Publications. Reprinted by permission of Blazing Publications, The Argosy Co.

SAM(UEL) MOSKOWITZ (1920–)

Moskowitz is best known as a historian of science fiction, having written a history of early science-fiction fandom (*The Immortal Storm,* 1954) and biographies of various writers. He has also edited numerous anthologies and has compiled collections of the work of Stanley G. Weinbaum, William Hope Hodgson, Edgar Page Mitchell, and others.

   1955   Hugo: Special Committee Award

TALBOT MUNDY *(William Lancaster Gibbon)* (1879–1940)

Mundy was a writer of adventure stories, generally set in India, which sometimes used lost worlds and fantastic inventions as plot elements.

Tros of Samothrace was published in one large hardcover volume by Gnome Press in the sixties. It was published as four paperback volumes by Avon Books in 1967 as *Tros, Helma, Liafail,* and *Helene.* Zebra Books republished it in three volumes in 1976 as *Tros of Samothrace Volume I: Lud of Lunden, Tros of Samothrace Volume II: Avenging Liafail,* and *Tros of Samothrace Volume III: The Praetor's Dungeon.*

Mundy's best-known novel, *King—of the Khyber Rifles,* is not a fantasy.

1924   *Om, the Secret of Abhor Valley*
1924   *The Caves of Terror*
1924   *The Nine Unknown*
1926   *The Devil's Guard*
1929   *Queen Cleopatra*
1930   *Black Light*
1931   *Jimgrim* (also as *Jimgrim Sahib*)
1934   *Tros of Samothrace* (see above)
1935   *The Purple Pirate* (sequel to *Tros*)
1935   *Full Moon*
1935   *The Mystery of Khufu's Tomb*
1937   *The Thunder Dragon Gate*
1940   *Old Ugly Face*

H(AROLD) WARNER MUNN (1903–1981)

Munn wrote for *Weird Tales* in the twenties and thirties, was rediscovered in 1966, and returned to writing after Ace reprinted *King of the World's Edge*.

1966   *King of the World's Edge*   **pb**
1967   *The Ship From Atlantis*   **pb**
1974   *Merlin's Ring*   **pb**
1976   *The Werewolf of Ponkert*   **ss   pb**
1976   *Merlin's Godson*   **ss   pb**
1979   *Tales of the Werewolf Clan*   **ss   hc$5.00**
1980   *The Lost Legion*   **hc$2.00**

LARRY NIVEN *(Laurence van Cott Niven)* (1938–)

Niven is known for the accuracy of his science. He achieved bestseller status in collaboration with Jerry Pournelle. He recently began a shared-universe series, *The Man-Kzin Wars*.

1967   Hugo (Short Story): "Neutron Star"
1970   Nebula (Novel): *Ringworld*
1971   Hugo (Novel): *Ringworld*

1972   Hugo (Short Story): "Inconstant Moon"

1975   Hugo (Short Story): "The Hole Man"

1976   Hugo (Novelette) "The Borderland of Sol"

1966   *World of Ptavvs*
1968   *A Gift From Earth*
1968   *Neutron Star*   ss
1969   *The Shape of Space*   ss
1970   *Ringworld*
1971   *All the Myriad Ways*   ss
1971   *The Flying Sorcerers* (with David Gerrold)
1973   *The Flight of the Horse*   ss
1973   *Protector*
1974   *The Mote in God's Eye* (with Jerry Pournelle)
1974   *A Hole in Space*
1975   *Tales of Known Space*   ss
1975   *Inferno* (with Jerry Pournelle)
1976   *The Long ARM of Gil Hamilton*   ss
1976   *A World Out of Time*
1976   *Inferno* (with Jerry Pournelle)
1977   *Lucifer's Hammer* (with Jerry Pournelle)
1979   *Convergent Series*   ss
1981   *Dream Park*   hc$1.00–
1982   *The Descent of Anansi* (with Steven Barnes)   pb only$1.00
1983   *The Integral Trees*
1984   *Niven's Laws*   ss   hc only$5.00
1984   *The Time of the Warlock*   ss   hc only$5.00
1985   *Limits*   ss
1985   *Footfall* (with Jerry Pournelle)
1987   *The Legacy of Heorot* (with Jerry Pournelle and Steven Barnes)
         $2.00–$6.00
1987   *The Smoke Ring* (seq to *The Integral Trees*) $1.00–$4.25

WILLIAM F(RANCIS) NOLAN (1928–)

Nolan began writing fiction rather late in life, after years as a fan (he wrote and published *The Ray Bradbury Review*). Besides his science fiction, he has written and edited for magazines. He has written biographies of Steve McQueen and Dashiell Hammett, edited several science-fiction anthologies, and written about auto racing. *Logan's Run* was made into a movie.

1963 *Impact 20* ss
1971 *Space for Hire*
1974 *Alien Horizons* ss
1977 *Wonderworlds* ss
Logan's Run series (trilogy hc 1986 *$4.25*)
   1967 *Logan's Run* (with George Clayton Johnson)
   1977 *Logan's World*
   1980 *Logan's Search*

JOHN NORMAN *(John Frederick Lange, Jr.)* (1931–)

Gor is a planet in Earth's orbit but it is always on the other side of the Sun, so we can't see it. This is called a counter-Earth, and several science-fiction/fantasy series are based on it. "Norman" populates his planet with warriors, sends Earthman Tarl Cabot there, and proceeds to tell stories full of bondage and women who love to be subjugated by big, strong men.

   Prices on back issues tend to begin at 50¢ for "Gor" books in "good" condition. They are pretty reliably kept in print.

1975 *Time Slave*
Gor series
   1966 *Tarnsmen of Gor*
   1967 *Outlaw of Gor*
   1968 *Priest-Kings of Gor*
   1969 *Nomads of Gor*
   1970 *Assassin of Gor*
   1971 *Raiders of Gor*
   1972 *Captive of Gor*
   1974 *Hunters of Gor* (20th printing by 1987)
   [9] *Marauders of Gor*
   1976 *Tribesmen of Gor*
   1977 *Slave Girl of Gor*
   [12] *Beasts of Gor*
   [13] *Explorers of Gor*
   [14] *Fighting Slave of Gor*
   [15] *Rogue of Gor*

[16]   *Guardsman of Gor*
1982   *Savages of Gor* (4th printing by 1987)
1982   *Blood Brothers of Gor* (6th printing by 1987)
[19]   *Kajira of Gor*
[20]   *Players of Gor*
[21]   *Mercenaries of Gor*
[22]   *Dancer of Gor*
[23]   *Renegades of Gor*
1987   *Vagabonds of Gor*

ANDRE NORTON *(Alice Mary Norton)* (1912–)

A retired Cleveland librarian, she has also written historical fiction and juvenile fiction. She has also written as "Andrew North," though most of those stories have been republished as by Andre Norton.

Most of her large output has been novel-length; virtually all her short fiction is included in *Garan the Eternal, The Book of Andre Norton* (published in hardcover as *The Many Worlds of Andre Norton*), and *Perilous Dreams*.

She also has edited some science-fiction anthologies and compiled a collection of stories by Malcolm Jameson, *Bullard of the Space Patrol.*

1983   SFWA Grand Master

1952   *Star Man's Son* (also as *Daybreak—2250* A.D.)
1953   *Star Rangers*
1955   *Star Guard*
1957   *Sea Siege   50¢–*
1958   *Star Gate*
1959   *Secret of the Lost Race*
1960   *Shadow Hawk*
1960   *The Sioux Spaceman*
1961   *Catseye*
1961   *Star Hunter*
1962   *Eye of the Monster*
1964   *Night of Masks   50¢–*
1965   *The X Factor   50¢–*
1967   *Operation Time Search*
1968   *Dark Piper*

1970 *Dread Companion*

1970 *Ice Crown*

1970 *High Sorcery* ss

1971 *Android at Arms* 50¢–

1972 *Breed to Come* pb50¢–

1972 *Garan the Eternal* ss 50¢–

1973 *Here Abide Monsters*

1974 *Iron Cage* pb (7th printing in 1986) 75¢–

1974 *The Many Worlds of Andre Norton* (aka *The Book of Andre Norton*) ss 50¢–

1974 *Outside*

1975 *Merlin's Mirror* (9th printing in 1987) 50¢–

1975 *The White Jade Fox*

1975 *The Day of the Ness* (with Michael Gilbert)

1975 *No Night Without Stars*

1975 *Knave of Dreams*

1976 *Star Ka'at* juv pb (with Dorothy Madlee) 50¢–

1976 *Perilous Dreams* ss (7th printing in 1987) 50¢–

1976 *Wraiths of Time*

1977 *The Opal-Eyed Fan*

1977 *Velvet Shadows*

1978 *Quag Keep* (5th printing in 1987) 50¢–

1978 *Yuth Burden* (6th printing in 1987) 50¢–

1979 *Star Ka'ats and the Plant People* juv (with Dorothy Madley)

1979 *Snow Shadow*

1979 *Seven Spells to Sunday* (with Phyllis Miller)

1980 *Iron Butterflies*

1980 *Voorloper*

Astra series

  1954 *The Stars Are Ours!*

  1957 *Star Born*

Blake Walker series

  1956 *The Crossroads of Time*

  1965 *Quest Crosstime*

Dane Thorson series

  1955 *Sargasso of Space* (originally as by Andrew North)

  1956 *Plague Ship* (originally as by Andrew North)

  1959 *Voodoo Planet* (originally as by Andrew North)

  1969 *Postmarked the Stars*

Hosteen Storm series
  1959   *The Beast Master*
  1962   *Lord of Thunder*
Janus series
  1963   *Judgment on Janus*   *50¢–*
  1966   *Victory on Janus*
Lantee series
  1960   *Storm Over Warlock*
  1964   *Ordeal in Otherwhere*
  1973   *Forerunner Foray*
Ross Murdock series
  1958   *The Time Traders*
  1959   *Galactic Derelict*   *50¢–*
  1962   *The Defiant Agents*
  1963   *The Key Out of Time*
Magic series   **juv**
  1965   *Steel Magic*
  1967   *Octagon Magic*
  1968   *Fur Magic*
  1972   *Dragon Magic*
  1974   *Lavender-Green Magic*
  1976   *Red Hart Magic*
Moon Singer series
  1966   *Moon of Three Rings*   *75¢–*
  1971   *Exiles of the Stars*
Murdock Jern series
  1968   *The Zero Stone*
  1969   *Uncharted Stars*
Time Traders series
  1958   *The Time Traders*   *50¢–*
  1963   *Key Out of Time*   *50¢–*
Witch World series
  1963   *Witch World*
  1964   *Web of the Witch World*
  1965   *Year of the Unicorn*
  1965   *Three Against the Witch World*
  1967   *Warlock of the Witch World*
  1968   *Sorceress of the Witch World*
  1972   *Spell of the Witch World*   ss (14th printing in 1987)   *50¢–*

1972   *The Crystal Gryphon*
1974   *The Jargoon Pard*
1978   *Trey of Swords*
1978   *Zarsthor's Bane*
1980   *Lore of the Witch World*   ss   75¢–
1981   *Horn Crown*   75¢–
Moon of Three Rings series
  Moon of Three Rings
  Exile of the Stars
1986   *Flight in Yiktor*   75¢

ALAN E(DWARD) NOURSE (1928–)

Dr. Nourse (a medical doctor whose last name is pronounced "nurse," he has undoubtedly heard all the jokes about "Doctor Nurse") has written a great deal of science fiction and some mainstream books about the medical profession.

1954   *Trouble on Titan*   juv
1955   *A Man Obsessed*
1957   *Rocket to Limbo*   juv pb75¢–
1959   *The Invaders Are Coming* (with J. A. Meyer)
1959   *Scavengers in Space*
1960   *Star Surgeon*
1961   *Tiger by the Tail and Other Stories*   ss
1962   *Raiders From the Rings*   juv
1964   *The Counterfeit Man and Other Stories*   ss
1965   *The Universe Between*   50¢–
1967   *Psi High and Others*   ss
1968   *The Mercy Men* (expanded version of *A Man Obsessed*)
1971   *Rx for Tomorrow*   ss
1974   *The Bladerunner*

PHILIP FRANCIS NOWLAN (1888–1940)

Nowlan wrote "Armageddon 2419 A.D." and "The Airlords of Han" for *Amazing Stories* in 1928 and 1929. These stories, which were combined into a novel with the title of the first story, introduced Anthony Rogers who, as Buck Rogers, became the hero of a comic strip and a synonym for science fiction in the minds of the general public.

1962   *Armageddon 2419*A.D.

ANDREW J. OFFUTT (1937–)

Offut has written sword-and-sorcery (including Conan pastiches) and sex novels (some of which are also science fiction), as well as science fiction. He edited the *Swords Against Darkness* series of heroic fantasy anthologies.

1970   *Evil Is Live Spelled Backwards*
1971   *The Great 24-Hour Thing*
1972   *The Castle Keeps*
1973   *The Galactic Rejects*
1973   *Messenger of Zhuvastou*
1973   *Ardor on Aros*
1975   *Genetic Bomb* (with D. Bruce Berry)
1976   *Chieftain of Andor*
1977   *My Lord Barbarian*
Conan series
   1979   *The Sword of Skelos*   50¢–
Cormac mac Art series
   1975   *Sword of the Gael*
   1976   *The Undying Wizard*
   1977   *Sign of the Moonbow*   **pb**
   1977   *The Mists of Doom*
   1980   *When Death Birds Fly* (with Keith Taylor)   50¢–
Thieves' World series
   1987   *Shadowspawn* $1.00
War of the Wizards series (with Richard Lyon)
   1978   *The Demon in the Mirror*
   1980   *The Eyes of Sarsis*

(SYMMES) CHAD(WICK) OLIVER (1928–)

Oliver's specialty is anthropological science fiction.

1952   *Mists of Dawn*   **juv**
1954   *Shadows in the Sun*

1955　*Another Kind*　ss
1957　*The Winds of Time*
1960　*Unearthly Neighbors*　ss
1971　*The Edge of Forever*　ss
1971　*The Shores of Another Sea*
1976　*Giants in the Dust*

GEORGE ORWELL *(Eric Arthur Blair)* (1903–1950)

"Orwell" was a noted mainstream novelist who wrote two classics in the science-fiction and fantasy fields.

1946　*Animal Farm*　hc/pb
1949　*Nineteen Eighty-Four*　hc/pb

RAYMOND A. PALMER (1910–1977)

Although he wrote a great deal of magazine science fiction, usually under pseudonyms, Palmer is best known as a magazine editor, particularly of *Amazing Stories, Fantastic Adventures,* and *Other Worlds.* His fascination with borderline matters—flying saucers and the Shaver Mystery—are detailed in the entries on those magazines.

EDGAR PANGBORN (1909–1976)

1953　*West of the Sun*
1954　*A Mirror for Observers* (winner International Fantasy Award)
1964　*Davy*
1966　*The Judgment of Eve*
1972　*Good Neighbors and Other Strangers*　ss
1975　*The Company of Glory*
1978　*Still I Persist in Wondering*　ss

ALEXEI PANSHIN (1940–)

In addition to his science fiction, Panshin is the author of a study of Robert A. Heinlein, *Heinlein in Dimension.* He married Cory Panshin in 1969, and what writing he has done in recent years has been in collaboration with her.

Fantastic Science-Fiction Art, 1926–1954, by Lester del Rey; about 8¾″ ×
11¾″; cover shown on the Ballantine book is by Frank R. Paul (1884–1963) and
is the cover for the November 1929 *Science Wonder Stories,* copyright 1929 by
Gernsback Publications, Inc. The book is copyright 1975 by Random House,
Inc.

1968   Nebula (Novel): *Rite of Passage*

1968   *Rite of Passage*
1975   *Farewell to Yesterday's Tomorrows*   ss
1978   *Earth Magic* (with Cory Panshin)
Anthony Villiers series
1968   *Star Well*
1968   *The Thurb Revolution*
1969   *Masque World*

FRANK R. PAUL (1884–1963)

Paul was the foremost artist of the early Hugo Gernsback magazines,
Amazing Stories and the various *Wonder* titles.

MERVYN PEAKE *(Lawrence)* (1911–1968)

Peake, a British writer and artist, is remembered for his Gormenghast trilogy of fantasies.

Gormenghast series
- 1946 *Titus Groan*
- 1950 *Gormenghast*
- 1959 *Titus Alone*

WENDY AND RICHARD PINI

Wendy is an artist and writer, and her husband, Richard, is a writer and editor on the graphic novel series of *Elfquest* volumes. At present, there are four graphic novels published by Starblaze Graphics; late in 1988, the Pinis began republishing the series themselves, with new material and a sequel, in six volumes.

   With Lynn Abbey and Robert Asprin, Richard Pini has edited a series of shared-world anthologies based on the world of *Elfquest*.

H(ENRY) BEAM PIPER (1904–1964)

Piper's "Little Fuzzy" series has been continued by other writers since his death (*Fuzzy Bones* by William Tuning and *Golden Dreams: A Fuzzy Odyssey* by Ardath Mayhar).

- 1957 *Crisis in 2140* (with John J. McGuire)
- 1958 *A Planet for Texans* (with John J. McGuire, also as *Lone Star Planet*)
- 1961 *Four-Day Planet*
- 1963 *The Cosmic Computer* (also as *Junkyard Planet*)
- 1963 *Space Viking*
- 1963 *Junkyard Planet* (also as *The Cosmic Computer*)
- 1979 *Four-Day Planet and Lone Star Planet*
- 1981 *Federation*
- 1981 *Empire* ss pb75¢–
- 1983 *Uller Uprising*
- 1983 *The Worlds of H. Beam Piper* ss

Little Fuzzy series
- 1962 *Little Fuzzy*
- 1964 *Fuzzy Sapiens* (also as *The Other Human Race*)

1977   *The Fuzzy Papers* (omnibus)
1984   *Fuzzies and Other People*
Paratime series
1965   *Lord Kalvan of Otherwhen*   **pb50ᶜ–**
1981   *Paratime*

EDGAR ALLAN POE (1809–1849)

First editions of the work of Poe are out of the reach of the average collector and will never show up in the catalogs of back-issue book and magazine sellers. These editions are sold by auction houses on rare, well-publicized occasions and sell for prices in excess of $100,000. There are several one-volume collections of the short stories and poems of Poe, including some editions illustrated by Harry Clarke (1889–1931), whose style was suited admirably to Poe's stories, whether they were mysteries, fantasies, horror, or science fiction—yes, Poe wrote some of each.

FREDERIK POHL (1919–)

In addition to his science fiction, which he has been writing for half a century, Pohl has written advertising copy (much of his fiction has satirized advertising) and books on politics. He collaborated frequently with C. M. Kornbluth, not only on science fiction, but on novels such as *Presidential Year* and *A Town Is Drowning*. The Pohl-Kornbluth collaborations continued even after Kornbluth's death, with Pohl completing stories left in fragmentary form or as notes by Kornbluth.

Pohl also edited a number of magazines, most notably *Galaxy* and *If,* and a number of anthologies. Del Rey books published his autobiography, *The Way the Future Was,* which gives a vivid picture of the science-fiction publishing scene of the forties and fifties in particular.

1973   Hugo (Short Story): ''The Meeting'' (with C. M. Kornbluth)
1976   Nebula (Novel): *Man Plus*
1977   Nebula (Novel): *Gateway*

1978 Hugo (Novel): *Gateway*
1986 Hugo (Short Story): "Fermi and Frost"

1953 *The Space Merchants* (with C. M. Kornbluth) *50¢–*
1954 *Search the Sky* (with C. M. Kornbluth)
1955 *Gladiator-at-Law* (with C. M. Kornbluth)
1955 *Preferred Risk* (with Lester del Rey as "Edson McCann")
1956 *Alternating Currents* ss
1956 *The Case Against Tomorrow* ss
1957 *Slave Ship*
1959 *Tomorrow Times Seven*
1959 *Wolfbane* (with C. M. Kornbluth)
1960 *Drunkard's Walk*
1960 *The Man Who Ate the World* ss
1961 *Turn Left at Thursday* ss
1962 *The Wonder Effect* ss (with C. M. Kornbluth)
1963 *The Abominable Earthman* ss
1965 *A Plague of Pythons*
1966 *Digits and Dastards* ss
1969 *The Age of the Pussyfoot* pb50¢
1970 *Day Million* ss
1972 *The Gold at The Starbow's End* ss
1975 *Farthest Star* (with Jack Williamson)
1975 *The Best of Frederick Pohl*
1976 *The Early Pohl*
1976 *In the Problem Pit* ss
1976 *Man Plus*
1977 *Critical Mass* ss (with C. M. Kornbluth)
Wall Around a Star (with Jack Williamson)
1979 *Jem*
1980 *Before the Universe* ss (with C. M. Kornbluth)
1981 *The Cool War*
1982 *Syzygy*
1982 *Bipohl (Drunkard's Walk* and *Age of the Pussyfoot)*
1982 *Planets Three* ss
1982 *Starburst*
1983 *Midas World* ss
1984 *Demon in the Skull* (revision of *Plague of Pythons*)
1984 *Pohlstars* ss

1985   *The Years of the City*
1985   *Black Star Rising*
1985   *Venus, Inc. (Space Merchants, Merchants' War)* **book club**$2.00
1986   *The Coming of the Quantum Cats*
1986   *Terror*
1987   *Our Best*   ss (with C. M. Kornbluth)
Heechee Saga
  1977   *Gateway*
  1980   *Beyond the Blue Event Horizon*
  1984   *Heechee Rendezvous*
  1987   *The Annals of the Heechee*   hc$4.25   pb$1.00
Starchild series (with Jack Williamson)
  1964   *The Reefs of Space*
  1965   *Starchild*
  1969   *Rogue Star*
  1977   *The Starchild Trilogy*
Undersea series   juv (with Jack Williamson)
  1954   *Undersea Quest*
  1955   *Undersea Fleet*
  1958   *Undersea City*

JERRY POURNELLE (1933–)

Pournelle has frequently collaborated with Larry Niven; those collaborations are listed under Niven's name. He has also edited a number of anthologies, mostly on a militaristic theme.

1973   *A Spaceship for the King* (later as *King David's Spaceship*)   50¢–
1974   *Escape from the Planet of the Apes* (movie novelization)
1976   *Birth of Fire*   50¢
1976   *West of Honor*   50¢
1977   *The Mercenary* (seq to *West*)   pb75¢
1977   *High Justice*   ss
1978   *Exiles to Glory*   pb75¢
1980   *King David's Spaceship*
Janissaries series
  [1]   *Janissaries I*
  [2]   *Janissaries II*

1987   *Janissaries III: Storms of Victory* (with Roland Green)   **hc$4.25**

E. HOFFMAN PRICE (1898–1988)

Price, who began selling to the pulps in 1924, spent a good part of his life traveling the world. He formed lasting friendships with many fantasy writers and was, in all probability, the only person ever to meet both Robert E. Howard and H. P. Lovecraft—since neither of those noted recluses traveled much, it took a traveling fantasist like Price to go to them.

   1984   WFA Life Achievement Award

1979   *The Devil Wives of Li Fong*
1980   *Operation Misfit*
1982   *The Jade Enchantress*
Operation Exile
Operation Longlife
1986   *Operation Isis*

SEABURY (GRANDIN) QUINN (1889–1969)

Seabury Quinn is best known for his *Weird Tales* stories, most of which featured an occult detective named Jules de Grandin (note the similarity to Quinn's own name) who encountered vampires and demons and defeated them to the accompaniment of a smattering of French expletives and interjections. Quinn was, for a time, an extremely popular author, though he is not widely known today.

1948   *Roads* (Arkham House)
Jules de Grandin series
   1966   *The Phantom Fighter*   **ss**
   1970   *Is the Devil a Gentleman?*   **ss**
   1976   *The Adventures of Jules de Grandin*   **ss**   **pb**
   1976   *The Casebook of Jules de Grandin*   **ss**   **pb**
   1976   *The Hellfire Files of Jules de Grandin*   **ss**   **pb**
   1976   *The Skeleton Closet of Jules de Grandin*   **ss**   **pb**
   1976   *The Devil's Bride*   **pb**
   1976   *The Horror Chambers of Jules de Grandin*   **pb**

ALEX RAYMOND (1909-1956)

Raymond, a comic-strip artist who based his style on the great magazine illustrators of the thirties, is best known for his art on the *Flash Gordon* comic strip. Don Moore wrote the strip, but it was Raymond's art which made the improbable plots work. Raymond spent years on the Graustarkian planet Mongo, where swords and rayguns shared an unlikely co-existence and where Ming the Merciless, the epitome of The Yellow Peril, ruled all but some diehard patches of rebels, all of whom tended to rally behind Flash Gordon (described only as a Yale graduate and polo player). Raymond joined the Marines in 1944 and left *Flash Gordon* in the hands of Austin Briggs (who had been drawing the daily strip and frequently ghosting Raymond's Sunday pages as well). On his return from the Marines, Raymond began a new strip about an ex-Marine private detective named *Rip Kirby*; he stayed on that strip until his death in an auto accident in 1956.

Currently, the entire *Flash Gordon* strip is being collected into large, generous volumes by Kitchen Sink Press, No. 2 Swamp Road, Princeton, Wisconsin. Unlike earlier attempts, which have concentrated exclusively on those strips alleged to be Raymond's, it is Publisher Denis Kitchen's avowed intent to publish the strip in its entirety. Also unlike earlier attempts, these strips are being published uncolored, shot from proofs, which allows the delicate feathering of Raymond's art to be seen to best advantage.

TOM REAMY (1935-1977)

Tom Reamy was a graphic designer and fanzine publisher (notably *Trumpet* and *Shayol*) who had a brief but memorable career as a professional writer of science fiction and fantasy. He won the John W. Campbell Award as most promising new science-fiction writer in 1976. Virtually all his writing is contained in his two books, one novel and one collection of short fiction, both published posthumously. (At this writing, he still has one unpublished story, slated for the long-delayed Harlan Ellison anthology, *The Last Dangerous Visions*.) Reamy literally died at his typewriter of a heart attack.

1975   Nebula (Novelette): "San Diego Lightfoot Sue"

Blind Voices
San Diego Lightfoot Sue   ss

MACK REYNOLDS *(Dallas McCord Reynolds)* (1917–1983)

Although he placed first in popularity in a poll of readers of *If*, Reynolds' popularity appears to be on the wane since his death. He was a member of the American Socialist Labor Party (his father, Verne L. Reynolds, was a presidential candidate) and many of his novels have a political setting.

Reynolds' 1951 novel, *The Case of the Little Green Men,* is a mystery novel set at a science-fiction convention. It is *not* science fiction, but it is one of a small number of books about fans; others include Anthony Boucher's *Rocket to the Morgue* (originally published as by H. H. Holmes), Robert Coulson and Gene DeWeese's *Now You See It/Him/Them* and *Charles Fort Never Mentioned Wombats,* and Sharyn McCrumb's *Bimbos of the Death Sun.* (The last three mentioned books are science fiction. McCrumb's book won the Mystery Writers of America's Edgar Award for Best Paperback Mystery.)

Reynolds spent several years living abroad and was a travel writer for various men's magazines. He also edited an anthology of science-fiction humor with Fredric Brown (*Science Fiction Carnival*) and wrote a *Star Trek* novel (*Mission to Horatius*) and some Gothic novels (*The House in the Kasbah* and *The Home of the Inquisitor*).

1962 *The Earth War*
1964 *Night is for Monsters*
1966 *Of Godlike Power*
1966 *Time Gladiator* (sequel to *The Earth War*)
1967 *After Some Tomorrow*
1967 *Computer War*
1967 *Space Pioneer*
1968 *Mercenary From Tomorrow* (sequel to *Time Gladiator)*
1969 *The Cosmic Eye*
1969 *The Space Barbarians*
1969 *Speakeasy*
1970 *Computer World*
1970 *Once Departed*
1973 *Looking Backward From the Year 2000*
1974 *Depression or Bust*
1974 *Commune 2000* A.D.
1975 *The Towers of Utopia*
1975 *Ability Quotient*

1975   *Tomorrow Might be Different*
1976   *Rolltown*
1976   *The Best of Mack Reynolds*   ss
1976   *Day After Tomorrow*
1976   *Galactic Medal of Honor*
1977   *Space Visitor*
1977   *Police Patrol: 2000* A.D.
1977   *Equality in the Year 2000*
1977   *After Utopia*
1977   *Perchance to Dream*
African series
   1972   *Black Man's Burden*
   1972   *Border, Breed, Nor Birth*
         The Best Ye Breed
Rex Bader series
   1975   *Five Way Secret Agent*
   1975   *Satellite City*
Section G series
   1965   *Planetary Agent X*
   1966   *Dawnman Planet*
   1967   *Amazon Planet*
   1967   *The Rival Rigelians*
   1968   *Code Duello*
   1976   *Section G: United Planets*

KEITH ROBERTS (1935–)

Roberts is a British advertising man, illustrator, and writer. Most of his books are made up of short stories and novelettes combined into novel format.

1966   *The Furies*
1968   *Pavane*
1969   *The Ice Schooner*
1970   *The Inner Wheel*
1970   *Anita*
1970   *The Chalk Giants*
1973   *Machines and Men*   ss
1976   *The Grain Kings*   ss
1977   *The Passing of the Dragons*   ss

FRANK M(ALCOLM) ROBINSON (1926–)

Much of Robinson's work has been done for men's magazines (he was an editor of *Playboy*), and his most successful work has been a series of "disaster" novels with Thomas M. Scortia (*The Glass Inferno* was combined with Richard Martin Stern's *The Tower* to make the movie, *The Towering Inferno*).

1956   *The Power*
1981   *A Life in the Day of* . . .   ss

KIM STANLEY ROBINSON

Robinson has been writing science fiction since 1976 and has produced, in addition to his novels and short magazine fiction, a critical study, *The Novels of Philip K. Dick*.

   1984   WFA (Novella): "Black Air"

1984   *The Wild Shore*
1984   *Icehenge*
1985   *Memory of Whiteness*
1986   *The Planet on the Table*   ss   trade pb$3.00   pb$1.00
1987   *The Gold Coast*

SPIDER ROBINSON (1948–)

Spider Robinson (that is his legal name) is an American writer living in Canada; he recently moved west after years in Nova Scotia. In addition to his fiction writing, he is a highly regarded critic who reviewed books for *Galaxy* for two years.

   1977   Hugo (Novella): "By Any Other Name"

   1977   Nebula (Novella): "Stardance" (with Jeanne Robinson)

   1978   Hugo (Novella): "Stardance" (with Jeanne Robinson)

   1983   Hugo (Short Story): "Melancholy Elephants"

1976   *Telempath*
Stardance (with Jeanne Robinson)
1980   *Antinomy*   ss
Melancholy Elephants   ss
Mindkiller

Night of Power
Callahan's Bar series
   1977   *Callahan's Crosstime Saloon*   ss
   1981   *Time Travelers Strictly Cash*   ss   75¢–
   1986   *Callahan's Secret*   ss   *$1.00*

SAX ROHMER *(Arthur Sarsfield Ward)* (1883–1959)

Rohmer's primary claim to fame is his series of Fu Manchu novels which contain some science-fiction elements; Rohmer also wrote a shorter series about a female version of Fu Manchu, Sumuru. Rohmer wrote many other fantasy novels, but only his Fu Manchu stories are readily available in paperback. (In the earliest books, the evil doctor's name is hyphenated as Fu-Manchu; that hyphen was dropped after the first three books.)

   1914   *The Sins of Severac Bablon*
   1918   *Brood of the Witch Queen*
   1918   *Tales of Secret Egypt*   ss
   1918   *The Orchard of Tears*
   1919   *The Quest of the Sacred Slipper*   ss (as by Hassan of Aleppo)
   1920   *The Dream Detective*   ss
   1920   *The Green Eyes of Bast*
   1920   *The Haunting of Low Fennel*   ss
   1921   *Bat-Wing*
   1921   *Fire-Tongue*
   1922   *Tales of Chinatown*   ss
   1924   *Grey Face*
   1928   *She Who Sleeps*
   1929   *The Emperor of America*
   1933   *Tales of East and West*   ss
   1935   *The Bat Flies Low*
   1938   *The Golden Scorpion Omnibus*   ss
   1938   *The Sax Rohmer Omnibus*   ss
   1939   *Salute to Bazarada and Other Stories*   ss
   1950   *Wulfheim* (as by Michael Furey)
   1954   *The Moon Is Red*
   1970   *The Secret of Holm Peel and Other Strange Stories*   ss
Fu Manchu series
   1913   *The Insidious Dr. Fu-Manchu*

1916   *The Return of Dr. Fu-Manchu*
1917   *The Hand of Fu-Manchu*
1931   *The Daughter of Fu Manchu*
1932   *The Mask of Fu Manchu*
1933   *The Bride of Fu Manchu*
1934   *The Trail of Fu Manchu*
1936   *President Fu Manchu*
1938   *The Drums of Fu Manchu*
1957   *Re-Enter Fu Manchu*   **pb** original
1959   *Emperor Fu Manchu*   **pb** original
1973   *The Wrath of Fu Manchu*   ss   **pb** original
Gaston Max series
1915   *The Yellow Claw*
1919   *The Golden Scorpion*
1930   *The Day the World Ended*
1943   *Seven Sins*
Sumuru series
1950   *Nude in Mink*
1951   *Sumuru*
1952   *The Fire Goddess*
1954   *Return of Sumuru*
1956   *Sinister Madonna*

JOANNA RUSS (1937–)

In addition to her highly acclaimed science fiction, Russ is a university professor, a book reviewer, and has a Master of Fine Arts degree in playwriting from Yale. Her work has a decided feminist slant, exemplified in her best-known book, *The Female Man*.

1972   Nebula (Short Story): "When It Changed"
1983   Hugo (Novella): "Souls"

1968   *Picnic on Paradise*
1970   *And Chaos Died*
1975   *The Female Man*
1976   *Alyx* (aka *The Adventures of Alyx*)   **pb75¢–**
1977   *We Who Are About To . . .*

ERIC FRANK RUSSELL (1905–1978)

Despite the laudable attempts of Del Rey Books to create a resurgence of interest in the work of this delightful British author (in 1985 and 1986, Del Rey reissued five Russell novels and *The Best of Eric Frank Russell*), Russell's work seems to be unfairly neglected since his death. His specialty was the humorous adventure story in which a lone Earthman is pitted against all the forces of a hostile planet.

1955   Hugo (Short Story): "Allamagoosa"

1943   *Sinister Barrier*
1951   *Dreadful Sanctuary*
1953   *Sentinels From Space*
1954   *Deep Space*
1956   *Three to Conquer* (Ace Double)
1956   *Men, Martians, and Machines*   ss
1957   *Wasp*
1958   *Six Worlds Yonder*   ss (Ace Double with *The Space Willies*)
1958   *The Space Willies* Ace Double with *Six Worlds Yonder*)
1961   *The Far Stars*
1962   *The Great Explosion*
1964   *The Mindwarpers*
1965   *Somewhere a Voice*   ss
1975   *Like Nothing on Earth*   ss
1978   *The Best of Eric Frank Russell*
1986   *Next of Kin* (expanded *The Space Willies*)

FRED (THOMAS) SABERHAGEN (1930–)

Saberhagen's most famous series involves the "Berserkers," about powerful, sentient alien weapons designed to eliminate all organic life. Other series include the various "books of swords" and a series of novels involving Dracula. The Dracula series began with *The Dracula Tapes*, in which Bram Stoker's Dracula gives his side of the story, very convincingly. Saberhagen later tried the same thing with Mary Wollstonecraft Shelley's *Frankenstein*.

1964   *The Golden People*
1968   *Empire of the East (Book I)*   50¢–
1968   *The Broken Lands*

1971 *The Black Mountains* (sequel to *Broken Lands*)
1973 *Changeling Earth* (sequel to *Black Mountains*)
1975 *The Book of Saberhagen* **pb only**
1976 *Specimens*
1978 *The Veils of Azlaroc* 75¢–
1979 *The Mask of the Sun* 75¢–
1980 *Thorn*
1981 *Octagon* 75¢
1981 *Earth Descended*
1982 *Dominion* **pb only** 90¢
1983 *A Century of Progress*
1984 *The Golden People*
1985 *Love Conquers All*
1985 *The Water of Thought* (expansion of Ace 1965 double) 75¢–
Coils (with Roger Zelazny)
The Earth Descended
1986 *The Frankenstein Papers*
1987 *Mask of the Sun*
1987 *Pyramids* **pb$1.00**
1987 *Saberhagen: My Best* **ss** 75¢
Berserker series
  1967 *Berserker* **ss**
  1969 *Brother Assassin*
  1979 *Berserker Man*
  1981 *The Berserker Wars*
  1985 *Berserker: Blue Death* 50¢
  1986 *The Berserker Throne*
  1987 *Berserker Base* (anthology with others) **$1.00**
Dracula series
  1975 *The Dracula Tape*
  1978 *The Holmes-Dracula File*
  1979 *An Old Friend of the Family* 75¢–
Swords series
  1983 *The First Book of Swords*
  1983 *The Second Book of Swords*
  1984 *The Third Book of Swords*
  1986 *The First Book of Lost Swords: Woundhealer's Story*
  1987 *The Second Book of Lost Swords: Sight-Binder's Story*

CARL SAGAN (1934–)

American astronomer and host of TV's *Cosmos*, Sagan has written only one science-fiction novel, though his science books and his precedent-making TV series have done a great deal to popularize science and science fiction.

1985   *Contact*

MARGARET ST. CLAIR (1911–)

Under her own name and that of "Idris Seabright," St. Clair has written a great deal of magazine science fiction and fantasy, beginning in 1946.

1956   *Agent of the Unknown*
1956   *The Green Queen*
1960   *The Games of Neith*
1963   *Sign of the Labrys*
1964   *Message From the Eocene*
1964   *Three Worlds of Futurity* ss
1967   *The Dolphins of Altair*
1969   *The Shadow People*
1973   *The Dancers of Noyo*
1974   *Change the Sky and Other Stories* ss
1985   *The Best of Margaret St. Clair* ss

SAKI *(Hector Hugh Munro)* (1870–1916)

Although he also wrote novels and plays, it is for his finely crafted short stories that Saki is remembered today. His work, as Anthony Boucher remarked, seems divided between apparent fantasies which turn out to be someone pulling someone else's leg and apparent leg-pulls which turn out to be fantasies. Saki's most reprinted story is "The Open Window"; it isn't a fantasy, but don't let that stop you from reading it.

The Complete Short Stories of Saki was reprinted in a Modern Library edition, which should be readily available. All the stories are short, making them ideal for bedtime reading.

Hector Hugh Munro was killed in action in World War I.

1914 *When William Came*
1904 *Reginald* ss
1910 *Reginald in Russia* ss
1911 *The Chronicles of Clovis* ss
1914 *Beasts and Super-Beasts* ss
1919 *The Toys of Peace* ss
1924 *The Square Egg* ss
1930 *The Complete Short Stories of Saki* ss

STUART DAVID SCHIFF

Schiff edits a semi-professional fantasy magazine called *Whispers* and has edited a number of anthologies of fantasy, including a series of stories from *Whispers*.

JAMES H. SCHMITZ (1911–1981)

Schmitz was noted for his frequent use of female protagonists, particularly his series character Telzey Amberdon.

1960 *Agent of Vega* ss
1962 *A Tale of Two Clocks*
1965 *A Nice Day for Screaming* ss
1966 *The Witches of Karres*
1968 *The Demon Breed*
1970 *A Pride of Monsters* ss
1973 *The Eternal Frontiers*
Telzey Amberdon series
  1964 *The Universe Against Her*
  1973 *The Lion Game*
  1973 *The Telzey Toy* ss

JOHN SCHOENHERR (1935–)

Although he has moved out of science-fiction art into children's book illustration and fine art, Schoenherr was for several years the primary cover artist for *Analog*. His best-known science-fiction illustrations were done for the magazine serialization of Frank Herbert's *Dune*.

  1965 Hugo (Professional Artist)

GEORGE SCITHERS (1929–)

A retired army officer, Scithers is in the unique position of having been the editor of the oldest science-fiction magazine (*Amazing Stories*) and the most famous fantasy magazine (*Weird Tales*). He was the first editor of *Isaac Asimov's Science Fiction Magazine*.

Scithers was editor of the fanzine *Amra,* devoted to heroic fantasy in general and the Conan stories of Robert E. Howard in particular. With L. Sprague de Camp, he edited two collections of pieces from *Amra: The Conan Swordbook* and *The Conan Grimoire*.

Scithers has also published books as the head of Owlswick Press, including editions of stories by Lord Dunsany and excellent books on writing science fiction.

1978   Hugo (Professional Editor)
1980   Hugo (Professional Editor)

ROD SERLING (1924–1975)

Serling, one of the first writers to earn a reputation as a major writer from television (*Requiem for a Heavyweight, Patterns*), will always be best remembered for the TV series he created and for which he was host, *The Twilight Zone.* (He later created another fantasy anthology series, *Night Gallery,* of which he was also host.) *Twilight Zone* has been revived as a TV series, was the basis for a movie (creatively titled *Twilight Zone: The Movie*), and exists today as the continuing fantasy magazine, *Rod Serling's The Twilight Zone Magazine*.

Most of the books credited to Serling are adaptations of his TV scripts into short-story form. He also edited three anthologies of stories which served as the basis for *TZ* scripts.

1960   *Stories From The Twilight Zone*   ss
1961   *More Stores From The Twilight Zone*   ss
1962   *New Stories From The Twilight Zone*   ss
1971   *Night Gallery*   ss
1972   *Night Gallery 2*   ss

BOB SHAW (1931–)

Shaw, who was born and lives in Northern Ireland, moved smoothly from science-fiction fan to science-fiction writer, turning out a number of successful novels. He is best known for a short story, "Light of Other Days," based on his concept of "slow glass," through which light passes so slowly that past events can be viewed through it. His "slow glass" stories were reworked into a novel, *Other Days, Other Eyes*. Marvel Comics licensed the concept and used it for a framing device on its black-and-white comics magazine, *Unknown Worlds of Science Fiction*, starting with an adaptation of "Light of Other Days."

1967	*Night Walk*
1968	*The Two-Timers*
1969	*The Palace of Eternity*
1969	*The Shadow of Heaven*
1970	*One Million Tomorrows*
1971	*Ground Zero Man*
1972	*Other Days, Other Eyes*
1973	*Tomorrow Lies in Ambush* ss
1975	*Orbitsville*
1976	*A Wreath of Stars*
1976	*Cosmic Kaleidoscope* ss
1977	*Medusa's Children*
1977	*Who Goes Here?*
1978	*Ship of Strangers*
1979	*Vertigo*
	A Better Mantrap
1982	*The Ceres Solution*
1987	*The Ragged Astronauts* hc$4.00

MICHAEL SHEA

1983 WFA (Novel): *Nifft the Lean*

1974	*A Quest for Simbilis*
1982	*Nifft the Lean*
1987	*Fat Face* $1.50–$16.75

ROBERT SHECKLEY (1928–)

Sheckley began as a short-story writer whose slick, satirical style made him the epitome of the *Galaxy* stories of the fifties. In later years, he left science fiction to write espionage and adventure novels, partly on the success of the movie version of his short story, "The Seventh Victim." (The movie was called *The Tenth Victim* and Sheckley subsequently wrote a novelization of the movie made from his short story.) Sheckley was an editor of *Omni* but has since returned to freelance writing, including a follow-up to *The Tenth Victim*.

1954	*Untouched by Human Hands*	ss
1955	*Citizen in Space*	ss
1957	*Pilgrimage to Earth*	ss
1958	*Immortality Delivered*	
1960	*Notions: Unlimited*	ss
1960	*The Status Civilization*	
1962	*Shards of Space*	ss
1963	*Journey Beyond Tomorrow*	
1966	*Mindswap*	
1966	*The Tenth Victim*	50¢–
1968	*Dimension of Miracles*	
1968	*The People Trap*	ss
1971	*Can You Feel Anything When I Do This?*	ss
1975	*Options*	
1978	*Crompton Divided*	
1978	*The Robot Who Looked Like Me*	ss
1981	*The People Trap/Mindswap* (2 novels)	**pb90¢**
1983	*Dramocles*	
1987	*Victim Prime* (sequel to *Tenth Victim*)	**90¢**

RACCOONA SHELDON *(see James Tiptree, Jr.)*

MARY WOLLSTONECRAFT SHELLEY (1797–1851)

The wife of poet Percy Bysshe Shelley owes her literary reputation primarily to a novel written as a lark. The Shelleys, Lord Byron, and Byron's physician, decided to try writing a ghost story. Shelley and Byron turned out nothing of note for the project, the physician wrote a good vampire short story—and Mary Shelley wrote *Frankenstein: or The Modern Prometheus*.

Her most famous novel is best known from various series of movies (primarily the Universal series and the Hammer Films series), so many have lost sight of the fact that her monster, far from being the mute shambler of the films, was literate and downright verbose.

She wrote one fantasy short story, "The Mortal Immortal," and a novel in which the population of Earth has been wiped out by a plague, *The Last Man*.

1818   *Frankenstein: or The Modern Prometheus*
1826   *The Last Man*

LUCIUS SHEPARD

Shepard began writing professionally in 1983; in 1985, he won the John W. Campbell Award as Most Promising Science Fiction Writer. He has been nominated for Hugo, World Fantasy, and Nebula awards.

    1986   Nebula (Novella): "R&R"

1984   *Green Eyes*   **pb original**
Life During Wartime
The Jaguar Hunter   ss

ROBERT SILVERBERG (1936–)

Silverberg began writing professionally before he was 20, turned out well over 100 books (not all science fiction) and hundreds of short stories, and retired before he was 40. The retirement didn't last and Silverberg returned to writing science fiction.

In his early years as a writer, Silverberg filled many a magazine with his stories, under his own name and more than a dozen pseudonyms. In later years, he began producing more serious books at a slower pace, remarking that he had worn off his fingerprints typing to produce his remarkably large body of work.

Many of Silverberg's books have been written under pseudonyms; he reportedly has ghost-written books as well. In addition to the books he has written, Silverberg has edited many anthologies, including the original-story series, *New Dimensions*. It may be that only Silverberg knows exactly how many books he has written and what their titles are.

1956 Hugo (New Author)

1969 Hugo (Novella): "Nightwings"

1969 Nebula (Short Story): "Passengers"

1971 Nebula (Novel): *A Time of Changes*

1971 Nebula (Short Story): "Good News From the Vatican"

1974 Nebula (Novella): "Born with the Dead"

1985 Nebula (Novella): "Sailing to Byzantium"

1987 Hugo (Novella): "Gilgamesh in the Outback"

1955 *Revolt on Alpha C* **juv**
1957 *The 13th Immortal*
1957 *Master of Life and Death*
1958 *Aliens From Space* (as by David Osborne)
1958 *Invisible Barriers* (as by David Osborne)
1958 *Lest We Forget Thee, Earth* (as by Calvin M. Knox)
1958 *Invaders From Earth* *50¢* (Ace Double)
1958 *Starhaven* (as by Ivar Jorgenson)
1958 *Stepsons as Terra*
1959 *The Planet Killers*
1959 *The Plot Against Earth* (as by Calvin M. Knox)
1959 *Starman's Quest*
1960 *Lost Race of Mars*
1961 *Collision Course* (Ace Double)
1962 *The Seed of Earth* (Ace Double with *Next Stop the Stars*)
1962 *Next Stop the Stars* **ss** (Ace Double with *Seed of Earth*)
1962 *Recalled to Life*
1963 *The Silent Invaders*
1964 *Godling Go Home* **ss**
1964 *One of Our Asteroids Is Missing* (as by Calvin M. Knox)
1964 *Regan's Planet*
1964 *Time of the Great Freeze*
1965 *Conquerors From the Darkness*
1965 *To Worlds Beyond* **ss**
1966 *Needle in a Timestack* **ss**
1967 *Thorns*

1967   *The Gate of Worlds*
1967   *Planet of Death*
1967   *Those Who Watch*
1967   *The Time Hoppers*
1967   *To Open the Sky*
1968   *Hawksbill Station*
1968   *The Masks of Time*
1969   *Nightwings* (3 novellas)   *50¢–*
1969   *The Man in the Maze*   *50¢–*
1969   *Up the Line*   *50¢–*
1969   *Across a Billion Years*   **juv**   **pb/hc75¢–**
1969   *The Calibrated Alligator*   **ss**
1969   *Dimension Thirteen*   **ss**
1969   *Three Survived*
1969   *To Live Again*
1970   *Parsecs and Parables*   **ss**
1970   *Downward to the Earth*
1970   *Tower of Glass*   *50¢–*
1970   *World's Fair 1992* (sequel to *Regan's Planet*)
1971   *A Time of Changes*
1971   *Son of Man*   *50¢–*
1971   *The World Inside*
1971   *The Cube Root of Uncertainty*   **ss**
1971   *Moonferns and Starsongs*   **ss**
1972   *The Second Trip*   *50¢–*
1972   *The Book of Skulls*
1972   *Dying Inside*
1972   *The Reality Trip and Other Implausibilities*   **ss**
1973   *Earth's Other Shadow*   **ss**
1973   *Valley Beyond Time*   **ss**
1973   *Unfamiliar Territory*   **ss**
1974   *Sundance and Other Science Fiction Stories*   **ss**
1974   *Born with the Dead*   **ss**
1975   *The Stochastic Man*   *75¢–*
1975   *The Feast of St. Dionysus*   **ss**
1975   *Sunrise on Mercury*   **ss**
1976   *Shadrach in the Furnace*
1976   *The Best of Robert Silverberg*   **ss**
1976   *Capricorn Games*   **ss**

1976   *The Shores of Tomorrow*   ss
1980   *Lord Valentine's Castle*   pb75¢–
1981   *The Desert of Stolen Dreams*   hc$3.00–$7.50
1982   *Majipoor Chronicles*   ss
1984   *The Conglomeroid Cocktail Party*   ss
Beyond the Safe Zone
Valentine Pontifex
Tom o'Bedlam
1986   *Star of Gypsies* $1.50–
At Winter's End

CLIFFORD D(ONALD) SIMAK (1904–1988)

Clifford Simak began writing science fiction in 1931 (his early science fiction has been cited by Isaac Asimov as a major influence on his own writing), quit writing a year later, then resumed in 1938, this time producing stories for John W. Campbell at *Astounding*. He became particularly productive during the fifties and sixties, writing novelettes for *Galaxy* and other magazines. In later years, he concentrated primarily on novels, continuing to write them until shortly before his death.

1959   Hugo (Novelette): "The Big Front Yard"

1964   Hugo (Novel): *Here Gather the Stars* (aka *Way Station*)

1980   Nebula (Short Story): "Grotto of the Dancing Bear"

1981   Hugo (Short Story): "Grotto of the Dancing Bear"

1976   SFWA Grand Master

1946   *The Creator*
1950   *Cosmic Engineers*
1951   *Time and Again*
1951   *Empire*
1952   *City*
1953   *Ring Around the Sun*
1956   *Strangers in the Universe*   ss
1960   *The Worlds of Clifford Simak*   ss
1961   *Time Is the Simplest Thing*
1961   *Trouble with Tycho*
1962   *All the Traps of Earth*   ss

1962   *They Walked Like Men*
1963   *Way Station*
1964   *Worlds Without End*   ss
1965   *All Flesh Is Grass*
1966   *Why Call Them Back from Heaven?*
1967   *Best SF Stories of Clifford Simak*   ss
1967   *The Werewolf Principle*
1968   *The Goblin Reservation*
1968   *So Bright the Vision*   ss (Ace Double)
1969   *Out of Their Minds*
1971   *Destiny Doll*
1972   *A Choice of Gods*
1973   *Cemetery World*
1974   *Our Children's Children*
1975   *Enchanted Pilgrimage*
1975   *The Best of Clifford D. Simak*   ss
1976   *Shakespeare's Planet*
1977   *A Heritage of Stars*
1977   *Skirmish: The Great Short Fiction*   ss
Mastodonia
Project Pope
The Fellowship of the Talisman
Special Deliverance
1980   *The Visitors*   pb75¢–
1982   *Where the Evil Dwells*
1986   *Highway of Eternity*

CLARK ASHTON SMITH (1893–1961)

Smith was a poet and sculptor but is best remembered as a fantasist of the adjective-rich school. He published collections of poetry (some of it fantastic) as well as of fiction.

1933   *The Double Shadow*   ss
1944   *Lost Worlds*   ss
1960   *The Abominations of Yondo*   ss
1964   *Poems in Prose*   ss
1964   *Tales of Science and Sorcery*   ss
1970   *Other Dimensions*   ss
1970   *Zothique*   ss

1971   *Hyperborea*   ss
1972   *Xiccarph*   ss
1973   *Poseidonis*   ss
1981   *The City of the Singing Flame*   ss
1981   *The Last Incantation*   ss
1983   *The Monster of the Prophecy*   ss

CORDWAINER SMITH *(psd. of Paul Myron Linebarger)* (1913–1966)

The first story by "Cordwainer Smith" was "Scanners Live in Vain," published in *Fantasy Book*. It went largely unnoticed because of the magazine's obscurity, but became famous shortly after it was anthologized by Frederik Pohl. The second story under the "Smith" name (Linebarger wrote fiction under other names, but dropped all the others before adopting the Cordwainer Smith persona) was "The Game of Rat and Dragon" in *Galaxy,* which began his long association with that magazine.

1963   *You Will Never Be the Same*   ss
1964   *The Planet Buyer*
1965   *Space Lords*   ss
1966   *Quest of the Three Worlds*   ss
1968   *The Underpeople*
1970   *Under Old Earth*   ss
1971   *Stardreamer*   ss
1975   *Norstrilia*
1975   *The Best of Cordwainer Smith*   ss
1979   *The Instrumentality of Mankind*   ss

EDWARD ELMER SMITH, Ph.D. (1890–1965)

Smith was a chemist (he specialized in doughnut mixes and was instrumental in developing a doughnut to which powdered sugar would adhere) who wrote slam-bang, no-holds-barred space opera. In his novels, he went beyond the previous limitations of science fiction, where one planet warred against another; in Smith's fiction, galaxies battled galaxies, using suns as weapons. Because of his extravagant stories, he was called "The Father of Space Opera."

The Lensman series is probably the most famous space opera. It involved a band of intrepid soldiers given special powers by the power of the Lens. The Skylark series, "Doc" Smith's other major work, involved an inventor hero who was able to whip together whatever advanced scientific weapon was needed under pressure of enemy attack—a tradition which today is found primarily in comic books (see Reed Richards of Marvel Comics' *The Fantastic Four* for a prime example).

Smith began writing *Skylark of Space* in 1915, in collaboration with Mrs. Lee Hawkins Garby, but it was not published in magazine form until 1928; it didn't come out in book form until 1946. (Mrs. Garby apparently contributed nothing to subsequent Smith books.) Unlike most science fiction of the twenties, the book—and all other Smith novels—has remained popular with each new generation of readers.

The demand for more has led other writers to produce sequels and related books using Smith's ideas and characters. Some of these (the "Family d'Alembert" series, for instance) have been published as if they were collaborations with Smith. Notable sequels to the Lensman novels have been written by David A. Kyle.

1947   *Spacehounds of IPC*
1965   *The Galaxy Primes*
1965   *Subspace Explorers*
1975   *The Best of E. E. "Doc" Smith* ss
1976   *Masters of Space* (with E. Everett Evans)
1983   *Subspace Encounter* (seq to *Explorers*, with Lloyd Arthur Eshbach)

Family d'Alembert series (with Stephen Goldin)

1976   *The Imperial Stars*
1976   *Stranglers' Moon*
1977   *The Clockwork Traitor*
1977   *Getaway World*
1978   *Appointment at Bloodstar*
1980   *The Purity Plot*

Lensman series

1948   *Triplanetary*
1950   *First Lensman*
1950   *Galactic Patrol*
1951   *Gray Lensman*

1953   *Second Stage Lensman   50¢–*
1954   *Children of the Lens*
1960   *The Vortex Blaster* (aka *Masters of the Vortex*)
Skylark of Space series
1946   *The Skylark of Space*
1948   *Skylark Three*
1949   *Skylark of Valeron*
1966   *Skylark DuQuesne*

NOTE: Listed prices are for items in *GOOD* condition.
Very Good = two times listed price.
Fine = three times listed price.
Mint = four times listed price.

GEORGE O(LIVER) SMITH (1911–1981)

Smith was an engineer whose best-known science-fiction work is the "Venus Equilateral" series of short stories.

1947   *Venus Equilateral* ss
1949   *Pattern for Conquest*
1950   *Nomad*
1950   *Operation Interstellar*
1953   *Hellflower*
1957   *Troubled Star*
1958   *Fire in the Heavens*
1959   *The Path of Unreason*
1959   *The Fourth "R"* (also as *The Brain Machine*)
1976   *The Complete Venus Equilateral* ss
1982   *The Worlds of George O.*   ss

THORNE SMITH (1892–1934)

Smith's specialty was the drunken fantasy. His characters always drank prodigious amounts of booze and got into extremely complicated situations as a result. The result was funny, though modern readers, more aware of the dangers of alcoholism, may have some difficulty ignoring the potential damage. Smith himself drank to excess; he claimed his publishers let him drink to his heart's content until they needed a new novel, then subjected him to drastic cold-water treatments to sober him up, keeping him sober until another book was produced. His heavy drinking contributed to his early death, another factor which diminishes the enjoyment of modern readers in reading about the drunken romps which characterized his work.

His most famous character was Cosmo Topper, the stuffy banker, and his private ghosts, George and Marian Kirby. The characters appeared in movies and in two different television series.

Smith's books usually were illustrated by Herbert Roese. For many years, Pocket Books reissued most of his novels every couple of years, but eventually let them all go out of print. A recent attempt by Del Rey Books to revive them met with discouraging sales. Perhaps it's hard for modern audiences to relate to stories set so obviously in the Jazz Age.

1926 *Topper*
1929 *The Stray Lamb*
1931 *Turnabout*
1932 *Topper Takes a Trip*
1933 *Rain in the Doorway*
1933 *Skin and Bones*
1934 *The Glorious Pool*
1939 *The Night Life of the Gods*
1941 *The Passionate Witch* (completed by Norman Matson after Smith's death)

NORMAN (RICHARD) SPINRAD (1940–)

Spinrad's reputation was made by his fourth novel, *Bug Jack Barron*. When it was serialized in *New Worlds*, it brought the wrath of censors down upon that magazine. Reading the novel today makes one wonder what all the complaints were about, but that's true of most censored material of bygone years.

Spinrad's other most famous book is *The Iron Dream*, which purports to be a novel written by Adolf Hitler in an alternate world in which he emigrated to the United States and became a science-fiction writer instead of remaining in Germany to become dictator.

1966 *The Solarians*
1967 *The Men in the Jungle*

1967 *Agent of Chaos*
1969 *Bug Jack Barron*
1970 *The Last Hurrah of the Golden Horde* ss
1972 *The Iron Dream*
1975 *No Direction Home* ss
1978 *Riding the Torch* (in *Binary Star #1*)
1979 *The Star-Spangled Future* ss
1979 *Passing Through the Flame*
1979 *A World Between*
1980 *The Mind Game*
1981 *Songs From the Stars*
1983 *The Void Captain's Tale*
1985 *Child of Fortune*
1987 *Little Heroes* hc$6.00

OLAF STAPLEDON (1886–1950)

Stapledon was an English writer whose cosmological science fiction
has a small but devoted following. His *Last and First Men* covers a
time span that few writers would attempt: two billion years. His best-
known work is *Odd John,* a novel about a superman.

1930 *Last and First Men*
1932 *Last Men in London*
1935 *Odd John*
1937 *Star Maker* 50¢–
1942 *Darkness and the Light*
1944 *Sirius*
1946 *Death into Life*
1947 *The Flames*

RICK STERNBACH (1951–)

Sternbach is best known for his astronomical paintings; he has worked
for *Astronomy Magazine* as well as for science-fiction magazines and
books—primarily as a cover artist.

His black-and-white work, if any, is not on the market; his paintings
go for $500–$1,600—"and could bring lots more," according to art
dealer Robert Weinberg.

1978 Hugo (Professional Artist)

ROBERT LOUIS STEVENSON (1850–1894)

The famous Scottish author is best known in the fantasy field for his 1886 novel, *The Strange Case of Dr. Jekyll and Mr. Hyde* (incidentally, while virtually everybody today pronounces "Jekyll" as "Jeckel," Stevenson himself pronounced it "Jeekel"), but he wrote a number of other fantasies. Collections of Stevenson's short stories generally contain the bulk of his fantasy work—usually including *Jekyll and Hyde*, which is not a very long novel.

BRAM STOKER (1847–1912)

Best known as the author of *Dracula*, Stoker also wrote a number of other fantasy novels and short stories. "Dracula's Guest," a segment cut out of the novel before publication, often appears in anthologies as a separate story.

Many editions of Stoker's most famous book are available; our recommendation is to try to find Leonard Wolf's *The Annotated Dracula*, which gives a great deal of the factual background Stoker incorporated into his novel. (Dracula was based on the historical Vlad Tepes [1432?–1477], ruler of Walachia [now a part of Romania]. Tepes signed himself "Drakula" or "Drakulya" and is remembered especially for using impalement as a punishment.)

1897 *Dracula*
1902 *The Mystery of the Sea*
1903 *The Jewel of the Seven Stars*
1909 *The Lady of the Shroud*
1911 *The Lair of the White Worm*
1914 *Dracula's Guest* ss

THEODORE STURGEON (1918–1985)

Theodore Sturgeon (that was his legal name, but some libraries still insist on listing him as a pseudonym for Edward Hamilton Waldo; he was born under that name but it was changed while he was still a child) made his reputation writing for John W. Campbell (*Astounding* and *Unknown*) but was writing primarily for *Galaxy* and *The Magazine of Fantasy and Science Fiction* when he was at his most prolific. *F&SF* devoted one of its special issues to him.

More Than Human by Theodore Sturgeon, about 4¼″ × 7″; cover by (Richard M.) Powers (1921–). The classic science-fiction novel was the 47th book in Ballantine Books' line; this first printing was published simultaneously with Farrar, Straus and Young's hardcover edition. Copyright 1953 by Theodore Sturgeon.

Sturgeon's most famous book is *More Than Human*. In addition to his science fiction and fantasy, Sturgeon wrote westerns, mysteries, and novelizations of movies (including the western movies *The Rare Breed* and *The King and Four Queens*).

In 1956, New York radio personality Jean Shepherd enlisted his listeners in creating a hoax on those not in his audience. They created a non-existent book, *I, Libertine* by Frederick R. Ewing, and succeeded in getting it condemned as obscene by various censoring groups. Sturgeon volunteered to actually write the book, a historical novel, under the Ewing byline, Kelly Freas painted a cover for it, and Ballantine Books printed it. It is a collector's item of interest to science-fiction fans even though it is not remotely science fiction or fantasy.

    1970   Nebula (Short Story): "Slow Sculpture"

    1971   Hugo (Short Story): "Slow Sculpture"

    1985   WFA Life Achievement Award

1948 *Without Sorcery* ss
1950 *The Dreaming Jewels* (also published as *The Synthetic Man*)

More Than Human by Theodore Sturgeon, about 5½″ × 8″; cover not credited. The hardcover was published simultaneously with Ballantine's paperback edition. "The low price of $2.00 is made possible by large printings of combined editions," said the statement of the publisher, Farrar, Straus and Young. Copyright 1953 by Theodore Sturgeon.

More Than Human by Theodore Sturgeon, about 5¼″ × 8¼″; cover by Paul Giovanopoulous. The first Ballantine Books trade edition of the novel was issued in October 1981. Copyright 1953 by Theodore Sturgeon.

More Than Human, The Graphic Story Version by Theodore Sturgeon, Alex Nino, and Doug Moench, about 8¼″ × 11″; cover by Michael Kanarek, published by Ballantine Books. Copyright 1953 (original novel) by Theodore Sturgeon and 1978 (*More Than Human, The Graphic Story Version*) by Byron Preiss Visual Publications, Inc.

1953 *More Than Human* (won International Fantasy Award) *50¢–*
1953 *E. Pluribus Unicorn* ss
1955 *A Way Home* ss
1955 *Caviar* ss
1958 *A Touch of Strange* ss
1958 *The Cosmic Rape* *50¢–*
1959 *Aliens 4* ss
1960 *Venus Plus X*
1960 *Beyond* ss
1961 *Some of Your Blood* (horror; borderline fantasy)
1961 *Voyage to the Bottom of the Sea* (movie novelization)
1964 *Sturgeon in Orbit* ss
1965 *And My Fear Is Great and Baby Is Three* ss
1966 *Starshine* ss
1971 *Sturgeon Is Alive and Well . . .* ss

More Than Human by Theodore Sturgeon, about 5¾″ × 8½″; cover by Gary Viskupic (1944–). The book-club edition was published by Farrar, Straus and Giroux, Inc. Copyright 1953 by Theodore Sturgeon.

Caviar by Theodore Sturgeon, about 4″ × 7″; cover by Darrell Sweet (1934–). The man depicted on the cover of this 1977 Ballantine edition is *not* Sturgeon; it is Lester del Rey.

1972   *The Worlds of Theodore Sturgeon*   ss
1973   *To Here and the Easel*   ss
1974   *Case and the Dreamer*   ss
1978   *Visions and Venturers*   ss
1979   *The Stars Are the Styx*   ss   pb*$1.00*
1979   *The Golden Helix*   ss
1979   *Maturity*   ss   hc*$5.00*
1984   *The Stars Are the Styx*   ss   pb75¢   trade pb*$3.00*
1985   *Godbody*   hc*$5.00*

THOMAS BURNETT SWANN (1928–1976)

Swann was born, lived, and died in Florida, but many of his historical fantasies were first published in the British magazine, *Science Fantasy*. Many of his books were published by DAW Books, usually with George Barr covers.

1966   *The Day of the Minotaur*
1967   *The Weirwoods*
1968   *The Dolphin and the Deep*
1968   *Moondust*
1970   *Where Is the Bird of Fire?*   ss
1971   *The Goat Without Horns*
1971   *The Forest of Forever*
1972   *Wolfwinter*
1972   *Green Phoenix*
1974   *How Are the Mighty Fallen*
1975   *The Not-World*
1976   *The Gods Abide*
1976   *The Minikins of Yam*
1976   *Lady of the Bees* (Sequel to *Green Phoenix*)
1976   *The Tournament of Thorns*
1976   *Will-o-the-Wisp*
1977   *Cry Silver Bells*
1977   *Queens Walk in the Dusk*

List of Color Plates

Plate 1. *Weird Tales,* March 1948, about 6½″ × 10″; cover by Lee Brown Coye (1907–1981). This is the 25th anniversary special of the long-running fantasy magazine. Defects include pencilling and price stamp. Copyright 1947 by Weird Tales. Used with permission of Weird Tales Ltd.

Plate 2. *Sumuru* by Sax Rohmer, about 4¼″ × 7¼″; cover of the Gold Medal Original is not credited. This is chosen to show the defect of loose cellophane, a common problem for paperbacks of this era, but there is also a cover corner crease and the binding glue is dry. Copyright 1951 by Fawcett Publications, Inc.

Plate 3. *Weird Tales,* December 1935, about 6¾″ × 9¾″; back cover. This is chosen to show the sort of defect occasionally found in old magazines—a large chunk missing from the back cover. Copyright 1935 by Popular Fiction Publications. Used with permission of Weird Tales Ltd.

Plate 4. *Weird Tales,* January 1950, about 6¾″ × 10″; cover not credited. The defects on this cover include a cover crease and, more importantly, a worn, scrubbed left edge, possibly combined with or caused by water damage. Copyright 1949 by Weird Tales. Used with permission of Weird Tales Ltd.

Plate 5. *Fahrenheit 451* by Ray Bradbury, about 5½″ × 8″; no jacket. The edition was limited to 200 signed and numbered copies, one of three "first" editions of the work. "It is specially bound in JOHNS-MANVILLE QUIN-TERRA, an asbestos material with exceptional resistance to pyrolysis." Copyright 1953 by Ray Bradbury.

Plate 6. *Fahrenheit 451* by Ray Bradbury, about 5½″ × 8″; cover by Joe Mugnaini. This is the hardcover "first" edition of the novel; priced at $2.50, "The low price of this new publication is made possible by simultaneous production with a 35¢ paperbound edition." Copyright 1953 by Ray Bradbury.

Plate 7. *Fahrenheit 451* by Ray Bradbury, about 5¼″ × 8¼″; cover design adapted from Joe Mugnaini's original design. This "Gold Seal" edition is

Ballantine's first trade edition (March 1981) and does not contain the short stories "The Playground" and "And the Rock Cried Out," which were in the early editions. Copyright 1953 by Ray Bradbury.

Plate 8. *Two Complete Science-Adventure Books,* Winter (October-December) 1951, about 10″ × 10″; cover by (Allen) Anderson. Copyright 1951 by Wings Publishing Co., Inc.

Plate 9. *Famous Fantastic Mysteries,* December 1940, about 7″ × 9½″; cover by (Frank R.) Paul (1884–1963). Copyright 1940 by Frank A. Munsey Company. Reprinted with permission of Blazing Publications, The Argosy Co.

Plate 10. *Famous Fantastic Mysteries,* August 1946, about 7″ × 9¼″; cover by Lawrence (Stern Stevens) (1886–1960). Defects include tape discoloration on cover top and cover crease. Listed as copyright 1946 by All-Fiction Field, Inc. Copyright 1946 by Popular Publications. Reprinted with permission of Blazing Publications, The Argosy Co.

Plate 11. *Two Complete Science-Adventure Books,* Winter 1950, about 7″ × 10″; cover by (Allen) Anderson. This is the first issue of the publication. Defects include cover wrinkling. Copyright 1950 by Wings Publishing Co., Inc.

Plate 12. *Fantastic Novels Magazine,* November 1940, about 7″ × 10″; cover by Virgil Finlay (1914–1971). Defects include tape discoloration on left side top and bottom and cover crease. Copyright 1940 by Frank A. Munsey Company. Reprinted with permission of Blazing Publications, The Argosy Co.

Plate 13. *Fantastic Novels,* July 1940, about 6¾″ × 9½″; cover not credited. This is the first issue of the publication. Defects include a name written on the cover, chipping, and tape discoloration in the corners. Copyright 1940 by Frank A. Munsey Company. Reprinted with permission of Blazing Publications, The Argosy Co.

Plate 14. *Fantastic Novels,* September 1940, about 6½″ × 9½″; cover not credited. Defects include a cover price written on the cover, chunks out of the cover, and a cover crease down the left side. Copyright 1940 by Frank A. Munsey Company. Reprinted with permission of Blazing Publications, The Argosy Co.

PLATE 1

PLATE 2

PLATE 3

PLATE 4

Defects reduce the value of collectibles.

PLATE 5

PLATE 6

PLATE 7

One work can appear in a variety of collectible forms.

PLATE 8

PLATE 9

PLATE 10

PLATE 11

Pulp magazines sometimes reprinted classic works and became collectible, themselves.

PLATE 12

PLATE 13

PLATE 14

PLATE 15

In the days before paperback science fiction was common, magazines specializing in reprinting novels flourished.

PLATE 16

PLATE 17

PLATE 18

PLATE 19

Some parents considered pulp magazines questionable reading, an opinion based largely on their appearance.

PLATE 20

PLATE 21

PLATE 22

PLATE 23

Weird Tales *is the longest-running fantastic horror magazine in America.*

PLATE 24

PLATE 25

PLATE 26

PLATE 27

Planet Stories *was the ultimate space-opera magazine, and* Tops in Science Fiction *reprinted from it.*

PLATE 28

PLATE 30

PLATE 29

The work of an artist (in this case, Frank Kelly Freas) can be collected in the form of original roughs, original finished art, or printed reproduction.

Plate 15. *Fantastic Novels Magazine,* September 1948, about 7″ × 9¼″; cover by Lawrence (Stern Stevens) (1886–1960). Listed as copyright 1948 by New Publications, Inc. Copyright 1948 by Popular Publications. Reprinted with permission of Blazing Publications, The Argosy Co.

Plate 16. *Fantastic Adventures,* October 1950, about 7″ × 10″; cover by Robert Gibson Jones illustrating L. Ron Hubbard's *The Masters of Sleep.* Defects include left-side cover crease and frayed right edge. Copyright 1950 by Ziff-Davis Publishing Company. "Fantastic" is a trademark owned by TSR, Inc. Copyright 1989 TSR, Inc. All rights reserved.

Plate 17. *Amazing Stories,* March 1945, about 7″ × 10″; cover by Robert Gibson Jones illustrating Richard S. Shaver's "I Remember Lemuria." Copyright 1944 by Ziff-Davis Publishing Company. "Amazing" is a registered trademark of TSR, Inc. Copyright 1989 TSR, Inc. All rights reserved.

Plate 18. *Fantastic Adventures,* July 1939, about 8½″ × 11¼″; cover by Leo Morey (?–1965). Copyright 1939 by Ziff-Davis Publishing Company. "Fantastic" is a trademark owned by TSR, Inc. Copyright 1989 TSR, Inc. All rights reserved.

Plate 19. *Fantastic Adventures,* July 1951, about 7″ × 10″; cover by Robert Gibson Jones, illustrating Robert Bloch's "The Dead Don't Die." Copyright 1951 by Ziff-Davis Publishing Company. "Fantastic" is a trademark owned by TSR, Inc. Copyright 1989 TSR, Inc. All rights reserved.

Plate 20. *Weird Tales,* December 1935, about 6¾″ × 9¾″; cover by Margaret Brundage (1900–1976), illustrating Robert E. Howard's "The Hour of the Dragon." Defects include two grease-pencilled prices and frayed bottom of the cover. Copyright 1935 by Popular Fiction Publishing Company. Used with permission of Weird Tales Ltd.

Plate 21. *Weird Tales,* July 1941, about 6¾″ × 10″; cover by Hannes Bok (1914–1964). Defects include frayed spine. Copyright 1941 by Weird Tales. Used with permission of Weird Tales Ltd.

Plate 22. *Weird Tales,* May 1951, about 6½″ × 9¾″; cover by Lee Brown Coye (1907–1981). Defects include cover crease and scuffing. Copyright 1951 by Weird Tales. Used with permission of Weird Tales Ltd.

Plate 23. *Weird Tales,* April 1934, about 6¾″ × 9¾″; cover by Margaret Brundage (1900–1976) illustrating E. Hoffman Price's "Satan's Garden."

Defects include some cover creasing. Copyright 1934 by Popular Fiction Publications. Used with permission of Weird Tales Ltd.

Plate 24. *Planet Stories,* Summer (March–May) 1946, about 7″ × 10″; cover not credited. Copyright 1946 by Love Romances Publishing Co., Inc.

Plate 25. *Tops in Science Fiction,* Spring 1953, about 7″ × 10″; cover not credited but by Alexander Leydenfrost (1889–1961). Compare the cover to *Planet Stories* for Spring 1942; such cover pickups are not common in the field. Copyright 1952 by Love Romances Publishing Co., Inc.

Plate 26. *Planet Stories,* May 1952, about 7″ × 10″; cover not credited. Defects include cover creases and fraying. Copyright 1952 by Love Romances Publishing Co., Inc.

Plate 27. *Planet Stories,* Spring 1942, about 7″ × 10″; cover by (Alexander) Leydenfrost (1889–1961). Defects include grease-pencilled number, cover loose from spine at bottom, frayed right edge. Note the cover on *Tops in Science Fiction* for Spring 1953.

Plate 28. *Planet Stories,* Summer 1954, about 7″ × 10″; cover by Kelly Freas (1922–). Copyright 1954 by Love Romances Publishing Co., Inc.

Plate 29. Original painting by (Frank) Kelly Freas (1922–) for the cover of the Summer 1954 *Planet Stories;* about 11″ × 15″; the painting contains the red-orange block on which the title print block appeared. The publication is copyright 1954 by Love Romances Publishing Co., Inc.; this first printing of the original painting is copyright 1989 by Kelly Freas.

Plate 30. Original cover rough by (Frank) Kelly Freas (1922–) for the cover of the April 1971 *Analog;* about 4¼″ × 6¼″; the painting bears almost no resemblance to the final, finished cover, although each picture illustrates Stanley Schmidt's "The Unreachable Stars." Copyright 1989 by Kelly Freas.

WILLIAM TENN *(Philip Klass)* (1920–)

Philip Klass joined the faculty of Pennsylvania State University in 1966 and, while he has done a great deal to further academic acceptance of science fiction, he has not written any science fiction since accepting that post. All of his published science fiction was written during the preceding twenty years.

In addition to his own fiction, he edited an anthology, *Children of Wonder*.

1955 *Of All Possible Worlds* ss
1956 *The Human Angle* ss
1958 *Time in Advance* ss
1968 *Venus and the Seven Sexes* ss
1968 *The Square Root of Man* ss
1968 *The Wooden Star*
1968 *A Lamp for Medusa*

JAMES TIPTREE, JR. *(psd. of Alice Sheldon)* (1915–1987)

Alice Sheldon (who also wrote under the name of Raccoona Sheldon) was a psychologist who successfully hid behind a masculine pseudonym from 1968 through 1977, when she revealed her identity.

Most of her writing was done in the shorter forms; an unusually large percentage of her stories won awards.

She killed her invalid husband and herself in a widely reported murder-suicide pact in 1987.

1973 Nebula (Short Story): "Love Is the Plan, the Plan Is Death"

1974 Hugo (Novella): "The Girl Who Was Plugged In"

1976 Nebula (Novella): "Houston, Houston, Do You Read?"

1977 Hugo (Novella): "Houston, Houston, Do You Read?"

1977 Nebula (Novelette): "The Screwfly Solution" (as Raccoona Sheldon)

1987 WFA (Collection): *Tales of the Quintana Roo*

1973 *Ten Thousand Light-Years From Home* ss
1975 *Warm Worlds and Otherwise* ss

1978   *Star Songs of an Old Primate*   ss
1978   *Up the Walls of the World*
1981   *Out of the Everywhere, and Other Extraordinary Visions*   ss   pb90¢
1986   *Tales of the Quintana Roo*   ss
1986   *The Starry Rift*   ss   hc/pb$1.25

J. R. R. TOLKIEN *(John Ronald Reuel Tolkien)* (1892–1973)

This fantasist's work provides such a rich field for exploration that many academic articles—including entire books—have been devoted to it. The first volume in *The Lord of the Rings* was a juvenile, *The Hobbit*. Although the second through fourth books are sometimes called a trilogy, they actually compose one long novel. Several authorized and unauthorized editions exist, since the basic three books were not protected by copyright in America.

The Ballantine edition was brought out as a set in 1965. The books are available in boxed sets, corrected, and with notes.

The Lord of the Rings series
   1937   *The Hobbit*   juv   50¢–
   1954   *The Fellowship of the Ring*   50¢–
   1954   *The Two Towers*   50¢–
   1955   *The Return of the King*   50¢–
   1968   *The Lord of the Rings* (omnibus of previous three books)
1949   *Farmer Giles of Ham*
1964   *Tree and Leaf*   ss
1966   *The Tolkien Reader*   ss
1967   *Smith of Wootton Major*
1969   *Smith of Wootton Major & Farmer Giles of Ham*   ss
1975   *Sir Gawain and the Green Knight/Pearl/Sir Orfeo*   ss
1976   *The Father Christmas Letters*
1977   *The Silmarillion*
1980   *Unfinished Tales*   hc$1.25–
1984   *The Book of Lost Tales*   ss
1986   *The Shaping of Middle Hearth: The Quenta, The Ambarkanta, and the Annals*   hc$4.25
1987   *The Lost Road and other Writings*   hc$6.00

(ARTHUR) WILSON TUCKER (1914–)

As fan Bob Tucker, he is a familiar figure at science fiction conventions, particularly in the Midwest. As Wilson Tucker, he began writing professionally in 1941. His first novel was not science fiction, but a mystery, *The Chinese Doll* (1946).

One of his characteristics is the use of names of real people, mostly science fiction fans, as names of characters in his books. Many people like—and imitate—these "Tuckerisms"; others are annoyed by them; a few are infuriated by them.

1951 *The City in the Sea*
1952 *The Long Loud Silence*
1953 *The Time Masters*
1954 *Science Fiction Subtreasury* ss (pb as *Time X*)
1954 *Wild Talent*
1955 *Time Bomb* ss (pb as *Tomorrow Plus X*)
1957 *The Lincoln Hunters*
1960 *To the Tombaugh Station*
1970 *The Year of the Quiet Sun*
1974 *Ice and Iron*
1981 *Resurrection Days*
1982 *The Best of Wilson Tucker* ss

LISA TUTTLE (1952–)

Tuttle was an early member of the Clarion Science Fiction Writers' Workship and won the John W. Campbell Award for Most Promising Science-Fiction Writer in 1974.

1981 Nebula (Short Story): "The Bone Flute"

1981 *Windhaven* (with George R. R. Martin) hc*$4.00*

MARK TWAIN *(psd. of Samuel Langhorne Clemens)* (1835–1910)

One of America's leading men of letters, Twain wrote a few fantasies, most notably *A Connecticut Yankee in King Arthur's Court,* which uses the notion of time travel as a vehicle for social satire.

1889   *A Connecticut Yankee in King Arthur's Court*
1909   *Captain Stormfield's Visit to Heaven*
1969   *The Mysterious Stranger*

JACK VANCE *(John Holbrook Vance)* (1920–)

Jack Vance is a hotly collected author; his work in a magazine doubles the price of the issue. While we will be listing only his fantasy and science-fiction books, it should be noted that he has also written mysteries, including three novels as Ellery Queen (*The Four Johns, The Madman Theory,* and *A Room to Die In*).

Fantasms: A Jack Vance Bibliography (1978) was published by Underwood/Miller, listing all of Vance's work. That bibliography is itself a collector's item.

1963   Hugo (Short Fiction): "The Dragon Masters"

1966   Nebula (Novella): "The Last Castle"

1967   Hugo (Novelette): "The Last Castle"

1984   WFA: Life Achievement Award

1953   *The Space Pirate*
1953   *Vandals of the Void* **hc**
1956   *To Live Forever* **hc/pb**
1957   *Big Planet* **hc/pb** (Ace Double—until 1977, all editions are abridged)
1958   *Slaves of the Klau* (Ace Double)
1958   *The Languages of Pao* **hc/pb**
1963   *The Dragon Masters* (Ace Double with *Five Gold Bands;* reissued 1972 with *The Last Castle* instead)
1963   *The Five Gold Bands* (Ace Double)
1964   *Future Tense* **ss**
1964   *The Houses of Iszm* (Ace Double)
1964   *Son of the Tree* (Ace Double)
1965   *Space Opera*
1965   *The World Between and Other Stories* **ss** (Ace Double)
1965   *Monsters in Orbit* **ss** (Ace Double)
1966   *The Blue World*
1966   *The Brains of Earth* (Ace Double)

1966 *The Many Worlds of Magnus Ridolph* ss
1967 *The Last Castle* (Ace Double; reissued 1972 with *The Dragon Masters*)
1969 *Eight Fantasms and Magics* ss
1969 *Emphyrio*
1972 *The Dragon Masters/The Last Castle* (Ace Double)
1973 *Trullion: Alastor 2262*
1973 *The Worlds of Jack Vance* ss
1974 *The Gray Prince*
1975 *Showboat World*
1975 *Marune: Alastor 993*
1976 *The Best of Jack Vance* ss
1976 *Maske: Thaery*
1978 *Wyst: Alastor 1716*
1978 *The Blue World*
1987 *Araminta Station* hc$5.00
Demon Princess series
  1964 *The Star King*
  1964 *The Killing Machine*
  1967 *The Palace of Love*
Durdane series
  1973 *The Anome* (aka *The Faceless Man*) 50¢–
  1973 *The Brave Free Men*
  1974 *The Asutra*
Dying Earth series
  1950 *The Dying Earth* ss pb/hc
  1966 *The Eyes of the Overworld*
        Cugel's Saga
  1984 *Rhialto the Marvellous* hc$3.00
Lyonesse series
  1983 *Lyonesse* (aka *Suldren's Garden*) pb/hc$2.00
  1985 *The Green Pearl* pb/hc$1.50–
Planet of Adventure series
  1968 *City of the Chasch*
  1969 *Servants of the Wankh*
  1969 *The Dirdir*
  1970 *The Pnume*

The Dying Earth by Jack Vance, about 4¼″ × 6½″; cover not credited. Defects include tiny puncture marks in the cover. Copyright 1950 by Hillman Periodicals, Inc.

A(LFRED) E(LTON) VAN VOGT (1912–)

Van Vogt is known for his extremely complicated novels, but his most famous novel is the relatively straightforward *Slan,* his first book. He was married to fellow science-fiction writer Edna Mayne Hull from 1939 until her death in 1975. He has subsequently remarried. In 1975, *Reflections of A. E. van Vogt,* an autobiography, was published.

1946   *Slan*   –*$45.00*
1946   *The Weapon Makers*
1947   *The Book of Ptath*
1948   *The World of Null-A*
1948   *Out of the Unknown* (with E. Mayne Hull)   ss
1950   *The House That Stood Still*
1950   *Masters of Time*   ss
1950   *The Voyage of the Space Beagle*   ss (also as *Mission Inter-planetary*)   *50¢–*
1951   *The Weapon Shops of Isher*

1952   *The Mixed Men* (reissued as *Mission to the Stars*)
1952   *Destination Universe*   ss
1952   *Away and Beyond*   ss
1953   *The Universe Maker*
1954   *Planets for Sale* (with E. Mayne Hull)
1956   *The Pawns of Null-A*
1956   *Empire of the Atom*
1957   *The Mind Cage*
1959   *The War Against the Rull*
1959   *Siege of the Unseen*
1960   *Earth's Last Fortress*
1962   *The Wizard of Linn*
1963   *The Beast*
1964   *The Twisted Men*   ss
1965   *Monsters*   ss
1965   *Rogue Ship*
1966   *The Winged Man* (with E. Mayne Hull)
1968   *The Far-Out Worlds of A. E. van Vogt*   ss
1969   *The Silkie*
1970   *Children of Tomorrow*
1970   *Quest for the Future*
1971   *The Battle of Forever*
1971   *More than Superhuman*   ss
1971   *The Proxy Intelligence and Other Mind Benders*   ss
1971   *M-33 in Andromeda*   ss
1972   *The Darkness on Diamondia*
1972   *The Book of van Vogt*   ss
1973   *Future Glitter*
1973   *The Three Eyes of Evil*   ss (British collection)
1974   *The Secret Galactics*
1974   *The Man with a Thousand Names*
1976   *The Gryb*   ss
1976   *The Best of A. E. van Vogt*   ss
1977   *Supermind*
1977   *The Anarchistic Colossus*

JOHN (HERBERT) VARLEY (1947–)

1978   Nebula (Novella): "The Persistence of Vision"

1979   Hugo (Novella): "The Persistence of Vision"

1982   Hugo (Short Story): "The Pusher"

1984   Nebula (Novella): "Press Enter ■"

1985   Hugo (Novella): "Press Enter ■"

1977   *The Ophiuchi Hotline*
1978   *The Persistence of Vision*   ss
1980   *The Barbie Murders*   ss (also as *Picnic on Nearside*)
Millennium
1986   *Blue Champagne*   ss   hc/pb75¢–
Gaean series
  1982   *Titan*
  1983   *Wizard*
  1984   *Demon*

JULES VERNE (1828–1905)

Verne is regarded as one of science fiction's founding fathers, though he never did much with his ideas except have his characters travel. Almost all of Verne's stories are voyages—in submarines, in balloons, in airships, or *Around the World in Eighty Days*. Possibly because of the translations, Verne's works are slow going for most modern readers, many of whom are disappointed by the books' lack of plot. (Virtually everything anyone remembers about *Twenty Thousand Leagues Under the Sea* comes from the Walt Disney movie; in the book, Nemo's origin is never explained, and everyone just travels around under the ocean looking at wondrous things.)

The passage of time has outdated most of Verne's books—it's hard to consider an account of travel in a balloon as science fiction. Many of his books have been published in paperback, particularly as movie tie-ins. (Verne has proven popular with movie-makers since 1902, when George Melies made a short film taken from *From the Earth to the Moon* which is invariably shown in histories of moviemaking.) Only a sampling of his books is listed here (dates given are of original publication in France; there have been different translations of some).

Those wishing a complete bibliography of Verne can find it in *Jules Verne: a Biography* by Jean Jules-Verne (his grandson).

1864 *Journey to the Center of the Earth*
1865 *From the Earth to the Moon*
1870 *Around the Moon* (seq to *From the Earth to the Moon*)
1870 *Twenty Thousand Leagues Under the Sea*
1875 *Mysterious Island* (seq to *20,000 Leagues*)

JOAN D. VINGE

The ex-wife of Vernor Vinge, since remarried, she keeps the name under which her reputation was made.

1978 Hugo (Novelette): "Eyes of Amber"
1980 Hugo (Novel): *The Snow Queen*

1978 *Fireship* ss
1978 *The Outcasts of Heaven Belt*
1979 *Eyes of Amber and Other Stories* ss
1980 *The Snow Queen* hc/pb75¢–
1980 *Legacy* (in *Binary Star #4*)
1985 *Return to Oz* (movie novelization)

VERNOR (STEFFAN) VINGE (1944–)

Vinge is best known for his "Realtime" novels.

1969 *Grimm's World*
1976 *The Witling* 50¢–
1981 *True Names* (in *Binary Star #5*)
1984 *The Peace War*
1986 *Marooned in Realtime* 90¢–
1986 *Across Realtime* (*Peace War*, *Marooned in Realtime*)
1987 *Tatja Grimm's World* $1.00–

KURT VONNEGUT, JR. (1922–)

Vonnegut is a major American novelist who, in the early days of his career, wrote occasionally for science-fiction magazines. His early novels were originally published as science-fiction novels; some of his earlier books (including *The Sirens of Titan, Canary in a Cat House,* and *Mother Night*) were originally published in paperback.

One of Vonnegut's recurring characters, a hack science-fiction writer named Kilgore Trout, took on a life of his own when Vonnegut allowed Philip Jose Farmer to write a book, *Venus on the Half Shell,* under the Trout byline. Permission was later withdrawn, and later editions of that book are credited to Farmer.

1952   *Player Piano* (also in pb as *Utopia 14*)
1959   *The Sirens of Titan*
1961   *Canary in a Cat House*   ss
1962   *Mother Night*
1963   *Cat's Cradle*
1968   *Welcome to the Monkey House*   ss
1969   *Slaughterhouse-Five*
1976   *Slapstick*

KARL EDWARD WAGNER (1945–)

Wagner was the editor of Carcosa, which published large volumes of short fantasy fiction by Manly Wade Wellman, E. Hoffman Price, and Hugh B. Cave. Wagner edits the annual *Year's Best Horror Stories* for DAW Books.

1983   WFA (Novella): "Beyond All Measure"

1984   *In a Lonely Place*   ss   hc$5.00
1987   *Why Not You and I?*   ss   pb$1.00
Bran Mak Morn series
   1976   *Legion From the Shadows*
   1977   *Queen of the Night*
Conan series
   1979   *The Road of Kings*
Kane series
   1970   *Darkness Weaves with Many Shades*
   1973   *Death Angel's Shadow*   ss
   1975   *Bloodstone*
   1976   *Dark Crusade*
   1985   *The Book of Kane*   hc$5.00   hc$12.50

HOWARD WALDROP

   1980   Nebula (Novelette): "The Ugly Chickens"
   1981   WFA (Short Fiction): "The Ugly Chickens"

1974   *The Texas-Israeli War: 1999* (with Jake Saunders)
1984   *Them Bones*   pb only$1.00
1987   *All about Strange Monsters of the Recent Past*   (hc, 600 copies)   *$12.00*

DONALD WANDREI

Wandrei was the co-founder, with August Derleth, of Arkham House.

   1984   WFA Life Achievement Award

IAN WATSON (1943–)

1973   *The Embedding*
1975   *The Jonah Kit*
1977   *The Martian Inca*   pb50¢
1977   *Alien Embassy*
1978   *The Miracle Visitors*
1979   *The Very Slow Time Machine*   ss
1980   *The Gardens of Delight*

LAWRENCE WATT-EVANS *(Lawrence Watt Evans)*

Lawrence Watt Evans adopted his pseudonym at the suggestion of Lester del Rey, who bought his first novels. In addition to his science fiction, he has written knowledgeably and well about comic books, in particular, horror comic books.

   1988   Hugo (Short Story): "Why I Left Harry's All-Night Hamburgers"

1982   *The Cyborg and the Sorcerers* (6 printings by 1987)   *50¢–*
1984   *The Chromosomal Code*
1985   *The Misenchanted Sword*
1986   *Shining Steel*   pb90¢–
1987   *With a Single Spell*   90¢–
1987   *The Wizard and the War Machine* (seq to *Cyborg*)   *$1.00*

The Lords of Dus series
   1980   *The Lure of the Basilisk*   pb75¢–
   1981   *The Seven Altars of Dusarra*   pb75¢–
   1982   *The Sword of Bheuleu*   pb75¢–
   1984   *The Book of Silence*   pb75¢–

STANLEY G(RAUMAN) WEINBAUM (1900–1935)

Weinbaum's career was brilliant and tragically short. His science-fiction writing period lasted a scant two years. Although he had published a mainstream novel before turning to science fiction, all of his science-fiction books were published posthumously. He died of cancer.

1936   *Dawn of Flame and Other Stories*   ss
1939   *The New Adam*
1948   *The Black Flame*
1949   *A Martian Odyssey*   ss
1950   *The Dark Other*
1952   *The Red Peri*   ss
1962   *A Martian Odyssey and Other Classics of Science Fiction*   ss
1974   *The Best of Stanley G. Weinbaum*   ss
1975   *A Martian Odyssey and Other Science Fiction Tales*   ss (combines *Odyssey* and *Peri*)

MANLY WADE WELLMAN (1903–1986)

Manly Wade Wellman was best known for his stories of the wandering folksinger John, who strung his guitar with silver and fought evil things that live in the southern hills.

In *Sherlock Holmes's War of the Worlds,* written with his son, he teamed Sir Arthur Conan Doyle's two greatest creations (something Doyle had never done) and pitted Holmes and Professor Challenger against H. G. Wells' Martian invaders.

   1975   WFA (Single-Author Collection): *Worse Things Waiting*
   1980   WFA Life Achievement Award

1932   *The Invading Asteroid*
1940   *Dr. Cyclops* (as by Will Garth)
1946   *Romance in Black* (as by Gans T. Field)

1949 *Sojarr of Titan*
1950 *The Beasts From Beyond*
1951 *The Devil's Planet*
1957 *Twice in Time*
1959 *Giants From Eternity*
1959 *The Dark Destroyers*
1961 *Island in the Sky*
1968 *The Solar Invasion*
1973 *Worse Things Waiting* **ss**
1975 *Sherlock Holmes's War of the Worlds* (with Wade Wellman) **pb**
1977 *The Beyonders*
1987 *The Valley So Low: Southern Mountain Stories* **ss** (collected by Karl Edward Wagner) **hc$4.00**

John the Balladeer (Silver John) series
1963 *Who Fears the Devil?* **ss** **hc** (Arkham House)
1963 *Who Fears the Devil?* **ss** **pb75¢**
1979 *The Old Gods Waken*
1980 *After Dark* **hc75¢–**
1981 *The Lost and the Lurking*
1982 *The Hanging Stones*
1983 *What Dreams May Come*

H(ERBERT) G(EORGE) WELLS (1866–1946)

The bulk of Wells' best science fiction can be found in two volumes: *Seven Science Fiction Novels of H. G. Wells* and *The Short Stories of H. G. Wells*.

His 1898 novel, *The War of the Worlds,* was the basis for Orson Welles' 1938 radio broadcast, *Invasion From Mars,* which caused widespread panic when some listeners thought it was real. It has also been the inspiration for movies, comic books, and television series.

Other movies based on Wells' novels include *The Time Machine, The Island of Dr. Moreau* (one version was called *The Isle of Lost Souls*; another kept the title but was so changed that Ron Goulart was hired to write a novelization of the movie, since Wells' original no longer fit it), *The Invisible Man* (which also has inspired TV series, comic strips, and comic books), *The Food of the Gods,* and *The First Men in the Moon.*

Famous Fantastic Mysteries, October 1946, about 7″ × 9½″; cover by Lawrence (Stern Stevens) (1886–1960). Defects include frayed right side of cover. Listed as copyright 1946 by All-Fiction Field, Inc. Copyright 1946 by Popular Publications. Reprinted by permission of Blazing Publications, The Argosy Co.

Famous Fantastic Mysteries, July 1951, about 6½″ × 9″; cover by Lawrence (Stern Stevens) (1886–1960), illustrating *The War of the Worlds.* Listed as copyright 1951 by All-Fiction Field, Inc. Copyright 1951 by Popular Publications. Reprinted by permission of Blazing Publications, The Argosy Co.

1895   *The Time Machine*
1895   *The Wonderful Visit*
1895   *The Stolen Bacillus and Other Incidents*   ss
1896   *The Island of Dr. Moreau*
1897   *The Invisible Man*
1897   *Thirty Strange Stories*
1897   *The Plattner Story and Others*   ss
1898   *The War of the Worlds*
1899   *When the Sleeper Wakes*
1899   *Tales of Space and Time*   ss
1901   *The First Men in the Moon*
1903   *Twelve Stories and a Dream*   ss
1904   *The Food of the Gods*
1905   *A Modern Utopia*
1906   *In the Days of the Comet*
1908   *The War in the Air*
1911   *The Country of the Blind and Other Stories*
1914   *The World Set Free*
1923   *Men Like Gods*
1927   *The Short Stories of H. G. Wells*
1933   *The Shape of Things to Come*
1933   *Seven Science Fiction Novels of H. G. Wells*
1935   *Things to Come*
1936   *The Croquet Player: A Story*
1936   *The Man Who Could Work Miracles*   ss
1937   *Star-Begotten*
1937   *The Camford Visitation*
1939   *The Holy Terror*
1941   *All Aboard for Ararat*

MICHAEL WHELAN (1950–)

Robert Weinberg's *A Biographical Dictionary of Science Fiction and Fantasy Artists* says, "In little more than ten years, Whelan has risen to the position of one of the most dominant forces in modern science-fiction art."

His black-and-white work, if any, is not on the market. His paintings go for $1,500–$15,000.

1980   Hugo (Professional Artist)
1981   Hugo (Professional Artist)
1981   WFA (Artist)
1982   Hugo (Professional Artist)
1982   WFA (Artist)
1983   Hugo (Professional Artist)
1983   WFA (Artist)
1984   Hugo (Professional Artist)
1985   Hugo (Professional Artist)
1986   Hugo (Professional Artist)
1988   Hugo (Professional Artist)
1988   Hugo (Non-Fiction: *Michael Whelan's Works of Wonder*

1987   *Michael Whelan's Works of Wonder*

JAMES WHITE (1928–)

White is a British writer best known for his medical stories of the far future.

1957   *The Secret Visitors*
1962   *Second Ending*
1964   *The Escape Orbit*
1964   *Deadly Litter*   ss
1966   *The Watch Below*
1968   *All Judgment Fled*
1969   *The Aliens Among Us*   ss
1971   *Tomorrow Is Too Far*
1972   *Dark Inferno*
1972   *Lifeboat*
1974   *The Dream Milennium*
1977   *Monsters and Medics*   ss
1982   *Futures Past*   ss
Sector General series
   1962   *Hospital Station*
   1963   *Star Surgeon*
   1971   *Major Operation*   50¢–
   1979   *Ambulance Ship*
   1983   *Sector General* $1.00–

1984   *Star Healer*
1987   *Code Blue—Emergency!*   *$1.00*

TED (EDWARD) WHITE (1938–)

Ted White was a well-known science-fiction fan who became a writer and editor (he edited *Amazing Stories, Fantastic,* and, briefly, *Heavy Metal*).

   1968   Hugo Fan Writer

1964   *Invasion From 2500* (with Terry Carr, as "Norman Edwards")
1965   *Android Avenger*
1966   *Phoenix Prime*
1966   *Sorceress of Qar* (sequel to *Phoenix Prime*)
1967   *The Jewels of Elsewhen*
1967   *Secret of the Marauder Satellite*
1967   *Lost in Space* (with Dave Van Arnam, as "Ron Archer")
1968   *The Spawn of the Death Machine* (sequel to *Android Avenger*)
1968   *The Great Gold Steal*
1968   *Sideslip* (with Dave Van Arnam)
1969   *No Time Like Tomorrow*
1970   *By Furies Possessed*
1971   *Starwolf!*
1971   *Trouble on Project Ceres*
1977   *The Oz Encounter* (with Marv Wolfman)

T(ERENCE) H(ANBURY) WHITE (1906–1964)

White's *The Sword in the Stone* was made into an animated Walt Disney feature. *The Once and Future King,* which incorporates *The Sword in the Stone* and two other books about King Arthur, was made into the Broadway and movie musical *Camelot*.

1934   *Earth Stopped*
1935   *Gone to Ground* (sequel to *Earth Stopped*)
1938   *The Sword in the Stone*
1939   *The Witch in the Wood*
1940   *The Ill-Made Knight*
1946   *Mistress Masham's Repose*
1947   *The Elephant and the Kangaroo*

1957   *The Master*
1958   *The Once and Future King* (revision of *Sword in the Stone,*
       Witch in the Wood, and *Ill-Made Knight*)
1977   *The Book of Merlyn*

KATE WILHELM (1928–)

Wilhelm, one of the first science-fiction writers to use cloning as a subject for stories, has been integrating mainstream fiction with science fiction in her novels. She is married to Damon Knight.

1986   Nebula (Short Story): "The Planners"

1977   Hugo (Novel): *Where Late the Sweet Birds Sang*

1986   Nebula (Novelette): "The Girl Who Fell into the Sky"

1963   *The Mile-Long Spaceship*   ss
1965   *The Clone* (with Theodore L. Thomas)
1966   *The Nevermore Affair*
1967   *The Killer Thing*
1968   *THe Downstairs Room and Other Speculative Fiction*   ss
1969   *Let the Fire Fall*
1970   *The Year of the Cloud* (with Theodore L. Thomas)
1971   *Margaret and I*
1971   *Abyss: Two Novellas*   ss
1975   *The Infinity Box*   ss
1976   *Where Late the Sweet Birds Sang*
1976   *The Clewiston Test*
1978   *Somerset Dreams and Other Fictions*   ss

JACK WILLIAMSON *(John Stewart Williamson)* (1908–)

In 1988, *Amazing Stories* featured Jack Williamson's 60th-anniversary story; his is one of the longest active careers as a science fiction writer on record. (His first story was "The Metal Man"; his anniversary story was called "The Mental Man.")

His *Beyond Mars* comic strip with Lee Elias ran for three years in *The New York Daily News*. That strip has been collected in its entirety in two black-and-white trade paperbacks from Blackthorne Publishing. He also has written books on teaching science fiction and an autobiography (the latter won a Hugo).

His "Seetee" stories are sometimes called the "Anti-Matter" series. "Seetee" is derived from contra-terrene (CT = Seetee), but that terminology gave way to "anti-matter."

1975   SFWA Grand Master

1985   Hugo (Non-Fiction Book): *Wonder's Child: My Life in Science Fiction*

1948   *Darker Than You Think*
1949   *The Humanoids*
1950   *The Green Girl*
1951   *Dragon's Island*
1952   *The Legion of Time*   ss
1952   *After World's End*
1955   *Dome Around America*
1955   *Star Bridge* (with James Gunn)
1962   *The Trial of Terra*
1964   *Golden Blood*
1965   *The Reign of Wizardry*
1967   *Bright New Universe*
1968   *Trapped in Space*   juv
1969   *The Pandora Effect*   ss
1971   *People Machines*   ss
1972   *The Moon Children*
1975   *The Early Williamson*
1975   *The Power of Blackness*
1975   *The Farthest Star* (with Frederik Pohl)
1978   *The Best of Jack Williamson*   ss
1980   *The Humanoid Touch* (seq to *The Humanoids*)
1981   *Brother to Demons, Brother to Gods*
1982   *Manseed*
1986   *Firechild* $1.25–$2.00
Seetee (Anti-Matter) series (originally as by "Will Stewart")
   1950   *Seetee Shock*
   1951   *Seetee Ship*
   Seetee Ship/Seetee Shock (omnibus)
Legion of Space series
   1947   *The Legion of Space*
   1950   *The Cometeers*

1951   *One Against the Legion*
1980   *Three From the Legion* (omnibus)
Starchild series (with Frederik Pohl)
1964   *The Reefs of Space*
1965   *Starchild*
1969   *Rogue Star*
1977   *The Starchild Trilogy* (omnibus of all three novels)
Undersea series (juveniles, with Frederik Pohl)
1954   *Undersea Quest*
1955   *Undersea Fleet*
1958   *Undersea City*

CONNIE WILLIS

1982   Nebula (Novelette): "Fire Watch"

1982   Nebula (Short Story): "A Letter From the Clearys"

1983   Hugo (Novelette): "Fire Watch"

1985   *Fire Watch*   ss
1987   *Lincoln's Dreams*   hc*$4.00*

F. PAUL WILSON (1946–)

Wilson is a medical doctor best known for his horror-fantasy novels.
His *The Keep* was made into a movie.

1976   *Healer*
1978   *Wheels Within Wheels*
1979   *The Tery* (in *Binary Star #2*)
1981   *The Keep*
1980   *An Enemy of the State*
1984   *The Tomb*   hc*$5.00*   pb*$1.00*
1986   *The Touch*   hc*$5.00*   pb*$1.00*

GAHAN WILSON

In addition to collections of his own stories and cartoons, Gahan Wilson has also edited anthologies of horror stories. He has also written and illustrated mystery novels, but this list is restricted to his fantasy cartoons and stories.

The price his cartoons bring is very dependent on the subject; the better the joke, the higher the price. His black-and-white cartoons bring $150–$300; his color cartoons bring $1,000.

1981   WFA (Special Convention Award)

1965   *Gahan Wilson's Graveside Manner* cartoons
1967   *The Man in the Cannibal Pot* cartoons
I Paint What I See cartoons
1973   *Playboy's Gahan Wilson*
1975   *Gahan Wilson's Cracked Cosmos* cartoons   ss
1975   *The Weird World of Gahan Wilson* cartoons
1978   *". . . And Then We'll Get Him!"* cartoons
1979   *Nuts* cartoons
1982   *Is Nothing Sacred?* cartoons

RICHARD WILSON (1920–1987)

A member of the Futurians, he wrote more than 100 published stories while pursuing a career in journalism.

1968   Nebula (Novelette): "Mother to the World"

1955   *The Girls From Planet Five*
1957   *Those Idiots From Earth*   ss
1960   *And Then the Town Took Off*
1960   *30-Day Wonder*
1962   *Time Out for Tomorrow*   ss

GENE WOLFE (1931–)

Wolfe is a mechanical engineer who is regarded—by an ever-increasing number of people—as one of the best writers in the field. He has an offbeat sense of humor, indicated by his trilogy of related stories, "The Island of Doctor Death and Other Stories," "The Death of Doctor Island," and "The Doctor of Death Island." As a topper, he published a collection called *The Island of Doctor Death and Other Stories and Other Stories*.

1973   Nebula (Novella): "The Death of Doctor Island"
1981   Nebula (Novel): *The Claw of the Conciliator*
1981   WFA (Novel): *The Shadow of the Torturer*

1970 *Operation ARES*
1972 *The Fifth Head of Cerberus* ss
1976 *The Devil in a Forest* juv
1980 *The Claw of the Conciliator*
1980 *The Island of Doctor Death and Other Stories and Other Stories* ss
Book of the Sun series
  1980 *The Shadow of the Torturer* 75¢–

DONALD A(LLEN) WOLLHEIM (1914–)

Wollheim's biggest contribution to the field has been as an editor—of magazines (including *Stirring Science Stories* and *Avon Fantasy Reader*), of early science-fiction anthologies (*The Pocket Book of Science Fiction*), and of books for Avon, Ace, and for his own publishing company, DAW Books.

Currently, in addition to heading DAW, he edits the long-running *Annual World's Best SF*. In 1971, he wrote a memoir, *The Universe Makers*.

  1975 Hugo (Special Award)

1954 *The Secret of Saturn's Rings*
1955 *Secret of the Martian Moons*
1956 *One Against the Moon*
1957 *Across Time* (as by David Grinnell)
1958 *Edge of Time* (as by David Grinnell)
1959 *The Martian Missile* (as by David Grinnell)
1959 *Secret of the Ninth Planet*
1969 *Two Dozen Dragon's Eggs* ss pb only
1970 *To Venus! To Venus!* (as by David Grinnell)
Ajax Calkins series (as by David Grinnell)
  1962 *Destiny's Orbit*
  1967 *Destination: Saturn* (with Lin Carter)
Mike Mars series juv
  1961 *Mike Mars, Astronaut*
  1961 *Mike Mars Flies the X-15*
  1961 *Mike Mars at Cape Canaveral*
  1961 *Mike Mars in Orbit*
  1962 *Mike Mars Flies the Dyna-Soar*

1962   *Mike Mars, South Pole Spaceman*
1963   *Mike Mars and the Mystery Satellite*
1964   *Mike Mars Around the Moon*

PHILIP (GORDON) WYLIE (1902–1971)

Wylie was a mainstream novelist best known for scandalous (at the time) books which accused the United States of being mother-dominated. His primary contributions to the science-fiction field—with which he was allied all his life; he boasted of being a charter subscriber to *Amazing Stories*—were *Gladiator,* said to be part of the inspiration for the creation of Superman by Cleveland high-school students Jerome Siegel and Joseph Shuster, and his doomsday books with Edwin Balmer. *When Worlds Collide* was made into a comic strip (it ended with the destruction of Earth) and a well-received George Pal movie. The lesser-known sequel has never been dramatized in comics or on film.

1930   *Gladiator*
1931   *The Murderer Invisible*
1933   *When Worlds Collide* (with Edwin Balmer)
1934   *After Worlds Collide* (with Edwin Balmer)
1951   *The Disappearance*
1955   *The Answer*
1971   *Los Angeles:* A.D. *2017*
1972   *The End of the Dream*

JOHN WYNDHAM *(John Wyndham Parkes Lucas Beynon Harris)* (1903–1969)

This multi-named author was frequently published in science-fiction magazines of the 1930s under the name of John Beynon. Around 1950, he decided to change his approach and adopted a new byline to set his new work apart from his old. He started a trend of British writers dealing with various worldwide catastrophes with his first books under the Wyndham name, all of which were published by Ballantine. *The Day of the Triffids* was made into a movie (*The Revolt of the Triffids*) and, more recently, into a television serial. *The Midwich Cuckoos* became the movie *Village of the Damned,* which spawned a sequel called *Children of the Damned.*

One of his books, *The Outward Urge,* was published as if it were a collaborative effort, but both names were pen names of Harris.

1935   *The Secret People* (as John Beynon, reprinted as by Wyndham)
1936   *Planet Plane* (as John Beynon, revised as *Stowaway to Mars*)
1951   *The Day of the Triffids* (also as *Revolt of the Triffids*)
1953   *Out of the Deeps*
1954   *Jizzle* ss
1955   *Re-Birth*
1956   *Tales of Gooseflesh and Laughter* ss
1956   *The Seeds of Time* ss
1957   *The Midwich Cuckoos*
1959   *The Outward Urge* ss (as by John Wyndham and Lucas Parkes)
1960   *Trouble with Lichen*
1961   *Consider Her Ways and Others* ss
1961   *The Infinite Moment*
1968   *Chocky*
1973   *Wanderers of Time*
1973   *Sleepers of Mars* ss

CHELSEA QUINN YARBRO (1942–)

Best-known for her historical fantasies about the vampire Count St. Germaine, Yarbro has also written science fiction and mysteries, often incorporating into them her love for and knowledge of opera.

1976   *Time of the Four Horsemen*
1978   *False Dawn*
1978   *Cautionary Tales* ss
1980   *Dead and Buried* (movie novelization)
1980   *Ariosto*
1983   *The Godforsaken*
1983   *Hyacinths*
1984   *Nomads*
1984   *Signs and Portents* ss *$1.00*
1985   *A Mortal Glamour*
1985   *To the High Redoubt*
1987   *A Flame in Byzantium*

St. Germaine series

1978   *Hotel Transylvania: A Novel of Forbidden Love*
1979   *The Palace*
1979   *Blood Games*
1981   *Path of the Eclipse*
1982   *Tempting Fate*   hc$5.00   pb$1.00
1983   *The Saint-Germain Chronicles*   ss

TIMOTHY ZAHN

1984   Hugo (Novella): "Cascade Point"

1985   *Spinneret*   pb95¢–

ROGER ZELAZNY (1937–)

A former civil servant in Cleveland, Zelazny has been a full-time writer for many years now. In addition to his science fiction, he has published some poetry.

A 1980 book on Zelazny is Joseph L. Sanders' *Roger Zelazny: A Primary and Secondary Bibliography.*

1965   Nebula (Novella): "He Who Shapes"

1965   Nebula (Novelette): "The Doors of His Face, the Lamps of His Mouth"

1966   Hugo (Novel): . . . *And Call Me Conrad* (aka *This Immortal*)

1968   Hugo (Novel): *Lord of Light*

1975   Nebula (Novella): "Home Is the Hangman"

1976   Hugo (Novella): "Home Is the Hangman"

1982   Hugo (Novelette): "Unicorn Variation"

1986   Hugo (Novella): "24 Views of Mount Fuji, by Hokusai"

1987   Hugo (Novelette): "Permafrost"

1966   *This Immortal*
1966   *The Dream Master*   50¢–
1967   *Four for Tomorrow*   ss
1967   *Lord of Light*
1969   *Isle of the Dead*

1969   *Creatures of Light and Darkness*
1969   *Damnation Alley*
1971   *The Doors of His Face, The Lamps of His Mouth, and Other Stories* ss
1971   *Jack of Shadows*
1973   *Today We Choose Faces*
1973   *To Die in Italbar*
1976   *Bridge of Ashes*
1976   *Deus Irae* (with Philip K. Dick)
1976   *My Name Is Legion* ss
1976   *Doorways in the Sand*
1978   *The Illustrated Roger Zelazny*   **trade pb$2.00**
1979   *Roadmarks*
1980   *Changeling*
1980   *The Last Defender of Camelot* ss
1981   *The Changing Land*   **hc$7.50   pb$1.00**
1981   *Madwand* (seq to *Changeling*)   **hc$9.00**
1982   *Dilvish, the Damned* ss
1982   *Coils* (with Fred Saberhagen)   **trade pb, book club$2.00**
1982   *Eye of Cat*
1983   *Unicorn Variations* ss   **$1.00–**
1987   *A Dark Traveling*   **$4.00**
Amber series
  1970   *Nine Princes in Amber*
  1972   *The Guns of Avalon*
  1975   *Sign of the Unicorn*
  1976   *The Hand of Oberon*
  1978   *The Courts of Chaos*
  1979   *The Chronicles of Amber Volume I* (book-club omnibus, *Princes, Guns*)   **$2.00**
  1979   *The Chronicles of Amber Volume II* (book club, *Sign, Hand, Courts*)   **$2.00**
  1985   *Trumps of Doom*
  1986   *Blood of Amber*   **$1.25–**
  1987   *Sign of Chaos*   **hc$5.00**

American Fiction Magazines

One of the best and simplest ways to get a feel for what's going on in science fiction and fantasy today is to buy current issues of science-fiction and fantasy magazines for a few months. It's a fast way to become familiar with themes in the field, writers of interest, hot topics of discussion, and (via letters columns) popular opinions.

American science-fiction and fantasy magazines available on many newsstands today and by subscription (for current subscription rates, send a self-addressed stamped envelope to the addresses given) are the following:

Aboriginal Science Fiction, P.O. Box 2449, Woburn, Massachusetts 01888. Published bi-monthly, bedsheet size.

Amazing Stories, TSR, Inc., P.O. Box 72089, Chicago, Illinois 60690. Published bi-monthly, digest size.

Analog Science Fiction/Science Fact, P.O. Box 1936, Marion, Ohio 43306. Published 13 times a year, digest size.

Isaac Asimov's Science Fiction Magazine, P.O. Box 1933, Marion, Ohio 43306. Published 13 times a year, digest size.

The Magazine of Fantasy and Science Fiction, Box 56, Cornwall, Connecticut 06753. Monthly, digest size.

Rod Serling's The Twilight Zone Magazine, P.O. Box 252, Mount Morris, Illinois 60154-9952. Bi-monthly, $8\frac{1}{2}'' \times 11''$.

Weird Tales, Terminus Publishing Company, P.O. Box 13418, Philadelphia, Pennsylvania 19101-3418. Published quarterly, pulp size.

Our coverage is limited to American magazines confining themselves to science-fiction or fantasy contents. Such early publications as *Argosy* and such recent publications as *Playboy* contain some fantasy and science-fiction material, but they are not, properly speaking, fantasy or science-fiction magazines and so are not included in this listing. In determining publications for inclusion, we consider back-up features. *Doc Savage* and *The Shadow,* for example, had mystery and crime-story back-ups, not science fiction and fantasy fiction. We are focusing on magazines available from newsstands and bookstores. (In a field with many amateur publishers, many amateur magazines have appeared over the years.)

Perhaps the collector's bargain today is the back-issue magazine in this field. Circulation was initially small on many publications, pulp paper degraded rapidly, covers seemed destined to fall from spines; outweighing these shortcomings is the fact that stories which today are regarded as classics originated in the magazines. For decades, virtually every great story, from novels to short stories, first appeared in the magazines. Yet, while comic-book prices have escalated wildly in the past 20 years—with many now bringing prices far in excess of a thousand dollars—magazine prices in science fiction and fantasy remain low.

One force at work has been back-issue retailers (collectors themselves) who have, in some cases, deliberately kept prices low. There have even been fears that a price guide will force prices artificially high. However, this edition—while our first and one which is *not* based on earlier editions—is actually the *third* edition of *The Official Price Guide to Science Fiction and Fantasy Collectibles*. A price guide has existed, and it has not driven prices beyond the reach of the average collector.

What has not been readily available to beginning collectors in the past was a list indicating the scope of what science-fiction and fantasy magazines could be collected. With some magazines using volume-and-number indications and others listing dates and a few others using whole numbers, collecting American magazines in the field has been confusing. And that's without even getting into the complexities of title changes.

Retailers most commonly list these magazines by date, and that is how we have listed them here. When necessary, we have added numbering information.

We have attempted to give some general information about the size of the science-fiction and fantasy magazines included in this list, following the designations in common usage among collectors.

A "bedsheet" magazine is one which is roughly the dimensions of a sheet of typing paper ($8\frac{1}{2}$ " x 11 "). Some bedsheet issues are a bit larger (9 " x 12 "). Generally, a bedsheet issue published before 1955 is on pulpwood paper; after that date, it may be on pulpwood paper, book paper, or even coated stock.

A "pulp" magazine is generally considered to be about 7″ x 9″ (about the same as a comic book). Again, this is an imprecise bit of terminology since a bedsheet magazine may be printed on pulp paper and a magazine designated as pulp size can be printed on excellent paper—as is the current incarnation of *Weird Tales,* for example.

A "digest" magazine is a magazine of about the dimensions of *Reader's Digest*—around 5¼″ x 7½″. Most of the science-fiction and fantasy magazines of the last 30 years have been published in this format.

A "paperback" magazine is one which is published in the format of a mass-market paperback book. There have been several attempts to publish periodicals in paperback format, a few of which are included here.

We are not including among magazines series of anthologies which present original fiction (Harry Harrison's *Nova* series, Damon Knight's *Orbit,* Terry Carr's *Universe,* Frederik Pohl's *Star Science Fiction Stories,* etc.). We are including only the ones which are published as magazines in paperback form—on a schedule, with departments, columns, continuing features, etc. (see *Destinies, New Destinies, Quark,* and *Weird Heroes,* for examples).

It is generally agreed that two publications led the way for mass-market fantasy and science fiction. *Weird Tales* was the first long-running magazine solely devoted to fantasy and was founded in 1923. *Amazing Stories,* founded by Hugo Gernsback in 1926, was the first magazine solely devoted to stories of what Gernsback then called "scientifiction." Both began as pulp magazines.

A slash mark (/) indicates the issue contains both indicated designations. Feb/Mar means the issue is dated February–March. #11/12 means the issue is designated as combining issues #11 and #12.

All prices are the averages of the prices *asked for the item by retailers selling it in "good" condition.* This means it is an average used copy, but nothing is missing. The magazine may be slightly dirtied and there may be minor tears. If glue was used in the binding process, it may be brittle. There may be *minor* tape repairs on pulp magazines—though not something as extreme as the entire front cover being taped on—and the repair is a definite defect.

If the magazine in question is in "very good" condition, retailers would ask about twice the price listed here. A "very good" copy will have no tape repairs and it will be clean. The cover may be loose, the spine on a pulp magazine may have considerable flaking, and there may be some wrinkling or slight creasing. Pages may have darkened, it may have minor marking, and it is a read copy.

If the magazine is in "fine" condition, retailers would ask about three times the price listed here. A "fine" issue is a very nice-looking item. It may have been read more than once, but there are no creases or writing (other than arrival date) on the cover. There may be some small flaking of the spine, but the cover is tight. There may be slight page darkening.

If the magazine is in "mint" condition, retailers would ask about four times the price listed here. This condition is about as good as it gets. The publication should look as good as you would find it if you bought it new today. It is entirely undamaged, although covers and untrimmed pulp pages may be slightly bent at the edges. There should be no spine damage. They may have pencilled arrival dates on the cover or stamped arrival dates on the back cover, and pre–1950s magazines may have slight color fading.

There are certain magazine contributors whose work increases the value of the magazine in which it is found. We have noted presence of their work by initials, as follows:

ERB: Edgar Rice Burroughs
JV: Jack Vance
B: Margaret Brundage (cover artist)
LRH: L. Ron Hubbard
PKD: Philip K. Dick
RAH: Robert A. Heinlein
REH: Robert E. Howard
SK: Stephen King

ABORIGINAL SF (1986–)

This magazine is named for the idea that human beings are the aborigines of planet Earth. The first three issues were tabloid size; with the fourth issue, it changed to bedsheet size.

1986 Oct Dec *50¢*
1987 Feb/Mar May/Jun Jul/Aug Sep/Oct Nov/Dec *50¢*

AIR WONDER STORIES (see *Wonder Stories*)

AMAZING DETECTIVE TALES (see *Scientific Detective Monthly*)

AMAZING STORIES/AMAZING SCIENCE FICTION (1926–)

The oldest science-fiction magazine in the world was founded in 1926 by Hugo Gernsback after he noted the popularity of the science-fiction stories he frequently published in his science and electronics magazines. It began in an 8½″ × 11″ format and continued that way until 1933, when it became a standard-sized (7″ x 10″) pulp magazine. Gernsback eventually lost the magazine in one of his business setbacks and went on to create other publications (see *Wonder Stories*) while *Amazing* continued with a series of different publishers and editors.

The magazine was edited for several years by T. O'Conor Sloane, an elderly and idiosyncratic man who frequently derided his readers for actually believing that space travel was possible.

From the late thirties through the war years and for a couple of years beyond, the magazine was edited for the Ziff-Davis publishing concern by Raymond A. Palmer, one of the most colorful and controversial editors in science-fiction. Palmer turned the magazine into an adventure-oriented publication largely indistinguishable from other magazines in the Ziff-Davis line. Many, if not most, of the stories were written by a stable of writers who also contributed to the Z-D mystery, adventure, and western pulp magazines, sometimes using the same plot for two or more publications, resulting in several science-fiction stories which were basically westerns set in a frontier town on Mars. Some were under contract to supply Z-D with a specific number of words per month for the various magazines, writing under a slew of pseudonyms, including "house names"—a pseudonym belonging to the publisher and used on stories by a number of different writers. If author A had two stories in the same issue, the editor could put a house name, such as "Alexander Blade," on one of them. This was done because it was felt readers did not like to think that the same author had two stories in the same issue; in fact, all the stories in an issue could be, and often were, by the same man using different names. Frequent contributors, who lived in the Chicago area near the magazine's editorial offices, included William P. McGivern, Robert

Bloch, and Rog Phillips (whose lesser-known real name was Roger P. Graham). Material from freelancers filled the few remaining holes in the magazines. *Amazing Stories* was able to survive the paper shortages of World War II and was generally successful.

With the publication of the March 1945 issue of *Amazing Stories,* Palmer became the most controversial editor the field has ever known. He published a story by Richard S. Shaver titled "I Remember Lemuria!" In this story, which Palmer later said he rewrote entirely from Shaver's rambling manuscript after another editor had tossed it in a wastebasket, Shaver postulated that the human race is menaced by "deros" (detrimental robots) which dwell in the caves and mines of this planet. Shaver apparently believed this was true and so did many of the magazine's readers; the circulation of *Amazing* soared to heights it had never attained before and which it has never reached since. The science-fiction fans were appalled.

Palmer went on to found his own magazines (see *Other Worlds*) which, along with some good fiction, pandered to the believers in various occult and idiosyncratic phenomena, including flying saucers, which Palmer helped popularize.

Since Palmer, *Amazing* has been edited by, among others, William L. Hamling, Howard Browne, Norman Lobsenz, Cele Goldsmith, Harry Harrison, Barry N. Malzberg, Ted White, George Scithers, and Patrick L. Price. *Amazing Stories* survived Palmer, as it had survived the Depression and World War II, and switched from the then-dying pulp format into a more popular digest-size format in 1953. Over the next 35 years, the magazine has changed editors and publishers several times (it currently is published by TSR, Inc., which is primarily known for its role-playing games, such as Dungeons and Dragons). Even the title was changed—to *Amazing Science Fiction*. In March 1986, after the magazine's original title was licensed for a TV series produced by Steven Spielberg, the magazine returned to its original title: *Amazing Stories*.

Stories by Edgar Rice Burroughs appeared in the issues for February 1927; January, March, June, July, August, and November 1941; February, March, and April 1942; February 1943; April 1961; November 1963; January 1964.

1926 Apr
1926 May Jun Jul Aug Sep Oct Nov Dec *$17.50*

1927   Jan Mar Apr May Jun Jul Aug Oct Nov Dec   *$12.50*
1927   Feb (ERB: "The Land That Time Forgot")   *$17.50*
1927   Sep (HPL: "The Colour Out of Space")   *$17.50*
1928   Jan Feb Mar Apr May Jun Jul Sep Oct Nov Dec   *$7.50*
1928   Aug (first Buck Rogers: "Armageddon—2419 A.D.")   *$62.50*
1929   Jan Feb Apr May Jun Jul Aug Sep Oct Nov Dec   *$6.00*
1929   Mar (second Buck Rogers: "The Airlords of Han")   *$27.50*
1930   Jan Feb Mar Apr May Jun Jul Aug Sep Oct Nov Dec   *$5.00*
1931   Jan Feb Mar Apr May Jun Jul Aug Sep Oct Nov Dec   *$5.00*
1932   Jan Feb Mar Apr May Jun Jul Aug Sep Oct Nov Dec   *$4.50*
1933   Jan Feb Mar Apr May Jun Jul Aug/Sep Oct Nov Dec   *$4.50*
1934   Jan Feb Mar Apr May Jun Jul Aug Sep Oct Nov Dec   *$4.00*
1935   Jan Feb Mar Apr May Jun Jul Aug Oct Dec   *$4.00*
1936   Feb Apr Jun Aug Oct Dec   *$3.75*
1937   Feb Apr Jun Aug Oct Dec   *$3.75*
1938   Feb Apr Jun Aug Oct Nov Dec   *$3.50*
1939   Jan Feb Mar Apr May Jun Jul Aug Sep Oct Nov Dec   *$3.50*
1940   Jan Feb Mar Apr May Jun Jul Aug Sep Oct Nov Dec   *$3.00*
1941   Feb Apr May Jul Sep Nov Dec   *$3.00*
1941   Jan (ERB: "John Carter and the Giant of Mars")   *$10.00*
1941   Mar (ERB: "The City of Mummies")   *$10.00*
1941   Jun (ERB: "Black Pirates of Barsoom")   *$10.00*
1941   Aug (ERB: "Yellow Men of Mars")   *$10.00*
1941   Oct (ERB: "Invisible Men of Mars")   *$9.00*
1942   Jan May Jun Jul Aug Sep Oct Nov Dec   *$2.75*
1942   Feb (ERB: "The Return to Pellucidar")   *$8.00*
1942   Mar (ERB: "Men of the Bronze Age")   *$8.00*
1942   Apr (ERB: "Tiger Girl")   *$10.00*
1943   Jan Mar Apr May Jun Jul Aug Sep Nov   *$2.75*
1943   Feb (ERB: "Skeleton Men of Jupiter")   *$8.00*
1944   Jan Mar May Sep Dec   *$2.50*
1945   Mar Jun Sep Dec   *$2.50*
1946   Feb May Jun Jul Aug Sep Oct Nov Dec   *$2.00*
1947   Jan Feb Mar Apr May Jun Jul Aug Sep Oct Nov Dec   *$2.00*
1948   Jan Feb Mar Apr May Jun Jul Aug Sep Oct Nov Dec   *$1.75*
1949   Jan Feb Mar Apr May Jun Jul Aug Sep Oct Nov Dec   *$1.75*
1950   Jan Feb Mar Apr May Jun Jul Aug Sep Oct Nov Dec   *$1.50*
1951   Jan Feb Mar May Jun Jul Aug Sep Oct Nov Dec   *$1.50*
1951   Apr (25th anniversary special)   *$2.00*

1952   Jan Feb Mar Apr May Jun Jul Aug Sep Oct Nov Dec   *$1.50*
1953   Jan Feb Mar Jun/Jul Oct/Nov   *$1.50*
1953   Apr/MayRAH Aug/SepPKD   *$3.00*
1953/54   Dec/JanPKD   *$3.00*
1954   Mar Sep Nov   *90¢*
1954   MayPKD JulPKD   *$1.80*
1955   Jan Mar May Jul Sep Nov Dec   *90¢*
1956   Jan Feb Mar May Jun Jul Aug Sep Oct Nov Dec   *75¢*
1956   AprRAH   *$1.50*
1957   Jan Feb Mar Apr May Jun Jul Aug Sep Oct Nov Dec   *75¢*
1958   Jan Feb Mar   *75¢*
(becomes *Amazing Science Fiction*)
1958   Apr   *75¢*
(becomes *Amazing Science Fiction Stories*)
1958   May Jun Jul Sep Oct Nov Dec   *75¢*

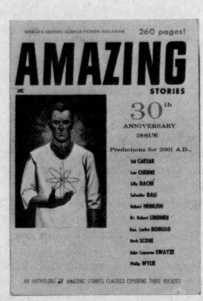

Amazing Stories, April 1956, about 5½″ × 7½″; cover by Edward (I.) Valigursky (1926–). The all-star issue celebrates the 30th anniversary of the longest-running science-fiction magazine. Copyright 1956 by Ziff-Davis Publishing Company. "Amazing" is a registered trademark of TSR, Inc. Copyright 1989 TSR, Inc. All rights reserved.

NOW IN ITS **30TH** STRAIGHT YEAR!

AMAZING STORIES

MAY 35¢

THE GIRL WHO HATED AIR by Milton Lesser

Amazing Stories, May 1956, about 5½″ × 7½″; cover by Edward (I.) Valigursky (1926–). The cover repeats the theme so common to science-fiction magazines of that era—a spaceman toting a scantily clad, well-built woman. Copyright 1956 by Ziff-Davis Publishing Company. "Amazing" is a registered trademark of TSR, Inc. Copyright 1989 TSR, Inc. All rights reserved.

1958   AugJV *$1.50*
1959   Jan Feb Mar Apr May Jun Jul Aug Sep Oct Nov Dec   *75¢*
1960   Jan Feb Mar Apr May Jun Jul Aug Sep   *75¢*
(becomes *Amazing Stories*)
1960   Oct Nov Dec   *75¢*
1961   Jan Feb Mar May Jun Jul Aug Sep Nov Dec   *65¢*
1961   Apr (35th anniversary special; ERB reprint)   *$2.50*
1961   OctJV *$1.25*
1962   Jan Feb Mar Apr May Jun Jul Sep Oct Nov Dec   *65¢*
1962   AugJV *$1.25*
1963   Jan Feb Mar Apr May Jun Jul Aug Sep Dec   *65¢*
1963   OctPKD DecPKD   *$1.25*
1963   NovPKD (ERB: "Savage Pellucidar")   *$1.25*
1964   Feb Mar Apr May Jun Aug Sep Oct Nov Dec   *65¢*
1964   Jan (ERB reprint: "John Carter and the Giant of Mars")   *$1.25*

1964   JulPKD   *$1.25*
1965   Jan Feb Mar Apr May Jun Aug Oct Dec   *65¢*
1966   Feb Apr Jun Aug Oct Dec   *65¢*
1967   Feb Apr Jun Aug Oct Dec   *65¢*
1968   Feb Jun Jul Sep Nov   *65¢*
1969   Jan Mar May Jul Sep Nov   *65¢*
1970   Jan Mar May Jul Sep Nov   *65¢*
1971   Jan Mar May Jul Sep Nov   *65¢*
1972   Jan Mar May Jul Sep Nov   *65¢*
1973   Jan Mar Jun Aug Oct Dec   *65¢*
1974   Feb Apr Jun Aug Oct Dec   *65¢*
1975   Mar May Jul Sep Nov   *65¢*
1976   Jan Mar Jun Sep Dec   *65¢*
1977   Mar Jul Oct   *65¢*
1978   Jan May Aug Nov   *65¢*
1979   Feb May Aug Nov   *65¢*
1980   Feb May Aug Nov   *65¢*
1981   Jan Mar May Jul Sep Nov   *65¢*
1982   Mar Jun Sep Nov   *50¢*
1983   Jan Mar May Jul Sep Nov   *50¢*
1984   Jan Mar May Jul Sep Nov   *50¢*
1985   Jan Mar May Jul Sep Nov   *50¢*
1986   Jan   *50¢*
(becomes *Amazing Stories*)
1986   Mar May Jul Sep Nov   *50¢*
1987   Jan Mar May Jul Sep Nov   *50¢*

AMAZING STORIES ANNUAL (1927)

1927   (ERB: "The Master Mind of Mars")   *$17.50*

AMAZING STORIES QUARTERLY (1928–1934)

1928   Win   *$17.50*
1928   Spr(Apr) Sum(Jul) Fal(Oct)   *$10.00*
1929   Win(Jan) Spr(Apr) Sum(Jul) Fal(Oct)   *$7.50*
1930   Win(Jan) Spr(Apr) Sum(Jul) Fal(Oct)   *$7.50*
1931   Win(Jan) Spr)Apr) Sum(Jul) Fal(Oct)   *$7.50*
1932   Win(Jan) Spr/Sum(Apr) Fal/Win(Sep)   *$7.50*

1933   Spr/Sum Win *$7.50*
1934   Fal *$7.50*

AMAZING STORIES SCIENCE FICTION NOVEL (1957)

There was only one issue of this projected series: an adaptation by the prolific Henry Slesar of a movie, *Twenty Million Miles to Earth*.
1957   no date *65¢*

A. MERRITT FANTASY (1949–1950)

Abraham Merritt was an editor of the long-running Sunday supplement magazine *American Weekly* and a popular writer of lush fantastic-adventure novels (*The Moon Pool, The Ship of Ishtar, The Metal Monster, Seven Footprints to Satan,* and *Burn, Witch, Burn!* among them) whose name was used, six years after his death, in the title of a fantasy-adventure pulp magazine. He holds the distinction of being the first English-language fantasy writer to have a magazine named for him, albeit posthumously. Although the mystery fiction magazine field currently has publications named for Ellery Queen and Alfred Hitchcock and has had periodicals named for Rex Stout, Ed McBain, and Craig Rice, the fantasy/science-fiction field has tended toward greater modesty. In addition to Merritt, only ''Vargo Statten'' (a pseudonym of John Russell Fearn) and Isaac Asimov have had English-language newsstand periodicals named for them. Asimov leads in sheer numbers, as he is wont to do, by having two new-fiction magazines and a series of reprint compilations which bear his name (see *Asimov's SF Adventure Magazine, Isaac Asimov's Science Fiction Magazine, Isaac Asimov's SF Anthology*).

1949   Dec *$4.00*
1950   Feb Apr Jul Oct *$3.00*

ANALOG (See *Astounding Stories*)

ANALOG ANNUAL (1976)

The magazine was a one-shot paperback book, published by Pyramid and edited by Ben Bova, which came complete with an editorial introduction, illustrations, stories, and an article.

1976 *$1.00*

ANALOG YEARBOOK (1978–1981)

This was another attempt (following *Analog Annual*) to provide a 13th issue of *Analog* each year. The first is a 5¼″ x 8¼″ trade paperback, published by Baronet. Again edited by Bova, it had an editorial, stories, articles, and illustrations.

The second was a standard-size, mass-market paperback, published by Ace Books and edited by Stanley Schmidt (who acknowledged that most of the editing had been done by Bova). Although it was completed in 1978, the book was not published until 1981. It was published as ''An Analog Book'' and belonged to a series which had begun in 1979 with two novels selected by Bova: *Capitol* by Orson Scott Card and *Maxwell's Demons* by Bova himself.

1978   #1   75¢
1981   #2   75¢

ANALOG ANTHOLOGIES (1981–1984)

These thick compilations of reprints from the magazine appeared both as newsstand publications and as hardcover books.

1981   #1   *$1.00*
1982   #2 #3   *$1.00*
1983   #4 Spr Sum Win   *$1.00*
1984   Sum Win   *$1.00*

ARGOSY

Argosy was a pulp magazine specializing in adventure stories, some of which were science fiction or fantasy. The magazine survived well beyond its pulp years as an adventure-oriented men's magazine. In its latter years, several one-shot special issues were published in an attempt to attract a new audience. One of those was a science-fiction special which reprinted stories by Chad Oliver, Leigh Brackett, John Jakes, and others from *Super Science Stories*.

Science Fiction special (1977)   *$1.00*

ARIEL (1976–1978)

Though published as a book, it called itself a magazine on the cover of its first issue but became *Ariel: The Book of Fantasy* with its second issue. It was heavily art-oriented, with much work by Frank Frazetta and other cover artists reproduced on quality paper stock

1976 Aut *$3.00*
1977 #2 *$2.00*
1978 #3 #4 *$2.00*

ARKHAM SAMPLER (1948–1949)

Although this publication was pulp size, it was not printed on pulp-wood paper but on book paper. It was edited by August Derleth and published by his Arkham House as a sampling of what he would be publishing in book form. It contains poetry, essays, and short stories by various Arkham House writers, including H. P. Lovecraft.

1948 Aut *$8.00*
1949 Win Spr Sum Aut *$7.00*

ASIMOV'S SF ADVENTURE MAGAZINE (1978–1979)

The short-lived companion magazine to *Isaac Asimov's Science Fiction Magazine* was the second—and, to date, the last—American magazine to be named for a living science-fiction writer. It was published in an 8½" x 11" format, something many science-fiction magazines have attempted over the years with, so far, a notable lack of success.

1978 Fal *$1.25*
1979 Spr Sum Fal *$1.25*

ASTONISHING STORIES (1940–1943)

The typical early-forties, adventure-oriented, science-fiction pulp was notable for its publication of early work by Isaac Asimov and others.

1940 Feb *$10.00*
1940 Apr *$6.00*
1940 Jun Aug Oct Dec *$5.00*
1941 Feb Sep *$4.00*
1941 AprRAH NovLRH *$10.00*

1942   Jun Oct Dec   *$4.00*
1942   MarRAH   *$10.00*
1943   Feb Apr   *$4.00*

ASTOUNDING SCIENCE FICTION (see *Astounding Stories*)

ASTOUNDING STORIES/ASTOUNDING SCIENCE FICTION/ANALOG (1930–)

This magazine, which began life as *Astounding Stories of Super-Science,* went on to be the leading science-fiction magazine—or, at least, one of the "Big Three" magazines in the field (the others being *The Magazine of Fantasy and Science Fiction* and, at various times, *Galaxy* or *Isaac Asimov's Science Fiction Magazine*).

The magazine had faltered and failed when it was purchased by Street & Smith in 1933. Five years later, S&S hired a young science-fiction writer named John W. Campbell, Jr. to edit the publication. Campbell, whose reputation to that time was built on interstellar adventure stories inspired by the galaxy-spanning novels of Edward Elmer Smith, Ph.D., changed the title from *Astounding Stories* (which, while more sedate than the publication's earliest title, was still a bit too suggestive of Martian westerns and pirates on the seas of Venus) to *Astounding Science Fiction*. Over the years, the first word of the title became smaller (and, for a time, was overprinted with a gray wash to make it even less noticeable) and the last two words became more prominent. It reputedly was Campbell's goal to change the publication's title to *Science Fiction,* but the need for a gradual transition and the revival of an earlier magazine of that title in the 1950s circumvented that plan.

Campbell changed the direction of the magazine even more drastically than he had altered the title, encouraging writers to try new ideas, new approaches, and to emphasize the human elements of their stories and to examine more fully the consequences of the scientific wonders which occurred in the course of stories. A part of Campbell's success must be attributed to luck—he was helped immeasurably by the appearance on the scene in the first three years of his editorship of such major writers as Robert A. Heinlein, A. E. van Vogt, L. Sprague de Camp, Lester del Rey, and Isaac Asimov. (Asimov developed into a Campbell writer more slowly than the others, though he frequently has cited Campbell as the editor all his stories were written for and has said that he felt any story which did not sell to Campbell was a failure, even if it sold to another market.) With these new writers and, with such older hands as Clifford D. Simak, L. Ron Hubbard, and Campbell's old role model, E. E. Smith, the new magazine was off to a flying start.

This was where virtually *all* of the classic science-fiction novels of the 1940s and 1950s first appeared. They were written as serials for *ASF* with no thought that they might eventually be published in book form, since it was rare for more than one or two science-fiction books to appear in a year. (This may be hard to believe for today's readers, who are used to large sections of bookstores being set aside for science fiction, but science-fiction books were as rare as dentures for Rhode Island Reds into the 1950s.) Such acknowledged classics as A. E. van Vogt's *Slan* and Hal Clement's *Mission of Gravity* were serialized, as were most of Heinlein's novels. Clifford D. Simak's *City* and Isaac Asimov's *Foundation, Foundation and Empire,* and *Second Foundation* first appeared as series of short stories and novelettes in *ASF.* Such other magazines as *Startling Stories* and *Thrilling Wonder Stories* achieved a notable success by printing Campbell's rejects—stories which didn't quite make it into *ASF.*

In 1960, Campbell changed the title of the magazine, gradually, over a period of months, to *Analog* (variously, it has been *Analog Science Fact & Fiction, Analog Science Fact & Science Fiction, Analog Science Fiction/Science Fact*). This was a controversial decision at the time among the tradition-minded science-fiction fans, but Campbell's will prevailed, and the magazine remains *Analog* to this day.

Campbell died in 1971 and was succeeded as editor by Ben Bova. When Bova left to edit *Omni,* Stanley Schmidt became editor of *Analog,* a post he still holds. The magazine currently is published by Davis Publications, which also publishes *Isaac Asimov's Science Fiction Magazine,* as well as the two leading mystery fiction publications, *Alfred Hitchcock's Mystery Magazine* and *Ellery Queen's Mystery Magazine.*

For the past few years, the magazine has been published thirteen times a year. Collectors will note that some issues in 1981 and 1982 have been dated like newspapers (Feb. 2, 1981, for instance). The magazine (like *Isaac Asimov's Science Fiction Magazine*) eventually settled down to publish that thirteenth issue as the ''mid-December'' issue.

    1953   Hugo

    1955   Hugo

    1956   Hugo

    1957   Hugo

    1961   Hugo

    1962   Hugo

    1964   Hugo

    1965   Hugo

1930   Jan *$400.00*

1930   Feb

1930   Mar *$75.00*

1930   Apr May Jun Jul Aug Sep Oct Nov Dec *$45.00*

1931   Jan Feb Mar Apr May Jun Jul Aug Sep Oct Nov Dec *$25.00*

1932   Jan Feb Mar Apr May Jun Sep Nov *$22.50*

1933   Jan Mar *$22.50*

1933   Oct (1st issue published by Street & Smith) *$47.50*

1933   Nov Dec *$37.50*

1934   Jan *$25.00*

1934   Feb Mar *$17.50*

1934   Apr May Jun Jul Aug Sep Oct Nov Dec *$15.00*

1935   Jan Feb Mar Apr May Jun Jul Aug Sep Oct Nov Dec *$10.00*

1936   Jan Feb Mar Apr May Jun Jul Aug Sep Oct Nov Dec *$8.75*

1937   Jan Feb Mar Apr May Jun Jul Aug Sep Oct Nov Dec *$7.50*

1938   Jan Feb *$7.50*

(becomes *Astounding Science Fiction*)

1938   Mar Apr May Jun Aug Dec *$7.50*

1938   JulLRH SepLRH OctLRH NovLRH *$19.00*

1939   Jan Feb Mar Apr May Jun Jul Sep Oct Dec *$5.00*

1939   AugRAH NovRAH *$12.50*

1940   Aug Oct Dec *$5.00*

1940   JanRAH FebRAH/LRH Mar AprLRH MayLRH JunRAH/LRH JulRAH/LRH SepRAH/LRH NovLRH *$12.50*

1941   Jun Nov Dec *$4.50*

1941   JanRAH/LRH FebRAH MarRAH AprLRH MayRAH(2)
       JulRAH(2) Aug SepRAH(2) OctRAH(2) *$11.00*
1942   Sep Nov Dec *$8.75*
1942   JanLRH FebLRH MarRAH AprRAH/LRH May JunLRH
       JulLRH AugRAH OctLRH *$22.00*
1943   Jan Feb *$8.75*
1943   Mar Apr May Jun Jul Aug Sep Oct Nov Dec *$4.50*
1944   Jan Feb Mar Apr May Jun Jul Aug Sep Oct Nov Dec *$4.00*
1945   Jan Feb Mar Apr May Jun Jul Aug Sep Oct Nov Dec *$3.00*
1946   Jan Feb Mar Apr May Jun Jul Aug Sep Oct Nov Dec *$3.00*
1947   Jan Feb Mar Apr May Jun Jul Dec *$2.25*
1947   AugLRH SepJV/LRH OctLRH(2) NovLRH *$4.50*
1948   Jan Feb MarLRH Apr MayLRH Jun Jul Aug SepLRH Oct Nov
       Dec *$2.25*
1949   Jan Feb Mar Jul Sep *$1.75*
1949   AprLRH MayLRH JunLRH AugLRH OctLRH NovRAH
       DecLRH *$3.50*
1950   Feb Jun Aug Sep Nov Dec *$2.00*
1950   JanLRH MarLRH AprLRH(2) JulRAH OctLRH *$2.00*
1950   MayJV/LRH (Dianetics, the Evolution of a Science)
1951   Feb Mar Apr May Jun Jul Aug Sep Oct Nov Dec *$1.00*
1951   JanLRH (Dianometry)
1952   Feb Mar Apr May Jun Jul Aug Sep Oct Nov Dec *$1.00*
1952   JanJV *$2.00*
1953   Jan Feb Mar Apr May Jul Aug Sep Oct Nov Dec *90¢*
1953   JunPKD *$2.00*
1954   Jan Feb Mar Apr May Jun Jul Aug Sep Oct Nov Dec *90¢*
1955   Jan Feb Mar Apr May Jun Jul Aug Oct Nov Dec *90¢*
1955   SepJV *$2.00*
1956   Jan May Jun Jul Aug Sep Oct Nov Dec *90¢*
1956   FebRAH MarRAH AprRAH *$2.00*
1957   Jan Feb Mar Apr May Jun Jul Aug *90¢*
1957   SepRAH OctRAH NovRAH DecRAH *$2.00*
1958   Jan Feb Mar Apr May Jun Aug Sep Oct Nov Dec *90¢*
1958   JulJV *$2.00*
1959   Jan Feb Mar Apr May Jun Jul Aug Sep Nov Dec *90¢*
1959   OctJV *$2.00*
1960   Jan *75¢*
(becomes *Astounding Science Fact & Fiction*)

1960   Feb Mar Apr May Jun Jul Aug Sep   *75¢*
(becomes *Analog Science Fact & Fiction*)
1960   Oct Nov Dec   *75¢*
1961   Jan Feb Mar Apr May Jun Jul Aug Sep Oct Nov   *75¢*
(becomes *Analog Science Fact & Science Fiction*)
1961   Dec   *75¢*
1962   Jan Feb Mar Apr May Jun Jul Aug Sep Oct Nov Dec   *75¢*
1963   Jan Feb   *75¢*
1963   Mar Apr May Jun Jul Aug Sep Oct Nov Dec   *$1.90*
1964   Jan Feb Mar Apr May Jun Jul Aug Sep Oct Nov Dec   *$1.90*
1965   Jan Feb   *$1.90*
1965   Mar   *50¢*
(becomes *Analog Science Fiction/Science Fact*)
1965   Apr May Jun Jul Aug Sep Oct Nov Dec   *50¢*
1966   Jan Feb Mar Apr May Jun Jul Aug Sep Oct Nov Dec   *50¢*
1967   Jan Feb Mar Apr May Jun Jul Aug Sep Oct Nov Dec   *50¢*
1968   Jan Feb Mar Apr May Jun Jul Aug Sep Oct Nov Dec   *50¢*
1969   Jan Feb Mar Apr May Jun Jul Aug Sep Oct Nov Dec   *50¢*
1970   Jan Feb Mar Apr May Jun Jul Aug Sep Oct Nov Dec   *50¢*
1971   Jan Feb Mar Apr May Jun Jul Aug Sep Oct Nov Dec   *50¢*
1972   Jan Feb Mar Apr May Jun Jul Aug Sep Oct Nov Dec   *50¢*
1973   Jan Feb Mar Apr May Jun Jul Aug Sep Oct Nov Dec   *50¢*
1974   Jan Feb Mar Apr May Jun Jul Aug Sep Oct Nov Dec   *50¢*
1975   Jan Feb Mar Apr May Jun Jul Aug Sep Oct Nov Dec   *50¢*
1976   Jan Feb Mar Apr May Jun Jul Aug Sep Oct Nov Dec   *50¢*
1977   Jan Feb Mar Apr May Jun Jul Aug Sep Oct Nov Dec   *50¢*
1978   Jan Feb Mar Apr May Jun Jul Aug Sep Oct Nov Dec   *50¢*
1979   Jan Feb Mar Apr May Jun Jul Aug Sep Oct Nov Dec   *50¢*
1980   Jan Feb Mar Apr May Jun Jul Aug Sep Oct Nov Dec   *50¢*
1981   Jan5 Feb2 Mar2 Mar30 Apr27 May25 Jun22 Jul20 Aug17
         Sep14 Oct12 Nov9 Dec7   *50¢*
1982   Jan4 Feb1 Mar1 Mar29 May Jun Jul Aug Sep mid-Sep Oct
         Nov Dec   *50¢*
1983   Jan Feb Mar Apr May Jun Jul Aug Sep mid-Sep Oct Nov
         Dec   *50¢*
1984   Jan Feb Mar Apr May Jun Jul Aug Sep Oct Nov Dec mid-
         Dec   *50¢*
1985   Jan Feb Mar Apr May Jun Jul Aug Sep Oct Nov Dec mid-
         Dec   *50¢*

1986   Jan Feb Mar Apr May Jun Jul Aug Sep Oct Nov Dec mid-
      Dec   *50¢*
1987   Jan Feb Mar Apr May Jun Jul Aug Sep Oct Nov Dec mid-
      Dec   *50¢*

ASTOUNDING STORIES YEARBOOK/ASTOUNDING SCIENCE FICTION (1970)

During the period when Sol Cohen was the owner and publisher of *Amazing* and *Fantastic*, he published a number of all-reprint titles made up of stories from the magazines. Some, like *Great Science Fiction*, had fairly long runs. Others lasted only one issue. This one lasted only two issues, with the second called *Astounding Science Fiction*. The title certainly raised a few eyebrows, evoking as it did a title of beloved memory among fans.

1970   #1 #2   *50¢*

AVON FANTASY READER (1947–1952)

This early digest-size periodical was edited by Donald A. Wollheim, who went on to edit the Ace Doubles series of paperbacks and then to establish his own science-fiction publishing company, DAW Books. *AFR* reprinted stories by Robert E. Howard, Robert Bloch, and others, often with new and extremely garish titles (''The Witch From Hell's Kitchen,'' ''Temptress of the Tower of Torture and Sin'') and with sexy (for its day) covers featuring scantily clad women being rescued from demons by bronze-skinned swordsmen.

1947   #1   *$5.00*
1947   #2REH #3 #4 #5   *$4.00*
1948   #6 #7REH #8REH   *$4.00*
1949   #9 #10REH #11   *$4.00*
1950   #12REH #13 #14REH   *$4.00*
1951   #15 #16 #17   *$4.00*
1952   #18REH   *$4.00*

AVON SCIENCE FICTION & FANTASY READER (1953)

The later incarnation of *Avon Fantasy Reader and Avon Science Fiction Reader* printed only original fiction, no reprints. It was not edited by Donald A. Wollheim, but by Sol Cohen, who later would become publisher of *Amazing*.

1953   Jan   *$2.00*
1953   AprJV   *$2.50*

AVON SCIENCE FICTION READER (1951–1952)

The companion magazine to *Avon Fantasy Reader* was also edited by Donald A. Wollheim and also featured some extravagant retitlings of older stories.

1951   #1   *$4.00*
1951   #2   *$3.75*
1952   #3   *$3.75*

THE BEST SCIENCE FICTION (1964)

The first issue of the digest-sized magazine was subtitled "From *Worlds of If*" and the second was subtitled "From *Worlds of Tomorrow*." Obviously, it contained reprints from those magazines.

1964   #1 #2   *50¢*

THE BEST OF OMNI SCIENCE FICTION (1980–1983)

Though it began as reprints selected from fiction published in the popularized science magazine, *Omni*, it began publishing new stories along with reprints with #2, including new fiction by Robert Silverberg, Spider Robinson, and Harlan Ellison. The first issue of this newsstand publication also was published in a hardcover edition for book stores.

1980   #1   *$1.00*
1981   #2   *$1.00*
1982   #3 #4   *$1.00*
1983   #5 #6   *$1.00*

BEYOND FANTASY FICTION/BEYOND FICTION (1953–1955)

Pure fantasy magazines have always had a rocky existence. While it is true that *Weird Tales* lasted for 32 years, it is also true that it was a marginal publication for most of that time. H. L. Gold, editor of *Galaxy*, attempted to publish an all-fantasy companion magazine which would replace *Unknown/Unknown Worlds* in the affections of fans and which would also be a financial success. Although neither goal was accomplished, the magazine did publish several good stories. The word "Fantasy" was dropped from the title for the final two, undated, issues.

1953 Jul *$2.50*
1953 Nov *$1.75*
1953 SeptPKD *$3.50*
1954 Jan Mar May Jul Sep *$1.75*
1954 #9PKD *$3.50*
1955 #10 *$1.75*

BEYOND INFINITY (1967)

The little-known, digest one-shot appeared and disappeared without fanfare.

1967 Dec *50¢*

BIZARRE! MYSTERY MAGAZINE (1965–1966)

Although ostensibly a mystery magazine, the fantasy content of *Bizarre!* was at least as strong as its mystery content. It was a digest-sized magazine and printed a mixture of new and reprinted stories.

1965 Oct HPL reprint *50¢*
1965 Nov *50¢*
1966 Jan *50¢*

CAPTAIN FUTURE (1940–1944)

The pulp magazine is the only American science-fiction magazine to feature in each issue the adventures of a continuing title hero, along the lines of *Doc Savage* and *The Shadow* (who, despite their frequent forays into the fantastic, belong more properly in the mystery/crime category). Captain Future was a super-scientist whose friends included a robot and a disembodied brain. All were the creations of Edmond Hamilton, whose long career included not only writing scores of interplanetary (and interstellar) adventure stories, but more than a decade of writing comic books featuring Batman and Superman.

It was customary in pulp adventure magazines for the publisher to play it safe by having the hero's adventures written under a house pseudonym, just in case the regular author missed a deadline. Walter Gibson, therefore, wrote all the Shadow stories under the house name of "Maxwell Grant," and Lester Dent wrote all but a handful of the 180 Doc Savage novels under the name of "Kenneth Robeson." ("Kenneth Robeson" also wrote all the adventures of another pulp hero, The Avenger, but that "Kenneth Robeson" was Paul Ernst. To further compound the confusion, when the Avenger stories were reprinted in paperback, Ron Goulart wrote a couple dozen new stories under the "Robeson" byline.)

Five of the seventeen Captain Future stories in the Captain's own magazine appeared as by "Brett Sterling." "Sterling" was, variously, Edmond Hamilton (Sum 43, Win 44, Spr 45) or Joseph Samachson (Spr 43, Spr 44). The remaining dozen stories were written by Hamilton under his own byline. A few other stories about Captain Future were written by Hamilton years later and published in *Thrilling Wonder Stories*.

(Only one non-Captain Future story appeared under the "Brett Sterling" pseudonym: "Referent," in *Thrilling Wonder Stories* for October 1948. That one was written by Ray Bradbury.)

1940	Win Spr Sum Fal	*$11.25*
1941	Win Spr Sum Fal	*$8.75*
1942	Win Spr Sum Fal	*$8.75*
1943	Win Spr Sum	*$8.75*
1944	Win Spr	*$8.75*

COMET STORIES (1940–1941)

The short-lived adventure pulp magazine included one of E. E. Smith's few short stories, "The Vortex Blaster" (July 1941), which later was incorporated into a novel of the same title.

1940 Dec *$6.00*
1941 Jan Mar May Jul *$5.00*

COSMIC STORIES/COSMIC SCIENCE FICTION (1941)

This magazine was edited by Donald A. Wollheim, whose budget was so low that he had to fill it largely with stories which he had talked his friends into donating. Since his friends included many greats in science fiction, its three issues are of interest to collectors. The title changed slightly with the second issue.

1941 Mar May Jul *$5.00*

COSMOS SCIENCE FICTION AND FANTASY (1953–1954)

In 1953, the science-fiction magazine field underwent a population explosion, with 39 magazines appearing on the stands. This was, obviously, more than the market could support, and most lasted only two to six issues. Some authors took advantage of this sudden glut to sell stories which had languished in their files for years; with 39 markets to choose from, it was easy for a "name" author to sell stories which were, to put it as charitably as possible, not up to his/her usual standard. Consequently, many of the short-lived magazines of 1953 contain stories by top authors—some of them good stories—which have never been reprinted. Collectors can find many a surprise in these magazines.

1953 SepPKD *$2.00*
1953 NovJV *$2.00*
1954 MarJV *$2.00*
1954 JulPKD *$2.00*

COSMOS SCIENCE FICTION AND FANTASY (1977)

This magazine is entirely unrelated to the earlier, digest-sized magazine of the same name. This was a "bedsheet" size (about 8½″ × 11″) magazine which contained stories by Frederik Pohl, Larry Niven, Fritz Leiber, and others. It was edited by David G. Hartwell, better known as an editor of science-fiction books.

1977 May *$2.50*
1977 Jul Sep Nov *$1.50*

COVEN 13/WITCHCRAFT & SORCERY (1969–1974)

The rocky road of this attempt to produce an all-fantasy magazine can best be traced by looking at its format changes. It began as a newsstand digest magazine, then became a thin, 8½″ × 11″ publication available only sporadically and usually only by mail or through specialty dealers. The later issues, because of their very low print runs, are hard to find.

1969   Sep Nov   75¢
1970   Jan Mar   75¢
(changes size and becomes *Witchcraft & Sorcery*)
1971   Jan/Feb May   75¢
1972   #7 #8 #9   75¢
1974   #10   75¢

DESTINIES (1978–1981)

''The paperback magazine of science fiction and speculative fact'' was edited by James Baen and published by Ace Books. While there may have been reprints of some issues, the listing here gives the date of the first printings.

There also was one volume of an original anthology (''A *Destinies* Special'') called *Proteus: Voices for the 80's.*

1978   Nov/Dec $1.50
1979   Jan/Feb Apr/Jun Aug/Sep Oct/Dec   75¢
1980   Feb/Mar Spr   75¢
1980   SumRAH FalRAH $1.50
1981   Win Aug   75¢

DREAM WORLD (1957)

Even in the field of fantasy and science fiction, this is an odd publication. It was published as a companion magazine to *Amazing Stories* and *Fantastic* and featured wish-fulfillment fantasies, mostly with a mild sexual content. What if you could walk through walls? Well, according to the cover of that issue, you could use your ability to walk into a ladies' shower room. What if you could become invisible? Again, a visit to the ladies' shower is called for. An excerpt from Thorne Smith's *Rain in the Doorway* (retitled, ''Sex, Love, and Mr.

Owen'') was published in the first issue; this is noteworthy because it is the *only* appearance of this noted fantasist in any fantasy magazine.

1957 Feb May Aug *50¢*

DYNAMIC SCIENCE FICTION (1952-1954)

One of the last of the true pulp magazines, *Dynamic* was one of several science-fiction magazines edited by Robert A. W. Lowndes. Like all his magazines (*Future, Science Fiction Stories, Startling Mystery,* etc.), it contains a surprising amount of readable, enjoyable science fiction. Surprising, because these publications had extremely low rates of payment; Lowndes got around this in part by using newer writers, some of whom went on to become major writers (see *Startling Mystery*).

1952 Dec *$1.50*
1953 Mar Jun Aug Oct *$1.50*
1954 Jan *$1.50*

DYNAMIC SCIENCE STORIES (1939)

This pulp magazine featured good adventure-oriented stories. It was revived, under a slightly different title, in 1952.

1939 Feb *$6.25*
1939 Apr/May *$6.00*

FAMOUS FANTASTIC MYSTERIES (1939-1953)

This was the longest-running (81 issues) of all the reprint fantasy magazines. With its companion publications (*Fantastic Novels* and *A. Merritt's Fantasy*), this reprinted famous fantasy stories which had appeared in such pulp magazines as *Argosy* and the various pulps published by the Munsey publishing line, along with rare books. Some of the novels reprinted in *FFM* were slightly abridged, although this was not acknowledged in the magazine. The reprints were illustrated by top fantasy pulp artists, including Virgil Finlay and Lawrence (L. Stern Stevens).

1939 Sep/Oct *$6.00*
1939 Nov Dec *$5.00*

Famous Fantastic Mysteries, September–October 1939, about 7″ × 10″; cover uncredited. This was the first issue of the publication which specialized in reprints of fantasies. Copyright 1939 by The Frank A. Munsey Company. Reprinted by permission of Blazing Publications, The Argosy Co.

1940   Jan Feb Mar Apr May/Jun Aug Oct Dec   *$5.00*
1941   Feb Apr Jun Aug Oct Dec   *$4.50*
1942   Feb Apr Jun Jul Aug Sep Oct Nov Dec   *$4.50*
1943   Mar Sep Dec   *$4.00*
1944   Mar Jun Sep Dec   *$4.00*
1945   Mar Jun Sep Dec   *$3.50*
1946   Feb Apr Jun Aug Oct Dec   *$3.50*
1947   Feb Apr Jun Aug Oct Dec   *$2.25*
1948   Feb Apr Jun Aug Oct Dec   *$2.00*
1949   Feb Apr Jun Aug Oct Dec   *$1.75*
1950   Feb Apr Jun Aug Oct   *$1.50*
1951   Jan Mar May Jul Oct   *$1.50*
1951   DecRAH   *$3.00*
1952   Feb   *$1.50*
(combines with *Fantastic Novels Magazine*)
1952   Apr Aug Oct DecREH   *$1.50*
1952   JunRAH/REH   *$3.00*
1953   Feb Apr Jun   *$1.50*

Famous Fantastic Mysteries, June 1953, about 7″ × 9¼″; cover by Lawrence (Stern Stevens) (1886–1960). Copyright 1953 by Popular Publications, Inc. Reprinted by permission of Blazing Publications, The Argosy Co.

FAMOUS SCIENCE FICTION (1966–1969)

Robert A. W. Lowndes edited the saddle-stitched, digest-sized magazine; it featured reprints from the science-fiction magazines of the twenties and thirties. It remains an inexpensive way for newer readers to familiarize themselves with early science-fiction stories.

1966/67 Win *75¢*
1967 Spr Sun Fal *75¢*
1967/68 Win *75¢*
1968 Spr Sum Fal *75¢*
1969 Spr *75¢*

FANTASTIC/FANTASTIC SCIENCE FICTION STORIES (1952–1980)

This digest-sized magazine was created as a companion magazine to *Amazing Stories* when that magazine switched to digest format. (As a pulp, *Amazing* had as its companion the similarly titled *Fantastic*

Famous Fantastic Mysteries, June 1944, about 7″ × 9¼″; cover by Lawrence (Stern Stevens) (1886–1960). Listed as copyright 1944 by All-Fiction Field, Inc. Copyright 1944 by Popular Publications. Reprinted by permission of Blazing Publications, The Argosy Co.

Adventures, which was later "combined" with *Fantastic.* Contrary to widely held opinion, however, *Fantastic* is *not* a retitling of *Fantastic Adventures; Fantastic* began with the Summer 1952 issue and *Fantastic Adventures* continued publishing until the following year, with March 1953 its last issue.) The first few issues are outstanding, containing a selection of excellent reprints and strong new stories—including B. Traven's "The Third Guest" (March/April 1953)—and some award-winning graphics and design.

Like *Amazing Stories, Fantastic* had a series of ups and downs, descending into the lower depths of hack space westerns for a few years, then pulling out to publish stories by Roger Zelazny, David R. Bunch, Thomas M. Disch, and others under the editorial direction of Cele Goldsmith. The frequency of title changes, including an attempt to de-emphasize its fantasy content and emphasize science fiction, indicated that its existence was troubled for years. Other indications of ill health (caused by poor circulation) were reductions in frequency

Fantastic, Summer 1952, about 5½″ × 7¾″; cover by Barye Phillips and L(eo) R(amon) Summers (1925–1985). This is the first issue of the magazine. Copyright 1952 by Ziff-Davis Publishing Company. "Fantastic" is a trademark owned by TSR, Inc. Copyright 1989 TSR, Inc. All rights reserved.

and the occasional skipped issue. Eventually, dwindling sales caused the magazine to be "combined" with *Amazing.*

1952   Sum   *$5.00*
1952   Fal Nov/Dec   *$1.00*
1953   Jan/Feb Mar/Apr   *$1.00*
(becomes *Fantastic combined with Fantastic Adventures*)
1953   May/Jun   *$1.00*
(becomes *Fantastic*)
1953   Jul/Aug Sep/Oct Nov/Dec   *$1.00*
1954   Jan/Feb Apr Jun Aug Oct Dec   *$1.00*
1955   Feb Apr Jun Aug Oct Dec   *$1.00*
1956   Feb Apr Jun Aug Oct Dec   *$1.00*
1957   Feb Mar Apr May Jun Jul Aug Sept Oct Nov Dec   *$1.00*
1958   Jan Feb Mar Apr May Jun Jul Aug Sept Oct Nov Dec   *$1.00*
1959   Jan Feb Mar Apr May Jun Jul Aug   *$1.00*
(becomes *Fantastic Science Fiction Stories*)
1959   Sep Oct Nov Dec   *$1.00*
1960   Jan Feb Mar Apr May Jun Jul Aug Sept   *75¢*
(becomes *Fantastic*)

1960   Oct Nov Dec   75¢
1961   Jan Feb Mar Apr MayREH Jun Jul Aug Sep Oct Nov DecREH   75¢
1962   Jan Feb Mar Apr May Jun Jul Aug Sep Oct Nov Dec   75¢
1963   Jan Feb Mar Apr May Jun Jul Aug Sep Oct Nov Dec   75¢
1964   Jan Mar Apr May Jun Aug Sep Oct Nov   75¢
1964   FebPKD JulJV DecPKD $1.50
1965   Jan Feb Mar Apr May Jun Sep Nov   75¢
1966   Jan Mar May Jul Sep Nov   75¢
1967   Jan Mar May Jul Sep Nov   75¢
1968   Jan Mar May Aug Oct Dec   75¢
1969   Feb Apr Jun Aug Oct Dec   75¢
1970   Feb Apr Jun Aug Oct Dec   60¢
1971   Feb Apr Jun Aug Oct Dec   60¢
1972   Feb Apr Jun Aug Oct Dec   60¢
1973   Feb Apr Jul Sep Nov   60¢
1974   Jan Mar May Jul Sep Nov   60¢
1975   Feb Apr Jun Aug Oct Dec   60¢
1976   Feb May Aug Nov   60¢
1977   Feb Jun Sep Dec   60¢
1978   Apr Jul Oct   60¢
1979   Jan Apr Jul Oct   60¢
1980   Jan Apr Jul Oct   60¢

FANTASTIC ADVENTURES (1939–1953)

Within a framework which never pretended to be anything but what the title promised, *FA* produced a lot of enjoyable stories, including some Edgar Rice Burroughs stories. (ERB stories appear in the issues of July 1939; March, July, November 1941; and March 1942.) A popular series of Damon Runyon-style stories by Robert Bloch, featuring a small-time drifter named Lefty Feep, also ran in *Fantastic Adventures* from 1942 through 1946. Most of the magazine's stories were written by a small group of writers who also wrote for the publisher's western, mystery, and adventure pulps; they used a number of pseudonyms and several of them wrote under house-owned names such as "Alexander Blade."

Of particular noteworthiness to collectors is the July 1939 issue, which contains the only story attributed to Edgar Rice Burroughs which has never been included in any of his books.

The first nine issues were ''bedsheet'' size (about 8½ ″ × 11 ″); the rest are standard pulp magazine size (7 ″ × 9 ″).

From 1941 through 1943 and again from 1948 to 1951, unsold issues were rebound, three issues to a volume, and sold as a reissue series, *Fantastic Adventures Quarterly Reissue*. These issues have mostly curiosity value—they do show how much magazine you could buy for 50¢ in the forties, since each issue is between two and three inches thick.

1939 May *$10.00*
1939 Jul (ERB: ''The Scientists Revolt'') *$12.00*
1939 Sep Nov *$7.50*
1940 Jan Feb Mar Apr May Jun Aug Oct *$7.50*
1941 Jan May Jun Aug Sep Oct Dec *$4.00*
1941 Mar (ERB: ''Slaves of the Fish Men'') *$9.00*
1941 Jul (ERB: ''Goddess of Fire'') *$9.00*
1941 Nov (ERB: ''The Living Dead'') *$9.00*
1942 Jan Feb Apr May Jun Jul Aug Sep Oct Nov Dec *$4.00*
1942 Mar (ERB: ''War on Venus'') *$9.00*
1943 Jan Feb Mar Apr May Jun Jul Aug Oct Dec *$3.50*
1944 Feb Apr Jun Oct *$3.50*
1945 Jan Apr Jul Oct *$2.75*
1946 Feb May Jul Sep Nov *$2.50*
1947 Jan Mar May Jul Sep Oct Nov Dec *$2.50*
1948 Jan Feb Mar Apr May Jun Jul Aug Sep Oct Nov Dec *$1.75*
1949 Jan Feb Mar Apr May Jun Jul Aug Sep Oct Nov Dec *$1.75*
1950 Jan Feb Mar Apr May Jun Jul Aug Sept Nov Dec *$1.25*
1950 OctLRH *$2.50*
1951 Jan Feb Mar Apr May Jun Jul Aug Sep Oct Nov Dec *$1.25*
1952 Jan Feb Mar Apr May Jun Jul Aug Sep Oct Nov Dec *$1.25*
1953 Jan Feb Mar *$1.25*

FANTASTIC ADVENTURES YEARBOOK (1970)

This is one of several digest-size publications which reprinted stories from *Amazing* and *Fantastic*.

1970 *50¢*

FANTASTIC NOVELS (1940–1951)

The companion pulp magazine to *Famous Fantastic Mysteries* published longer stories than *FFM*. Selections came primarily from pulp magazines of the 1920s and from books.

1940   Jul Sep Nov   *$5.00*
1941   Jan Apr Mar   *$5.00*
1948   May Jul Sep Nov   *$2.25*
1949   Jan Mar May Jul Sep Nov   *$1.75*
1950   Jan Mar May Jul Sep Nov   *$1.50*
(becomes *Fantastic Novels Magazine*)
1951   Jan Apr Jun   *$1.50*

FANTASTIC SCIENCE FICTION (1952)

The very thin (48 pages) publication is extremely hard to find, particularly in collectible condition. It is approximately 9″ × 12″ ("bedsheet" size) and contains exceptionally bad stories. It is too thin to support itself upright on shelves and is larger than most other science-fiction magazines, which adds to its storage problems. It was edited by Walter B. Gibson, creator of The Shadow, and published by Charlton, which also published the Monarch line of paperbacks and the Charlton line of comics, which included *Space Western*. Because of its odd, awkward size, the curiosity item is easily damaged.

1952   Aug   *$7.50*
1952   Dec   *$7.50*

FANTASTIC STORY QUARTERLY/FANTASTIC STORY MAGAZINE (1950–1955)

The companion to *Startling Stories* and *Thrilling Wonder Stories*, the pulp magazine reprinted stories from its sister publications.

1950   Spr Sum Fal   *$1.40*
1951   Win   *$1.40*
(becomes *Fantastic Story Quarterly/Magazine*)
1951   Spr   *$1.40*
(becomes *Fantastic Story Magazine*)
1951   Sum Fal   *$1.40*
1952   Win Spr Sum Sep(Fal) Nov   *$1.40*

1953   Jan Mar May Sep   *$1.40*
1953   JulPKD   *$2.80*
1954   Win Spr Sum Fal   *$1.40*
1955   Spr   *$1.40*
1955   WinJV   *$2.80*

FANTASTIC UNIVERSE (1953–1960)

It began as a thick digest magazine with the then-unheard-of cover price of 50¢. Resistance to that "high" price resulted in the magazine cutting pages (from 192 pages in the first three issues to 160 pages for each of the next four and then to 128 pages) so it could reduce the cover price to 35¢.

Fantastic Universe was a companion magazine to *The Saint Detective Magazine* but, unlike its companion, did not include any reprinted stories. Several series which ordinarily ran in other magazines had one or two episodes appear in *Fantastic Universe* (Robert Sheckley's "AAA Ace" series, which ordinarily ran in *Galaxy*; H. Nearing, Jr.'s "Ransom and MacTate" series, which customarily appeared in *F&SF*), which would indicate that the magazine was receptive to other editors' rejected stories. It published a number of noteworthy stories, including several "Conan" stories by Robert E. Howard.

In its latter days, the magazine changed to a sort of thin pulp size, but on better-than-pulp paper. Its last six issues appeared in this format. The first part of Fredric Brown's *The Mind Thing* appeared in the last issue of the magazine, making it one of several science-fiction/fantasy publications to cease publishing with a serial in progress.

1953   Jun/JulPKD   *$3.00*
1953   Aug/Sep   *$1.25*
1953   Oct/NovPKD   *$2.50*
1954   Mar Jul Sep Nov Dec   *$1.25*
1954   JanPKD MayPKD OctPKD   *$2.50*
1955   Jan Feb Apr May Jun Aug Sep Nov   *$1.25*
1955   MarJV JulPKD OctREH DecREH   *$2.50*
1956   Feb Mar May Jun Jul Aug Sep Nov   *$1.25*
1956   JanPKD AprREH OctJV DecREH   *$2.50*
1957   Jan Feb Mar Apr May Jun Jul Aug Sep Oct Nov Dec   *$1.25*
1958   Jan Feb Mar Apr May Jun Jul Aug Sep Oct Nov   *$1.25*

1959   Jan Mar May Jul Sep Oct Nov Dec   *$1.25*
1960   Jan Feb Mar   *$1.25*

FANTASY AND SCIENCE FICTION (see *The Magazine of Fantasy and Science Fiction*)

FANTASY BOOK (1947–1951)

One of two magazines with the title, *Fantasy Book* from the late forties changed sizes and shapes with almost every issue; the first two issues were 9″ × 12″ and the next two were 5½″ × 8½″. Subsequent issues shrank even more, with the last two being about 3″ × 4″. In addition, there were variant printings, with different cover colors, on #5, at least. There were issues printed on book paper, as well. The editor and publisher was William Crawford, who also published books as Fantasy Publishing Company, Inc. (FPCI).

1947   Vol. 1 #1; Vol. 1 #2   *$2.50*
1948   Vol. 1 #3; Vol. 1 #4   *$1.50*
1949   Vol. 1 #5 (LRH: "Battle of Wizards")   *$5.00*
1950   Vol. 1 #6; Vol. 1 #7   *$1.50*
1951   Vol. 1 #8   *$1.50*

FANTASY BOOK (1981–1987)

There is no connection between this *Fantasy Book* and the one from 1947–1951. This 8½″ × 11″ publication offered a mixture of fiction and comics between heavy cardboard cover stock. It was published by Dennis Mallonee, whose Heroic Publishing Co. also published a line of color comic books, one of which featured *Eternity Smith,* a science-based super-hero at least partially inspired by the works of E. E. Smith, Ph.D. (Eternity Smith's daughter is named Skylark, and *Skylark of Space* is a classic E. E. Smith novel.)

1981   Oct Dec   *$1.50*
1982   Feb May Aug Nov   *$1.50*
1983   Feb May Aug Dec   *$1.50*
1984   Mar Jun Sep Dec   *$1.50*
1985   Mar Jun Sep Dec   *$1.50*
1986   Mar Jun Sep Dec   *$1.50*
1987   Mar   *$1.50*

FANTASY FICTION/FANTASY STORIES (1950)

You can't tell a book by its cover and you can't tell the quality of a story by its title—particularly when the title has been altered to sensationalize it. This magazine featured extremely good reprinted stories under new, garish titles: "She Said, 'Take Me If You Dare' " and "Blood Brother of the Swamp Cats" among them. Despite some good stories and a superficial resemblance to *The Magazine of Fantasy and Science Fiction,* this publication came and went virtually unnoticed, pausing only long enough to change its title between issues.

1950   May   *$2.00*
(becomes *Fantasy Stories*)
1950   Nov   *$2.00*

FANTASY MAGAZINE/FANTASY FICTION (1953)

Part of the science-fiction magazine glut of 1953 was a line of magazines which was edited by Lester del Rey and Harry Harrison, among others. The line included *Science Fiction Adventures, Space Science Fiction, Rocket Stories,* and *Fantasy Magazine/Fantasy Fiction.* A lot of good stories by top authors are to be found in these magazines, which were more or less lost in the crowd in 1953, when 39 science-fiction magazines elbowed each other for newsstand space.

1953   Feb/MarREH   *$2.00*
(becomes *Fantasy Fiction*)
1953   Nov   *$1.25*
1953   JunPKD Aug PKD/REH   *$2.50*

FANTASY STORIES (see *Fantasy Fiction*)

FEAR! (1960)

This was a digest-sized, terror-suspense magazine.

1960   May Jul   *$3.50*

FLASH GORDON STRANGE ADVENTURE MAGAZINE (1936)

Only one "bedsheet" (about 8½" × 11") pulp magazine was published of this little-known title. It attempted to transfer the success of the comic strip to magazines and is also of interest to comics collectors. It is extremely rare.

1936   Dec   *$35.00*

FLYING SAUCERS FROM OTHER WORLDS (see *Other Worlds Science Stories*)

FORGOTTEN FANTASY (1970–1971)

This digest-sized publication attempted to follow in the footsteps of *Famous Fantastic Mysteries* and *Fantastic Novels* by reprinting older stories. It had one problem *FFM* and *FN* had not had, however— paperback reprints of science fiction and fantasy were common by the time *Forgotten Fantasy* came along, making it hard to find good-but-unavailable novels to reprint. It ran one serial (*The Goddess of Atvatabar*, an 1891 novel by William R. Bradshaw) in its first four issues and began—but never completed—*Hartmann, the Anarchist*, an 1893 novel by E. Douglas Fawcett, in its last.

1970   Oct Dec   *$1.50*
1971   Feb Apr Jun   *$1.50*

FROM UNKNOWN WORLDS (see *Unknown*)

FUTURE COMBINED WITH SCIENCE FICTION (see *Future Fiction*)

FUTURE COMBINED WITH SCIENCE FICTION STORIES (see *Future Fiction*)

FUTURE FANTASY AND SCIENCE FICTION (see *Future Fiction*)

FUTURE FICTION/FUTURE COMBINED WITH SCIENCE FICTION/FUTURE FANTASY AND SCIENCE FICTION/FUTURE COMBINED WITH SCIENCE FICTION STORIES (1939–1960)

When it comes to name changes, this is the champion, though the honor is dubious at best. Lurking behind all these changes is a good pulp science-fiction adventure magazine line which suffered from a serious case of undercapitalization, which caused titles to fold, combine, and re-emerge.

There is quite a bit of good fiction (James Blish, C. M. Kornbluth, Donald A. Wollheim) and art (Hannes Bok) in its pages.

With the June 1954 issue, *Future* became a digest-sized magazine.

1939   Nov   *$5.00*
1940   Mar Jul Nov   *$4.00*
1941   Apr Aug   *$4.00*
(becomes *Future Combined with Science Fiction*)
1941   Oct Dec   *$4.00*
1942   Apr Jun Aug   *$4.00*
1942   FebRAH   *$10.00*
(becomes *Future Fantasy and Science Fiction*)
1942   Oct Dec   *$4.00*
1943   Feb   *$4.00*
(becomes *Future Combined with Science Fiction Stories*)
1950   May/Jun   *$2.50*
1950   Jul/Aug Sep/Oct Nov   *$1.40*
1951   Jan Mar May Jul Sep Nov   *$1.40*
(becomes *Future Science Fiction Stories*)
1952   Jan Mar May   *$1.40*
(becomes *Future Science Fiction*)
1952   Jul   *$1.40*
(becomes *Future Science Fiction Stories*)
1952   Sep   *$1.40*
(becomes *Future Science Fiction*)
1952   Nov   *$1.40*
1953   Jan Mar Sep Nov   *$1.40*
1953   MayJV JulJV   *$2.80*

1954   Jan Mar Aug Oct   *$1.00*
1954   JunPKD   *$2.00*
1955   #28   *$1.00*
1956   #30   *$1.00*
1956   #29PKD   *$2.00*
1956/57   Win   *$1.00*
1957   Spr Sum Fal   *$1.00*
1958   Feb Apr Jun Aug Oct Dec   *$1.00*
1959   Feb Apr Jun Aug Oct Dec   *$1.00*
1960   Feb Apr   *$1.00*

GALAXY MAGABOOKS (see *Magabook*)

GALAXY SCIENCE FICTION (1950–1980)

At one time, *Galaxy* was one of The Big Three science-fiction magazines (the others being *Astounding* and *The Magazine of Fantasy and Science Fiction*). In fact, *Galaxy* was a leading contender for the top spot under editor Horace Gold. The publication was brash and brassy and very, very modern during the 1950s, with a bold cover design, top authors, and a breezy contemporary style. Social satire was the magazine's stock in trade, epitomized by the work of Frederik Pohl and Robert Sheckley. Advertising came in for a lot of attention, since the world was newly aware of the manipulative tricks of *The Hidden Persuaders* as used by *The Man in the Gray Flannel Suit*. Translated into if-this-goes-on science fiction, the examination of and satire on advertising hit its peak with *The Space Merchants* by Frederik Pohl and C. M. Kornbluth (serialized in *Galaxy* as ''Gravy Planet''). Many stories from *Galaxy* were dramatized on the radio program *X Minus One*.

Gold made no secret of his intention of unseating *Astounding* as the field's top magazine. He went after—and got—most of *ASF*'s writers. He signed Willy Ley to write a science column. He ran serials by Clifford D. Simak, Isaac Asimov, and Robert A. Heinlein. The magazine and many of the stories it published won awards.

But Gold's health, precarious at best, curtailed his editorship. His successors, all talented people, lacked his fire and drive, although their work was technically excellent and they published many great stories and discovered many top talents. Frederik Pohl edited the magazine for a while. So did Lester del Rey. Judy-Lynn Benjamin learned the editing business at the magazine, then went to Ballantine Books where she quickly demonstrated that she was now the field's top editor. She married Lester del Rey, and Ballantine renamed its science-fiction line for her: Del Rey Books. (Lester edited the fantasy line, also under the Del Rey imprint.) Various others edited the magazine but, somehow, it wasn't the same.

Companion magazines (*If, Worlds of Tomorrow, Beyond, Galaxy Science Fiction Novels, International Science Fiction*) came and went. Paperback books replaced the magazines in importance within the field. Major novels, which once would certainly have had magazine serialization before book publication, bypassed the magazines entirely, some of them appearing as paperback originals.

At the end of 1977, the magazine began putting only its volume and number on the covers although the date still appeared in the indicia at the bottom of the contents pages (Volume 38, No. 8 was the first, designated on the contents pages as the October 1977 issue). Clearly, this was an indication of troubled times even though the magazine still appeared on a sometimes monthly basis.

In 1979, after almost 30 years of publication, the magazine died, not with the bang it started out with, but with a whimper. It was still laboring to complete a serial, Frederik Pohl's *Jem*, which had already come out in hardcover book form between the time the serial started and the final (as of then) issue of *Galaxy*, which contained part four of five installments (it was originally announced as a four-part serial).

A year later, after *Jem* had been reprinted in paperback, the next—truly final—issue of *Galaxy* was published, in a radically different format, by the publisher of *Galileo*. The 8½" × 11" magazine even contained the final installment of *Jem*. That final issue was never distributed to newsstands; copies are available only through specialists in back-issue science fiction.

1953   Hugo

1950   Oct   *$20.00*
1950   Nov Dec   *$1.25*
1951   Jan Feb Mar Apr May Jun Jul Aug   *90¢*
1951   SepRAH OctRAH NovRAH DecJV   *$2.00*
1952   Jan Apr May Jun Jul Aug Sep Oct Nov Dec   *90¢*
1952   FebRAH MarRAH   *$2.00*
1953   Feb Mar Apr May Jul Aug Sep Oct Nov Dec   *90¢*

1953   JanPKD JunPKD   *$2.00*
1954   Jan Feb Mar Apr May Jun Jul Aug Nov Dec   *75¢*
1954   SepPKD OctPKD   *$1.50*
1955   Jan Feb Mar Apr May Jun Jul Aug Sep Oct   *75¢*
1955   NovPKD   *$1.50*
1956   Jan Feb Mar Apr May Jun Jul Aug Sep Oct Nov Dec   *75¢*
1957   Jan Feb Mar Apr May Jun Jul Aug Sep Oct Nov Dec   *75¢*
1958   Jan Feb Mar Apr May Jun Jul Aug Sep   *75¢*
(becomes *Galaxy Magazine*)
1958   Oct Nov   *75¢*
1958   DecJV   *$1.50*
1959   Feb Apr Jun Aug Oct   *75¢*
1959   DecPKD   *$1.50*
1960   Feb Apr Jun Aug Oct Dec   *75¢*
1961   Feb Apr Jun Oct Dec   *60¢*
1961   AugJV   *$1.20*
1962   Feb Apr Jun Oct Dec   *60¢*
1962   AugJV   *$1.20*
1963   Feb Apr Jun Aug Oct   *60¢*
1963   DecPKD   *$1.20*
1964   Apr Jun Aug Dec   *60¢*
1964   FebPKD OctPKD   *$1.20*
1965   Feb Apr Jun Aug Oct Dec   *60¢*
1966   Feb Apr Jun Aug Oct Dec   *60¢*
1967   Feb Apr Jun Aug Oct Dec   *60¢*
1968   Feb Apr Jun Jul Aug Sep Oct Nov Dec   *60¢*
1969   Jan Feb Mar Apr May Jul Sep Oct Nov Dec   *60¢*
1970   Feb Mar Apr May Jun Jul Aug/Sep Oct/Nov Dec   *60¢*
1971   Jan Feb Mar Apr Jul Sep Nov   *60¢*
1972   Jan Mar May Jul Sep Nov   *60¢*
1973   Jan Mar May Jul Sep Oct Nov Dec   *60¢*
1974   Jan Feb Mar Apr May Jun Jul Aug Sep Oct Nov Dec   *60¢*
1975   Jan Feb Mar Apr May Jun Jul Aug Sep Oct   *60¢*
1976   Jan Feb Mar May Jul Sep Oct Nov Dec   *60¢*
1977   Mar Apr May Jun Jul Aug Sep Oct Nov   *60¢*
1978   Dec/Jan Feb Mar Apr May Jun Sep Nov/Dec   *60¢*
1979   Mar/Apr Jun/Jul Sep/Oct   *60¢*
1980   Vol. 40, #1 (final issue, never distributed)   *$2.50*

GALAXY SCIENCE FICTION NOVELS (1950–1961)

This line of digest-sized novels began concurrently with *Galaxy* and mixed reprints and new novels. With #32 in the series, the format changed to that of paperback books. With #36, there was a team-up with Beacon Books, the books got slightly taller, and there was a sudden emphasis on softcore sex on the covers, though not always in the contents. A favorite of fans at the time was the blurb on the cover of #39:

> "Randall Garrett and Larry M. Harris
> Forced to make love to beautiful women!
> This is adult Science Fiction at its best."

Note: Most of these are reprints. The copyright, for example, on #9–#13 is 1951, but these editions were actually on sale in 1952.

1950   #1 *Sinister Barrier* by Eric Frank Russell   *$1.50*
1950   #2 *The Legion of Space* by Jack Williamson   *$1.50*
1951   #3 *Prelude to Space* by Arthur C. Clarke   *$1.50*
1951   #4 *The Amphibians* by S. Fowler Wright   *$1.50*
1951   #5 *The World Below* by S. Fowler Wright   *$1.50*
1951   #6 *The Alien* by Raymond F. Jones   *$1.50*
1951   #7 *Empire* by Clifford D. Simak   *$1.50*
1951   #8 *Odd John* by Olaf Stapledon   *$1.50*
1951   #9 *Four Sided Triangle* by William F. Temple   *$1.50*
1951   #10 *(The) Rat Race* by Jay Franklin   *$1.50*
1951   #11 *The City in the Sea* by Wilson Tucker   *$1.50*
1951   #12 *The House of Many Worlds* by Sam Merwin, Jr.   *$1.50*
1951   #13 *Seeds of Life* by John Taine   *$1.50*
1953   #14 *Pebble in the Sky* by Isaac Asimov   *$1.50*
1932[53]   #15 *Three Go Back* by J. Leslie Mitchell   *$1.50*
1953   #16 *The Warriors of Day* by James Blish   *$1.50*
1953   #17 *Well of the Worlds* by Lewis Padgett   *$1.50*
1953   #18 *City at World's End* by Edmond Hamilton   *$1.50*
1953   #19 *Jack of Eagles* by James Blish   *$1.50*
1954   #20 *The Black Galaxy* by Murray Leinster   *$1.50*
1954   #21 *The Humanoids* by Jack Williamson   *$1.50*
1954   #22 *Killer to Come* by Sam Merwin, Jr.   *$1.50*
1954   #23 *Murder in Space* by David V. Reed   *$1.50*
#24   *Lest Darkness Fall* by L. Sprague de Camp   *$1.50*
#25   *The Last Spaceship* by Murray Leinster   *$1.50*

#26   *Chessboard Planet* by Lewis Padgett   *$1.50*
1956   #27 *Tarnished Utopia* by Malcolm Jameson   *$1.50*
#28   *Destiny Times Three* by Fritz Leiber   *$1.50*
1957   #29 *Fear* by L. Ron Hubbard   *$3.00*
#30   *Double Jeopardy* by Fletcher Pratt   *$1.50*
#31   *Shambleau* by C. L. Moore   *$1.50*
#32   *Address: Centauri* by F. L. Wallace   *$1.50*
#33   *Mission of Gravity* by Hal Clement   *$1.50*
1958   #34 *Twice in Time* by Manly Wade Wellman   *$1.50*
1958   #35 *The Forever Machine* by Mark Clifton and Frank Riley   *$1.50*
1959   (#36) *Odd John* by Olaf Stapledon   *$1.50*
1959   (#37) *The Deviates* by Raymond F. Jones   *$1.50*
1959   (#38) *Troubled Star* by George O. Smith   *$1.50*
1959   (#39) *Pagan Passions* by Randall Garrett and Larry M. Harris   *$1.50*
1960   (#40) *Virgin Planet* by Poul Anderson   *$1.50*
1960   (#41) *Flesh* by Philip Jose Farmer   *$1.50*
1960   (#42) *The Sex War* by Sam Merwin, Jr.   *$1.50*
1960   (#43) *A Woman a Day* by Philip Jose Farmer   *$1.50*
1960   (#44) *The Mating Cry* by A. E. van Vogt   *$1.50*
1961   (#45) *The Male Response* by Brian Aldiss   *$1.50*
1961   (#46) *Sin in Space* by Cyril Judd   *$1.50*

GALILEO (1976–1980)

The 8½″ × 11″ magazine had stiff cardboard covers and fairly cheap interior paper. It contained a number of articles, interviews, columns, and continuing features in addition to its fiction.

1976   #1 #2   *$1.25*
1977   #3 #4 #5   *$1.25*
1978   #6 #7 #8 #9 #10   *$1.25*
1979   #11/12 #13(Jul) #14(Sep) #15(Nov)   *$1.25*
1980   #16(Jan)   *$1.25*

> *NOTE:* Listed prices are for items in *GOOD* condition.
> *Very Good = two times listed price.*
> *Fine = three times listed price.*
> *Mint = four times listed price.*

GAMMA (1963-1965)

The digest magazine offered a few reprints and a number of newer stories. Most of its contributors lived in California.

1963 #1 (Spr) *$2.75*
1963 #2 (Fal) *$2.50*
1964 #3 *$2.50*
1965 Feb Sep *$2.50*

GHOST STORIES (1926-1932)

The early pulp magazine printed, obviously, ghost stories.

1926 Jul *$15.00*
1926 Aug Sep Oct Nov Dec *$10.00*
1927 Jan Feb Mar Apr May Jun Jul Aug Sep Oct Nov Dec *$10.00*
1928 Jan Feb Mar Apr May Jun Jul Aug Sep Oct Nov Dec *$10.00*
1929 Jan Feb Mar Apr May Jun Jul Aug Sep Oct Nov Dec *$10.00*
1930 Jan Feb Mar Apr May Jun Jul Aug Sep Oct Nov Dec *$10.00*
1931 Jan Feb Mar Apr May Jun Jul Sep Nov *$10.00*
1932 Jan *$10.00*

GOLDEN FLEECE (1938-1939)

Note that Margaret Brundage did the cover on the last issue. This was an adventure magazine, but it printed a considerable amount of fantasy and a number of stories by the fantasy-related Robert E. Howard.

1938 Oct *$20.00*
1938 Nov Dec *$15.00*
1939 Jan Feb Mar Spr May *$15.00*
1939 Jun*B* *$30.00*

GREAT SCIENCE FICTION/SCIENCE FICTION GREATS/S.F. GREATS (1965–1971)

Sometimes the sub-head, *From Amazing* or *From Fantastic,* was added to the series of reprints from those magazines.

1965   #1   *50¢*
1966   #2 #3 #4 #5   *50¢*
1967   #6 #7 #8(Fal) #9(Win)   *50¢*
1968   #10(Spr) #11(Sum) #12(Fal)   *50¢*
(becomes *Science Fiction Greats*)
1969   #13(Win)   *50¢*
1969   #14(Spr) (unauthorized all-Harlan Ellison issue)   *50¢*
1969   #15(Sum) #16(Win)   *50¢*
1970   #17(Spr)   *50¢*
(becomes *S.F. Greats*)
1970   #18(Sum) #19(Fal) #20(Win)   *50¢*
1971   #21(Spr)   *50¢*

GREAT SCIENCE FICTION STORIES (see *A Treasury of Great Science Fiction Stories*)

HAUNT OF HORROR, THE (1973)

Marvel Comics published the digest-sized magazine, using a mixture of established science-fiction writers and artists and some comics writers and artists. The magazine was seriously overprinted and lasted only two issues—both of which print Harlan Ellison's story, "Neon." The printing was botched in the first issue, reversing the order of Ellison's last two pages, so the entire story was reprinted, correctly, in the second issue, with a new illustration.

Incidentally, Marvel Comics also published a black-and-white comics magazine called *The Haunt of Horror* (1974–1975). It is unrelated to this magazine.

1973   JuneREH   *$1.50*
1973   Aug   *$1.50*

HORROR SEX TALES (1972)

For more information, see the listing for *Sex Tales*. This magazine had a story credited to Edward D. Wood, Jr., fabled as the author and director of the cult-classic bad movie, *Plan 9 From Outer Space*. It seems likely that other stories in this and the other *Sex Tales* magazines were also written by Wood—the contents pages are replete with names which *have* to be pseudonyms.

1972   #1   *50¢*

IF WORLDS OF SCIENCE FICTION/WORLDS OF IF SCIENCE FICTION (1952–1986)

The digest-sized magazine began life under the editorship of Paul W. Fairman, who had been a writer and editor for the pulp *Amazing,* and it began as a digest version of *Amazing*. Under other editors—and *If* had quite a few, including Larry T. Shaw and Damon Knight—it developed in other directions. Eventually, it was taken over by the publisher of *Galaxy* and made into a sort of little-sister publication of that magazine. In various fan polls, however, *If* proved to be more popular than its sibling, though that did not prevent it from pre-deceasing (being "combined with") *Galaxy.*

Of particular note to collectors is the March 1969 issue, which celebrates the magazine's winning of the Hugo Award for Best Magazine for the third year in a row by publishing an issue featuring the Hugo Award-winning authors and artists of 1968, including Roger Zelazny, Harlan Ellison, Philip Jose Farmer, Anne McCaffrey, Fritz Leiber, Ted White, George Scithers, Jack Gaughan, and George Barr.

In 1986, one issue of *If* appeared, continuing the numbering where the original series left off. More issues were promised, but they have so far failed to materialize.

   1966   Hugo
   1967   Hugo
   1968   Hugo

1952   Mar   *$5.00*
1952   May Jul Nov   *$1.50*
1952   SepPKD   *$3.00*
1953   Jan Mar May Nov   *$1.10*

1953   JulJV SepPKD   *$2.20*
1954   Jan Mar Jun Jul Sep Oct Dec   *$1.10*
1954   AprPKD MayPKD AugPKD NovPKD   *$2.20*
1955   Jan Feb May Jun Aug Oct Dec   *$1.00*
1955   MarPKD AprPKD   *$2.00*
1956   Feb Apr Jun Aug Oct Dec   *$1.00*
1957   Feb Apr Jun Aug Oct Dec   *$1.00*
1958   Feb Apr Jun Aug Oct   75¢
1958   DecPKD   *$1.50*
1959   Feb Nov   75¢
1959   JulPKD SepPKD   *$1.50*
1960   Jan Mar May Jul Sep Nov   75¢
1961   Jan Mar May Jul Sep   75¢
(becomes *Worlds of If Science Fiction* on cover logo)
1961   Nov   75¢
1962   Jan Mar May Jul Sep   75¢
1962   NovRAH   *$1.50*
1963   May Jul Sep Nov   75¢
1963   JanRAH MarRAH   *$1.50*
1964   Mar May Nov Dec   75¢
1964   JanPKD JulRAH AugRAH OctRAH   *$1.50*
1965   Jan Feb Mar Apr May Jun Jul Aug Sep Oct Nov   75¢
1965   DecRAH   *$1.50*
1966   May Jun Jul Aug Sep Oct Nov Dec   60¢
1966   JanRAH FebRAH MarRAH AprRAH   *$1.20*
1967   Jan Feb Mar Apr May Jun Jul Aug Sep Oct Nov Dec   60¢
1968   Jan Feb Mar Apr May Jun Jul Aug Sep Oct Nov Dec   60¢
1969   Jan Feb Mar Apr May Jun Jul Aug Sep Oct Nov Dec   60¢
1970   Jan Feb Mar Apr May/Jun Jul/Aug Sep/Oct Nov/Dec   50¢
1971   Jan/Feb Mar/Apr Jun Aug Oct Dec   50¢
1972   Feb Apr Jun Aug Oct Dec   50¢
1973   Feb Apr Jun Aug Oct Dec   50¢
1974   Feb Apr Jun Aug Oct Dec/#175   50¢
1986   Fal(Sep/Nov) (Vol 23 #1) (#176)   *$1.50*

IMAGINATION (1950–1958)

William L. Hamling, former editor of *Amazing* and *Fantastic Adventures* and future editor of the men's magazine *Rogue*, was the editor of this magazine, which features mostly first-draft, thud-and-blunder space opera. Few fans have much good to say about the hastily written stories published in *Imagination,* but it did provide a training ground for several young authors who were earning a living while learning a trade; those authors included Randall Garrett, Robert Silverberg, and Harlan Ellison.

In addition, several of the early issues of this digest-sized magazine contain good stories, stories many editors would have been proud to print, including frequently reprinted stories by Ray Bradbury and Theodore Sturgeon.

1950	Oct *$3.00*
1950	Nov *$1.00*
1951	Feb Apr Jun Sep Nov *$1.00*
1952	Jan Mar May Jul Sep Oct Dec *75¢*
1953	Apr May Aug Sep *75¢*
1953	JanPKD FebPKD JunPKD JulPKD OctPKD NovRAH DecPKD *$1.50*
1954	Jan Feb Mar Apr May Jun Aug Sep Oct Nov *75¢*
1954	JulPKD DecPKD *$1.50*
1955	Jan Feb Mar Apr May Oct Dec *75¢*
1955	JunPKD JulPKD *$1.50*
1956	Apr Jun Aug Oct Dec *75¢*
1956	FebPKD *$1.50*
1957	Feb Apr Jun Aug Oct Dec *75¢*
1958	Feb Apr Jun Aug Oct *75¢*

IMAGINATIVE TALES/SPACE TRAVEL (1954–1958)

The digest-sized companion to *Imagination* began as a vehicle for reprinting light-comedy fantasies from *Fantastic Adventures* but soon switched to publishing the same sort of space opera as its sister magazine.

1954	Sep Nov *$1.75*
1955	Jan Mar May Jul Sep *$1.40*
1955	NovPKD *$2.80*
1956	Jan Mar May Jul Sep Nov *$1.40*
1957	Jan Mar May Jul Sep Nov *$1.40*
1958	Jan Mar May *$1.40*

(becomes *Space Travel*)
1958   July Sep Nov   *$1.40*

INFINITY (1970–1973)

An anthology of original science-fiction stories published on a periodical basis was an attempt at a paperback magazine. The publisher,
Lancer Books (also noted as the original paperback publisher of most
of Robert E. Howard's "Conan" books), went bankrupt after five
volumes of this series were published. The editor was Robert Hoskins
and the series was called a "lineal descendant" of *Infinity Science
Fiction* magazine and Arthur C. Clarke's "The Star," which appeared
in the magazine's first issue, was reprinted in the paperback's first
volume.

1970   Infinity One   *75¢*
1971   Infinity Two   *75¢*
1972   Infinity Three Infinity Four   *75¢*
1973   Infinity Five   *75¢*

INFINITY SCIENCE FICTION (1955–1958)

Larry Shaw edited the digest-sized magazine, which printed a number
of good stories by writers destined for greatness. For example, it was
the first magazine to publish a story by Harlan Ellison ("Glow
Worm," in the February 1956 issue). It also printed Arthur C. Clarke's
"The Star," which has since become a classic, in its first issue. It is,
in sum, an extremely enjoyable magazine.

1955   Nov   *$2.00*
1956   Feb Jun Aug Oct Dec   *$1.00*
1957   Feb Apr Jun Sep Oct Nov   *90¢*
1957   JulJV   *$1.80*
1958   Jan Mar Apr Jun Aug Oct Nov   *60¢*

INTERNATIONAL SF (1967–1968)

The short-lived, digest-sized companion to *Galaxy* offered translations
of science-fiction stories from other countries.

1967   Jan   *$1.00*
1968   Jun   *$1.00*

ISAAC ASIMOV'S SCIENCE FICTION ANTHOLOGY (1979–1983)

This thick, digest-sized newsstand publication offered reprints from *Isaac Asimov's Science Fiction Magazine*; copies were also published in hardcover for book stores.

1979   (1)Fal/Win(2)   *$1.00*
1980   Spr/Sum(3) Fal/Win(4)   *$1.00*
1982   (5) (6)   *$1.00*
1983   Spr/Sum(7) Fal/Win(8)   *$1.00*

ISAAC ASIMOV'S SCIENCE FICTION MAGAZINE (1977–)

Isaac Asimov is, of course, a famed and prolific author and editor (at this writing, he is bearing down on 400 published books, including novels, story collections, anthologies, limerick collections, joke collections, and a variety of non-fiction books on subjects including religion, history, literature, and, of course, various branches of science). He is also the only living American author to have a science-fiction magazine named for him—two, including the now-defunct *Asimov's SF Adventure Magazine* (see *A. Merritt's Fantasy*).

IASFM grew quickly. In its first year, it was published quarterly. In its second year, it was bi-monthly. It went to monthly publication in its third year. Since 1981, it has been published thirteen times a year, as has its companion publication, *Analog*. The digest-sized magazine has won several Hugo Awards.

Each issue of the magazine has at least an editorial by Dr. Asimov and he often contributes a story as well, but he leaves the actual editing up to others, starting with George H. Scithers (who has also edited *Amazing* and *Weird Tales*), followed by Shawna McCarthy, and, currently, Gardner F. Dozois.

1977   Spr Sum Fal Win   *$1.50*
1978   Jan/Feb Mar/Apr May/Jun Jul/Aug Sep/Oct Nov/Dec   *60¢*
1979   Jan Feb Mar Apr May Jun Jul Aug Sep Oct Nov Dec   *60¢*
1980   Jan Feb Mar Apr May Jun Jul Aug Sep Oct Nov Dec   *60¢*
1981   Jan19 Feb16 Mar16 Apr13 May11 Jun8 Jul6 Aug3 Aug31
      Sep28 Oct26 Nov23 Dec21   *60¢*
1982   Jan18 Feb15 Mar15 Apr May Jun Jul Aug Sep Oct Nov Dec
      mid-Dec   *60¢*

1983 Jan Feb Mar Apr May Jun Jul Aug Sep Oct Nov Dec mid-Dec *60¢*

1984 Jan Feb Mar Apr May Jun Jul Aug Sep Oct Nov Dec mid-Dec *60¢*

1985 Jan Feb Mar Apr May Jun Jul Aug Sep Oct Nov Dec mid-Dec *60¢*

1986 Jan Feb Mar Apr May Jun Jul Aug Sep Oct Nov Dec mid-Dec *60¢*

1987 Jan Feb Mar Apr May Jun Jul Aug Sep Oct Nov Dec mid-Dec *60¢*

ISAAC ASIMOV'S SF ADVENTURE MAGAZINE (See *Asimov's SF Adventure Magazine*)

LAST WAVE (1983–1986)

Scott Edelman edited *Last Wave*, and the first four are 8½″ × 11″, while the fifth is digest size.

1983 Oct *75¢*
1984 Win Spr Aut *75¢*
1986 Win *75¢*

MAGABOOK (1963)

This odd-sized publication (at 4¾″ × 7¼″, it was somewhere between a digest magazine and a paperback book) is often listed in back-issue dealers' catalogs as *Galaxy Magabooks,* since it was published by Galaxy Publishing Co., but that was not its actual name. It ran three issues, each reprinting two short novels by a single author. The first issue featured Lester del Rey, the second Jack Williamson, the third and final one had Theodore Sturgeon.

1963 #1 #2 #3 *75¢*

MAGAZINE OF FANTASY/THE MAGAZINE OF FANTASY AND SCIENCE FICTION (1949–)

The companion publication to *Ellery Queen's Mystery Magazine* was originally edited by Anthony Boucher and J. Francis McComas. After McComas left, Boucher edited it for several years and was followed by Avram Davidson, Robert P. Mills, and the current editor, Edward L. Ferman. Under all its editors, *F&SF* has emphasized literary values and is widely respected. Initially, it published a mixture of new and reprinted stories, but, with rare exceptions, it now publishes only new stories. It rarely publishes serials.

Most of the top names in science fiction and fantasy—and many famous names from outside those fields as well—have had stories in *F&SF*. It is the science-fiction/fantasy publication most likely to appeal to newer readers.

From October 1967 on and erratically before that, *F&SF*'s October issues have been special anniversary issues featuring all-star author line-ups. For more than two decades, Isaac Asimov has contributed a science column in every issue; in recent years, Harlan Ellison has contributed a media commentary in most issues. Other issues deserving special collector attention are the single-author issues in which the cover, at least one article, and some fiction is devoted to a particular author. Those issues—and the author involved—are indicated in parentheses following the cover date.

1958   Hugo

1959   Hugo

1960   Hugo

1963   Hugo

1969   Hugo

1970   Hugo

1971   Hugo

1972   Hugo

1949   Fal   *$20.00*
(becomes *The Magazine of Fantasy and Science Fiction*)
1950   Win-Spr Sum   *$4.00*
1950   Fal Dec   *$2.50*
1951   Feb Apr Jun Aug Oct Dec   *$1.75*
1952   Feb Apr Jun Aug Sep Oct Dec   *$1.25*
1952   NovPKD   *$2.50*
1953   Jan Mar Apr May Aug Sep Oct Nov Dec   *$1.00*
1953   FebPKD JunPKD JulPKD   *$2.00*
1954   Feb Mar Apr Aug Sep Oct Nov   *90¢*

1954   JanPKD MayRAH JunRAH JulRAH DecPKD   *$1.80*
1955   Jan Feb Mar Apr May Jun Jul Aug Sep Oct Nov Dec   *90¢*
1956   Jan Feb Mar Apr May Jun Jul Aug Sep   *90¢*
1956   OctRAH NovRAH DecRAH   *$1.80*
1957   Jan Feb Mar Apr May Jun Jul Sep Oct Nov Dec   *90¢*
1957   AugRAH   *$1.80*
1958   Jan Feb Mar Apr May Jun Jul Nov Dec   *90¢*
1958   AugRAH SepRAH OctRAH   *$1.80*
1959   Feb Apr May Jun Jul Aug Sep Dec   *90¢*
1959   JanPKD MarRAH OctRAH NovRAH   *$1.80*
1960   Jan Feb Mar Apr May Jun Jul Aug Sep Oct Nov Dec   *75¢*
1961   Jan Feb Mar Apr May Jun Jul Aug Sep Oct Nov Dec   *75¢*
1962   Jan Feb Mar Apr May Jun Jul Aug Sep(Sturgeon) Oct Nov Dec   *75¢*
1963   Jan Feb Mar Apr May(Bradbury) Oct Nov Dec   *75¢*
1963   JunJV JulRAH AugRAH SepRAH   *$1.50*
1964   Jan Feb Mar Apr May Jun Aug Sep Oct Nov Dec   *75¢*
1964   JulPKD   *$1.50*
1965   Jan Feb Mar Apr May Jun Jul Aug Sep Oct Nov   *75¢*
1965   DecJV   *$1.50*
1966   Jan Mar May Sep Oct(Asimov) Nov Dec   *60¢*
1966   FebJV AprPKD JunJV JulJV AugREH   *$1.20*
1967   Jan Mar Apr May Jun Jul Aug Sep Oct Nov Dec   *60¢*
1967   FebREH   *$1.20*
1968   Jan Feb Mar Apr May Jun Jul Aug Sep Oct Nov Dec   *60¢*
1969   Jan Feb Mar Apr May Jun Jul Aug Sep Nov Dec   *60¢*
1969   OctPKD   *$1.20*
1970   Jan Feb Mar Apr May Jun Jul Aug Sep Oct Nov Dec   *60¢*
1971   Jan Mar Apr(Anderson) May Jun Jul Aug Sep Oct Nov Dec   *60¢*
1971   FebJV   *$1.20*
1972   Jan Feb Mar Apr(Blish) May Jun Sep Oct Nov Dec   *60¢*
1973   JulJV AugJV   *$1.20*
1973   Jan Feb Mar Apr Jun Jul Aug Sep(Pohl) Oct Nov Dec   *60¢*
1973   MayJV   *$1.20*
1974   Jan Feb Mar Apr(Silverberg) May Jun Jul Aug Sep Nov Dec   *60¢*
1974   OctPKD   *$1.20*
1975   Jan Feb Mar Apr May Jun Jul Aug Sep Oct Nov Dec   *60¢*

1976 Jan Feb Mar Apr May Jun Jul Aug Sep Oct Nov(Knight) Dec *60¢*

1977 Jan Feb Mar Apr May Jun Jul(Ellison) Aug Sep Oct Nov Dec *60¢*

1978 Jan Mar Apr May Jun Jul Aug Sep Nov Dec *60¢*

1978 FebSK OctSK *$5.00*

1979 Jan Feb Mar Apr May Jun Jul Aug Sep Oct(30th anniv/double-sized) Nov Dec *60¢*

1980 Jan Feb Mar May Jun Jul Aug Sep Oct Nov Dec *60¢*

1980 AprSK *$5.00*

1981 Jan Mar Apr May Jun Aug Sep Nov Dec *60¢*

1981 FebSk JulSK OctSK *$5.00*

1982 Jan Feb Mar Apr May Jun Jul Aug Sep Oct Nov Dec *60¢*

1983 Jan Feb Mar Apr May Jun Jul Aug Sep Oct Nov Dec *60¢*

1984 Jan Feb Mar Apr May Jun Jul Aug Sep Oct Nov Dec *60¢*

1984 JunSK *$5.00*

1985 Jan Feb Mar Apr May Jun Jul Aug Sep Oct Nov Dec *60¢*

1986 Jan Feb Mar Apr May Jun Jul Aug Sep Oct Nov Dec *60¢*

1987 Jan Feb Mar Apr May Jun Jul Aug Sep Oct Nov Dec *60¢*

MAGAZINE OF FANTASY AND SCIENCE FICTION (see *Magazine of Fantasy*)

MAGAZINE OF HORROR (1963–1971)

For the most part, this digest-sized magazine edited by Robert A.W. Lowndes reprinted stories from *Weird Tales* and other fantasy and horror pulp magazines. It did, however, also publish several new stories. A companion magazine, *Startling Mystery,* published similar stories.

1963 Aug Nov *$1.00*

1964 Feb MayHPL Sep Nov *$1.00*

1965 JanHPL Apr JunREH Aug NovREH Win 65/66REH *$1.00*

1966 SumREH Win *$1.00*

1967 SprREH Sum Fal NovREH *$1.00*

1968 JanREH Mar MayREH JulREH Sep NovHPL *$1.00*

1969 Jan Mar May JulREH Sep DecHPL *$1.00*

1970 FebREH May Sum FalREH *$1.00*

1971 Feb *$1.00*

MAGIC CARPET (see *Oriental Stories*)

MARVEL SCIENCE FICTION (see *Marvel Science Stories*)

MARVEL SCIENCE STORIES/MARVEL TALES/MARVEL STORIES/MARVEL SCIENCE FICTION (1938–1952)

In its pulp incarnation, this magazine was a part of the same publishing firm as Timely Comics (where Captain America, The Human Torch, and The Sub-Mariner appeared), the forerunner to today's Marvel Comics. It changed sizes almost as often as it changed its title: The May, August, and November 1951 issues are digest-sized; all previous issues and the final issue are pulp size.

1938   Aug   *$5.00*
1938   Nov   *$4.00*
1939   Feb Apr/May Aug   *$4.00*
(becomes *Marvel Tales*)
1939   Dec   *$17.50*
1940   May Nov   *$5.00*
(becomes *Marvel Stories*)
1941   Apr   *$3.50*
(becomes *Marvel Science Stories*)
1950   Nov   *$1.50*
1951   Feb   *$1.50*
1951   MayJV/LRH   *$3.00*
(becomes *Marvel Science Fiction*)
1951   Aug (Dianetics discussion)   *$2.50*
1951   Nov   *$1.50*
1952   May   *$1.50*

MARVEL STORIES (see *Marvel Science Stories*)

MARVEL TALES (see *Marvel Science Stories*)

MARVEL TALES (1934–1935)

William L. Crawford published, edited, and typeset the semi-professional magazine. It printed (or reprinted) fiction by H. P. Love-craft, Robert E. Howard, Robert Bloch (his first story), and Clifford D. Simak, but it was not widely distributed or generally available. Copies are extremely rare. P. Schuyler Miller's short novel, "The Titan," was being serialized when the magazine ceased publication.

1934   May Jul/Aug Dec   *$15.00*
1935   Win(Apr/May) Sum   *$15.00*

MIRACLE SCIENCE AND FANTASY STORIES (1931)

This is perhaps the rarest of science-fiction pulp magazines. The lead story in the first issue was by editor Douglas M. Dold; the lead story in the second was by Elliott Dold, Douglas's brother. Elliott Dold was best known as an artist.

1931   Apr/May Jun/Jul   *$40.00*

MONSTER SEX TALES (1972) (see also *Sex Tales*)

This is one of at least four softcore sex-fantasy magazines, each of which apparently lasted for one issue. See *Sex Tales* for details.

1972   #1   *50¢*

THE MOST THRILLING SCIENCE FICTION EVER TOLD/ THRILLING SCIENCE FICTION/THRILLING SCIENCE FICTION ADVENTURES (1966–1975)

Another of Sol Cohen's digest-sized reprint magazine boasts (if that's the right word) one of the longest and most stupid titles of any science-fiction magazine; it reissued stories from *Amazing* and *Fantastic*.

The final issue was trumpeted as a "Big All-Star Issue," with stories by Harlan Ellison, Keith Laumer, Randall Garrett, Robert Silverberg, and Jack Sharkey; an article by Ben Bova, and an article *about* Robert A. Heinlein by Sam Moskowitz.

1966   #1 #2 #3 #4   *50¢*
1967   #5 #6 Win(#7)   *50¢*
1968   Spr Sum Fal Win   *50¢*
1969   Spr Sum Fal   *50¢*
1970   Spr Sum Fal Win   *50¢*
1971   Spr Sum Fal Dec   *50¢*
1972   Feb Apr Jun Aug Oct Dec   *50¢*

1973   Feb Apr Jun Aug Oct Dec   *50¢*
1974   Feb Apr Jun Aug Oct Dec   *50¢*
1975   Apr Jul   *50¢*

THE MYSTERIOUS TRAVELER MAGAZINE/THE MYSTERIOUS TRAVELER MYSTERY READER (1951–1952)

This is a borderline magazine for this listing. It is basically a mystery magazine with some science-fiction and fantasy content. However, it is based on a radio series which was primarily fantasy-oriented and there is at least one fantasy or science-fiction story in every issue. Still, it is borderline; if it had run for as long as *Argosy,* we wouldn't list it but there were only five issues.

1951   Nov   *$4.00*
1952   Jan Mar Jun   *$4.00*
(becomes *The Mysterious Traveler Mystery Reader*)
1952   #5   *$4.00*

NEW DESTINIES (1987–)

Destinies was edited by James Baen for Ace Books. This was, in effect, a continuation for his own firm, Baen Books.

1987   Spr Fal   *$1.00*

NEW WORLDS (1974–1975)

Following the demise of *New Worlds Quarterly,* from Berkley Books, Avon published two volumes of the same series in trade paperback editions (about digest size, only thicker) in its Equinox line. The first of these was edited by Michael Moorcock and Charles Platt, the second by Platt and Hilary Bailey. They continued their numbering from *New Worlds Quarterly.*

1974   #5   *$1.00*
1975   #6   *$1.00*

NEW WORLDS QUARTERLY (1971–1972)

In a sense, this paperback series is a continuation of the British magazine, *New Worlds*. Michael Moorcock edited this series for Berkley Books.

1971   #1 #2   50¢
1972   #3 #4   50¢

NEW WORLDS SCIENCE FICTION MAGAZINE (1960)

This digest-sized magazine reprinted stories from the British science-fiction magazine, *New Worlds,* for American audiences.

1960   Mar Apr May Jun Jul   65¢

NIGHT CRY (1984–1987)

The digest-size magazine began life as a vehicle for reprinting stories from *Rod Sterling's Twilight Zone Magazine*. The first issue is also titled *Twilight Zone Special* #1; there was a *Twilight Zone Special* #2 (a collection of trivia about the TV series) but apparently there was no separate *Night Cry* #1. This magazine printed many new stories.

1984   TZ Special #1 $1.00
1985   Sum Fal Win   65¢
1986   Spr Sum Fal Win   65¢
1987   Spr Sum   65¢

ODYSSEY (1976)

Roger Elwood edited the bedsheet magazine; he is one of the science-fiction field's more prolific anthologists. It lasted only two issues and contained no outstanding fiction, articles, or artwork.

1976   Spr Sum   75¢

ORBIT SCIENCE FICTION (1953–1954)

A lot of science fiction came along in 1953 (there were 39 titles published that year) and most of them went away as quickly as they came. This extremely slim-looking digest magazine was one of them. At five issues, it lasted longer than some.

1953   #1   *$2.00*
1953   #2PKD   *$3.00*
1954   Jul/Aug   *$1.50*
1954   Sep/OctPKD Nov/DecPKD/JV   *$3.00*

ORIENTAL STORIES/MAGIC CARPET (1930–1934)

This pulp magazine specialized in exotic fantasies, *Arabian Nights*-style stories set in far-off lands.

1930   Oct/Nov Dec/Jan   *$65.00*
1931   Feb/Mar Apr/May/Jun Sum Fal   *$62.50*
1932   Win Spr Sum   *$62.50*
(becomes *Magic Carpet*)
1933   Jan Apr Jul Oct   *$50.00*
1934   Jan   *$50.00*

ORIGINAL SCIENCE FICTION STORIES (see *Science Fiction Stories*)

OTHER WORLDS/SCIENCE STORIES/UNIVERSE SCIENCE FICTION/OTHER WORLDS SCIENCE FICTION (1949–1957)

Ray Palmer (see *Amazing Stories* for background on this most colorful of editors) left *Amazing* and *Fantastic Adventures* to publish his own science-fiction magazines. The first two issues of *Other Worlds* appeared with Robert N. Webster's name on the masthead as editor, but Palmer later said that he was the editor from the first issue on— Webster's name (apparently another of numerous Palmer pen names) appeared as editor because Palmer was still under contract to Ziff-Davis.

Whoever the editor of the first two issues had been, it didn't take Palmer long to put his own distinctive stamp on the magazine. Fiction ranged wildly in quality, from stories hastily written by Palmer himself under one of his many pseudonyms to first-class stories by top writers. In his editorials, Palmer happily made outrageous claims about having a captured flying saucer stored in his barn in Amherst, Wisconsin, and delighted in the outraged reaction of the science-fiction

Flying Saucers From Other Worlds, June 1957, about 6½″ × 9¼″; cover is a photo-composite using stills from *Forbidden Planet* and *Captive Women.* This is the "flying saucers" version of the title for the period; the cover trimming, which deleted part of the title of "Saucer Over Paris," was done by the printer and is not a defect. No copyright notice.

fans—and of federal agencies; according to Palmer's former son-in-law, the FBI sent agents to Amherst to search Palmer's barn.

The magazine was never particularly successful and Palmer tried some characteristically unusual methods of improving its chances. He split it into two magazines, *Science Stories* and *Universe Science Fiction.* He then reunited them as *Other Worlds Science Fiction* and later still alternated his science-fiction issues of *Other Worlds* with *Flying Saucers From Other Worlds,* designed to appeal to the people who had made the Shaver Mystery such a success. He said he was attempting to fool his distributors into thinking they were handling only one magazine instead of two.

From the November 1954 issue on, *Other Worlds* (and *Flying Saucers From Other Worlds*) were pulp size; all other issues were digest-sized.

Palmer died without writing his autobiography, which is a great loss; it would have been a fascinating book.

1949 Nov *$3.50*
1950 Jan Mar May Jul Sep Oct Nov *$1.00*
1951 Jan Mar May Jun/Jul Sep Oct Dec *$1.00*

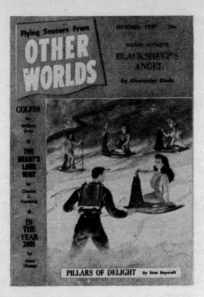

Flying Saucers From Other Worlds, October 1957, about 6½″ × 9¼″; cover by Robert Gibson Jones. This is the "Other Worlds" version of the title for the period. No copyright notice.

1952   Jan Mar Apr Jun Jul Aug Oct Nov Dec   *$1.00*
1953   Jan Feb Mar Apr May Jun Jul   *$1.00*
(becomes two titles, *Science Stories*)
1953   Oct Dec   *$1.25*
1954   Feb Apr   *$1.25*
(as *Universe Science Fiction*)
1953   Jun Sep Dec   *$1.00*
1954   Mar May Jul Sep Nov   *$1.00*
1955   Jan Mar   *$1.00*
(both become *Other Worlds Science Fiction*)
1955   May Jul Sep Nov   *90¢*
1956   Feb Apr Jun Sep Nov   *90¢*
1957   Jan Mar May   *90¢*
(becomes *Other Worlds*)
1957   Jul Sep/Oct   *90¢*

OUT OF THIS WORLD ADVENTURES (1950)

This otherwise undistinguished pulp magazine has the unusual distinction of being the only science-fiction magazine to have a comic book bound into it. The comic book was pretty undistinguished, too, although it did contain a rip-off of Conan called "Crom the Barbarian." (The Canadian edition of this magazine contains a different comic book in the second issue.)

1950   Jul Dec   *$6.25*

PERRY RHODAN (1969–1978)

Perry Rhodan is a long-running German magazine featuring the pulp-style adventures of an Earthman involved in setting up a Solar Empire. Many of the hundreds of stories in the series were translated and published in a paperback book/magazine series from Ace Books. The series was edited by Wendayne and Forrest J. Ackerman. In addition to the "Rhodan" stories, the books contained short stories, columns, film reviews, letter columns, and other impedimenta of magazines, hence it is included here.

Of particular noteworthiness to the collector is the serialization of *Cosmos*, a round-robin novel written by Ralph Milne Farley, David H. Keller, Arthur J. Burks, Bob Olsen, Francis Flagg, John W. Campbell, Jr., Rae Winters, Otis Adelbert Kline, E. Hoffmann Price, Abner J. Gelula, Raymond A. Palmer, A. Merritt, Edward E. Smith, J. Harvey Haggard, P. Schuyler Miller, Lloyd Arthur Eshbach, Eando Binder, and Edmond Hamilton. It ran in books #32 through #60.

Some of these books may have had more than one printing; the dates given are for first printings. For a major portion of the series' run, it was issued twice a month.

After #108, the Rhodan "novels" were printed two to a book through #117/118. After that, the Rhodan stories were included with a "novel" in the related "Atlan" series for three books; there were two "Atlan" stories in the fourth of these books. The series ended with the publication of what was called "the first full-length Perry Rhodan novel," *In the Center of the Galaxy.*

1969   #1 2 3   *50¢*
1970   #4 5   *50¢*
1971   #6 7 8 9 10   *50¢*

1972 #11 12 13 14 15 16 17 18 19 20 *50¢*

1973 #20 21 22 23 24 25 26 27 28 29 30 31 32 33 35 36 *50¢*

1974 #37 38 39 40 41 42 43 44 45 46 47 48 49 50 51 52 53 54 55
56 57 58 59 60 *50¢*

1975 #61 62 63 64 65 66 67 68 69 70 71 72 73 74 75 76 77 78 79
80 81 82 83 84 85 *50¢*

1976 #86 87 88 89 90 91 92 93 94 95 96 97 98 99 100 101 102 103
104 105 106 *50¢*

1977 #107 108 109/110 111/112 113/114 115/116 117/118 *50¢*

(becomes *Perry Rhodan* and *Atlan*; *Rhodan* series not numbered)

1977 Atlan #1 Atlan #2 Atlan #3 Atlan #4/5 *50¢*

1978 *In the Center of the Galaxy* ends series *50¢*

PLANET STORIES (1939–1955)

In many ways, *Planet Stories* is the ultimate pulp magazine. It certainly is, hands down, the ultimate space opera pulp, with stories like "Beast Jewel of Mars" (*Planet* used that title on two entirely different stories by two different authors—Leigh Brackett [Win 48] and V. E. Theissen [Spr 55]) and garish covers featuring bronze-brassiered bimbos and noble—albeit dim—heroes battling alien hordes. The shaggy-edged pulp paper left the reader salted with flecks of shredded paper, and the stories, for the most part, had no pretense at having redeeming social value. Occasionally, an excellent story would find its way into *Planet*'s flaking pages (the young Ray Bradbury had to sell his idiosyncratic stories *somewhere*) and some of the magazine's leading action-adventure writers plied a craft rather than a trade: Leigh Brackett always wrote better fiction than the medium required.

Most of Ray Bradbury's best early stories appeared in this publication, which also (June 1952) printed Philip K. Dick's first story.

1939 Win(Nov) *$20.00*

1940 Spr(Feb) Sum(May) Fal(Aug) *$11.25*

1940/41 Win(Nov40) *$11.25*

1941 Spr(Feb) Sum(May) Fal(Aug) *$8.75*

1941/42 Win(Nov41) *$8.75*

1942 Spr(Feb) Sum(May) Fal(Aug) *$8.75*

1942/43 Win(Nov42) *$8.75*

1943 Mar May Fal Win *$7.50*

1944 Spr Sum Fal Win *$7.50*

Planet Stories, Winter 1939, about 7″ × 9¾″; cover uncredited. This is the first issue. Copyright 1939 by Fiction House, Inc.

1944/45 Spr(Dec/Feb) *$7.50*

1945 Sum(Mar/May) Fal(Jun/Aug) Win(Sep/Nov) *$7.50*

1946 Spr(Mar/May) Sum(Mar/May) Fal(Jun/Aug) Win(Sep/Nov) *$6.25*

1946/47 Spr47(Dec/Feb) *$6.25*

1947 Sum(Mar/May) Fal(Jun/Aug) Win(Sep/Nov) *$6.25*

1947/48 Spr(Dec/Feb) *$5.00*

1948 Sum Fal Win *$5.00*

1949 Spr Sum Fal Win *$5.00*

1950 Spr Sum Fal Nov *$5.00*

1951 Jan Mar May Sep Nov *$4.00*

1951 JulJV *$8.00*

1952 Jan Mar May Nov *$3.75*

1952 JulPKD SepPKD *$7.50*

1953 Jan Mar Jul Sep Nov *$3.75*

1953 MayPKD *$7.50*

1954 Mar Sum Fal *$3.75*

Planet Stories, Spring 1944, about 7″ × 9¾″; cover by Graham Ingels (1915–). Copyright 1943 by Love Romances Publishing Co., Inc.

Planet Stories, Winter 1948, about 7″ × 10″; cover by (Allen) Anderson. *Planet* ran two different stories titled "The Beast-Jewel of Mars." This was by Leigh Brackett, and the other was by V. E. Thiessen and ran in the Spring 1955 issue. Copyright 1948 by Love Romances Publishing Co., Inc.

1954   JanPKD MayPKD   *$7.50*
1954/55 Win   *$3.75*
1955   Spr Sum   *$3.75*

QUARK (1970–1971)

More of a literary review than a science-fiction or fantasy magazine, *Quark* was also a paperback series, published by Paperback Library, not a standard-format magazine. It was edited by Samuel R. Delany and his then-wife, Marilyn Hacker. It contained a considerable amount of fantasy.

1970   #1   *65¢*
1971   #2 #3 #4   *65¢*

RIGEL SCIENCE FICTION (1981–1983)

This 8½″ × 11″ magazine offered a variety of fiction from professional writers but probably qualifies as a semi-professional publication, done more as a hobby than a business.

1981   Sum Fal   *65¢*
1982   Win(#3) Spr Fal Win(#6)   *65¢*
1983   Spr Sum   *65¢*

ROCKET STORIES (1953)

The digest-sized magazine was deliberately aimed at the audience for space opera, juvenile science fiction.

1953   Apr   *$2.50*
1953   Jul Sep   *$1.25*

ROD SERLING'S THE TWILIGHT ZONE MAGAZINE (1981–)

This 8½″ × 11″ magazine attempts to capture fans of the TV series and also the audience for science-fiction, fantasy, and horror movies; as a consequence, the publication is heavily weighted toward movie articles and checklists of such TV series as *The Twilight Zone, Night Gallery,* and *The Outer Limits*. The February 1986 issue has an article with many details on collecting the work of Stephen King, but there is no specific list of that writer's magazine appearances.

1981   Apr May Jun Jul Aug Sep Oct Nov Dec   *$1.25*
1982   Jan Feb Mar Apr May Jun Jul(review by SK) Aug Sep Oct Dec   *$1.25*
1982   NovSK   *$5.00*
1983   Feb Apr Aug Oct Dec   *$1.25*
1983   JunSK   *$5.00*
1984   Feb Apr Jun Aug Oct Dec   *$1.25*
1985   Feb Apr Jun Aug Oct   *$1.25*
1985   DecSK   *$5.00*
1986   FebSK (spec ed)   *$5.00*
1986   Apr Jun Aug Oct Dec   *$1.25*
1987   Feb Apr Jun Aug Oct Dec   *$1.25*

SATELLITE SCIENCE FICTION (1956–1959)

It began life as a digest-sized publication, specializing in one long story and several very short ones per issue. With the February 1959 issue, it changed its format and became an $8^{1}/_{2}$ ″ × 11 ″ magazine.

Note: The final (June 1959) issue was not distributed to the public, though it was printed. Norm Metcalf's *The Index of Science Fiction Magazines 1951–1965* called it ''a very rare collector's item'' in 1968. It still is.

1956   OctPKD   *$2.00*
1956   DecPKD   *$2.00*
1957   Feb Apr Jun Aug Oct   *$1.00*
1957   DecJV   *$2.00*
1958   Feb Apr Jun Aug Oct   *$1.00*
1959   ($8^{1}/_{2}$ ″ × 11 ″ size) Feb Mar Apr May   *$1.00*
1959   Jun

SATURN (1957–1958)

Donald A. Wollheim was editorial consultant on this publication, which offered ''new'' (hitherto untranslated) Jules Verne stories in its first and third issues.

Saturn, subtitled *The Magazine of Science-Fiction*
1957   Mar   *$1.25*
(becomes *Saturn, Magazine of Fantasy and Science Fiction*)
1957   May   *$1.25*
(becomes *Saturn, Magazine of Science Fiction and Fantasy*)
1957   Jul   *$1.25*
1957   OctJV,RAH   *$2.50*
1958   Mar   *$1.25*

SCIENCE FANTASY *(see Science Fantasy Yearbook)*

SCIENCE FANTASY YEARBOOK/SCIENCE FANTASY *(1970–1971)*

1970   #1   *50¢*
(becomes *Science Fantasy*)
1970   Fal   *50¢*
1971   Win Spr   *50¢*

SCIENCE FICTION *(1939–1941)*

This pulp magazine faded out and in again rather rapidly, then faded out for good. It was revived, after a fashion, as *Science Fiction Stories,* a digest magazine, years later.

1939   Mar   *$6.00*
1939   Jun Aug Oct Dec   *$4.00*
1940   Mar Jun Oct   *$3.75*
1941   Jan Mar Jun Sep   *$3.75*
(combines with *Future Fiction*—see *Future Fiction*)
(changes back to *Science Fiction*)
1943   AprLRH   *$7.00*
1943   Jul   *$3.50*

SCIENCE FICTION ADVENTURES *(1952–1954)*

Four digest-sized magazines have borne this title; this one, edited by Harry Harrison and Lester del Rey at one time or another, was a companion to *Fantasy Fiction/Fantasy Magazine, Rocket Stories,* and *Space Science Fiction.* It contained a number of excellent stories.

1952   Nov   *$1.25*
1953   Feb Mar May Jul Sep   *75¢*
1953   DecPKD   *$1.50*
1954   Feb/Mar May   *75¢*

SCIENCE FICTION ADVENTURES (1956–1958)

This was the second digest-sized magazine to bear this title (the third was a British magazine which began its existence reprinting stories from this version) and was a companion magazine to *Infinity Science Fiction*. Like *Infinity*, this magazine printed a good deal of early work by such writers as Robert Silverberg and Harlan Ellison.

1956   Dec   *$1.50*
1957   Feb Apr Jun Aug Sep Oct Dec   *90¢*
1958   Jan Mar Apr Jun   *90¢*

SCIENCE FICTION ADVENTURES (see *Science Fiction Classics*)

SCIENCE FICTION CLASSICS/SCIENCE FICTION ADVENTURE CLASSICS/SCIENCE FICTION ADVENTURES/SCIENCE FICTION ADVENTURES CLASSICS/SCIENCE FICTION ADVENTURES (1967–1974)

This is yet another multi-titled Sol Cohen digest-sized magazine which reprinted stories from *Amazing* and *Fantastic*.

1967   #1 Fal Win   *50¢*
1968   Spr Sum Fal   *50¢*
(becomes *Science Fiction Adventure Classics*)
1969   Win Fal   *50¢*
1971   Win Spr Sum Fal   *50¢*
1972   Jan Mar May Jul Sep Nov   *50¢*
(becomes *Science Fiction Adventures*)
1973   Jan Mar May   *50¢*
(becomes *Science Fiction Adventures Classics*)
1973   Jul Sep Nov   *50¢*
1974   Jan Mar May Jul   *50¢*
(becomes *Science Fiction Adventures*)
1974   Sep Nov   *50¢*

SCIENCE FICTION DIGEST (1954)

This reprint magazine was a companion to *Vortex Science Fiction*. It printed a number of articles and squibs about science as well as some science fiction from general magazines.

1954 #1(Spr)JV *$1.30*
1954 #2(Fal) *65¢*

SF DIGEST (1981–1982)

The digest publication, intended as a companion periodical to *Isaac Asimov's Science Fiction Magazine*, printed a condensed version of Stephen King's *Cujo* as well as abridgments of and selections from books by Isaac Asimov, Robert Heinlein, and others.

1981 Oct/Nov *75¢*
1982 Jan/FebSK *$5.00*
1982 May/Jun *75¢*
1982 Sep/Oct RAH (double-sized) *$1.50*

SCIENCE FICTION GREATS (see *Great Science Fiction*)

SCIENCE FICTION PLUS (1953)

Hugo Gernsback intended the magazine to be his triumphant return to science-fiction magazine editing and publishing. Unfortunately, time had passed him by, and it was a bit as though D. W. Griffith were to attempt to make a movie in 1945 without taking any notice of the progress which had been made since his silent epics had been filmed. Many of the stories and features were tedious, and some newer writers complained that their stories were ruined by heavy-handed editing.

On the plus side, the magazine—particularly in its later issues, when it switched to book paper instead of enameled stock—was attractive and many of its covers were excellent. Anne McCaffrey's first science-fiction story appeared in the October 1953 issue.

1953 Mar *$5.00*
1953 Apr May Jun Aug Oct Dec *$3.75*

SCIENCE FICTION QUARTERLY (1940-1958)

This was a companion pulp magazine to *Future* and *Science Fiction*, specializing in longer lead stories.

1940   Sum *$5.00*
1941   Win Spr Sum *$4.50*
1941/42 Win *$4.50*
1942   Spr Sum Fal Win *$4.00*
1943   Spr *$4.00*
(new series)
1951   May Aug Nov *$1.25*
1952   Feb May Aug Nov *$1.25*
1953   Feb Aug Nov *$1.25*
1953   MayPKD *$2.50*
1954   Feb May Aug Nov *$1.25*
1955   Feb May Aug Nov *$1.25*
1956   Feb May Aug Nov *$1.25*
1957   May Aug Nov *$1.25*
1957   FebPKD *$2.50*
1958   Feb *$1.25*

SCIENCE FICTION STORIES (1953-1960)

The digest magazine, a revival of a pulp which ran from 1939 to 1943, was labeled "The Original *Science Fiction Stories*" in an attempt to emphasize its ties to the past. Unfortunately, the result was that many people think the magazine is called *Original Science Fiction Stories* and you sometimes will find it listed that way in sale lists.

1953   1PKD *$2.50*
1954   2PKD *$2.00*
1955   Jan Mar May Sep Nov *$1.00*
1955   JulPKD *$2.00*
1956   Jan Mar May Jul Sep Nov 75¢
1957   Mar May Jul Sep Nov 75¢
1957   JanPKD *$1.50*
1958   Jan Mar May Jun Jul Aug Sep Nov 75¢
1959   Jan Feb Mar May Jul Sep Nov 75¢
1960   Jan Mar May 75¢

SCIENCE FICTION YEARBOOK (see *SF Yearbook*)

SCIENCE STORIES (see *Other Worlds Science Stories*)

SCIENCE WONDER QUARTERLY (1929-1933)

This is one of the pulp magazines Hugo Gernsback founded after he lost the rights to *Amazing Stories*.

1929   Fal   *$17.50*
1930   Win Spr   *$10.00*
(becomes *Wonder Stories Quarterly*)
1930   Sum Fal   *$10.00*
1931   Win Spr Sum Fal   *$10.00*
1932   Win Spr Sum Fal   *$10.00*
1933   Win   *$10.00*

SCIENCE WONDER STORIES (see *Wonder Stories*)

SCIENTIFIC DETECTIVE MONTHLY (1930)

Somewhere between a science-fiction magazine and a mystery magazine, *SDM* leaned a little more toward science fiction.

1930   Jan Feb Mar Apr May   *$20.00*
(becomes *Amazing Detective Tales*)
1930   Jun Jul Aug Sep Oct   *$20.00*

SEX TALES (1972)

These are the final two words of a series of four 8½ ″ × 11 ″ magazines: *Horror Sex Tales*, *Legendary Sex Tales*, *Monster Sex Tales*, and *Weird Sex Tales*. At least some of the material published was by cult movie producer Edward D. Wood, Jr.—some of it probably pseudonymously. See the actual titles. Apparently there was only one issue of each.

SF GREATS (see *Great Science Fiction*)

SF YEARBOOK/SCIENCE FICTION YEARBOOK (1967–1971)

This was an annual which reprinted stories from the Standard magazines, *Startling Stories* and *Thrilling Wonder Stories*. It was in a standard pulp format, but with much better paper. It was similar to the earlier *Treasury of Great Science Fiction Stories/Great Science Fiction Stories*.

1967 #1 *$1.50*
1968 #2 *$1.00*
1969 #3 *$1.00*
1970 #4 *$1.00*
1971 #5 *$1.00*

SHOCK (1960)

Packaged as a suspense magazine (with excellent covers by Jack Davis), this digest magazine contained a number of fine fantasies, mostly reprints.

1960 May Jul Sep *$3.00*

SKY WORLDS (1977–1978)

This was a very thin, saddle-stitched digest magazine which reprinted mostly from *Marvel,* with some brief news squibs and a comic-book story. The first two issues are subtitled "Classics in Science Fiction"; the second two are subtitled "Marvels in Science Fiction."

1977 Nov *50¢*
1978 Feb May Aug *50¢*

SPACE ADVENTURES (1970–1971)

Apparently this was a retitling of *Science Fiction Adventure Classics* (a look at that entry will show an odd gap in 1970), it picked up the numbering with #9 and continued through #14—but *Science Fiction Adventure Classics* resumed with its own #9 while *Space Adventures* was still running, making life more challenging for collectors, indexers, and historians. This was another of Sol Cohen's several digest-sized magazines which published reprints from *Amazing* and *Fantastic*.

1970 Win(#9) Spr Sum Win(#12) *50¢*
1971 Spr Sum *50¢*

SPACE SCIENCE FICTION (1952–1953)

This was one of a group of digest magazines edited by Lester del Rey which, despite the presence of many good stories, got lost in the crowd during the glut of 1953.

1952 May *$1.50*
1952 SepREH Nov *$1.00*
1953 Feb Mar Jul *$1.00*
1953 MayPKD SepPKD *$2.00*

SPACE SCIENCE FICTION MAGAZINE (1957)

Lyle Kenyon Engle edited this undistinguished digest science-fiction magazine but later found fame and fortune as a book packager. One of his triumphs was conceiving the "Kent Family Chronicles" series of historical novels, which brought fame and fortune to science-fiction writer John Jakes.

1957 Spr *$1.50*
1957 AugPKD *$3.00*

SPACE STORIES (1952–1953)

This was an unabashed space-opera magazine from the publisher of *Startling Stories* and *Thrilling Wonder Stories*. It was the equivalent of juvenile science-fiction novels but in shorter form.

1952 OctJV *$2.50*
1952 Dec *$1.50*
1953 Feb Apr Jun *$1.50*

SPACE TRAVEL (see Imaginative Tales)

SPACEWAY (1953-1970)

This was another strange, undercapitalized publication from William Crawford. It was consistently digest-sized throughout its first incarnation, in the 1950s, but the 1969 and 1970 issues are a bit taller than most digest magazines. This publication featured several predictions by the California "psychic," Jeron King Criswell (of *Plan 9 From Outer Space* fame), which are even sillier today than they were when he made them (Mae West was destined not only to become President of the United States, but to be the first Woman on the Moon).

In its 1969–1970 incarnation, the magazine changed size with its second issue; the final four issues were in a sort of tall digest format.

Incidentally, in the last issue of the original series (June 1955), the magazine began a serial, "Radio Minds of Mars," by Ralph Milne Farley. In the January 1969 issue, "Radio Minds of Mars" is published in its entirety.

1953	Dec	*$1.50*
1954	Apr Jun Dec	*$1.00*
1954	FebLRH	*$2.00*
1955	Feb Apr Jun	*$1.00*
1969	Jan Jun OctREH	*$1.00*
1970	Jun	*$1.00*

STAR SCIENCE FICTION MAGAZINE (1958)

As if to prove that quality is not enough, this digest-sized magazine was published by Ballantine Books, edited by Frederik Pohl, and designed to carry on the success of the *Star* paperback book series published by Ballantine and edited by Pohl. It lasted only one issue.

1958   Jan   *$1.00*

STARTLING MYSTERY (1966-1969)

This digest-sized magazine featured reprints of mysteries, usually with a fantasy element, and weird stories, with and without a fantasy element.

It was an entertaining magazine, but what is most noteworthy about it is that it published the first *two* stories by Stephen King, in issue

#6 ("The Glass Floor") and #12 ("The Reaper's Image"). King's name appears on the cover of #12.

1966   Sum(#1)   *$5.00*
1966   Fal(#2)   *$3.75*
1966/67   Win(#3)   *$3.75*
1967   Spr(#4) Sum(#5)   *$3.75*
1967   Fal(#6) first published Stephen King story   *$10.00*
1967/68   Win(#7)   *$3.75*
1968   Spr(#8) Sum(#9) Fal(#10)   *$2.50*
1968/69   Win(#11)   *$2.50*
1969   Spr(#12) second published Stephen King story   *$10.00*
1969   Sum(#13) Win(#14)   *$2.50*

STARTLING STORIES (1939–1955)

One of the best of the pulp science-fiction magazines, *SS* achieved greatness through a fortuitous series of good editors—chief among them Sam Merwin, Jr. and Samuel Mines—and being in a position to get second look (right after John W. Campbell, Jr. at *Astounding*) at virtually all science-fiction manuscripts. There is an impressive amount of good science fiction in the pages of *SS,* including a lot of the best adventure stories of Henry Kuttner and an equally impressive amount of work by Fredric Brown and Ray Bradbury.

With its companion, *Thrilling Wonder Stories,* this was one of the leading science-fiction magazines of the forties. They were known as the Standard Twins (they were published by Standard Magazines).

1939   Jan   *$12.50*
1939   Mar May Jul Sep Nov   *$7.50*
1940   Jan Mar May Jul Sep Nov   *$5.25*
1941   Jan Mar May Jul Sep Nov   *$4.25*
1942   Jan Mar May Jul Sep Nov   *$3.25*
1943   Jan Mar Jun Fal(Sep)   *$3.25*
1944   Win(Dec 43) Spr(Mar) Sum(Jun) Fal(Sep)   *$3.25*
1945   Win(Dec 44) Spr(Mar) Sum(Jun) Fal(Sep)   *$2.50*
1946   Win(Dec 45) Mar Spr(May) Sum(Jul)JV Fal   *$2.50*
1947   Jan Mar Jul Sep Nov   *$2.00*
1947   MayRAH   *$4.00*

1948   Jan Mar May   *$2.00*
1948   JulJV/LRH SepJV NovJV   *$4.00*
1949   JanJV/LRH MarJV/LRH MayLRH JulLRH SepLRH NovJV/
       LRH   *$4.00*
1950   Mar May   *$1.50*
1950   JanLRH JulJV SepJV NovJV/LRH   *$3.00*
1951   Jan May Jul Nov   *$1.50*
1951   MarJV SepJV   *$3.00*
1952   Jan Feb Mar Apr May Jul Oct Nov Dec   *$1.50*
1952   JunJV AugJV SepJV   *$3.00*
1953   Feb Mar Apr May Jun Aug Oct   *$1.50*
1953   JanJV   *$3.00*
1954   Sum Fal   *$1.50*
1954   JanPKD SprJV   *$3.00*
1955   Sum Fal   *$1.50*
1955   WinPKD SprPKD   *$3.00*

STIRRING SCIENCE STORIES (1941–1942)

Donald A. Wollheim was editor-without-budget for this pulp magazine which, despite the handicap of not having anything to pay for
stories, managed to get some good ones. This was a companion magazine to *Cosmic Stories*. It printed a number of stories by Cyril M.
Kornbluth and other members of the Futurians science-fiction club.
Damon Knight's first story appeared in this magazine. The first three
issues are pulp size, the fourth and final issue is bedsheet size.

1941   Feb   *$6.25*
1941   Apr Jun   *$4.00*
1942   Apr   *$4.00*

STRANGE FANTASY (1969–1970)

This is yet another Sol Cohen digest magazine reprinting stories from
Fantastic. The first issue was #8, suggesting that it was a retitling of
yet another of these magazines, but it is unclear which one.

1969   Spr Sum Fal   *50¢*
1970   Spr Sum Fal   *50¢*

STRANGE STORIES (1939–1941)

The pulp adventure-fantasy magazine was a companion to *Startling Stories* and *Thrilling Wonder*; it printed some good Henry Kuttner stories.

1939　Feb Mar Jun Aug Oct Dec　*$3.00*
1940　Feb Apr Jun Aug Oct Dec　*$3.00*
1941　Feb　*$3.00*

THE STRANGEST STORIES EVER TOLD (1970)

The one-shot digest magazine from Sol Cohen reprinted stories from *Fantastic* and *Fantastic Adventures*.

1970　Sum　*50¢*

STRANGE TALES (1931–1933)

The pulp fantasy magazine was a companion publication to *Astounding Stories*. It is entirely unrelated to the British publication of the same name.

1931　Sep Nov　*$4.00*
1932　Jan Mar Jun Oct　*$4.00*
1933　Jan　*$4.00*

SUPER-SCIENCE FICTION (1956–1959)

This was another of those minor digest magazines which served primarily to provide eating money and writing experience for young writers Harlan Ellison and Robert Silverberg. It hasn't much to offer modern readers except the chance to see these writers in their salad years, when they were fresh and green.

1956　Dec　*$2.00*
1957　Feb Apr Jun Aug Oct Dec　*$1.50*
1958　FebJV　*$3.00*
1958　Apr Jun Aug Oct Dec　*$1.50*
1959　Feb Apr Jun Aug Oct　*$1.50*

SUPER SCIENCE NOVELS MAGAZINE (see *Super Science Stories*)

SUPER SCIENCE STORIES/SUPER SCIENCE NOVELS MAGAZINE (1940–1951)

This was a companion pulp magazine to *Famous Fantastic Mysteries* and *Fantastic Novels*; however, *SSS* published science fiction, not fantasy, and new stories, not reprints. It was a better-than-average science-fiction adventure magazine.

1940   Mar   *$6.25*
1940   Jul Sep Nov   *$5.00*
1940   MayRAH   *$12.50*
1941   Jan   *$4.00*
(becomes *Super Science Novels Magazine*)
1941   Mar May Aug   *$3.50*
(becomes *Super Science Stories*)
1941   NovRAH   *$10.50*
1942   Feb May Aug Nov   *$3.50*
1943   Feb May   *$3.50*
1949   Jan Apr Jul Sep Nov   *$1.50*
1950   Mar May Jul Nov   *$1.50*
1950   JanLRH SepJV/LRH   *$3.00*
1951   Jan Apr Jun Aug   *$1.50*

SUSPENSE (1951–1952)

Suspense is a borderline publication for inclusion here. Based on the radio show of the same name, this was primarily a mystery-story magazine, but it printed a respectable amount of fantasy and even some science fiction. Authors represented included Ray Bradbury and William Tenn.

1951   Spr   *$2.00*
1951   Sum Fal   *$2.00*
1952   Win   *$2.00*

Super Science Stories, March 1940, about 7″ × 9½″; cover uncredited. Defect is a pencilled "S" on this first issue of the publication. Listed as copyright 1940 by Fictioneers, Inc. Copyright 1940 by Popular Publications. Reprinted by permission of Blazing Publications, The Argosy Co.

Super Science Stories, May 1940, about 7″ × 9½″; cover by Gabriel Mayorga. Defects include a store stamp and grease-pencilled "15"—but there is an interior defect: The right side of the cover is reinforced by a glued strip of white paper; collectors must check magazine interiors, as well as exteriors, for condition. Listed as copyright 1940 by Fictioneers, Inc. Copyright 1940 by Popular Publications. Reprinted by permission of Blazing Publications, The Argosy Co. .

Super Science Stories, April 1949, about 7″ × 10″; cover by Lawrence (Stern Stevens) (1886–1960). Pulp writer John D. MacDonald's "novel" *Death Quotient* is also in this issue. Listed as copyright 1949 by Fictioneers, Inc. Copyright 1949 by Popular Publications. Reprinted by permission of Blazing Publications, The Argosy Co.

Super Science Novels Magazine, May 1941, about 7″ × 9½″; cover by Gabriel Mayor. Listed as copyright 1941 by Fictioneers, Inc. Copyright 1941 by Popular Publications. Reprinted by permission of Blazing Publications, The Argosy Co.

Super Science Stories, March 1950, about 7″ × 9½″; cover by (Norman) Saunders (1907–). Listed as copyright 1950 by Fictioneers, Inc. Copyright 1950 by Popular Publications. Reprinted by permission of Blazing Publications, The Argosy Co.

SWORD & SORCERY ANNUAL (1971)

This was another of the many Sol Cohen digests which reprinted stories from *Fantastic*.

1971   no number REH   *50¢*

TALES OF MAGIC & MYSTERY (1927–1928)

This was a pulp fantasy magazine edited (anonymously) by Walter B. Gibson, creator of The Shadow.

1927   Dec   *$25.00*
1928   Jan Feb MarHPL Apr   *$20.00*

TALES OF THE FRIGHTENED (1957)

This digest-sized magazine was made up entirely of short stories based on a radio program starring Boris Karloff.

1957 Spr Aug *$3.50*

10 STORY FANTASY (1951)

This was a one-shot pulp magazine in the same vein as *Avon Fantasy Reader*. It contained more than ten stories but three of them were novelettes, one of which was labeled a novel. There were ten short stories and presumably that's what the person who dreamed up the title really meant. One of the stories was "Sentinel of Eternity," a short-short story by Arthur C. Clarke which formed part of the basis for the movie, *2001: A Space Odyssey*; this was the first publication of that story.

1951 Spr *$5.00*

THRILLING SCIENCE FICTION (see *The Most Thrilling Science Fiction Ever Told*)

THRILLING SCIENCE FICTION ADVENTURES (see *The Most Thrilling Science Fiction Ever Told*)

THRILLING WONDER STORIES (see *Wonder Stories*)

TOPS IN SCIENCE FICTION (1953)

This magazine—the first issue was a pulp, the second was digest-sized—reprinted stories from *Planet Stories*.

1953 Spr Fal *$1.75*

TREASURY OF GREAT SCIENCE FICTION STORIES/ GREAT SCIENCE FICTION STORIES (1964–1966)

This pulp-format magazine was printed on very good paper. It reprinted stories from *Startling Stories* and *Thrilling Wonder Stories*, as did the earlier *Wonder Stories* (1957–1963) and the later *SF Yearbook/ Science Fiction Yearbook* (1967–1971).

1964   #1   *$1.75*
1966   #2JV/RAH   *$3.50*
(becomes *Great Science Fiction Stories*)
1966   #3   *$1.25*

TWILIGHT ZONE (see *Rod Serling's The Twilight Zone Magazine*)

TWILIGHT ZONE SPECIAL (1984)

1984   #1 (See *Night Cry*)   *$1.00*
1984   #2 *Trivia from Rod Serling's The Twilight Zone*   50¢

TWO COMPLETE SCIENCE ADVENTURE NOVELS/TWO COMPLETE SCIENCE-ADVENTURE BOOKS (1950–1954)

This pulp companion magazine to *Planet Stories* offered two stories per issue; some of them were reprints of previously published stories and books, others were originals. Really, the title says it all.

1950   WinLRH   *$3.00*
(becomes *Two Complete Science-Adventure Books*)
1951   Spr Sum Win   *$1.50*
1952   Spr Sum WinRAH   *$1.50*
1953   Spr Sum Win   *$1.50*
1954   Spr   *$1.50*

UNCANNY STORIES (1941)

This was a one-shot fantasy pulp magazine.

1941   Apr   *$15.00*

UNIVERSE SCIENCE FICTION (see *Other Worlds Science Stories*)

NOTE: Listed prices are for items in *GOOD* condition.
Very Good = *two times listed price.*
Fine = *three times listed price.*
Mint = *four times listed price.*

UNKNOWN/UNKNOWN WORLDS/FROM UNKNOWN WORLDS (1939–1943)

In the minds and hearts of many fantasy fans, this is the ultimate fantasy magazine. Edited by John W. Campbell, Jr. as a companion magazine to *Astounding, Unknown* took the approach of modernizing traditional fantasy figures: What would a ghost be like in a modern city? How would a vampire operate in modern-day America instead of in an ancient Carpathian castle? How would World War II affect vampires in central Europe?

The result was to render ancient myths and fables meaningful to modern readers and, above all, to instill a sense of fun in fantasy.

Unfortunately, reality—in the form of wartime paper shortages— won out in the end. The magazine began and ended in a pulp-size format but the issues from October 1941 through April 1943 were bedsheet size.

1939   Mar Jun Sep Oct Nov Dec   *$30.00*
1939   AprLRH MayLRH JulLRH AugLRH   *$75.00*
1940   Jan Mar May Jun   *$12.50*
1940   FebLRH AprLRH   *$31.00*
1940   Aug   *$10.00*
1940   JulLRH SepRAH OctLRH NovLRH DecLRH   *$25.00*
1941   Jun   *$10.00*
1941   FebLRH AprRAH AugLRH   *$25.00*
(becomes *Unknown Worlds*)
1941   Dec   *$10.00*
1941   OctLRH   *$25.00*
1942   Jun Aug Dec   *$10.00*
1942   FebLRH AprLRH OctRAH   *$25.00*
1943   Feb Apr Jun Aug Oct   *$10.00*

FROM UNKNOWN WORLDS (collection *From Unknown Worlds*) *(1948)*

1948 $7.50

VANGUARD SCIENCE FICTION (1958)

This digest magazine should have gone into orbit. It was edited by James Blish, a writer, critic, and editor of impeccable taste. The first issue was excellent and came out at the same time that the Vanguard satellite was successfully launched. There never was a second issue.

1958 Jun $1.00

VENTURE SCIENCE FICTION (1957–1958, 1969–1970)

Twice to date, this digest-sized, adventure-oriented, companion magazine to *F&SF* has been attempted. Both times, despite a preponderance of good stories by top names in the field, it has failed to get off the ground. It gives you some idea of the odds against any new science-fiction magazine gaining a foothold.

1957 Jan Mar May Jul Sep Nov *$1.35*
1958 Jan Mar May Jul *$1.25*
1969 May Aug Nov *$1.00*
1970 Feb May Aug *$1.00*

VERTEX (1973–1975)

This 8½" × 11" magazine came from the publishers of *Mankind*, a magazine which tried to do for world history what *American Heritage* does for American history. Despite quality paper, heavy cardboard cover stock, and good newsstand display, *Vertex* did not sell well.

In a peculiar move, the publisher switched for the last three issues to a tabloid newspaper format on cheap paper. Those issues are *extremely* hard to find today in any condition; they are almost impossible to find in mint condition.

1973 Apr Jun Aug Oct Dec *$2.00*
1974 Feb Apr Jun Aug Oct Dec *$2.00*
1975 Feb Apr *$2.00*

tabloid newspaper format:
1975   Jun Aug Oct   *$5.00*

VORTEX SCIENCE FICTION (1953)

Even in the glut of 1953, this publication was singled out by many fans as the worst of the lot. The magazine featured 20 stories in each issue and most were just space-fillers. Even here though, there are some top authors and some good stories. Marion Zimmer Bradley, who rarely writes short stories, has two in the second issue.

This was a companion magazine to *Science Fiction Digest*. It is entirely unrelated to a later British magazine called *Vortex Science Fiction*. (For that matter, it is unrelated to *Vertex*.)

1953   #1JV   *$1.50*
1953   #2   *75¢*

WEIRD HEROES (1975–1977)

This was a series of paperback books, subtitled "A New American Pulp!" which attempted to revive the tradition of the pulp magazine hero. It was packaged by Byron Preiss and relied heavily on stories and graphics from people associated with comics (Steve Englehart, Marv Wolfman, Jim Steranko, Howard Chaykin) and with people known to have a fondness for pulps (Ted White, Ron Goulart, Philip Jose Farmer). The result was an entertaining package of stories and novels, but none of them had the hoped-for staying power of The Shadow or Doc Savage. The series was published by Pyramid Books.

Volumes 1, 2, 6, and 8 were collections of stories; the rest were novels, usually featuring characters introduced in the short stories. Those novels were *Quest of the Gypsy* (Volume 3) and *Eye of the Vulture* (Volume 7) by Ron Goulart; *Nightshade* (Volume 4) by Tappan King and Beth Meacham; *Doc Phoenix: The Oz Encounter* (Volume 5) by Ted White and Marv Wolfman. In addition—related to the series but not published as part of it—there were two novels, *Guts* by Preiss and *I, Alien* by J. Michael Reaves.

1975   Volume 1 Volume 2   *75¢*
1976   Volume 3 Volume 4   *75¢*
1977   Volume 5 Volume 6 Volume 7 Volume 8   *75¢*

Vortex Science Fiction, 1953, about 5¼″ × 7½″; cover by Martin. This is the first issue. Copyright 1953 by Specific Fiction Corp.

Vortex Science Fiction, 1953, about 5½″ × 7¾″; cover by Martin. This is the final issue. Copyright 1953 by Specific Fiction Corp.

WEIRD SEX TALES (1972) (see *Sex Tales*)

1972   #1   *50¢*

WEIRD TALES (1923–1954)

This is the classic horror fantasy magazine in the field—longest-running, most famous, and probably most widely collected. Issues at a premium tend to include those with cover art by Margaret Brundage (q.v. in the chapter of names in the field). Those issues are followed by a *"B"* in the listings, and they cost up to $5 more each than the price given for the year (including those years in which all issues contained Brundage covers).

Weird Tales also was a primary market for such collectible writers as H. P. Lovecraft, Robert E. Howard, Robert Bloch, and Ray Bradbury. But the author whose early work for *Weird Tales* is most hotly sought is Tennessee Williams; at the age of 14, he sold a story, "The Vengeance of Nitocris," to *Weird Tales*. It appeared under the name of "Thomas Lanier" (his real name was Thomas Lanier Williams).

Famous and revered as the magazine is and was, it spent virtually all of its 32 years on the brink of extinction. In its last years, it switched from pulp size to digest size in the vain hope of attracting a market. The magazine was digest-sized from September 1953 through September 1954.

Under the editorship of Sam Moskowitz, a revival in a sort of pulp format was tried, but it failed after only four issues. Lin Carter edited a series of four paperback books, continuing the numbering from Moskowitz, who had continued *his* numbering from the last "real" issue of the magazine.

Recently, there were two issues of a revised magazine version, but copies were never widely distributed. All copies were sold to collectors at high prices.

In 1988, George Scithers (who had earlier edited the world's oldest science-fiction magazine, *Amazing Stories*) began editing and publishing the world's oldest fantasy-horror magazine, *Weird Tales*. Since the first issue under his aegis was dated 1988, it does not come under the scope of this book (our cut-off date is December 1987), but an address for subscription information appears at the beginning of this section of the book.

Weird Tales, July 1946, about 6¾″ × 10″; cover by Matt(hew) Fox (1906–). Defects include water damage on the right side and the cover loose from the body. Copyright 1946 by Weird Tales. Used with permission of Weird Tales Ltd.

Weird Tales, January 1953, about 6½″ × 10″; cover by Frank Kelly Freas (1922–). Copyright 1952 by Weird Tales. Used with permission of Weird Tales Ltd.

1923   Mar *$600.00*
1923   Apr *$400.00*
1923   May Jun *$300.00*
1923   Jul/Aug Sep Oct Nov *$200.00*
1924   Jan Feb Mar Apr *$125.00*
1924   May/Jun/Jul (anniversary issue) *$200.00*
1924   Nov Dec *$125.00*
(Vol. 4 #1 was not published)
1925   Jan Feb Mar Apr May Jun Jul Aug Sep Oct Nov Dec *$75.00*
1926   Jan Feb Mar Apr May Jun Jul Aug Sep Oct Nov Dec *$50.00*
1927   Jan Feb Mar Apr May Jun Jul Aug Sep Oct Nov Dec *$45.00*
1928   Jan Feb Mar Apr May Jun Jul *$33.00*
1928   Aug (Tennessee Williams' first published story: "The Vengeance of Nitocris"; REH: "Red Nails") *$50.00*
1928   Sep Oct Nov Dec *$33.00*
1929   Jan Feb Mar Apr May Jun Jul Aug Sep Oct Nov Dec *$30.00*
1930   Jan Feb Mar Apr May Jun Jul Aug Sep Oct Nov Dec *$27.50*
1931   Jan Feb/Mar Apr/May Jun/Jul Aug Sep Oct Nov Dec *$26.00*
1932   Jan Feb Mar Apr May Jun Jul Aug Sep*B* Oct*B* Nov Dec *$26.00*
1933   Jan Feb Mar*B* Apr*B* May Jun*B* Jul*B* Aug*B* Sep*B* Oct*B* Nov*B* Dec*B* *$22.00*
1934   Jan*B* Feb*B* Mar*B* Apr*B* May*B* Jun*B* Jul*B* Aug*B* Sep*B* Oct*B* Nov*B* Dec*B* *$15.00*
1935   Jan*B* Feb*B* Mar*B* Apr*B* May*B* Jun*B* Jul*B* Aug*B* Sep*B* Oct*B* Nov*B* Dec*B* *$15.00*
1936   Jan*B* Feb*B* Mar*B* Apr*B* May*B* Jun*B* Jul*B* Aug–Sep*B* Oct Nov*B* Dec *$10.00*
1937   Jan*B* Feb Mar*B* Apr May*B* Jun*B* Jul Aug*B* Sep*B* Oct*B* Nov*B* Dec *$7.50*
1938   Jan*B* Feb Mar*B* Apr May*B* Jun*B* Jul Aug*B* Sep*B* Oct*B* Nov Dec *$12.50*
1939   Jan Feb Mar Apr May Jun/Jul Aug Sep Oct Nov Dec *$12.50*
1940   Jan Mar May Jul*B* Sep Nov*B* *$10.00*
1941   Jan Mar*B* May Jul Sep*B* Nov *$10.00*
1942   Jan Mar May Jul*B* Sep Nov *$8.50*
1943   Jan Mar*May*B* Jul Sep Nov *$8.50*
1944   Jan Mar May*B* Jul Sep Nov *$8.50*
1945   Jan*B* Mar May Jul Sep Nov *$8.50*

Weird Tales, September 1953, about
5½″ × 7½″; cover by Jon (D.)
Arfstrom (1928–). Copyright 1953
by Weird Tales. Used with permission of Weird Tales Ltd.

Weird Tales, November 1953, about
5½″ × 7½″; cover uncredited (but
by Jon D. Arfstrom [1928–]).
Copyright 1953 by Weird Tales.
Used with permission of Weird
Tales Ltd.

Weird Tales, January 1954, about 5½″ × 7½″; cover by W. H. Silvey. Copyright 1953 by Weird Tales. Used with permission of Weird Tales Ltd.

Weird Tales, March 1954, about 5½″ × 7½″; cover by Evan Singer. Copyright 1953 by Weird Tales. Used with permission of Weird Tales Ltd.

Weird Tales, May 1954, about 5½″ × 7½″; cover by W. H. Silvey. Defects include some creasing. Copyright 1954 by Weird Tales. Used with permission of Weird Tales Ltd.

Weird Tales, July 1954, about 5½″ × 7½″; cover uncredited. Cover is worn. Copyright 1954 by Weird Tales. Used with permission of Weird Tales Ltd.

Weird Tales, September 1954, about 5½″ × 7½″; cover by Virgil Finlay (1914–1971). Copyright 1954 by Weird Tales. Used with permission of Weird Tales Ltd.

1946   Jan Mar May Jul Sep Nov   *$8.50*
1947   Jan Mar May Sep Nov   *$8.50*
1948   Jan Mar May Jul Sep Nov   *$5.00*
1949   Jan Mar May Jul Sep Nov   *$5.00*
1950   Jan Mar May Jul Sep Nov   *$4.25*
1951   Jan Mar May Jul Sep Nov   *$4.25*
1952   Jan Mar May Jul Sep Nov   *$4.25*
1953   Jan Mar May Jul Sep Nov   *$4.25*
1954   Jan Mar May Jul Sep   *$4.25*
(series edited by Sam Moskowitz, 1973–1974)
1973   Sum Fal Win   *$3.00*
1974   Sum   *$3.00*
(paperback series edited by Lin Carter for Zebra Books, 1980–1983)
1980   #1HPL #2   *$6.00*
1981   #3REH   *$5.00*
1983   #4REH   *$5.00*
(limited distribution magazine)

1984 Fal *$17.00* (very hard to find; most will be higher in better shape)

1985 Win *$17.00* (very hard to find; most will be higher in better shape)

WEIRD TERROR TALES (1969–1970)

This three-issue, saddle-stitched, digest magazine was edited by Robert A. W. Lowndes and reprinted fantasy stories, some of which were in the public domain. (There is a story by Edgar Allan Poe in the first issue and one by Edward Bulwer-Lytton in the second.)

1969/70 WinHPL *$1.00*
1970 Sum Fal *$1.00*

WITCHCRAFT & SORCERY (see *Coven 13*)

WONDER STORIES/AIR WONDER STORIES/SCIENCE WONDER STORIES/THRILLING WONDER STORIES (1929–1955)

After Hugo Gernsback lost *Amazing Stories*, he founded new magazines, all of which had "Wonder" in the title. Most of these combined eventually, and the combined magazine was sold and became part of the "Thrilling" group of pulp magazines—which included *Thrilling Adventure, Thrilling Western,* and *Thrilling Detective.* As a predictable consequence, *Wonder Stories* became *Thrilling Wonder Stories.* When the same publisher began a companion magazine, *Startling Stories,* a division of material was set up—*Startling* published a novel and enough short stories to fill out an issue; *Thrilling Wonder* published about three novelettes and enough short stories to fill out an issue. The results, to those who bought both magazines, was a nice mix of stories. For most of their existence, *Startling* and *Thrilling Wonder* ranked right behind *Astounding*—as Number Two and Number Three science-fiction magazines.

Under Gernsback, the magazines were published on pulp paper in the bedsheet size. When the magazine became *Thrilling Wonder Stories,* it was converted to the standard pulp size. The later incarnation of *Wonder Stories* (in 1957 and 1963) was a digest-sized collection of material reprinted from *TWS* and *SS,* presumably to test the market

to see if it would support a regular magazine. The same is true of *Treasury of Great Science Fiction Stories, Great Science Fiction Stories, SF Yearbook,* and *Science Fiction Yearbook,* which also contained reprints from "the Standard Twins," as *Startling Stories* and *Thrilling Wonder* (both published by Standard Magazines) were sometimes called.

Science Wonder Stories (1929–1930)

1929   Jun   *$25.00*
1929   Jul Aug Sep Oct Nov Dec   *$8.75*
1930   Jan Feb Mar Apr May   *$8.75*
(combines with *Air Wonder Stories,* becomes *Wonder Stories*)

Air Wonder Stories (1929–1930)

1929   Jul   *$25.00*
1929   Aug Sep Oct Nov Dec   *$12.50*
1930   Jan Feb Mar Apr May   *$12.50*
(combines with *Science Wonder Stories* as)

Wonder Stories (1930–1936)

1930   Jun Jul Aug Sep Oct Nov Dec   *$7.50*
1931   Jan Feb Mar Apr May Jun Jul Aug Sep Oct Nov Dec   *$6.50*
1932   Jan Feb Mar Apr May Jun Jul Aug Sep Oct Nov Dec   *$6.25*
1933   Jan Feb Mar Apr May Jun Aug Oct Nov Dec   *$6.25*
1934   Jan Feb Mar Apr May Jun Jul Aug Sep Oct Nov Dec   *$5.50*
1935   Jan Feb Mar Apr May Jun Jul Aug Sep Oct Nov/Dec   *$5.50*
1936   Jan/Feb Mar/Apr   *$5.00*
(becomes)

Thrilling Wonder Stories (1936–1955)

1936   Aug Oct Dec   *$5.00*
1937   Feb Apr Jun Aug Oct Dec   *$4.50*
1938   Feb Apr Jun Aug Oct Nov   *$4.00*
1939   Feb Apr   *$4.00*
1939   Jun (10th anniversary issue)   *$7.50*
1939   Aug Oct Dec   *$4.00*
1940   Jan Feb Mar Apr May Jun Jul Aug Sep Oct Nov Dec   *$3.50*

1941   Jan Feb Mar Apr Jun Aug Oct Dec   *$3.50*
1942   Feb Apr Jun Aug Oct Dec   *$3.00*
1943   Feb Apr Jun Aug Fal(Nov)   *$3.00*
1944   Win(Feb) Spr(May) Sum(Aug) Fal(Nov)   *$3.00*
1945   Win(Feb) Spr(May) Sum(Aug)JV Fal(Nov)   *$2.50*
1946   Win(Feb) Spr(Apr) Sum(Jun) Fal(Oct) DecJV   *$2.50*
1947   Feb Apr Jun Aug Dec   *$1.50*
1947   OctRAH   *$3.00*
1948   Feb Apr Jun Aug Oct   *$1.50*
1948   DecLRH   *$3.00*
1949   Feb Apr Jun Aug Dec   *$1.50*
1949   OctLRH   *$3.00*
1950   Feb Apr Jun Oct Dec   *$1.40*
1950   AugJV/LRH   *$2.80*
1951   Apr Aug Dec   *$1.40*
1951   FebJV JunJV OctJV   *$2.80*
1952   Apr Jun Dec   *$1.40*
1952   FebJV AugJV OctJV   *$2.80*
1953   Feb Apr Jun Aug Nov   *$1.40*
1954   Sum Fal   *$1.40*
1954   WinPDK SprPKD   *$2.80*
1955   Win   *$1.40*

WONDER STORIES (1957, 1963)

This was a digest-sized magazine reprinting stories from *Startling Stories* and *Thrilling Wonder Stories*.

1957   *$1.50*
1963   *$1.50*

WONDER STORIES QUARTERLY (see *Science Wonder Quarterly*)

WONDER STORY ANNUAL (1950–1953)

This was an annual pulp collection of reprints from *Thrilling Wonder Stories* and *Startling Stories*.

1950   *$1.25*
1951   *$1.25*

1952   *$1.25*
1953RAH   *$2.50*

WORLD OF IF (1957–1958)

This digest-sized publication reprinted stories from *If*. The first was called *The First World of If* and the second was titled *The Second World of If*. It could be argued that they are books, but they are in the same format as the magazine and are reprinted by the then-publisher of the magazine, Quinn Publishing Company.

1957   First World of If   *$1.50*
1958   Second World of If   *$1.50*

WORLDS BEYOND (1950–1951)

Damon Knight edited this digest-sized magazine and has written of the frustrations of dealing with a publisher who knows nothing of science and wants to put pictures of Saturn into the sky on the cover "so it looks like science fiction." It proves you can't tell a book—or a magazine—by its cover, because Knight managed to get some fine science fiction and fantasy—a mixture of new stories and reprints—

Worlds Beyond, December 1950, about 5½″ × 7½″; cover by Paul Calle (1928–). Defects of this first issue include a frayed right side and rolled spine. Copyright 1950 by Hillman Periodicals, Inc.

Worlds Beyond, January 1951, about 5¹/₂″ × 7¹/₂″; cover by (Henry Richard) Van Dongen. Copyright 1950 by Hillman Periodicals, Inc.

Worlds Beyond, February 1951, about 5¹/₂″ × 7¹/₂″; cover by (Henry Richard) Van Dongen. Defects in this last issue include spotting, pencilling, and a slight gouge. Copyright 1951 by Hillman Periodicals, Inc.

into the short-lived magazine, including Harry Harrison's first published science-fiction story ("Rock Diver," February 1951). Harrison, who had been a comic-book artist and writer (for EC Comics,
among other publishers), also did illustrations for the magazine.

1950   DecJV   *$4.00*
1951   Jan   *$1.50*
1951   FebJV   *$3.00*

WORLDS OF FANTASY (1968–1971)

This was another attempt at creating a digest-size fantasy magazine
from the publisher and editor of *Galaxy* and *If*.

1968   #1REH   *$2.00*
1970   #2   *$1.00*
1970/71   *$1.00*
1971   Spr   *$1.00*

WORLDS OF IF SCIENCE FICTION (see *If Worlds of Science Fiction*)

WORLDS OF TOMORROW (1963–1971)

This digest-sized companion to *Galaxy* and *If* was intended to be more
adventure-oriented. It printed some notable stories, including several
installments of Philip Jose Farmer's "Riverworld" series and a Philip
K. Dick serial, "All We Marsmen," which was published in book
form as *Martian Time-Slip*.

1963   Apr   *$1.50*
1963   Jun   75¢
1963   AugPKD OctPKD DecPKD   *$1.50*
1964   Feb Apr Nov   75¢
1964   JunPKD AugPKD   *$1.50*
1965   Mar May Jul Sep   75¢
1975   JanPKD NovPKD   *$1.50*
1966   Mar Aug Nov   75¢

1966   JanPKD MayPKD   *$1.50*
1967   Feb May   75¢
1970   #24 #25   75¢
1971   Spr   75¢

British Fiction Magazines

As noted in this book's introductory remarks, the scope of this guide is *American* science fiction and fantasy. However, there are enough British magazines in circulation among American science-fiction and fantasy collectors that we felt it necessary to add this section on British magazines.

It is frustrating enough to collect such magazines when one has a listing of what is available; at present many collectors own a few scattered issues without any idea of the total breadth of the field.

None of these are in truly plentiful American supply—nor is the American demand for them high. Their dollar value does not really indicate the ease with which a collector will locate copies; therefore we have not listed any prices in this section, but we promise to add them in the next edition should there be more information available. We are *not* listing here publications which are simply British reprints of American titles, often with sharply abbreviated contents—but rather British magazines with noticeable British material.

ALIEN WORLDS (1966)

There was only one issue of this digest-sized magazine; it was undated, but came out in the summer of 1966.

1966

AMERICAN SCIENCE FICTION (1944–1946)

This pocketbook magazine reprinted American science fiction stories in 12 volumes of about 36 pages each. The first issue was unnumbered.

1944 Sep #2 #3
1945 #4 #5 #6 #7 #8 #9 #10 #11
1946 Jan

AUTHENTIC SCIENCE FICTION SERIES (1950?–1957)

This magazine underwent a number of name changes. The first two, undated and unnumbered, issues were called *Authentic Science Fiction Series;* issues #3–8 were called *Science Fiction Fortnightly;* a change in frequency necessitated the next name change, to *Science Fiction Monthly,* for issues #9–12; issues #13–28 were called *Authentic Science Fiction Monthly;* #69–77 were called *Authentic Science Fiction;* issues #78–85 were called *Authentic Science Fiction Monthly.* Issue #85 was the last. All issues except the first two were numbered.

1950? no date or number
(becomes *Science Fiction Fortnightly*)
1951 Feb/3 Feb/4 Mar 1 Mar 15 Apr 1 Apr 15
(becomes *Science Fiction Monthly*)
1951 May Jun Jul Aug
(becomes *Authentic Science Fiction*)
1951   Sep Oct Nov Dec
1952   Jan Feb Mar Apr May Jun 22 (Jul) Aug Sep Oct Nov Dec
1953   Jan Feb Mar Apr May Jun Jul Aug Sep Oct Nov Dec
1954   Jan Feb Mar Apr May Jun Jul Aug Sep Oct Nov Dec
1955   Jan Feb Mar Apr May Jun Jul Aug Sep Oct Nov Dec
1956   Jan Feb Mar Apr May Jun Jul Aug Sep Nov Dec
1957   Jan Feb Mar Apr May Jun Jul Aug Sep Oct

A BOOK OF WEIRD TALES (1960)

An odd digest one-shot, the magazine reprinted stories from a number of old pulps and cover-featured a brief article about Bela Lugosi by Forrest J Ackerman which is reprinted from *Famous Monsters of Filmland.* Ackerman is listed on the cover as "associate (American) editor."

The magazine has no date.

#1

THE BRITISH SCIENCE FICTION MAGAZINE (see *Vargo Statten Science Fiction Magazine*)

THE BRITISH SPACE FICTION MAGAZINE (see *Vargo Statten Science Fiction Magazine*)

COSMIC SCIENCE STORIES (1950)

The one-shot pulp magazine published an abridged reprint of the American *Super Science Stories* for September 1949.

1950

FANTASY (1938–1939)

The pulp magazine published three issues.

1938   #1
1939   #2 #3

FANTASY (1946–1947)

Fantasy was a digest magazine which also lasted only three issues.

1946   Dec
1947   Apr Aug

FANTASY TALES (1977)

It was a digest-sized one-shot.

1977   Sum

FUTURE SCIENCE FICTION (1953–1967)

Contents of the Australian digest-sized magazine were a mixture of U.S. reprints and new Australian stories.

1953   #1 #2
1954   #3 #4 #5
1955   #6
1967   #7 #8

FUTURISTIC SCIENCE STORIES (1950–1954)

This pocketbook magazine published juvenile science fiction.

#1 #2 #3 #4 #5 #6 #7 #8 #9 #10 #11 #12 #13 #14 #15 #16

FUTURISTIC STORIES (1946–1947)

This was a juvenile pulp-size magazine, a companion to *Strange Adventures*.

1946 #1
1947 #2

IMPULSE/SF IMPULSE (1966–1967)

The paperback-format successor to *Science Fantasy* is sometimes listed in back-issue catalogs under *Science Fantasy*.

1966 Mar Apr May Jun Jul
(becomes *SF Impulse*)
1966 Aug Sept Oct Nov Dec
1967 Jan Feb

INTERZONE (1982–)

This literary publication is a sort of spiritual descendant of the latter-day *New Worlds* (when that magazine published "speculative fiction" instead of science fiction).

1982 Spr Sum Aut
1983 Spr Aut
1983/84 Win
1984 Spr Sum Aut
1984/85 Win
1985 Spr Sum Aut
1985/86 Win
1986 Spr Sum Aut
1986/87 Win
1987 Spr Sum Aut
1987/88 Win

NEBULA SCIENCE FICTION (1952–1959)

The first and, to date, the only Scottish science-fiction magazine was published in a tall digest format.

1952 Aut
1953 Spr Sum Aut
(becomes *Nebula Science-Fiction*)

1953   Sep Dec
1954   Feb Apr AugRAH Oct Dec
1955   AprRAH Sep Nov
1956   JanRAH Mar Jul Nov Dec
1957   Mar May Jul Aug Sep Oct
1958   Jan Feb Mar Apr May Jun Jul Aug Sep Oct Nov Dec
1959   Jan Feb May Jun

NEW WORLDS (1946–1970)

New Worlds has had a long and varied career. It began as a pulp (there were two different versions of #1, with different covers). There were three issues in this format and then the magazine disappeared for two years. When it returned in 1949, it was in a tall-digest format (5″ × 8½″), which lasted through the March 1953 issue (#20). It then switched to a standard digest format. It switched again to a paperback format and finished its days as a bedsheet "literary" magazine. Following the demise of the magazine, there was a series of American paperbacks (see *New Worlds Quarterly* and the *New Worlds* trade paperback editions in the American magazine listings) which reprinted six of a series of ten paperbacks published in England.

Those ten original anthologies were published by Sphere Books in England from 1971–1975. There was an attempt to revive the magazine by fans, starting with #212 (counting the original 201 issues and the ten anthologies), but this is not a professional publication and certainly not a science-fiction magazine.

During the period when it was printing science fiction (as opposed to "speculative fiction"), it became the only British magazine to have an American reprint edition (see the American listing for *New Worlds Science Fiction*), reversing a long-standing trend.

Unlike American science-fiction magazines, British magazines tend to be more prominently numbered than dated and it is easier to collect them by numbers. The numbering does not change even when volume-and-numbers are given. (For instance: Volume One had three issues; Volume Two then began with Volume 2 #4.) There were 201 issues of *New Worlds*. Numbers 1–3 were pulps. Numbers 4 through 20 were tall digests. Numbers 21 through 141 were standard-size digests. From #142 through #171, it was published in a paperback format. From #172 through #201, it was published in a bedsheet format

under a grant from the Arts Council. The final issue, #201, was sent only to subscribers and was never available on newsstands.

1946   #1 (#1 had two different covers) #2
1947   #3
1949   #4 #5
1950   Spr Sum Win
1951   Spr Sum Aut Win
1952   Jan Mar May Jul Sep Nov
1953   Jan
(becomes *New Worlds Science Fiction*)
1953   Mar Jun
1954   Apr May Jun Jul Aug Sep Oct Nov Dec
1955   Jan Feb Mar Apr May Jun Jul Aug Sep Oct Nov Dec
1956   Jan Feb Mar Apr May Jun Jul Aug Sep Oct Nov Dec
1957   Jan Feb Mar Apr May Jun Jul Aug Sep OctRAH Nov Dec
1958   Jan Feb Mar Apr May Jun Jul Aug Sep Oct Nov Dec
1959   Jan Feb Mar Apr May Jun Jul Aug/Sep Oct Nov DecPKD
1960   JanPKD FebPKD Mar Apr May Jun Jul Aug Sep Oct Nov Dec
1961   Jan Feb Mar Apr May Jun Jul Aug Sep Oct Nov Dec
1962   Jan Feb Mar Apr May Jun Jul Aug Sep Oct Nov Dec
1963   Jan Feb Mar Apr May Jun Jul Aug Sep Oct Nov Dec
1964   Jan Feb Mar Apr
(becomes *New Worlds SF* in a paperback format)
1964   May/Jun Jul/Aug Sep/Oct Nov/Dec
1965   Jan Feb Mar Apr MayJV Jun Jul Aug Sep Oct Nov Dec
1966   Jan Feb Mar Apr May Jun Jul Aug Sep Oct Nov Dec
1967   Jan Feb Mar
(becomes bedsheet size, *New Worlds*)
1967   Aug Sep Oct Nov
1967/68   Dec/Jan
1968   Jan Feb Mar Apr Jul Oct Nov Dec
1969   Jan Feb Mar Apr May Jun Jul Aug Sep/Oct Nov Dec
1970   Jan Feb Mar Apr
1971   Mar (#201, sent to subscribers only)

NEW WORLDS ANTHOLOGIES (1971–1975)

Sphere Books published a series of original stories after the demise of *New Worlds* magazine. The first five were edited by Michael Moorcock, the sixth was edited by Moorcock and Charles Platt, the seventh by Platt and Hilary Bailey, and the remainder by Bailey.

Some of these books were reprinted in the United States. Four of the Moorcock-edited books were published as *New Worlds Quarterly* #1–4 by Berkley Books. The sixth British book (edited by Moorcock and Platt) was published as *New Worlds #5* by Avon. Avon published the seventh British book (edited by Platt and Bailey) as *New Worlds #6.* The fifth Moorcock book and the three Bailey books were not published in the United States.

1971   #1 #2
1972   #3 #4
1973   #5 #6
1974   #7
1975   #8 #9
1976   #10

PHANTOM (1957–1958)

Ghost stories found a home in this magazine, published in a tall digest format (5″ × 8½″). The stories were mostly very traditional—and consequently predictable. The magazine was subtitled "A magazine of weird tales," which indicates what publication it was attempting to emulate.

1957   Apr May Jun Jul Aug Sep Oct Nov Dec
1958   Jan Feb Mar Apr May Jun Jul

POPULAR SCIENCE FICTION (1953–1967)

Published on the same erratic schedule as *Future Science Fiction,* this Australian digest magazine was similar to that companion magazine.

1953   #1 #2
1954   #3 #4 #5
1955   #6
1967   #7 #8

SCIENCE-FANTASY/SCIENCE FANTASY (1950–1966)

This was a companion magazine to *New Worlds,* concentrating on fantasy stories—including the ''Elric'' stories of Michael Moorcock. This magazine is highly regarded by collectors because of the large number of excellent stories it contains; even American collectors, who tend to be less likely to praise British magazines, have likened this magazine to such venerated fantasy titles as *Unknown/Unknown Worlds* and *The Magazine of Fantasy and Science Fiction.* The magazine published the first stories of Brian Aldiss and J. G. Ballard and much of the early work of John Brunner and Kenneth Bulmer. It also published more work by the American fantasist Thomas Burnett Swann than appeared in any other magazine.

The magazine began life with a hyphen in its title and as a thin digest magazine. After two issues, it became a tall digest (5″ × 8½″) for four issues, then switched to a standard digest size from March 1954 (the first issue without a hyphen) until 1964, when it switched to a paperback size.

When it suspended publication with #81 (February 1966), it was continued (in a sense) as *Impulse/SF Impulse,* but that periodical did not continue *Science Fantasy*'s numbering. For purposes of this index, they are regarded as separate publications, but some back-issue catalogs list them together.

1950   Sum
1951   Win 50/51
1952   Win 51/52 Spr Aut
1953   Spr
(becomes *Science Fantasy*)
1954   Mar May Jul Sep Dec
1955   Feb Apr Jun Sep Nov
1955/56   Feb
1956   May Aug Dec
1957   Feb Apr Jun Aug Oct Dec
1958   Feb Apr Jun Aug Oct Dec
1959   Feb Apr Jun Aug Nov Dec
1960   Feb Apr Jun Aug Oct Dec
1961   Feb Apr Jun Aug Oct Dec
1962   Feb Apr Jun Aug Oct Dec
1963   Feb Apr Jun Aug Oct Dec

1964   Feb Apr
(switches to a paperback format)
1964   Jun/Jul Jul/Aug Sep/Oct
1964/65   Dec/Jan
1965   Jan/Feb Mar Apr May Jun Jul Aug Sep Oct Nov Dec
1966   Jan Feb

SCIENCE FICTION ADVENTURES (1958–1963)

The digest-size magazine started as a reprint edition of the American magazine (the second to bear this title) which was a companion publication to *Infinity Science Fiction*. The British edition, however, lasted far longer than the twelve issues of its American progenitor.

Only the first five issues of the British *SFA* reprinted material from the U.S. version. The remaining issues concentrated on British writers and the magazine became a worthy companion to its sister magazines, *New Worlds* and *Science Fantasy*.

1958   Mar May Jul Sep Nov
1959   Jan Mar May Jul Oct Nov Dec
1960   Feb May Jul Sep Nov
1961   Jan Mar May Jul Sep Nov
1962   Jan Mar May Jul Sep Nov
1963   Jan Mar May

SCIENCE FICTION DIGEST (1976)

Despite the title, it was not a digest-sized magazine, but a bedsheet publication. It lasted only one issue.

1976   #1

SCIENCE FICTION FORTNIGHTLY (see *Authentic Science Fiction*)

SCIENCE FICTION LIBRARY (1960)

The paperback magazine used some new stories and some reprints from the American magazine *Science Fiction Quarterly*. Those reprints were then twenty years old.

1960   #1 #2 #3

SCIENCE FICTION MONTHLY (see *Authentic Science Fiction*)

SCIENCE FICTION MONTHLY (1955-1957)

Three British magazines used this title, including *Authentic Science Fiction*, which used it briefly. This one was an Australian digest which primarily reprinted from American magazines.

```
1955   #1 #2 #3 #4 #5
1956   #6 #7 #8 #9 #10 #11 #12 #13 #14 #15 #16 #17
1957   #18
```

SCIENCE FICTION MONTHLY (1974-1976)

The third magazine to use this title was a tabloid-size publication featuring pull-out posters of science-fiction art and some good biographical articles on major science-fiction writers. It apparently was aimed at a youthful audience, one more attracted by graphics than by the printed word. It was published in three volumes; the first two have twelve issues each, the third has four, making twenty-eight issues in all.

```
1974   Feb Mar Apr May Jun Jul Aug Sep Oct Nov Dec
1975   Jan Feb Mar Apr May Jun Jul Aug Sep Oct Nov Dec
1976   Jan Feb Mar Apr May
```

SCOOPS (1934)

The weekly bedsheet publication for boys is regarded as the first British science-fiction magazine. There were twenty weekly issues, all hard to find and expensive. It included a serial, *The Poison Belt*, by Sir Arthur Conan Doyle.

```
1934   10Feb 17Feb 24Feb 3Mar 10Mar 17Mar 24Mar 31Mar 7Apr
       14Apr 21Apr 28Apr 5May 12May 19May 26May 2Jun 9Jun
       16Jun 23Jun
```

SELECTED SCIENCE FICTION (1955)

The Australian digest magazine was a companion to *American Science Fiction*. Like that magazine, it reprinted from the U.S. science-fiction magazines.

1955   May Jun Jul Aug Sep

SF IMPULSE (see *Impulse*)

SPACE FACT AND FICTION (1954)

This pulp magazine reprinted stories from decade-old issues of the American magazines *Future Fiction* and *Science Fiction*.

1954   Mar Apr May Jun Jul Aug Sep Oct

STRANGE ADVENTURES (1946–1947)

The very thin pulp magazine featured juvenile science fiction; it was a companion publication to *Futuristic Stories*. Neither issue is dated and the only help we can give on telling which issue is which is that the cover of the first issue has a man in a red shirt pointing a rifle at a huge gray beast which seems to have wings.

1946   #1
1947   #2

STRANGE TALES (1946–1947)

The thin digest reprinted fantasy stories by Ray Bradbury, H. P. Lovecraft, Robert Bloch, and others. The issues are not dated; however, the words ''first selection'' or ''second selection'' appear on the covers.

1946   first selection
1947   second selection

SUPERNATURAL STORIES

There were at least 67 issues of the paperback-format magazine from John Spencer & Co., the publisher of *Tales of Tomorrow, Futuristic Science Stories,* and other periodicals. The majority of the stories (perhaps all the stories?) were written by the extremely prolific Robert

Lionel Fanthorpe under his own name and various of his pseudonyms. (Fanthorpe has dozens of pseudonyms, including Trebor Thorpe, Max Chartair, Ray Cosmic, and Lionel Roberts.) The stories were hastily written, naturally, and are not very good. Fans generally regard the John Spencer & Co. publications as being for completist collectors only.

Supernatural Stories proclaimed itself as a bi-monthly publication (and, later, as a monthly), but we can't find any dates on any of the copies we have seen. Judging from the dates on the other publications from the same firm, we would guess that it began around 1950 and continued for an unknown period. This publication obviously outlasted the other John Spencer & Co. titles we have cited, but we have no idea by how long.

#1–67—at least.

TALES OF TOMORROW (1950–1954)

The paperback magazine was published on an irregular schedule.

#1 #2 #3 #4 #5 #6 #7 #8 #9 #10 #11

TALES OF WONDER (1937–1942)

This is generally regarded as the first British science-fiction magazine aimed at an adult audience (*Scoops,* a boys' weekly, was the first British science-fiction magazine). Largely because of World War II, its publishing history was extremely erratic. The first issue is unnumbered and undated, but was published in June 1937.

1937   no # #2
1938   Sum Aut Win
1939   Spr Sum Aut Win
1940   Spr Sum Aut
1941   Win Spr Aut
1942   Spr

THRILLS, INC. (1950–1952)

The Australian magazine was published in a variety of sizes, from bedsheet through pulp size to digest size. The first 12 issues were published in the larger sizes, the next 11 in digest, making 23 issues.

#1 #2 #3 #4 #5 #6 #7 #8 #9 #10 #11 #12 #13 #14 #15 #16 #17 #18 #19 #20 #21 #22 #23

UNCANNY TALES (1940–1943)

Lyle Kenyon Engel edited the Canadian pulp magazine. He eventually achieved fame and fortune as a book packager (he created the Kent Family Chronicles series and assigned science-fiction writer John Jakes to produce the actual books). *Uncanny* reprinted a good deal from U.S. magazines, but also contained some original material.

#1 #2 #3 #4 #5 #6 #7 #8 #9 #10 #11 #12 #13 #14 #15 #16 #17 #18 #19 #20 #21

VARGO STATTEN BRITISH SCIENCE FICTION MAGAZINE (see *Vargo Statten Science Fiction Magazine*)

VARGO STATTEN SCIENCE FICTION MAGAZINE/ VARGO STATTEN BRITISH SCIENCE FICTION MAGAZINE/THE BRITISH SCIENCE FICTION MAGAZINE/THE BRITISH SPACE FICTION MAGAZINE (1954–1956)

Vargo Statten was a pen name of the prolific John Russell Fearn, and this publication makes him the first writer to have a science-fiction magazine named for him while he was alive. (*A. Merritt's Fantasy Magazine* came along years after Merritt had died and *Isaac Asimov's Science Fiction Magazine* did not begin until 1977.)

This publication, a pulp for the first three issues, then a digest, changed names several times, phasing Vargo out completely. There were nineteen issues (Volume One, #1–12, and Volume Two, #1–7).

Volume 1 #1–3 (pulp size)
(becomes *Vargo Statten British Science Fiction Magazine,* digest)
Volume 1 #4–5
(becomes *The British Science Fiction Magazine*)
Volume 1 #6–12
(becomes *The British Space Fiction Magazine*)
Volume 2 #1–7

Vargo Statten Science Fiction Magazine, January 1954, about 7¼″ × 9¾″; cover not credited. This is the first issue of the British magazine named after a pseudonym of the editor, John Russell Fearn. Copyright, apparently, by Scion Limited.

Vargo Statten Science Fiction Magazine, February 1954, about 7¼″ × 9¾″; cover not credited. Copyright, apparently, by Scion Limited.

VISION OF TOMORROW (1969–1970)

The attractive bedsheet magazine used its large cover space to showcase art by Eddie Jones and David Hardy. It was the first English-language magazine to publish a story by Stanislaw Lem.

1969   Aug Nov Dec
1970   Jan Feb Mar Apr May Jun Jul Aug Sep

VORTEX (1977)

The bedsheet magazine was printed on glossy paper and contained some colored illustrations.

1977   Jan Feb Mar Apr May

WEIRD AND OCCULT LIBRARY (1960)

The companion publication to *Science Fiction Library* was a paperback magazine.

1960   #1 #2 #3

WEIRD WORLD (1955)

The short-lived pulp magazine printed new and reprint fantasy and science fiction.

1955   #1 #2

WONDERS OF THE SPACEWAYS (1950–1954)

The paperback format for magazines seems to be more popular in Britain than it has been in the United States. This was from the same publisher as *Futuristic Science Stories* and *Tales of Tomorrow*.

#1 #2 #3 #4 #5 #6 #7 #8 #9 #10

WORLDS OF FANTASY (1950–1954)

This was yet another paperback-format magazine from the publisher of *Futuristic Science Stories*, *Tales of Tomorrow*, and *Wonders of the Spaceways*.

#1 #2 #3 #4 #5 #6 #7 #8 #9 #10 #11 #12 #13 #14

WORLDS OF THE UNIVERSE (1953)

Worlds was a paperback-format one-shot.

1953 #1

Science Fiction and Fantasy in Comic Books

Anyone collecting comic books can use as a primary source of information Robert M. Overstreet's *The Official Overstreet Comic Book Price Guide*. The House of Collectibles title has been the standard in the industry for more than a decade and a half and indicates the prices collectors can expect to pay in comics shops, by mail order, and at comics conventions.

The other publication that will provide you with the most recent listings by specialty dealers in the field is the weekly comics industry newspaper we edit: *Comics Buyer's Guide*.

It is true that many highly collectible comics are science-fiction or fantasy titles: *Superman*, after all, is based on a science-fiction concept by creators Jerry Siegel and Joe Shuster, science-fiction fans themselves. Science-fiction writer Otto Binder wrote most of the adventures of Superman's rival super-hero of the forties, *Captain Marvel*, and the Captain himself had a fantasy origin.

But there isn't room in this volume to go into great detail on comics with fantasy and science-fiction elements. What we list are publications more specifically tied to the science-fiction and fantasy fields than by general theme.

Prices are for publications in "good" condition.

PUBLICATIONS

Elfquest

What began as a virtual fanzine production became a cottage industry, even including licensing arrangements with Marvel Comics and gaming manufacturers. The project is rare in that it spans comics, science fiction, role-playing games, and fantasy fandoms. The comic books have not generally commanded "hot" prices, because of the efforts of creators Wendy and Richard Pini to keep the material in print.

The series began in a publication called *Fantasy Quarterly* #1 but quickly went to self-publishing via Warp (for Wendy and Richard Pini) Graphics. The story is available in collected, colored form.

First printing in *Fantasy Quarterly* #1   *$6.00*
#1-#21   *25¢*
Marvel reprints #1-#36   *25¢*
Elfquest: Siege at Blue Mountain
#1-#8   *25¢*

Heavy Metal

The publication is a slick-paper comics magazine largely featuring translations of European comics stories, along with some work by American comics writers and artists. The content is primarily fantasy; there is some true science fiction, but fantasy predominates. Some fiction by writers such as Theodore Sturgeon and Harlan Ellison appears, primarily in the earlier issues.

In the following list, all except the issues marked with an asterisk (*) may be available from the publisher (Heavy Metal, 635 Madison Avenue, New York, NY 10022). Those issues marked with an asterisk are sold out from the publisher. Prices from the publisher will be roughly three times those given here, since our price guide lists items in only "good" condition.

1977   *Apr   *$3.00*
1977   May   *$1.50*
1977   *Jun   *$2.50*
1977   Jul   *$1.50*
1977   Aug Sep Oct Nov Dec   *$1.50*
1978   Jan Feb Mar   *$1.50*
1978   Apr May Jun Jul   *$1.50*
1978   (all*) Sep Oct Nov Dec   *$2.50*
1979   (all*) Jan Feb Apr May Jun Jul Sep Dec   *$2.50*
1979   Mar Aug Oct Nov   *$1.50*
1980   *Jan   *$2.50*
1980   (all*) Feb Apr Jun Jul Sep Oct Nov Dec   *$1.75*
1980   Mar May Aug   *$1.25*
1981   (all*) Jan Feb Mar Jul Aug Sep Oct Dec   *$1.75*
1981   Apr May Jun Nov   *$1.25*

1982   Jan Feb Mar Apr May Jun Jul Aug Sep Oct Nov Dec   *$1.25*
1983   *May $1.25*
1983   Jan Feb Mar Apr Jun Jul Aug Sep Oct Nov Dec   *$1.00*
1984   Jan Feb Mar Apr May Jun Jul Aug Sep Oct Nov Dec   *$1.00*
1985   Jan Feb Mar Apr May Jun Jul Aug Sep Oct Nov Dec   *$1.00*
1986   Win Spr Sum Fal   *$1.50*
1987   Win Spr Sum Fal   *$1.50*

Unknown Worlds of Science Fiction

In the mid-seventies, the Marvel Comics Group experimented with a string of black-and-white magazine-format comic books. The company aimed the line at older readers and, with this title, hoped to attract science-fiction buffs to its line. Many stories were adaptations of existing science-fiction stories.

1975   Jan Mar May Jul Sep Nov   *40c*
1976   Special (100 pp.)   *40c*

COMICS IN BOOK FORM

Especially in an era in which comic books are becoming more widely accepted as a legitimate art form, book publications of comic-book stories are increasingly seen. With limited space available for listings, we list only a tiny portion of the published material. Once again, we recommend checking Overstreet's guide to comics.

Harlan Ellison

1986   *Demon with a Glass Hand* (with artist Marshall Rogers)   *$1.20*
1987   *Night and the Enemy* (with artist Ken Steacy)   *$3.00*

Crockett Johnson

1985   *Barnaby #1: Wanted: A Fairy Godfather*   *75¢*
1985   *Barnaby #2: Mr. O'Malley and the Haunted House*   *75¢*
1985   *Barnaby #3: Jackeen J. O'Malley for Congress*   *75¢*
1986   *Barnaby #4: Mr. O'Malley Goes for the Gold*   *75¢*
1986   *Barnaby #5: Mr. O'Malley, Wizard of Wall Street*   *75¢*
1986   *Barnaby #6: J. J. O'Malley Goes to Hollywood*   *75¢*

Alan Moore and Dave Gibbons

1988   Hugo (''Best in Other Forms''): *Watchmen*

1986   *Watchmen* (coll in pb 1987)   *$3.00*

Science-Fiction
and Fantasy Drama

By the early fifties, there had still not been enough high-quality science-fiction movies made to lead droves of thinking members of the national audience to explore published science fiction. *The Day the Earth Stood Still* was acknowledged by science-fiction fans as being a classic; *The Thing* was a good movie—though it dropped much of the subtlety of John W. Campbell's *Who Goes There?*, on which it was based. Fantasy films were more accepted, and many collectors of the work of L. Frank Baum were initially drawn into the Oz series by *The Wizard of Oz;* James Stewart still says he considers *It's a Wonderful Life* his favorite film.

Hollywood has always tended to lag about 30 years behind the magazines when it comes to science fiction, and in the fifties most science-fiction movies were giant-insect stories of the type which most science-fiction magazines had abandoned by the end of the twenties.

By the mid-sixties, science-fiction fandom had few women among its numbers; the field was still primarily limited to men reading material many considered inaccessible to a female audience—and men writing material for that audience. Though the cheesecake pulp covers were pretty much a thing of the past by that point, there was little in the field to attract the attention of many women.

At the 1966 World Science Fiction Convention, something happened that changed that: In Cleveland, Ohio, Gene Roddenberry almost shyly introduced *Star Trek* to a roomful of devotees of science fiction who had been, time after time, disappointed in Hollywood's version of science fiction. That same convention saw a hard-sell promotion of another television show due for network showing that fall: *Time Tunnel*—which disappointed the attendees.

Time Tunnel came and went, but *Star Trek* was a delightful surprise to most fans at that convention (who were shown both the pilot and the "Charlie X" episode) and, eventually, brought science fiction to

the attention of a wide, enthusiastic viewing audience. That audience, in turn, meant the entry of thousands of young women—most of them drawn by the complex character of Mr. Spock, performed by Leonard Nimoy—into what had been an almost exclusively male fandom. (It also showed the networks for the first time that viewer activism was a power to be reckoned with—when science-fiction fan Bjo Trimble led a successful campaign to return the show to the air after the network had canceled the program.)

In this chapter, we scratch the surface of a few publications connected with hotly collected science-fiction and fantasy dramas. Many collectors are forced to limit their collecting to what has been shown on television; others collect books and other memorabilia associated with them. Again, entire books have been devoted to this material, and we have only indicated some of interest.

DOCTOR WHO

By the end of the twenty-fourth season—on December 7, 1987—this BBC-TV series had become the longest-running prime-time television drama in the world. While the program originates in England, it is hotly collected in America. Many British viewers consider the series limited in its interest to children; American viewers have been drawn to its basic premise and many fresh concepts to view it as adult entertainment.

The premise is that The Doctor (who is *not* called "Doctor Who" on the show—the title is a joke, indicating the mystery surrounding the character) is centuries old and a member of a two-hearted race of humanoid extra-terrestrials who are masters of space and time but who have devoted themselves to non-interference in the affairs of other residents of the universe. Initially, The Doctor was an outlaw—and there was even a question as to whether he was truly humanoid in appearance. When William Hartnell, who originated the role, became too ill to continue the role, the problem of continuing the show was solved by taking advantage of the possibilities of science fiction: Members of The Doctor's species were able to regenerate bodies when they wore out. William Hartnell's Doctor collapsed and changed—into Patrick Troughton, who continued the role.

The list that follows gives the actor who played the role, the span of appearances by story, the number of episodes each story ran

(whether or not The Doctor was in each episode). The list does *not* use the official BBC code. "H1" is William Hartnell's first story. The number at the end of each story title is the number of episodes each story ran; "H1" had four episodes. (The BBC did not broadcast the story titles for the first 25 stories, only episode titles for each chapter. The story titles given here are the accepted ones for each.)

Dates given are those of the original British broadcasts; "The Five Doctors" was shown in England after it had been shown in America; the American broadcast was November 23, 1983.

What is a classic to the audience is not always immediately regarded that way by a series' owner. Although even the never-broadcast pilot for the program was preserved in the BBC's archives, many episodes were destroyed before it was realized that a market might exist for them. In recent years, American audiences have rejoiced to see stories from earlier incarnations of the series—although those stories often seemed to jump from one situation to another.

The reason for the jumps is the unavailability of broadcast-quality prints of some stories. The story was originally in black and white, but with the advent of Jon Pertwee's Doctor, the material was made available both from black-and-white film and from color videotape. In the latter case, some color videotape seems to be no longer available, and the episodes were shown in recent American syndication only in black and white.

We have marked the absence of story in American syndication by "*"; in many cases, this absence indicates a continuing search for missing episodes. In Pertwee's tenure, the following stories are a current part of syndication packages only in black and white: P2 (The Silurians); P5 (Terror of the Autons), P6 (The Mind of Evil); and P9 (The Daemons). In addition, the opening episode of P21 (Invasion of the Dinosaurs) was accidentally destroyed, and the story in syndication begins with the second episode.

Many of the stories have been novelized by Target Books in England, and those books have been released in America. A brief attempt to Americanize the stories and release them in the United States in that form by Pinnacle Books was made in 1979, but the series was abandoned after only a few titles were released. The introduction which ran in each volume was by Harlan Ellison. (The same introduction runs in all volumes.)

The first *Doctor Who* novelization in America occurred as long ago

as 1967, when a paperback edition of *Doctor Who in an Exciting Adventure with the Daleks* was issued by Avon, a novelization of the first story in the series—with many changes. There was a British edition in 1965 and by the early 1980s it was available again—from Target—as *Doctor Who and the Daleks*.

The Target novelizations have been listed following the listing of the broadcast stories. Target novelizations are now numbered in sequence, but that sequence is not chronological with reference to broadcasts: The novelization of *Vengeance on Varos* (broadcast in 1985) is numbered 106; the novelization of *Time and the Rani* (broadcast in 1987) is numbered 127; and the novelization of *The Underwater Menace* (broadcast in 1967) is numbered 129.

Some of the book titles have been changed slightly—from "Doctor Who and the—" to "Doctor Who:."

There are other books of interest to the *Doctor Who* collector: A "Find Your Fate" series is available from Ballantine *(Crisis in Space, Garden of Evil, Mission to Venus,* and *Search for The Doctor)*. Such affiliated books from Target as *Travel Without the TARDIS* by Jean Airey and Laurie Haldeman, *The Doctor Who Programme Guide* (in two volumes) by Jean-Marc Lofficier, and *The Doctor Who Quiz Book* by Nigel Robinson are among them.

Also of interest is the *Doctor Who* magazine, which began as a weekly and later became a monthly in England; it is available through many specialty retailers, including comics specialty shops. Larry Charet (who sells books, monthlies, comics, and fanzines devoted to the show and will provide his sale list for a self-addressed, stamped envelope to Larry's Comic Book Store, 1219A West Devon Avenue, Chicago, Illinois 60660) comments that, although most of the books are currently in print, prices are higher for earlier editions, most with covers by Chris Achilleos. Though there are lower-priced later editions, we've indicated the presence of such earlier editions and the price in "good" condition as follows: "**$1.25.*" (The price in "good" condition of in-print items is $1.00.) In some cases, earlier editions can be determined by earlier logos; in some cases the title "Doctor Who and . . ." has been replaced by "Doctor Who:" or "Doctor Who—" on the cover.

Charet and other retailers confirm that many collectors now simply collect the books by book numbers placed on them by the publisher, Target. Target apparently took its titles, arranged them alphabetically,

and then numbered them. Later books continued the numbering—out of chronological or alphabetical order. We have indicated the Target number in parentheses following the book title.

William Hartnell as The Doctor (134 episodes)

Season I (November 23, 1963–September 12, 1964)
H1 An Unearthly Child 4 *Doctor Who and an Unearthly Child* (68)
H2 The Dead Planet 7 *Doctor Who and the Daleks* (16) *$1.75
H3 The Edge of Destruction 2 *Doctor Who and the Edge of Destruction*
H4 * Marco Polo 7 *Doctor Who: Marco Polo* (94)
H5 The Keys of Marinus 6 *Doctor Who and the Keys of Marinus* (38)
H6 The Aztecs 4 *Doctor Who: The Aztecs* (88)
H7 The Sensorites 6 *Doctor Who and the Sensorities* (118)
H8 * The Reign of Terror 6 *Doctor Who and the Reign of Terror* (119)
Season II (October 31, 1964–July 24, 1965)
H9 Planet of Giants 3
H10 Dalek Invasion of Earth 6 *Doctor Who and the Dalek Invasion of Earth* (17)
H11 The Rescue 2 *Doctor Who and the Rescue* (124)
H12 The Romans 4 *Doctor Who and the Romans* (120)
H13 The Web Planet 6 *Doctor Who and the Zarbi* (73) *$1.75
H14 * The Crusaders 4 *Doctor Who and the Crusaders* (12) *$1.75
H15 The Space Museum 4 *Doctor Who and the Space Museum* (117)
H16 The Chase 6
H17 The Time Meddler 4 *Doctor Who and the Time Meddler* (126)
Season III (September 11, 1965–July 16, 1966)
H18 * Galaxy Four 4 *Doctor Who: Galaxy Four* (104)
H19 * Mission to the Unknown 1
H20 * The Myth Makers 4 *Doctor Who and the Myth Makers* (97)
H21 * The Dalek Master Plan 12
H22 * The Massacre 4 *Doctor Who and the Massacre* (122)
H23 The Ark 4 *Doctor Who and the Ark* (114)
H24 * The Celestial Toymaker 4 *Doctor Who: The Celestial Toymaker* (111)
H25 The Gunfighters 4 *Doctor Who: The Gunfighters* (101)

H26 * The Savages 4 *Doctor Who: The Savages* (109)
H27 The War Machines 4

Season IV (September 10, 1966–July 1, 1967)

H28 * The Smugglers 4 *Doctor Who and the Smugglers*
H29 * The Tenth Planet 4 *Doctor Who and the Tenth Planet* (62)

Patrick Troughton as The Doctor (119 episodes)

T1 * The Power of the Daleks 6
T2 * The Highlanders 4 *Doctor Who: The Highlanders* (90)
T3 * The Underwater Menace 4 *Doctor Who: The Underwater Menace* (129)
T4 * The Moonbase 4 *Doctor Who and the Cybermen* (14) *$1.75
T5 * The Macra Terror 4 *Doctor Who and the Macra Terror* (123)
T6 * The Faceless Ones 6 *Doctor Who and the Faceless Ones* (116)
T7 * The Evil of the Daleks 7

Season V (September 2, 1967–June 1, 1968)

T8 * The Tomb of the Cybermen 4 *Doctor Who and the Tomb of the Cybermen* (66)
T9 * The Abominable Snowmen 6 *Doctor Who and the Abominable Snowmen* (1) *$1.75
T10 * The Ice Warriors 6 *Doctor Who and the Ice Warriors* (33)
T11 * The Enemy of the World 6 *Doctor Who and the Enemy of the World* (24)
T12 * The Web of Fear 6 *Doctor Who and the Web of Fear* (72) *$1.75
T13 * Fury From the Deep 6 *Doctor Who and the Fury From the Deep* (110)
T14 * The Wheel in Space 6 *Doctor Who and the Wheel in Space* (130)

Season VI (August 10, 1968–June 21, 1969)

T15 The Dominators 5 *Doctor Who: The Dominators* (86)
T16 The Mind Robber 5 *Doctor Who and the Mind Robbers* (115)
T17 * The Invasion 8 *Doctor Who and the Invasion* (98)
T18 The Krotons 4 *Doctor Who: The Krotons* (99)
T19 The Seeds of Death 6 *Doctor Who: Seeds of Death* (112)
T20 * The Space Pirates 6
T21 The War Games 10 *Doctor Who and the War Games* (70)

Jon Pertwee as The Doctor (128 episodes)

Season VII (January 3, 1970–June 20, 1970)

   P1 Spearhead From Space 4 *Doctor Who and the Auton Invasion* (6) *$1.75

   P2 The Silurians 7 *Doctor Who and the Cave-Monsters* (9) *$1.75

   P3 The Ambassadors of Death 7 *Doctor Who and the Ambassadors of Death* (121)

   P4 Inferno 7 *Doctor Who: Inferno* (89)

Season VIII (January 2, 1971–June 19, 1971)

   P5 Terror of the Autons 4 *Doctor Who and the Terror of the Autons* (63) *$3.50

   P6 The Mind of Evil 6 *Doctor Who: The Mind of Evil* (96)

   P7 The Claws of Axos 4 *Doctor Who and the Claws of Axos* (10) *$4.00

   P8 Colony in Space 6 *Doctor Who and the Doomsday Weapon* (23) *$3.50

   P9 The Daemons 5 *Doctor Who and the Daemons* (15) *$3.50

Season IX (January 1, 1972–June 24, 1972)

   P10 Day of the Daleks 4 *Doctor Who and the Day of the Daleks* (18) *$1.75

   P11 The Curse of Peladon 4 *Doctor Who and the Curse of Peladon* (13)

   P12 The Sea Devils 6 *Doctor Who and the Sea-Devils* (54) *$3.50

   P13 The Mutants 6 *Doctor Who and the Mutants* (44)

   P14 The Time Monster 6 *Doctor Who: The Time Monster* (102)

Season X (December 20, 1972–June 23, 1973)

   P15 The Three Doctors 4 *Doctor Who and the Three Doctors* (64) *$5.00

   P16 Carnival of Monsters 4 *Doctor Who and the Carnival of Monsters* (8)

   P17 Frontier in Space 6 *Doctor Who and the Space War* (57)

   P18 Planet of the Daleks 6 *Doctor Who and the Planet of the Daleks* (46)

   P19 The Green Death 6 *Doctor Who and the Green Death* (29) *$3.50

Season XI (December 15, 1973–June 8, 1974)

   P20 The Time Warrior 4 *Doctor Who and the Time Warrior* (65)

P21 Invasion of the Dinosaurs 6 *Doctor Who and the Dinosaur Invasion* (22) *\$4.00

P22 Death to the Daleks 4 *Doctor Who: Death to the Daleks* (20)

P23 The Monster of Peladon 6 *Doctor Who and the Monster of Peladon* (43)

P24 Planet of the Spiders 6 *Doctor Who and the Planet of the Spiders* (48) (original cover hardest to find) *\$5.00

Tom Baker as The Doctor (172 episodes)

Season XII (December 28, 1974–May 10, 1975)

B1 Robot 4 *Doctor Who and the Giant Robot* (28) *\$3.50

B2 The Ark in Space 4 *Doctor Who and the Ark in Space* (4)

B3 The Sontaran Experiment 2 *Doctor Who and the Sontaran Experiment* (56)

B4 Genesis of the Daleks 6 *Doctor Who and the Genesis of the Daleks* (27)

B5 Revenge of the Cybermen 4 *Doctor Who and the Revenge of the Cybermen* (51)

Season XIII (August 30, 1975–March 6, 1976)

B6 Terror of the Zygons 4 *Doctor Who and the Loch Ness Monster* (40)

B7 Planet of Evil 4 *Doctor Who and the Planet of Evil* (47) *\$1.75

B8 Pyramids of Mars 4 *Doctor Who and the Pyramids of Mars* (50) *\$1.75

B9 The Android Invasion 4 *Doctor Who and the Android Invasion* (2)

B10 The Brain of Morbius 4 *Doctor Who and the Brain of Morbius* (7)

B11 The Seeds of Doom 6 *Doctor Who and the Seeds of Doom* (55)

Season XIV (September 4, 1976–April 2, 1977)

B12 The Masque of Mandragora 4 *Doctor Who and the Masque of Mandragora* (42)

B13 The Hand of Fear 4 *Doctor Who and the Hand of Fear* (30)

B14 The Deadly Assassin 4 *Doctor Who and the Deadly Assassin* (19)

B15 The Face of Evil 4 *Doctor Who and the Face of Evil* (25)

B16 The Robots of Death 4 *Doctor Who and the Robots of Death* (53)

B17 The Talons of Weng-Chiang 6 *Doctor Who and the Talons of Weng-Chiang* (61)

Season XV (September 3, 1977– March 11, 1978)

B18 Horror of Fang Rock 4 *Doctor Who and the Horror of Fang Rock* (32)

B19 The Invisible Enemy 4 *Doctor Who and the Invisible Enemy* (36)

B20 Image of the Fendahl 4 *Doctor Who and the Image of the Fendahl* (34)

B21 The Sun Makers 4 *Doctor Who and the Sunmakers* (60)

B22 Underworld 4 *Doctor Who and the Underworld* (67)

B23 The Invasion of Time *Doctor Who and the Invasion of Time* (35)

Season XVI (September 2, 1978–February 24, 1979)

B24 The Ribos Operation 4 *Doctor Who and the Ribos Operation* (52)

B25 The Pirate Planet 4

B26 The Stones of Blood 4 *Doctor Who and the Stones of Blood* (59)

B27 The Androids of Tara 4 *Doctor Who and the Androids of Tara* (3)

B28 The Power of Kroll 4 *Doctor Who and the Power of Kroll* (49)

B29 The Armageddon Factor 6 *Doctor Who and the Armageddon Factor* (5)

Season XVII (September 1, 1979–January 12, 1980)

B30 Destiny of the Daleks 4 *Doctor Who and the Destiny of the Daleks* (21)

B31 City of Death 4

B32 The Creature From the Pit 4 *Doctor Who and the Creature From the Pit* (11)

B33 Nightmare of Eden 4 *Doctor Who and the Nightmare of Eden* (45)

B34 The Horns of Nimon 4 *Doctor Who and the Horns of Nimon* (31)

Season XVIII (August 30, 1980–March 21, 1981)

B35 The Leisure Hive 4 *Doctor Who and the Leisure Hive* (39)

B36 Meglos 4 *Doctor Who: Meglos* (75)

B37 Full Circle 4 *Doctor Who: Full Circle* (26)

B38 State of Decay 4 *Doctor Who and the State of Decay* (58)

B39 Warriors' Gate 4 *Doctor Who and the Warriors' Gate* (71)

B40 The Keeper of Traken 4 *Doctor Who and the Keeper of Traken* (37)

B41 Logopolis 4 *Doctor Who: Logopolis* (41)

Peter Davison as The Doctor (71 episodes)

Season XIX (January 4, 1982–March 30, 1982)

D1 Castrovalva 4 *Doctor Who: Castrovalva* (76)

D2 Four to Doomsday 4 *Doctor Who: Four to Doomsday* (7)

D3 Kinda 4 *Doctor Who: Kinda* (84)

D4 The Visitation 4 *Doctor Who and the Visitation* (69)

D5 Black Orchid 2 *Doctor Who and the Black Orchid* (113)

D6 Earthshock 4 *Doctor Who: Earthshock* (78)

D7 Time Flight 4 *Doctor Who: Time-Flight* (74)

Season XX (January 3, 1983–March 16, 1983)

D8 Arc of Infinity 4 *Doctor Who: Arc of Infinity* (80)

D9 Snakedance 4 *Doctor Who: Snakedance* (83)

D10 Mawdryn Undead 4 *Doctor Who: Mawdryn Undead* (82)

D11 Terminus 4 *Doctor Who: Terminus* (79)

D12 Enlightenment 4 *Doctor Who: Enlightenment* (85)

D13 The King's Demons 2 *Doctor Who: The King's Demons* (108)

Twentieth Anniversary Special (November 25, 1983)

D14 The Five Doctors 1 *Doctor Who: The Five Doctors* (81)

Season XXI (January 5, 1984–March 30, 1984)

D15 Warriors of the Deep 4 *Doctor Who: Warriors of the Deep* (87)

D16 The Awakening 2 *Doctor Who: The Awakening* (95)

D17 Frontios 4 *Doctor Who: Frontios* (91)

D18 Resurrection of the Daleks 4

D19 Planet of Fire 4 *Doctor Who and the Planet of Fire* (93)

D20 Caves of Androzani 4 *Doctor Who: The Caves of Androzani* (92)

Colin Baker as The Doctor (31 episodes)

CB1 The Twin Dilemma 4 *Doctor Who and the Twin Dilemma* (103)

Season XXII (January 5, 1985–March 30, 1985)

CB2 Attack of the Cybermen 2 (double-length) *Doctor Who and the Attack of the Cybermen*

CB3 Vengeance on Varos 2 (double-length) *Doctor Who: Vengeance on Varos* (106)

CB4 The Mark of the Rani 2 (double-length) *Doctor Who: The Mark of the Rani* (107)

CB5 The Two Doctors 3 (double-length) *Doctor Who and the Two Doctors* (100)

CB6 Timelash 2 (double-length) *Doctor Who and Timelash* (105)

CB7 Revelation of the Daleks 2 (double-length)

Season XXIII (September 6, 1986–December 6, 1986)

(Trial of a Time Lord, with titles not individually broadcast)

CB8 4 (The Mysterious Planet) *Doctor Who and the Mysterious Planet*

CB9 4 (Mindwarp)

CB10 4 (Terror of the Vervoids) *Doctor Who and the Terror of the Vervoids* (125)

CB11 2 (The Ultimate Foe)

Sylvester McCoy as The Doctor (14 episodes)

Season XXIV (–December 7, 1987)

Mc1 Time and the Rani 4 *Doctor Who: Time and the Rani*

Mc2 Paradise Towers 4

Mc3 Delta and the Bannermen 3

Mc4 Dragonfire 3

DOCTOR WHO MAGAZINE

There is also a British *Doctor Who* magazine in fairly wide circulation in the direct-sales comic-book market in America. It began as *Doctor Who Weekly* and with #44 became *Doctor Who Monthly*. Prices in "good" condition tend to average about $1.00, although some are higher priced. The highest prices are for #44, which is priced at around $3.75 in "good," and #45, which is about $3.50.

STAR TREK

This is a media success story: a science-fiction series to which both the general public and science-fiction fans are attracted. At this point, all episodes (including what remains of the never-aired pilot) are available on pre-recorded videotape, as are the four motion pictures which followed the series. The cartoons are a rarity, in that the Saturday-

morning series was closely tied to the original, live-action series and consistent with its continuity. It also used the voices of the original cast.

Moreover, it was a series which employed established science-fiction writers in production of several of the episodes and an established science-fiction writer and critic in some of the earliest paperback adaptations. Collectors are rewarded for their interest with material of acknowledged substance.

Reference books on the series are plentiful, some of them collectors' items in their own right. Bjo Trimble is the author of one of the most basic, initially self-published: *Star Trek Concordance,* of which the 1976 Ballantine edition contains information on the television series *and* the animated episodes.

1967   Hugo (Best Dramatic Presentation): ''The Menagerie''

1968   Hugo (Best Dramatic Presentation): ''City on the Edge of Forever''

Season I (September 8, 1966–April 13, 1967)
1   The Man Trap (by George Clayton Johnson)
2   Charlie X (by D. C. Fontana, story by Gene Roddenberry)
3   Where No Man Has Gone Before (by Samuel A. Peeples)
4   The Naked Time (by John D. F. Black)
5   The Enemy Within (by Richard Matheson)
6   Mudd's Women (by Stephen Kandel, story by Gene Roddenberry)
7   What Are Little Girls Made Of? (by Robert Bloch)
8   Miri (by Adrian Spies)
9   Dagger of the Mind (by Shimon Wincelberg [S. Bar-David])
10   The Corbomite Maneuver (by Jerry Sohl)
11   The Menagerie (two-parter by Gene Roddenberry)
12   The Conscience of the King (by Barry Trivers)
13   Balance of Terror (by Paul Schneider)
14   Shore Leave (by Theodore Sturgeon)
15   The Galileo Seven (by Oliver Crawford and S. Bar-David)
16   The Squire of Gothos (by Paul Schneider)
17   Arena (by Gene L. Coon, story by Fredric Brown)
18   Tomorrow Is Yesterday (by D. C. Fontana)

19 Court-Martial (by Don M. Mankiewicz and Stephen W. Carabatsos)
20 The Return of the Archons (by Boris Sobelman)
21 Space Seed (by Gene L. Coon and Carey Wilbur)
22 A Taste of Armageddon (by Robert Hamner and Gene L. Coon, story by Robert Hamner)
23 This Side of Paradise (by D. C. Fontana)
24 The Devil in the Dark (by Gene L. Coon)
25 Error of Mercy (by Gene L. Coon)
26 The Alternative Factor (by Don Ingalls)
27 The City on the Edge of Forever (by Harlan Ellison)
28 Operation—Annihilate! (by Stephen W. Carabatsos)

Season II (September 15, 1967–March 29, 1968)

29 Amok Time (by Theodore Sturgeon)
30 Who Mourns for Adonais? (by Gilbert Ralston and Gene L. Coon, story by Gilbert Ralston)
31 The Changeling (by John Meredyth Lucas)
32 Mirror, Mirror (by Jerome Bixby)
33 The Apple (by Max Erlich and Gene L. Coon)
34 The Doomsday Machine (by Norman Spinrad)
35 Catspaw (by Robert Bloch)
36 I, Mudd (by Stephen Kandel and David Gerrold)
37 Metamorphosis (by Gene L. Coon)
38 Journey to Babel (by D. C. Fontana)
39 Friday's Child (by D. C. Fontana)
40 The Deadly Years (by David P. Harmon)
41 Obsession (by Art Wallace)
42 Wolf in the Fold (by Robert Bloch)
43 The Trouble with Tribbles (by David Gerrold)
44 The Gamesters of Triskelion (by Margaret Armen)
45 A Piece of the Action (by David P. Harmon and Gene L. Coon)
46 The Immunity Syndrome (by Robert Sabaroff)
47 A Private Little War (by Gene Roddenberry, story by Judd Crucis)
48 Return to Tomorrow (by Gene Roddenberry)
49 Patterns of Force (by John Meredyth Lucas)
50 By Any Other Name (by D. C. Fontana and Jerome Bixby, story by Jerome Bixby)

51   The Omega Glory (by Gene Roddenberry)
52   The Ultimate Computer (by D. C. Fontana, story by Lawrence N. Wolfe)
53   Bread and Circuses (by Gene L. Coon and Gene Roddenberry)
54   Assignment: Earth (by Art Wallace, story by Gene Roddenberry and Art Wallace)

Season III (September 20, 1968–June 3, 1969)

55   Spock's Brain (by Lee Cronin)
56   The Enterprise Incident (by D. C. Fontana)
57   The Paradise Syndrome (by Margaret Armen)
58   And the Children Shall Lead (by Edward J. Lakso)
59   Is There in Truth No Beauty? (by Jean Lissette Aroeste)
60   Spectre of the Gun (by Lee Cronin)
61   Day of the Dove (by Jerome Bixby)
62   For the World Is Hollow and I Have Touched the Sky (by Rick Vollaerts)
63   The Tholian Web (by Judy Burns and Chet Richards)
64   Plato's Stepchildren (by Meyer Dlinsky)
65   Wink of an Eye (by Arthur Heinemann, story by Lee Cronin)
66   The Empath (by Joyce Muskat)
67   Elaan of Troyius (by John Meredyth Lucas)
68   Whom Gods Destroy (by Lee Erwin, story by Jerry Sohl and Lee Erwin)
69   Let That Be Your Last Battlefield (by Oliver Crawford, story by Lee Cronin)
70   The Mark of Gideon (by George F. Slavin and Stanley Adams)
71   That Which Survives (by John Meredyth Lucas, story by "Michael Richards")
72   The Lights of Zetar (by Jeremy Tarcher and Shari Lewis)
73   Requiem for Methuselah (by Jerome Bixby)
74   The Way to Eden (by Arthur Heinemann, story by "Michael Richards" and Arthur Heinemann)
75   The Cloud-Minders (by Margaret Armen, story by David Gerrold and Oliver Crawford)
76   The Savage Curtain (by Gene Roddenberry and Arthur Heinemann)
77   All Our Yesterdays (by Jean Lissette Aroeste)
78   Turnabout Intruder (by Gene Roddenberry)

Animated Cartoons (September 15, 1973–October 12, 1974)

1 Yesteryear (by D. C. Fonana)
2 One of Our Planets Is Missing (by Marc Daniels)
3 The Lorelei Signal (by Margaret Armen)
4 More Tribbles, More Troubles (by David Gerrold)
5 The Survivor (by James Schmerer)
6 The Infinite Vulcan (by Walter Koenig)
7 The Magicks of Megas-Tu (by Larry Brody)
8 Once Upon a Planet (by Len Jenson and Chuck Menville)
9 Mudd's Passion (by Stephen Kandel)
10 The Terratin Incident (by Paul Schneider)
11 Time Trap (by Joyce Perry)
12 The Ambergris Element (by Margaret Armen)
13 Slaver Weapon (by Larry Niven)
14 Beyond the Farthest Star (by Samuel A. Peeples)
15 The Eye of the Beholder (by David P. Harmon)
16 Jihad (by Stephen Kandel)
17 The Pirates of Orion (by Howard Weinstein)
18 Bem (by David Gerrold)
19 Practical Joker (by Chuck Menville)
20 Albatross (by Dario Finelli)
21 How Sharper Than a Serpent's Tooth (by Russell Bates and David Wise)
22 The Counter-Clock Incident (by John Culver)

Films

1979 *Star Trek—The Motion Picture*
1982 *Star Trek II: The Wrath of Khan*
1984 *Star Trek III: The Search for Spock*
1986 *Star Trek IV: The Voyage Home*

Second Series—*Star Trek: The New Generation*

Season I (October 1987–May 1988)

1 Encounter at Farpoint (2 hours)
2 The Naked Now
3 Code of Honor
4 The Last Output
5 Where No One Has Gone Before

6   Lonely Among Us
7   Justice
8   The Battle
9   Hide and Q
10 Haven
11 The Big Goodbye
12 Datalore
13 Angel One
14 11001001
15 Too Short a Season
16 When the Bough Breaks
17 Home Soil
18 Coming of Age
19 Heart of Glory
20 The Arsenal of Freedom
21 Symbiosis
22 Skin of Evil
23 We'll Always Have Paris
24 Conspiracy
25 The Neutral Zone

STAR TREK BOOKS

James Blish Numbered Series—ss (adaptations of episodes [Bantam])

1967   *Star Trek*
1968   *Star Trek 2*
1969   *Star Trek 3*
1971   *Star Trek 4*
1972   *Star Trek 5*
1972   *Star Trek 6*
1972   *Star Trek 7*
1972   *Star Trek 8*
1973   *Star Trek 9*
1974   *Star Trek 10*
1975   *Star Trek 11*
1977   *Star Trek 12* (with J. A. Lawrence)
1978   *Mudd's Angels* (by J. A. Lawrence alone, completing the adaptations)

The Science Fiction Book Club collected the first nine books into three omnibus volumes but, for some reason, scrambled the order of the reprints. *Star Trek Reader* contains Blish's books 2, 3, and 8; *Star Trek Reader 2* contains books 1, 4, and 9; *Star Trek Reader III* contains books 5, 6, and 7.

Alan Dean Foster "Log" Numbered books—ss (adaptations of animated episodes [Ballantine])

1974	*Star Trek Log One*
1974	*Star Trek Log Two*
1975	*Star Trek Log Three*
1975	*Star Trek Log Four*
1975	*Star Trek Log Five*
1976	*Star Trek Log Six*
1976	*Star Trek Log Seven*
1976	*Star Trek Log Eight*
1977	*Star Trek Log Nine*
1978	*Star Trek Log Ten*

Fotonovels (Bantam)

1977	(1)	*The City on the Edge of Forever*
1977	(2)	*Where No Man Has Gone Before*
1977	(3)	*The Trouble with Tribbles*
1978	(4)	*A Taste of Armageddon*
1978	(5)	*Metamorphosis*
1978	(6)	*All Our Yesterdays*
1978	(7)	*The Galileo 7*
1978	(8)	*A Peice of the Action*
1978	(9)	*The Devil in the Dark*
1978	(10)	*Day of the Dove*
1978	(11)	*The Deadly Years*
1978	(12)	*Amok Time*

Other Fiction (Bantam and Pocket)

1970   *Spock Must Die!* by James Blish
1976   *Spock, Messiah!* by Theodore R. Cogswell and Charles A. Spano, Jr.
1976   *Star Trek: The New Voyages* ed. by Sondra Marshak and Myrna Culbreath
1977   *Star Trek: The New Voyages 2* ed. by Sondra Marshak and Myrna Culbreath
1977   *The Price of the Phoenix* by Sondra Marshak and Myrna Culbreath
1977   *Planet of Judgment* by Joe Haldeman
1978   *Vulcan!* by Kathleen Sky
1978   *The Starless World* by Gordon Eklund
1979   *Devil World* by Gordon Eklund
1979   *The Fate of the Phoenix* by Sondra Marshak and Myrna Culbreath
1979   *World Without End* by Joe Haldeman
1979   *Trek to Madworld* by Stephen Goldin
1980   *Perry's Planet* by Jack C. Haldeman III
19??   *The Galactic Whirlpool* by David Gerrold
1981   *Death's Angel* by Kathleen Sky
1986   *Enterprise: The First Adventure* by Vonda N. McIntyre   **$1.00**
1986   *Star Trek IV: The Voyage Home* by Vonda N. McIntyre

Timescape (later just Pocket, new novels [Pocket Books])

Initially, the Pocket *Star Trek* books were not numbered. Later editions—and volumes that came later in the series—carried the numbering; some fans carry want lists by number, rather than title. This series has several titles with the distinction of capturing a spot on national bestseller lists. Prices initially ranged from $2.25 to $3.50; prices in only "good" condition should range from about 75¢ to $1.00.

1979   (1) *Star Trek: The Motion Picture* by Gene Roddenberry
1981   (2) *The Entropy Effect* by Vonda N. McIntyre
1981   (3) *The Klingon Gambit* by Robert E. Vardeman
1981   (4) *The Covenant of the Crown* by Howard Weinstein

1982   (5) *The Prometheus Design* by Sondra Marshak and Myrna Culbreath

1982   (6) *The Abode of Life* by Lee Correy

1982   (7) *Star Trek II: The Wrath of Khan* by Vonda N. McIntyre

1983   (8) *Black Fire* by Sonni Cooper

1983   (9) *Triangle* by Sondra Marshak and Myrna Culbreath

1983   (10) *Web of the Romulans* by M. S. Murdock

1983   (11) *Yesterday's Son* by A. C. Crispin *90¢*

1983   (12) *Mutiny on the Enterprise* by Robert E. Vardeman

1983   (13) *The Wounded Sky* by Diane Duane (4th printing by 1987) *90¢*

1984   (14) *The Trellisane Confrontation* by David Dvorkin

1984   (15) *Corona* by Greg Bear

1984   (16) *The Final Reflection* by John M. Ford

1984   (17) *Star Trek III: The Search for Spock* by Vonda N. McIntyre

1984   (18) *My Enemy, My Ally* by Diane Duane

1984   (19) *The Tears of the Singers* by Melenda Snodgrass

1984   (20) *The Vulcan Academy Murders* by Jean Lorrah

1985   (21) *Uhura's Song* by Janet Kagan

1985   (22) *Shadow Lord* by Laurence Yep

1985   (23) *Ishmael* by Barbara Hambly

1985   (24) *Killing Time* by Della Van Hise

1985   (25) *Dwellers in the Crucible* by Margaret Wander Bonanno

1985   (26) *Pawns and Symbols* by Majliss Larson

1986   (27) *Mindshadow* by J. M. Dillard

1986   (28) *Crisis on Centaurus* by Brad Ferguson

1986   (29) *Dreadnought!* by Diane Carey

1986   (30) *Demons* by J. M. Dillard

1986   (31) *Battlestations!* (seq to #29) by Diane Carey

1987   (32) *Chain of Attack* (seq to #6) by Gene DeWeese

1987   (33) *Deep Domain* by Howard Weinstein *90¢*

1987   (34) *Dreams of the Raven* by Carmen Carter

1987   (35) *The Romulan Way* by Diane Duane and Peter Morwood

1987   (36) *How Much for Just the Planet?* by John M. Ford

Nonfiction

1968 *The Making of Star Trek* by Stephen E. Whitfield and Gene Roddenberry

1973 *The World of Star Trek* by David Gerrold

1973 *The Trouble with Tribbles* by David Gerrold

1975 *Star Trek Lives!* by Jacqueline Lichtenberg, Sondra Marshak, and Joan Winston

1977 *I Am Not Spock* by Leonard Nimoy

1977 *Letters to Star Trek* ed. by Susan Sackett

1978 *Official Star Trek Cooking Manual* by Mary Ann Piccard

1980 *Chekov's Enterprise* by Walter Koenig

1980 *Star Trek Maps*   *$5.00*

1980 *The Monsters of Star Trek* by Daniel Cohen

1983 *On the Good Ship Enterprise: My 15 Years with Star Trek* by Bjo Trimble (5th printing by 1986)

Games

1976 *Star Trek Puzzle Manual* by James Razzi, Sondra Marshak, and Myrna Culbreath

1977 *The Star Trek Quiz Book* by Bart Andrews with Brad Dunning

1980 *The Official Star Trek Trivia Book* by Rafe Needleman

STAR WARS

1977 SFWA (Special Award): *Star Wars*

1977 Hugo (Special Award): George Lucas

1978 Hugo (Dramatic Presentation): *Star Wars*

1981 Hugo (Dramatic Presentation): *The Empire Strikes Back*

1984 Hugo (Dramatic Presentation): *Return of the Jedi*

1976 *Star Wars* by George Lucas (this has had many printings; the most valuable by far is its first edition, which was on sale months before the movie was released)   *$1.00–*

1979 *Han Solo at Stars' End* by Brian Daley   pb75¢

1980 *The Empire Strikes Back* by Donald F. Glut   *$1.00–*

1983 *Return of the Jedi* by James Kahn   *$1.00–*

1986 *The Star Wars Trilogy* (trade pb omnibus)   *$2.00*

Star Wars by George Lucas, about 4¹/₄″ × 7″; cover by Ralph Mc-Quarrie. The first edition was released a half-year before the movie was released. (The release did very well, indeed, for Ballantine, which had bought the rights; the editor who made the purchase was the canny Judy-Lynn del Rey.) Copyright 1976 by The Star Wars Corporation.

Nonfiction

1977 *The Star Wars Sketchbook* by Joe Johnston   trade pb$5.00
1978 *The Star Wars Storybook*   trade pb$3.00
1980 *Once Upon a Galaxy: A Journal of the Making of The Empire Strikes Back* by Alan Arnold   pb$1.00
1980 *The Empire Strikes Back Sketchbook* by Joe Johnston and Nilo Rodis-Jamero   trade pb$5.00
1983 *The Making of Return of the Jedi* ed. by John Phillip Peecher pb$1.00

U.N.C.L.E.

The Man From U.N.C.L.E. was a television show followed by many science-fiction fans—and many of the books emphasized the science-fictional aspects of the television show. Copyrights on the books were not necessarily publication dates. Most of the books can be purchased for $1.00 or less in "good" condition. A few go for more. David McDaniel was the real name of a fan who used the pen name of Ted

Johnstone for his fan activities; McDaniel dedicated one of his *U.N.C.L.E.* books to Ted Johnstone. "Thomas Stratton" was a pen name for the team of Robert Coulson and Gene DeWeese, who had both their proposed title (*The Invisible Dirigible Affair*) and their proposed dedication ("To my wives and child") rejected for #11.

Michael Avallone wrote two *The Girl From U.N.C.L.E.* paperbacks for Signet. There were 24 issues of *The Man From U.N.C.L.E. Magazine* and 7 issues of *The Girl From U.N.C.L.E.* magazine. There were 22 issues of *The Man From U.N.C.L.E.* comic book and 5 issues of *The Girl From U.N.C.L.E.* comic book.

The Man From U.N.C.L.E. Paperbacks (Ace)

1965 (1) *The Man From U.N.C.L.E.* by Michael Avallone
1965 (2) *The Doomsday Affair* by Harry Whittington
1965 (3) *The Copenhagen Affair* by John Oram
1965 (4) *The Dagger Affair* by David McDaniel
1966 (5) *The Mad Scientist Affair* by John T. Phillifent
1966 (6) *The Vampire Affair* by David McDaniel
1966 (7) *The Radioactive Camel Affair* by Peter Leslie
1967 (8) *The Monster Wheel Affair* by David McDaniel
1967 (9) *The Diving Dames Affair* by Peter Leslie
1967 (10) *The Assassination Affair* by J. Hunter Holly
1967 (11) *The Invisibility Affair* by Thomas Stratton
1967 (12) *The Mind Twisters Affair* by Thomas Stratton
1967 (13) *The Rainbow Affair* by David McDaniel
1968 (14) *The Cross of Gold Affair* by Fredric Davies
1968 (15) *The Utopia Affair* by David McDaniel
1968 (16) *The Splintered Sunglasses Affair* by Peter Leslie
1969 (17) *The Hollow Crown Affair* by David McDaniel
1968 (18) *The Unfair Fare Affair* by Peter Leslie
1968 (19) *The Power Cube Affair* by John T. Phillifent
1967 (20) *The Corfu Affair* by John T. Phillifent
1967 (21) *The Thinking Machine Affair* by Joel Bernard
1966 (22) *The Stone Cold Dead in the Market Affair* by John Oram
1966 (23) *The Finger in the Sky Affair* by Peter Leslie
      (24) *The Final Affair* by David McDaniel (So far, this is a nonexistent collectible. When book sales dwindled, a final, series-ending novel was written. However, it was understandably felt at Ace that a series being discontinued for

lack of sales did not cry out for one *more* book just to wrap up the story. Later, a private edition of the McDaniel novel was proposed and a sign-up list established in case the book was published—but the book has not yet been printed.)

Filksongs and
Other Recordings

Filksong retailer and collector Robert Coulson told us, "Like science fiction itself, filksongs are what we mean when we point to them. In general, they relate to science fiction and fantasy. They can be about published stories or authors; conventions or other fan activity; individual fans; current, past, or projected space events; or original ballads of a fantastic nature.

"They can also, now and then, be existing poems set to music by a fan; or a parody of a well-known song; or, actually, anything that a filksinger wants to sing about. Folk songs, preferably obscure, are sometimes included on filk tapes."

Filksongs are folksongs of a science-fictional or fantastic ilk—hence, the coined term. The usage is comparable to that of the world of folksongs and is easily picked up, as is apparent from our use here: Filksongs are sung by filksingers, they are passed on from filksinger to filksinger, etc.

They grew out of some science-fiction fans' interest in folk music; indeed, Coulson and his wife, Juanita, maintained a collection of recorded folk music for years before she became known as one of the foremost filksingers. Juanita Coulson is a well-known science-fiction author, but she also plays acoustic guitar and is known in filksong circles for her skills as a singer. Today, they also retail filksong tapes, and he has acted as recording engineer on two tapes. More information is available from Coulson Publications, 2677W-500N, Hartford City, Indiana 47348.

Recording of filksong performances began in relatively recent years; Coulson puts the first professional filk tape release at 1979, although filksinging has existed at least since the mid-fifties.

"Because of this," he said in mid-1988, "most filk tapes are still available from the publisher at the list price, and inflated prices for collectors are, in all but a few cases, a thing of the future.

"There is no particular premium on first editions."

Commercially recorded tapes have been released primarily from the following companies:

DAG Productions, 1810 14th Street, #102, Santa Monica, California 90404
Magic Granny Line, Route 4, Box 192-E, Huntsville, Arkansas 72740
Pegasus Music, P.O. Box 150471, Arlington, Texas 76015
Wail Songs, P.O. Box 19888, Oakland, California 94604

One other releasing company was called Off Centaur, Inc., until late in 1988. However, its name was then changed and before long it was known as Firebird Arts & Music, Inc., P.O. Box 124, El Cerrito, California 94530.

There have been changes over the years, too, in material released from some of the companies. Coulson said, "Off Centaur began replacing its original, single-color inserts with full-color ones in 1985, but most originals are still available." Because of this, no notations of insert variations are given in this listing. Coulson said that collectors' interest in this field has so far focused on the songs recorded, rather than the rarity of a specific "edition."

The larger filksong releasing companies offer catalogs including their own tapes and those from smaller, independent ones. Almost all current tapes and songbooks—and a few folk music tapes and related material—may be obtained from one or more of the sources previously listed.

Pricing information was researched and provided by Robert Coulson. Coulson notes that the prices for Off Centaur/Firebird tapes listed here are those which are in the process of being established; tapes may be available at $1.00 cheaper on the $9.00 tapes and at $2.00 cheaper on the $11.00 tapes, depending on the process of price hikes at the time of ordering.

SINGERS ON VIDEOTAPE

Suzette Haden Elgin

Suzette Haden Elgin Talks About Science Fiction's Filkmusic 50 min., VHS only (Magic Granny Line) sample songs by Elgin ***$22.50***

SINGERS ON RECORDS

Sheldon Allman

Folk Songs for the 21st Century lp (High Fidelity Recordings, Inc.) o/p commercial release *$11.00*

The Caltech Stock Company

Let's Advance on Science lp (no publisher listed) o/p *$17.00*

Meg Davis

Captain Jack and the Mermaid lp (Fretless) same as Off Centaur tape *$9.00*

Leslie Fish

Folk Songs for Folk Who Ain't Even Been Yet with the Dehorn Crew lp (T. J. Phoenix Co.) o/p *$50.00*
Solar Sailors with the Dehorn Crew lp (Bandersnatchi Press) available from Off Centaur *$9.00*

The Dehorn Crew (see Leslie Fish)

Chuck Rein

"The Green Hills of Earth"/flip side unknown 45 rpm (Fantasy Record Co.) o/p *$20.00*
"In Western Lands"/"Oh, the Planets We've Seen" 45 rpm (Fantasy Record Co.) o/p *$17.50*

SINGERS ON AUDIO TAPE

Condition: In this particular case, since virtually all material is available and is being collected for its content, the condition is assumed to be "as new" (at least "fine") at that price. A tape may not be sealed in cellophane. Coulson says, "Very few filk tapes are sealed by the publisher." The tape should play without problem and contain whatever notes or packaging were included with the tape.

These releases are listed by singer, the way they are primarily collected. Unless otherwise noted, the tapes are 60 minutes long.

Robert Asprin (performing as "Yang the Nauseating")

Kha-Khan's Lament (Pegasus Music) SCA songs **$9.00**

Avenydd

Pot Luck (Wail Songs) **$9.00**

Robin Bailey

Almost Alive, Sometimes (Bailey) **$8.00**
Dreamflight (Bailey) **$8.00**

Martie Benedict (sends tape in return for blank tape and postage)

All the listed tapes involve Harrison Ford. "VHF" stands for "Very Harrison Ford."

Communion (Benedict) **$2.00**
Love Songs/Star Songs (Benedict) **$2.00**
More VHF I 90 min. (Benedict) **$2.00**
More VHF II 90 min. (Benedict) **$2.00**
More VHF III (Benedict) **$2.00**
More VHF IV (Benedict) **$2.00**
More VHF V (Benedict) **$2.00**
VHF (Benedict) **$2.00**

Marty Burke

ConClave at Sweeny's, Spasm 1 (Margaret Middleton) o/p field recording from convention **$11.50**
ConClave at Sweeny's, Spasm 2 (Margaret Middleton) o/p field recording from convention **$11.50**

M. Dorothy Breen

Turnabout narrated by Mary Mason, songs by Breen and Kirstoph Klover, written by Mercedes Lackey (Off Centaur) **$7.50**

Barry and Sally Childs-Helton

Escape From Mundania (Space Opera House) **$9.00**

Juanita Coulson

Juanita Coulson Live at Filkcon West (Off Centaur) field recording from convention **$9.00**

Rifles & Rhymes (Off Centaur) poems of history and folklore by Martha Keller set to music **$11.00**

Meg Davis

Captain Jack and the Mermaid 45 min. (Off Centaur tape) **$11.00**
———(Fretless 1p record) **$9.00**
Dream of Light Horses 45 min. (Off Centaur) **$11.00**
Swing the Cat 45 min. (Off Centaur) **$11.00**

The Dehorn Crew (see Leslie Fish)

Dennis Drew

The Final Reality (Drew) **$10.00**
The Pride of the Angry Sea (Drew) **$9.00**

Julia Ecklar

A Wolfrider's Reflections (Off Centaur) songs are affiliated with Wendy and Richard Pini's *Elfquest* series **$11.00**

Divine Intervention (Air Craft Records) **$9.00**

Genesis (Off Centaur) **$11.00**

The Horse-Tamer's Daughter (Off Centaur) **$11.00**

Space Heroes and Other Fools with Anne Harlan Prather (Off Centaur) **$9.00**

Traveller First Edition (Ecklar) o/p; will be scarce **$12.50**
———Second Edition (Off Centaur) o/p; much better recording **$16.00**

Suzette Haden Elgin

Dragons, Cows, and Kudzus with Randy Farran (Magic Granny Line) **$8.50**

Industrious Strength Songs and Stories 45 min. (Magic Granny Line) temporarily o/p **$7.00**

Song at the Ready (Magic Granny Line) temporarily o/p **$8.00**

Songs From the Ozark Trilogy (Magic Granny Line) temporarily o/p **$7.00**

Soon to Be a Major Embarrassment with Randy Farran (Magic Granny Line) **$8.50**

Randy Farran (see Suzette Haden Elgin)

Leslie Fish

Chickasaw Mountain (Off Centaur) **$11.00**

Cold Iron Kipling poems set to music (Off Centaur) **$11.00**

It's Sister Jenny's Turn to Throw the Bomb with the Dehorn Crew (Off Centaur) Filk, folk, and IWW songs **$11.00**

Sykbound **$9.00**

The Undertaker's Horse (Off Centaur) Kipling poems set to music **$11.00**

Clif Flynt

Fragile Wall with Mary Ellen Wessels (Wail Songs) **$9.00**

Liftoff to Landing with Bill Roper (STI Studios) **$9.00**

Diana Gallagher

Cosmic Concepts Complete 45 min. (Gallagher) o/p **$7.50**

Cosmic Concepts More Complete (Off Centaur) re-mastering and expansion of *Cosmic Concepts Complete* **$11.00**

Star Song 45 min. First Edition (Gallagher) o/p **$7.00**

———Second Edition (Off Centaur) **$7.50**

The Great Broads of the Galaxy

Cosmic Connection 45 min. (Great Broads) **$5.00**

Frank Hayes

Don't Ask (Off Centaur) **$11.00**

Heather Rose Jones

Ecotone (Wail Songs) **$9.00**

Kathleen Kingslight

Dragonsongs with narration by Anne McCaffrey (Performing Arts Press) *$8.00*

Kristoph Klover (see M. Dorothy Breen)

L. A. Filkharmonics

In Space, No One Can Hear You Sing 70 min. (Nick Smith) o/p; productions stopped due to copyright difficulties, media oriented *$10.00*

Cynthia McQuillan

Crystal Memories with Phil Wayne (Off Centaur) o/p *$7.50*
Crystal Singer (Off Centaur) *$11.00*
Dark Moon Circle (Unlikely Productions) *$9.00*
Shadow Spun (Off Centaur) *$11.00*
Singer in the Shadow Southern California Version (Off Centaur) o/p *$9.00*
Singer in the Shadow Northern California Version (Off Centaur) same songs as other version, but back-up musicians are different *$11.00*

Kathy Mar

Bamboo Wind (Off Centaur) *$11.00*
On a Bright Wind (Off Centaur) *$11.00*
Songbird (Off Centaur) *$11.00*

Bill Maraschiello

Magnetic Elixir 45 min. (Starwind Productions) folk and filk *$6.50*

Mary Mason (see M. Dorothy Breen)

Margaret Middleton

Margaret Middleton at Bayfilk I (Off Centaur) *$9.00*

Anne Harlan Prather

Storyteller (Off Centaur)   *$11.00*
(see also Julia Ecklar)

Jane Robinson

Dr. Jane's Science Notes (Off Centaur)   *$11.00*

Roberta Rogow

People and Places (Rogow)   *$8.00*
Rec-Room Rhymes (Rogow) *Star Trek* songs   *$8.00*
Rec-Room Rhymes #2 (Rogow) *Star Trek* songs   *$8.00*
Rogow and Company (Rogow) media-oriented   *$8.00*

Bill Roper

The Grim Roper (Off Centaur)   *$11.00*
(see also Clif Flynt)

Linda Short

Ditties From the Edge of the World (Short) songs about BBC-TV SF
   series *Blake's 7*   *$6.00*
Songs of the Seven (Short) songs about BBC-TV series *Blake's
   7*   *$6.00*

Valondis Stareagle

Star Shadows (Pegasus Music)   *$9.00*

Edward Starlinglathe (available from Pegasus Music)

Errantry: Fantasy/Reality   *$10.00*
Errantry: Others   *$10.00*
Errantry: Quartz   *$10.00*
Errantry: Tresses   *$10.00*

Beth Stevens

Lady of Lies with Janet Wilson 45 min. (Caliche Records)   *$9.00*

Bill Sutton

Past Due (Off Centaur) *$11.00*

Technical Difficulties

Please Stand By 45 min. (Technical Difficulties) *$9.00*

Phil Wayne (see Cynthia McQuillan)

Chris Weber

I Filk (DAG Productions) *$8.00*

Mary Ellen Wessels (see Clif Flynt)

Karen Willson

Children of the Future (ed. number on insert) First edition (Hourglass
   Productions) o/p *$9.00*
———Second edition (Hourglass Productions) o/p *$9.00*
———Third edition (DAG Productions) *$9.00*

Janet Wilson (see Beth Stevens)

CONVENTION AND ANTHOLOGY RECORDINGS ON TAPE

"Convention" refers to material recorded at a convention—in folk
music terms, a field recording. "Anthology" recordings are done in
a studio with a variety of singers. Anthology tapes have better production values and less ambiance than convention tapes (which frequently have audience noises and interruptions). If not identified in
the tape title, the name of the specific convention is included in the
notes. The notation "o/p" indicates a recording that is out of print.

Austin Ditty Limits (Off Centaur) convention: LACon II (1984 World-
   con) *$9.00*
Bayfilk Concert (Off Centaur) convention: Bayfilk I *$9.00*
Bayfilk Crazies (Off Centaur) convention: Bayfilk I *$9.00*
Bayfilk II: Concert 1 (Off Centaur) convention *$9.00*
Bayfilk II: Concert 2 (Off Centaur) convention *$9.00*

Bayfilk II: Dredgings (Off Centaur) convention   **$9.00**

Bayfilk III: Back Stage (Off Centaur) convention   **$9.00**

Bayfilk III: Center Stage (Off Centaur) convention   **$9.00**

Bayfilk III: On Stage (Off Centaur) convention   **$9.00**

Bayfilk III: Stage Struck (Off Centaur) convention   **$9.00**

The Best of Bayfilk (Off Centaur) convention   **$9.00**

Best of Bayfilk II (Off Centaur) convention   **$9.00**

Best of Chicon IV (Off Centaur) convention: 1982 Worldcon   **$9.00**

Best of Constellation (Off Centaur) convention: 1983 Worldcon   **$9.00**

The Best of Filkcon I (Filk Foundation, Inc.) convention; sold only to members First Edition o/p   **$12.50**

———Second Edition o/p (Side B of Second Edition is revised. Side B of First Edition starts with "Reminder" and "Memorandum" by Juanita Coulson; Side B of Second Edition starts with "Reminder" and "The Tzen" by Robert Asprin) o/p   **$12.50**

The Best of Filkcon West (Off Centaur) convention   **$9.00**

The Best of OVFF (Off Centaur) convention: Ohio Valley Filk Fest #1   **$9.00**

The Black Unicorn (DAG Productions) convention: ConChord III   **$9.00**

Brandywine (Off Centaur) anthology: songs of conflict   **$11.00**

Challenger Memorial (Off Centaur) anthology: requiem for the shuttle   **$11.00**

Con-Chord Concert (Tera Mitchel) convention: Con-Chord I o/p   **$10.00**

Dreams and Nightmares (Wail Songs) convention: Con-Chord II   **$9.00**

Filkcon 5.2 East Concert (The Filk Foundation) convention   **$8.00**

Filks That Pass in the Night (Wail Songs) convention: Ohio Valley Filk Fest #2   **$9.00**

Finity's End (Off Centaur) anthology: songs written by C. J. Cherryh or about her fiction   **$11.00**

Flying Island (Wail Songs) convention: Marcon 22   **$9.00**

Free Fall and Other Delights (Off Centaur) anthology: songs about space travel, insert illo by Kelly Freas   **$9.00**

Friends of Kushyon Flyte House (Tera Mitchel) anthology   **$7.00**

Heralds, Harpers, and Havoc (Off Centaur) anthology: songs written by Mercedes Lackey   **$11.00**

Highlights of Filkcon 2 (Filk Foundation) convention; sold only to members o/p **$10.00**

Highlights of Filkcon 4.2 (Filk Foundation) convention; sold only to members o/p **$9.00**

The Joy of Singing (Wail Songs) convention: ConChord II **$9.00**

KFH Presents (Tera Mitchel) anthology; limited edition; not sold o/p **$12.50**

A Little Rat Music (Off Centaur) convention: LACon II (1984 WorldCon) **$9.00**

Manifilk Destiny (Wail Songs) convention: Westercon XXXX **$9.00**

Marcon Grows Up (Wail Songs) convention: Marcon 21 **$9.00**

Minus Ten and Counting 65 min. (Off Centaur) anthology: musical history of past and future space development **$11.00**

Mister Author (Wail Songs) convention: ConChord II **$9.00**

Murder, Mystery and Mayhem (Off Centaur) anthology: songs written by Mercedes Lackey **$11.00**

Other Times, Other Places (DAG Productions) anthology **$9.00**

OVFF Concert 1 (Off Centaur) convention: Ohio Valley Filk Fest #1 **$9.00**

OVFF Concert 2 (Off Centaur) convention: Ohio Valley Filk Fest #1 **$9.00**

Rat Mastersongs (Off Centaur) convention: LACon II (1984 WorldCon) **$9.00**

Rebel Yells (Off Centaur) convention: Confederation (1986 WorldCon) **$9.00**

Snow Magic (Off Centaur) anthology **$11.00**

Song of the Stars (DAG Productions) convention: ConChord III **$9.00**

Songs of the Dorsai (Off Centaur) anthology: songs about the writings of Gordon R. Dickson **$11.00**

Songs That Go Filk in the Night (Wail Songs) convention: Ohio Valley Filk Fest #2 **$9.00**

Star Trek Comedy 50 min. (Vince Emery) anthology: mostly comedy routines, some music **$9.00**

There's a Filksing Here Tonight (Wail Songs) convention: ConChord II **$9.00**

Time Winds Tavern (Off Centaur) anthology: songs about mythological beasts **$11.00**

The Wail From Down Under (Wail Songs) convention: Aussiecon II
   (1985 WorldCon) *$9.00*
Where No Man . . . (Off Centaur) anthology: mostly humorous songs
   about *Star Trek* *$11.00*
Yankee Doodles (Off Centaur) convention: Confederation (1986
   WorldCon) *$11.00*

SPOKEN WORD

In recent years, there has been an explosion in the availability of
spoken-word tapes in the science-fiction and fantasy fields. Bookstores have increasing rack space devoted to such material, and it is
possible to get stories, cut and uncut, read by the original author or
by professional actors.

There have even been amateur productions. *Outworlds* #50 was a
cassette edition of Bill Bowers' fanzine produced "live" at the 1987
Corflu convention. The audio version is $6.50; the VHS or Beta ver-
sion is $12.50 from Bowers, 1874 Sunset Ave. #56 Cincinnati, Ohio
45238. Larry Tucker (3358 Chelsea Circle, Ann Arbor, Michigan
48108) produces *Uncle Albert's Electric Talking Fanzine*. In either
case, interested purchasers should send the fans a self-addressed,
stamped envelope and ask for current availability and prices.

Hourglass Productions produced a series of interviews and discussions with science-fiction authors; Coulson says they are out of print
but lists the following:

An Hour with Isaac Asimov *$9.00*
An Hour with Marion Zimmer Bradley *$9.00*
An Hour with Randall Garrett *$5.00*
An Hour with David Gerrold *$5.00*
An Hour with Stephen Goldin *$3.00*
An Hour with Katherine Kurtz *$5.00*
An Hour with Fritz Leiber *$7.00*
An Hour with Kathleen Sky *$3.00*

At least in this volume, we will not provide any sort of complete
list of recorded material; this portion of the chapter indicates only the
type of material available.

Obviously, the range of potential recorded material for science-
fiction and fantasy fans can range from original cast recordings of *The*

Rocky Horror Picture Show to the anthroporphic humorous songs in *The Bestiary of Flanders & Swann* to recordings of performances of *The Tempest* and soundtracks of science-fiction movies.

This listing focuses on readings of the work of science-fiction and fantasy professionals. Where possible, the year of copyright of the recording is given. Retailers typically charge *$15.00* for new copies of most of the records listed below.

Brian W. Aldiss. *Frankenstein Unbound* "a dramatization narrated by the author, produced in cooperation with the BBC" (Alternate World Recordings AWR 5911, 1976)

Isaac Asimov. *Foundation* ("The Psychohistorians") read by William Shatner (Caedmon TC 1508, 1976)
The Isaac Asimov Recorded Library ("The author reads favorite stories with commentary") ("I Just Make Them Up, See?" "The Feeling of Power," "Someday," "Satisfaction Guaranteed," "Living Space," "The Last Question," "Jokester," "The Immortal Bard," "Spell My Name with an 'S'," "The Ugly Little Boy") (designed for use in schools, 6-cassette set Listening Library CXL 505)
The Mayors (from *Foundation*) read by Isaac Asimov (Caedmon TC 1527, 1977)

Robert Bloch. *Gravely, Robert Bloch* read by Robert Bloch (Alternate World Recordings AWR 3210)
The Life and Future Times of Jack the Ripper ("from the works of and read by Robert Bloch and Harlan Ellison") (Alternate Worlds Recordings AWR 6925)

Ray Bradbury. *The Martian Chronicles* ("There Will Come Soft Rains," "Usher II") read by Leonard Nimoy (Caedmon TC 1466, 1975)

Lewis Carroll. *Alice's Adventure in Wonderland* (complete on 4 lp records) read and sung by Cyril Ritchard (Riverside SDP 22, recorded 1957)
Through the Looking Glass (complete on 4 lp records) read and sung by Cyril Ritchard (Murray Hill M-2387, recorded 1964) Noel Coward. *Blithe Spirit* performed by Noel Coward, Claudette Colbert, Lauren Bacall, and Mildred Natwick. (Sandpiper 1)

Harlan Ellison. *Harlan!* read by Harlan Ellison (Alternate Worlds Recordings AWR 6922) (see also Robert Bloch)

Kenneth Grahame. *The Reluctant Dragon* read by Boris Karloff (Caedmon TC 1074)

Robert A. Heinlein. *The Green Hills of Earth* (and "Gentlemen, Be Seated") read by Leonard Nimoy (Caedmon TC 1526, 1977)

Robert E. Howard. *From the Hells Beneath the Hells* read by Ugo Toppo (Alternate World Recordings AWR 4810)

Shirley Jackson. *The Lottery and Other Stories by Shirley Jackson* ("My Life with R. H. Macy," "The Witch," "Charles") read by Maureen Stapleton (Caedmon TC 1491, 1976)

Rudyard Kipling. *How Fear Came* read by Boris Karloff (Caedmon TC 1100)

Henry Kuttner. *Mimsy Were the Borogoves* read by William Shatner (Caedmon TC 1509, 1976)

Ursula K. LeGuin. *The Ones Who Walk Away From Omelas* read by Ursula K. LeGuin (Alternate World Recordings AWR 7476)

Fritz Leiber. *Gonna Roll the Bones* read by Fritz Leiber (Alternate Worlds Recordings AWR 3239)

A. A. Milne. *The Most of Winnie-the-Pooh* read by Maurice Evans (Pathways of Sound POS 1038)

C. L. Moore. *Shambleau* read by C. L. Moore (Caedmon TC1667)

Joanna Russ. *Joanna Russ Interpreting Her Stories* (Alternate Worlds Recordings AWR 6913)

Robert Silverberg. *Robert Silverberg Reads "To See the Invisible Man" and "Passengers"* read by Robert Silverberg. (Pelican Records LP 2003)

Theodore Sturgeon. *Theodore Sturgeon Reads His Stories* read by Theodore Sturgeon (Alternate Worlds Recordings AWR 3340)

H. G. Wells. *Jeff Wayne's Musical Version of The War of the Worlds* (2-record set, Columbia PC2 35290)

Oscar Wilde. *Oscar Wilde Fairy Tales* ("The Selfish Giant," "The Happy Prince," "The Nightingale and the Rose") read by Basil Rathbone (Caedmon TC 1044)

Collecting the Best

A practical method of beginning to collect—or getting the feeling of what a field has to offer—is to collect the award-winning material in that field. Awards have been given in America since 1953 (for the year 1952), but there are even collections of the cream of the crop from years preceding that.

An outstanding work (which lists nominees, as well as winners) for collectors in this field is *A History of the Hugo, Nebula, and International Fantasy Awards* by Donald Franson and Howard DeVore; see the chapter on reference works. We list winners here.

HUGO AWARDS

The Hugo Awards are voted on by members of the World Science Fiction Convention each year and began in conjunction with the WorldCon in 1953. (In early years, voting was not limited to paid members, but that limitation was in force within a decade.) They were not picked up the following year, but in 1955, they were reinstated and have run in every succeeding year. The awards are given for work published in the previous year.

Technically, the awards are the Science Fiction Achievement Awards and are nicknamed ''Hugos'' (after Hugo Gernsback, the father of magazine science fiction).

The categories have changed over the years. A detailed history of the developments in the field can be found in *A History of the Hugo, Nebula, and International Fantasy Awards* by Donald Franson and Howard DeVore.

1953

Best Novel: *The Demolished Man* by Alfred Bester
Best Professional Magazine: *Astounding* and *Galaxy*
Best Interior Illustrator: Virgil Finlay
Best Cover Artist: Ed Emshwiller and Hannes Bok

Excellence in Fact Articles: Willy Ley
Best New Author: Philip Jose Farmer
#1 Fan Personality: Forrest J. Ackerman

1955

Best Novel: *They'd Rather Be Right* (also known as *The Forever Machine*) by Mark Clifton and Frank Riley
Best Novelette: "The Darfsteller" by Walter M. Miller, Jr.
Best Short Story: "Allamagoosa" by Eric Frank Russell
Best Professional Magazine: *Astounding*
Best Professional Artist: Frank Kelly Freas
Best Fanzine: *Fantasy-Times*
Special Committee Award: Sam Moskowitz
Special Hugo (a joke, the category being "Best Unpublished Story"): "Sven" by Lou Tabakow, which had been listed on the cover of a magazine but did not appear therein. It eventually was published.

1956

Best Novel: *Double Star* by Robert A. Heinlein
Best Novelette: "Exploration Team" by Murray Leinster (also known as "Combat Team")
Best Short Story: "The Star" by Arthur C. Clarke
Best Professional Magazine: *Astounding*
Best Professional Artist: Frank Kelly Freas
Best Fanzine: *Inside & Science Fiction Advertiser*
Best Feature Writer: Willy Ley
Best Book Reviewer: Damon Knight
Best New Author: Robert Silverberg

1957

Best American Professional Magazine: *Astounding*
Best British Professional Magazine: *New Worlds*
Best Fanzine: *Science-Fiction Times*

1958

Best Novel or Novelette: *The Big Time* by Fritz Leiber
Best Short Story: "Or All the Seas with Oysters" by Avram Davidson
Best Professional Magazine: *The Magazine of Fantasy and Science Fiction*
Best Artist: Frank Kelly Freas
Outstanding Movie: *The Incredible Shrinking Man*
Outstanding Actifan: Walt Willis

1959

Best Novel: *A Case of Conscience* by James Blish
Best Novelette: "The Big Front Yard" by Clifford D. Simak
Best Short Story: "That Hell-Bound Train" by Robert Bloch
Best Professional Magazine: *The Magazine of Fantasy and Science Fiction*
Best Professional Artist: Frank Kelly Freas
Best Science Fiction or Fantasy Movie: No Award
Best Fanzine: *Fanac*
Best New Author: No Award (Runner-up Brian W. Aldiss received a plaque.)

1960

Best Novel: *Starship Troopers* by Robert A. Heinlein
Best Short Fiction: "Flowers for Algernon" by Daniel Keyes
Best Professional Magazine: *The Magazine of Fantasy and Science Fiction*
Best Professional Artist: Ed Emshwiller
Best Dramatic Presentation: *Twilight Zone*
Best Fanzine: *Cry of the Nameless*
Special Hugo Award: Hugo Gernsback as "The Father of Magazine Science Fiction"

1961

Best Novel: *A Canticle for Leibowitz* by Walter M. Miller, Jr.
Best Short Fiction: "The Longest Voyage" by Poul Anderson
Best Professional Magazine: *Astounding/Analog*
Best Professional Artist: Ed Emshwiller

Best Dramatic Presentation: *Twilight Zone*
Best Fanzine: *Who Killed Science Fiction?*

1962

Best Novel: *Stranger in a Strange Land* by Robert A. Heinlein
Best Short Fiction: *The Hothouse Series* (also known as *The Long Afternoon of Earth*) by Brian Aldiss
Best Professional Magazine: *Analog*
Best Professional Artist: Ed Emshwiller
Best Dramatic Presentation: *Twilight Zone*
Best Fanzine: *Warhoon*
Special Committee Awards: Cele Goldsmith; Donald H. Tuck; and Fritz Leiber and the Hoffman Electronic Corporation

1963

Best Novel: *The Man in the High Castle* by Philip K. Dick
Best Short Fiction: "The Dragon Masters" by Jack Vance
Best Professional Magazine: *The Magazine of Fantasy and Science Fiction*
Best Professional Artist: Roy Krenkel
Best Dramatic Presentation: No Award
Best Fanzine: *Xero*
Special Hugo Awards: P. Schuyler Miller (for book reviews in *Analog*) and Isaac Asimov (for "adding science to science fiction" for his column in *The Magazine of Fantasy and Science Fiction*)

1964

Best Novel: *Here Gather the Stars* by Clifford D. Simak (also known as *Way Station*)
Best Short Fiction: "No Truce with Kings" by Poul Anderson
Best Professional Magazine: *Analog*
Best Professional Artist: Ed Emshwiller
Best Dramatic Presentation: Dropped from final ballot for lack of interest on nominating ballot
Best Fanzine: *Amra*
Best Science-Fiction Book Publisher: Ace

1965

Best Novel: *The Wanderer* by Fritz Leiber
Best Short Story: "Soldier, Ask Not" by Gordon R. Dickson
Best Professional Magazine: *Analog*
Best Professional Artist: John Schoenherr
Special Drama: *Dr. Strangelove or: How I Learned to Stop Worrying and Love the Bomb*
Best Fanzine: *Yandro*
Best Science-Fiction Book Publisher: Ballantine

1966

Best Novel: . . . *And Call Me Conrad* by Roger Zelazny (also known as *This Immortal*)
Best Short Fiction: " 'Repent, Harlequin!' Said the Ticktockman" by Harlan Ellison
Best Professional Magazine: *If*
Best Professional Artist: Frank Frazetta
Best Dramatic Presentation: Dropped from final ballot because of overwhelming "No Award" vote on nominating ballot
Best Fanzine: *ERB-dom*
Best All-Time Series: *Foundation Series* by Isaac Asimov

1967

Best Novel: *The Moon Is a Harsh Mistress* by Robert A. Heinlein
Best Novelette: "The Last Castle" by Jack Vance
Best Short Story: "Neutron Star" by Larry Niven
Best Professional Magazine: *If*
Best Professional Artist: Jack Gaughan
Best Dramatic Presentation: "The Menagerie" from *Star Trek*
Best Fanzine: *Niekas*

1968

Best Novel: *Lord of Light* by Roger Zelazny
Best Novella: "Riders of the Purple Wage" by Philip Jose Farmer and "Weyr Search" by Anne McCaffrey
Best Novelette: "Gonna Roll the Bones" by Fritz Leiber

Best Short Story: "I Have No Mouth, and I Must Scream" by Harlan
  Ellison
Best Professional Magazine: *If*
Best Professional Artist: Jack Gaughan
Best Dramatic Presentation: "City on the Edge of Forever" from *Star
  Trek*
Best Fanzine: *Amra*
Best Fan Artist: George Barr
Best Fan Writer: Ted White
Special Committee Awards: Harlan Ellison and Gene Roddenberry

1969

Best Novel: *Stand on Zanzibar* by John Brunner
Best Novella: "Nightwings" by Robert Silverberg
Best Novelette: "The Sharing of Flesh" by Poul Anderson
Best Short Story: "The Beast that Shouted Love at the Heart of the
  World" by Harlan Ellison
Best Professional Magazine: *The Magazine of Fantasy and Science
  Fiction*
Best Professional Artist: Jack Gaughan
Best Dramatic Presentation: *2001: A Space Odyssey*
Best Fanzine: *Science Fiction Review*
Best Fan Artist: Vaughn Bode
Best Fan Writer: Harry Warner, Jr.
Special Committee Awards: Neil Armstrong, Michael Collins, and
  Edwin Aldrin

1970

Best Novel: *The Left Hand of Darkness* by Ursula K. LeGuin
Best Novella: "Ship of Shadows" by Fritz Leiber
Best Short Story: "Time Considered as a Helix of Semi-Precious
  Stones" by Samuel R. Delany
Best Professional Magazine: *The Magazine of Fantasy and Science
  Fiction*
Best Professional Artist: Frank Kelly Freas
Best Dramatic Presentation: News coverage of Apollo XI
Best Fanzine: *Science Fiction Review*

Best Fan Artist: Tim Kirk
Best Fan Writer: Wilson (Bob) Tucker

1971

Best Novel: *Ringworld* by Larry Niven
Best Novella: "Ill Met in Lankhmar" by Fritz Leiber
Best Short Story: "Slow Sculpture" by Theodore Sturgeon
Best Professional Magazine: *The Magazine of Fantasy and Science Fiction*
Best Professional Artist: Leo and Diane Dillon
Best Dramatic Presentation: No Award
Best Fanzine: *Locus*
Best Fan Artist: Alicia Austin
Best Fan Writer: Richard E. Geis

1972

Best Novel: *To Your Scattered Bodies Go* by Philip Jose Farmer
Best Novella: "The Queen of Air and Darkness" by Poul Anderson
Best Short Story: "Inconstant Moon" by Larry Niven
Best Professional Magazine: *The Magazine of Fantasy and Science Fiction*
Best Professional Artist: Frank Kelly Freas
Best Dramatic Presentation: *A Clockwork Orange*
Best Fanzine: *Locus*
Best Fan Artist: Tim Kirk
Best Fan Writer: Harry Warner, Jr.
Special Committee Award: Club du Livre d'Anticipation, Harlan Ellison, and Nueva Dimension

1973

Best Novel: *The Gods Themselves* by Isaac Asimov
Best Novella: "The Word for World Is Forest" by Ursula K. LeGuin
Best Novelette: "Goat Song" by Poul Anderson
Best Short Story: "Eurema's Dam" by R. A. Lafferty and "The Meeting" by Frederik Pohl and Cyril M. Kornbluth
Best Professional Editor: Ben Bova
Best Professional Artist: Frank Kelly Freas

Best Dramatic Presentation: *Slaughterhouse-Five*
Best Fanzine: *Energumen*
Best Fan Artist: Tim Kirk
Best Fan Writer: Terry Carr
Special Committee Award: Pierre Versins

1974

Best Novel: *Rendezvous with Rama* by Arthur C. Clarke
Best Novella: "The Girl Who Was Plugged In" by James Tiptree, Jr.
Best Novelette: "The Deathbird" by Harlan Elison
Best Short Story: "The Ones Who Walk Away From Omelas" by
  Ursula K. LeGuin
Best Professional Editor: Ben Bova .
Best Dramatic Presentation: *Sleeper*
Best Professional Artist: Frank Kelly Freas
Best Fanzine: *Algol* and *The Alien Critic*
Best Fan Artist: Tim Kirk
Best Fan Writer: Susan Wood
Special Committee Award: Chesley Bonestell

1975

Best Novel: *The Dispossessed* by Ursula K. LeGuin
Best Novella: "A Song for Lya" by George R. R. Martin
Best Novelette: "Adrift Just Off the Islets of Langerhans: Latitude 38°
  54′N, Longitude 77° 00′13″W" by Harlan Ellison
Best Short Story: "The Hole Man" by Larry Niven
Best Dramatic Presentation: *Young Frankenstein*
Best Professional Editor: Ben Bova
Best Professional Artist: Frank Kelly Freas
Best Fanzine: *The Alien Critic*
Best Fan Writer: Richard E. Geis
Best Fan Artist: Bill Rotsler
Special Committee Award: Donald A. Wollheim and Walt Lee

1976

Best Novel: *The Forever War* by Joe Haldeman
Best Novella: "Home is the Hangman" by Roger Zelazny
Best Novelette: "The Borderland of Sol" by Larry Niven
Best Short Story: "Catch that Zeppelin!" by Fritz Leiber
Best Dramatic Presentation: *A Boy and His Dog*
Best Professional Editor: Ben Bova
Best Professional Artist: Frank Kelly Freas
Best Fanzine: *Locus*
Best Fan Writer: Richard E. Geis
Best Fan Artist: Tim Kirk
Special Committee Award: James E. Gunn

1977

Best Novel: *Where Late the Sweet Birds Sang* by Kate Wilhelm
Best Novella: "By Any Other Name" by Spider Robinson and "Houston, Houston, Do You Read?" by James Tiptree, Jr.
Best Novelette: "The Bicentennial Man" by Isaac Asimov
Best Short Story: "Tricentennial" by Joe Haldeman
Best Dramatic Presentation: No Award
Best Professional Editor: Ben Bova
Best Professional Artist: Rick Sternbach
Best Fan Writer: Richard E. Geis and Susan Wood
Best Fanzine: *Science Fiction Review*
Best Fan Artist: Phil Foglio
Special Committee Award: George Lucas

1978

Best Novel: *Gateway* by Frederik Pohl
Best Novella: "Stardance" by Spider and Jeanne Robinson
Best Novelette: "Eyes of Amber" by Joan D. Vinge
Best Short Story: "Jefty Is Five" by Harlan Ellison
Best Dramatic Presentation: *Star Wars*
Best Professional Editor: George Scithers
Best Professional Artist: Rick Sternbach
Best Fan Writer: Richard E. Geis

Best Fanzine: *Locus*
Best Fan Artist: Phil Foglio

1979

Best Novel: *Dreamsnake* by Vonda N. McIntyre
Best Novella: "The Persistence of Vision" by John Varley
Best Novelette: "Hunter's Moon" by Poul Anderson
Best Short Story: "Cassandra" by C. J. Cherryh
Best Dramatic Presentation: *Superman*
Best Professional Editor: Ben Bova
Best Professional Artist: Vincent DiFate
Best Fanzine: *Science Fiction Review*
Best Fan Writer: Bob Shaw
Best Fan Artist: Bill Rotsler

1980

Best Novel: *The Fountains of Paradise* by Arthur C. Clarke
Best Novella: "Enemy Mine" by Barry Longyear
Best Novelette: "Sandkings" by George R. R. Martin
Best Short Story: "The Way of Cross and Dragon" by George R. R. Martin
Best Non-Fiction Book: *The Science Fiction Encyclopedia* by Peter Nicholls
Best Dramatic Presentation: *Alien*
Best Professional Artist: Michael Whelan
Best Professional Editor: George Scithers
Best Fanzine: *Locus*
Best Fan Writer: Bob Shaw
Best Fan Artist: Alexis Gilliland

1981

Best Novel: *The Snow Queen* by Joan D. Vinge
Best Novella: "Lost Dorsai" by Gordon R. Dickson
Best Novelette: "The Cloak and the Staff" by Gordon R. Dickson
Best Short Story: "Grotto of the Dancing Bear" by Clifford D. Simak
Best Non-Fiction Book: *Cosmos* by Carl Sagan
Best Dramatic Presentation: *The Empire Strikes Back*

Best Professional Artist: Michael Whelan
Best Professional Editor: Ed Ferman
Best Fanzine: *Locus*
Best Fan Writer: Susan Wood
Best Fan Artist: Victoria Poyser

1982

Best Novel: *Downbelow Station* by C. J. Cherryh
Best Novella: "The Saturn Game" by Poul Anderson
Best Novelette: "Unicorn Variation" by Roger Zelazny
Best Short Story: "The Pusher" by John Varley
Best Non-Fiction Book: *Danse Macabre* by Stephen King
Best Dramatic Presentation: *Raiders of the Lost Ark*
Best Professional Artist: Michael Whelan
Best Professional Editor: Ed Ferman
Best Fanzine: *Locus*
Best Fan Writer: Richard E. Geis
Best Fan Artist: Victoria Poyser

1983

Best Novel: *Foundation's Edge* by Isaac Asimov
Best Novella: "Souls" by Joanna Russ
Best Novelette: "Fire Watch" by Connie Willis
Best Short Story: "Melancholy Elephants" by Spider Robinson
Best Non-Fiction Book: *Isaac Asimov: The Foundations of Science Fiction* by James Gunn
Best Professional Editor: Edward L. Ferman
Best Professional Artist: Michael Whelan
Best Dramatic Presentation: *Blade Runner*
Best Fanzine: *Locus*
Best Fan Writer: Richard E. Geis
Best Fan Artist: Alexis Gilliland

1984

Best Novel: *Startide Rising* by David Brin
Best Novella: "Cascade Point" by Timothy Zahn
Best Novelette: "Blood Music" by Greg Bear

Best Short Story: "Speech Sounds" by Octavia Butler
Best Non-Fiction Book: *The Encyclopedia of SF & Fantasy,* Vol. III,
    by Donald H. Tuck
Best Dramatic Presentation: *Return of the Jedi*
Best Professional Editor: Shawna McCarthy
Best Professional Artist: Michael Whelan
Best Semi-Professional Magazine: *Locus*
Best Fanzine: *File 770*
Best Fan Writer: Mike Glyer
Best Fan Artist: Alexis Gilliland

1985

Best Novel: *Neuromancer* by William Gibson
Best Novella: "Press Enter ■" by John Varley
Best Novelette: "Bloodchild" by Octavia Butler
Best Short Story: "The Crystal Spheres" by David Brin
Best Non-Fiction Book: *Wonder's Child: My Life in Science Fiction*
    by Jack Williamson
Best Dramatic Presentation: *2010*
Best Professional Editor: Terry Carr
Best Professional Artist: Michael Whelan
Best Semi-Professional Magazine: *Locus*
Best Fanzine: *File 770*
Best Fan Writer: Dave Langford
Best Fan Artist: Alexis Gilliland

1986

Best Novel: *Ender's Game* by Orson Scott Card
Best Novella: "24 Views of Mount Fuji, by Hokusai" by Roger Ze-
    lazny
Best Novelette: "Paladin of the Lost Hour" by Harlan Ellison
Best Short Story: "Fermi and Frost" by Frederik Pohl
Best Non-Fiction: *Science Made Stupid* by Tom Weller
Best Dramatic Presentation: *Back to the Future*
Best Professional Editor: Judy-Lynn del Rey (refused by Lester del
    Rey)
Best Professional Artist: Michael Whelan
Best Semi-Professional Magazine: *Locus*

Best Fanzine: *Lan's Lantern*
Best Fan Writer: Mike Glyer
Best Fan Artist: Joan Hanke-Woods

1987

Best Novel: *Speaker for the Dead* by Orson Scott Card
Best Novella: "Gilgamesh in the Outback" by Robert Silverberg
Best Novelette: "Permafrost" by Roger Zelazny
Best Short Story: "Tangents" by Greg Bear
Best Non-Fiction: *Trillion Year Spree* by Brian Aldiss with David Wingrove
Best Dramatic Presentation: *Aliens*
Best Professional Artist: Jim Burns
Best Professional Editor: Terry Carr
Best Semi-Professional Magazine: *Locus*
Best Fanzine: *Ansible*
Best Fan Writer: David Langford
Best Fan Artist: Brad Foster

1988

Best Novel: *The Uplift War* by David Brin
Bet Novella: "Eye for Eye" by Orson Scott Card
Best Novelette: "Buffalo Gals, Won't You Come Out Tonight" by Ursula K. LeGuin
Best Short Story: "Why I Left Harry's All-Night Hamburgers" by Lawrence Watt-Evans
Best Non-Fiction: *Michael Whelan's Works of Wonder* by Michael Whelan
Best Dramatic Presentation: *The Princess Bride*
Best in Other Forms: *Watchmen* by Alan Moore and Dave Gibbons
Best Professional Artist: Michael Whelan
Best Professional Editor: Gardner Dozois
Best Semi-Professional Magazine: *Locus*
Best Fanzine: *Texas SF Inquirer*
Best Fan Writer: Mike Glyer
Best Fan Artist: Brad Foster
Special Award: SF Oral History Society

NEBULA AWARDS

These awards are voted on by the professionals in the field, members of the Science Fiction Writers of America. The nominees are supposed to be science fiction, not fantasy, but it is left up to the voters what qualifies.

Awards are given the year following the year of the award. For example, the 1985 awards were announced in 1986.

1965

Best Novel: *Dune* by Frank Herbert
Best Novella: "He Who Shapes" by Roger Zelazny
Best Novelette: "The Doors of His Face, the Lamps of His Mouth" by Roger Zelazny
Best Short Story: " 'Repent, Harlequin!' Said the Ticktockman" by Harlan Ellison

1966

Best Novel: *Babel-17* by Samuel R. Delany and *Flowers for Algernon* by Daniel Keyes
Best Novella: "The Last Castle" by Jack Vance
Best Novelette: "Call Him Lord" by Gordon R. Dickson
Best Short Story: "The Secret Place" by Richard McKenna

1967

Best Novel: *The Einstein Intersection* by Samuel R. Delany
Best Novella: "Behold the Man" by Michael Moorcock
Best Novelette: "Gonna Roll the Bones" by Fritz Leiber
Best Short Story: "Aye, and Gomorrah" by Samuel R. Delany

1968

Best Novel: *Rite of Passage* by Alexei Panshin
Best Novella: "Dragonrider" by Anne McCaffrey
Best Novelette: "Mother to the World" by Richard Wilson
Best Short Story: "The Planners" by Kate Wilhelm

1969

Best Novel: *The Left Hand of Darkness* by Ursula K. LeGuin
Best Novella: "A Boy and His Dog" by Harlan Ellison
Best Novelette: "Time Considered as a Helix of Semi-Precious Stones" by Samuel R. Delany
Best Short Story: "Passengers" by Robert Silverberg

1970

Best Novel: *Ringworld* by Larry Niven
Best Novella: "Ill Met in Lankhmar" by Fritz Leiber
Best Novelette: "Slow Sculpture" by Theodore Sturgeon
Best Short Story: No Award ("Island of Dr. Death" by Gene Wolfe was second.)

1971

Best Novel: *A Time of Changes* by Robert Silverberg
Best Novella: "The Missing Man" by Katherine MacLean
Best Novelette: "The Queen of Air and Darkness" by Poul Anderson
Best Short Story: "Good News from the Vatican" by Robert Silverberg

1972

Best Novel: *The Gods Themselves* by Isaac Asimov
Best Novella: "A Meeting with Medusa" by Arthur C. Clarke
Best Novelette: "Goat Song" by Poul Anderson
Best Short Story: "When It Changed" by Joanna Russ

1973

Best Novel: *Rendezvous with Rama* by Arthur C. Clarke
Best Novella: "The Death of Doctor Island" by Gene Wolfe
Best Novelette: "Of Mist, and Grass, and Sand" by Vonda N. McIntrye

Best Short Story: "Love Is the Plan, the Plan Is Death" by James Tiptree, Jr.
Best Dramatic Presentation: *Soylent Green*

1974

Best Novel: *The Dispossessed* by Ursula K. LeGuin
Best Novella: "Born with the Dead" by Robert Silverberg
Best Novelette: "If the Stars Are Gods" by Gordon Eklund and Gregory Benford
Best Short story: "The Day Before the Revolution" by Ursula K. LeGuin
Best Dramatic Presentation: *Sleeper*
Grand Master: Robert A. Heinlein

1975

Best Novel: *The Forever War* by Joe Haldeman
Best Novella: "Home Is the Hangman" by Roger Zelazny
Best Novelette: "San Diego Lightfoot Sue" by Tom Reamy
Best Short Story: "Catch That Zeppelin!" by Fritz Leiber
Best Dramatic Presentation: *Young Frankenstein*
Grand Master: Jack Williamson

1976

Best Novel: *Man Plus* by Frederik Pohl
Best Novella: "Houston, Houston, Do You Read?" by James Tiptree, Jr.
Best Novelette: "The Bicentennial Man" by Isaac Asimov
Best Short Story: "A Crowd of Shadows" by C. L. Grant
Best Dramatic Presentation: No Award
Grand Master: Clifford D. Simak

1977

Best Novel: *Gateway* by Frederik Pohl
Best Novella: "Stardance" by Spider and Jeanne Robinson
Best Novelette: "The Screwfly Solution" by Raccoona Sheldon

Best Short Story: "Jefty is Five" by Harlan Ellison
Special Award (not a Nebula): *Star Wars*

1978

Best Novel: *Dreamsnake* by Vonda N. McIntrye
Best Novella: "The Persistance of Vision" by John Varley
Best Novelette: "A Glow of Candles, a Unicorn's Eye" by
  C. L. Grant
Best Short Story: "Stone" by Edward Bryant
Grand Master: L. Sprague de Camp

1979

Best Novel: *The Fountains of Paradise* by Arthur C. Clarke
Best Novella: "Enemy Mine" by Barry Longyear
Best Novelette: "Sandkings" by George R. R. Martin
Best Short Story: "giANTS" by Edward Bryant

1980

Best Novel: *Timescape* by Gregory Benford
Best Novella: "Unicorn Tapestry" by Suzy McKee Charnas
Best Novelette: "The Ugly Chickens" by Howard Waldrop
Best Short Story: "Grotto of the Dancing Bear" by Clifford D. Simak
Grand Master: Fritz Leiber

1981

Best Novel: *The Claw of the Conciliator* by Gene Wolfe
Best Novella: "The Saturn Game" by Poul Anderson
Best Novelette: "The Quickening" by Michael Bishop
Best Short Story: "The Bone Flute" by Lisa Tuttle

1982

Best Novel: *No Enemy but Time* by Michael Bishop
Best Novella: "Another Orphan" by John Kessel
Best Novelette: "Fire Watch" by Connie Willis
Best Short Story: "A Letter From the Clearys" by Connie Willis

1983

Best Novel: *Startide Rising* by David Brin
Best Novella: "Hardfought" by Greg Bear
Best Novelette: "Blood Music" by Greg Bear
Best Short story: "The Peacemaker" by Gardner Dozois
Grand Master Award: Andre Norton

1984

Best Novel: *Neuromancer* by William Gibson
Best Novella: "Press Enter ■" by John Varley
Best Novelette: "Bloodchild" by Octavia Butler
Best Short Story: "Morning Child" by Gardner Dozois

1985

Best Novel: *Ender's Game* by Orson Scott Card
Best Novella: "Sailing to Byzantium" by Robert Silverberg
Best Novelette: "Portraits of His Children" by George R. R. Martin
Best Short Story: "Out of All Them Bright Stars" by Nancy Kress
Grand Master Award: Arthur C. Clarke

1986

Best Novel: *Speaker for the Dead* by Orson Scott Card
Best Novella: "R&R" by Lucius Shepard
Best Novelette: "The Girl Who Fell into the Sky" by Kate Wilhelm
Best Short Story: "Tangents" by Greg Bear
Grand Master Award: Isaac Asimov

WORLD FANTASY AWARDS

These award winners are chosen by a panel of judges and awarded at the World Fantasy Convention. The awards are dated for the year they are given; they cover material issued the preceding year.

1975 (honoring material from 1973–1974)

Best Novel: *The Forgotton Beasts of Eld* by Patricia McKillip
Best Short Fiction: "Pages From a Young Girl's Diary" by Robert Aickman
Best Single-Author Collection: *Worse Things Waiting* by Manly Wade Wellman
Special Award (Professional): Ian and Betty Ballantine
Special Award (Non-Professional): Stuart David Schiff
Best Artist: Lee Brown Coye
Life Achievement Award: Robert Bloch

1976 (honoring material from 1975)

Best Novel: *Bid Time Return* by Richard Matheson
Best Short Fiction: "Belsen Express" by Fritz Leiber
Best Single-Author Collection: *The Enquiries of Dr. Eszterhazy* by Avram Davidson
Special Award (Professional): Donald M. Grant
Special Award (Non-Professional): Carcosa
Best Artist: Frank Frazetta
Life Achievement Award: Fritz Leiber

1977

Best Novel: *Doctor Rat* by William Kotzwinkle
Best Short Fiction: "There's a Long, Long Trail a-Winding" by Russell Kirk
Best Collection/Anthology: *Frights* ed. by Kirby McCauley
Special Award (Professional): Alternate World Recording, Inc.
Special Award (Non-Professional): Stuart David Schiff
Best Artist: Roger Dean
Life Achievement Award: Ray Bradbury

1978

Best Novel: *Our Lady of Darkness* by Fritz Leiber
Best Short Fiction: "The Chimney" by Ramsey Campbell
Best Collection/Anthology: *Murgunstrumm and Others* by Hugh B. Cave
Special Award (Professional): E. F. Bleiler
Special Award (Non-Professional): Robert Weinberg
Best Artist: Lee Brown Coye
Life Achievement Award: Frank Belknap Long

1979

Best Novel: *Gloriana* by Michael Moorcock
Best Short Fiction: "Naples" by Avram Davidson
Best Collection/Anthology: *Shadows* ed. by Charles L. Grant
Special Award (Professional): Ed Ferman
Special Award (Non-Professional): Donald H. Tuck
Best Artist: Alicia Austin and Dale Enzenbacher
Special Award: Kirby McCauley
Life Achievement Award: Jorge Luis Borges

1980

Best Novel: *Watchtower* by Elizabeth A. Lynn
Best Short Fiction: "The Woman Who Loved the Moon" by Elizabeth A. Lynn and "Mackintosh Willy" by Ramsey Campbell
Best Collection/Anthology: *Amazons!* ed. by Jessica Amanda Salmonson
Special Award (Professional): Donald M. Grant
Special Award (Non-Professional): Paul Allen
Best Artist: Don Maitz
Life Achievement Award: Manly Wade Wellman

1981

Best Novel: *The Shadow of the Torturer* by Gene Wolfe
Best Short Fiction: "The Ugly Chickens" by Howard Waldrop
Best Anthology: *Dark Forces* ed. by Kirby McCauley

Special Award (Professional): Donald A. Wollheim
Special Award (Non-Professional): Pat Cadigan and Arnie Fenner
Best Artist: Michael Whelan
Special Convention Award: Gahan Wilson
Life Achievement Award: C. L. Moore

1982 (8th, announced Dec '82 for '81)

Best Novel: *Little, Big* by John Crowley
Best Novella: "The Fire When It Comes" by Parke Godwin
Best Short Story: "The Dark Country" by Dennis Etchison and "Do the Dead Sing?" by Stephen King
Best Anthology/Collection: *Elsewhere* ed. by Terri Windling and Mark Allan Arnold
Best Artist: Michael Whelan
Special Award (Professional): Ed Ferman
Special Award (Non-Professional): Paul Allen and Robert Collins
Special Convention Award: Roy Krenkel and Joseph Payne Brennan
Life Achievement Award: Italo Calvino

1983

Best Novel: *Nifft the Lean* by Michael Shea
Best Novella: "Beyond All Measure" by Karl Edward Wagner and "Confess the Seasons" by Charles L. Grant
Best Short Fiction: "The Gorgon" by Tanith Lee
Best Anthology/Collection: *Nightmare Seasons* by Charles L. Grant
Best Artist: Michael Whelan
Special Award (Professional): Donald M. Grant
Special Award (Non-Professional): Stuart David Schiff
Special Award: Arkham House
Life Achievement Award: Roald Dahl

1984 (10th)

Best Novel: *The Dragon Waiting* by John M. Ford
Best Novella: "Black Air" by Kim Stanley Robinson
Best Short Fiction: "Elle Est Trois (La Mort)" by Tanith Lee
Best Anthology/Collection: *High Spirits* by Robinson Davies

Best Artist: Steve Gervais
Special Award (Professional): Ian and Betty Ballantine, Joy Chant, George Sharp, and David Larkin
Special Award (Non-Professional): Stephen Jones and David Sutton
Special Award: Donald M. Grant
Life Achievement Award: L. Sprague de Camp, Richard Matheson, E. Hoffman Price, Jack Vance, and Donald Wandrei

1985

Best Novel: *Mythago Wood* by Robert Holdstock and *Bridge of Birds* by Barry Hughart
Best Novella: "The Unconquered Country" by Geoff Ryman
Best Short Story: "Still Life with Scorpion" by Scott Baker and "The Bones Wizard" by Alan Ryan
Best Anthology/Collection: *Clive Barker's Books of Blood*, Volumes I–III, by Clive Barker
Best Artist: Edward Gorey
Special Award (Professional): Chris Van Allsburg
Special Award (Non-Professional): Stuart David Schiff
Special Award: Evangeline Walton
Life Achievement Award: Theodore Sturgeon

1986

Best Novel: *Song of Kali* by Dan Simmons
Best Novella: "Nadelman's God" by T. E. D. Klein
Best Short Story: "Paper Dragons" by James Blaylock
Best Anthology/Collection: *Imaginary Lands* ed. by Robin McKinley
Special Award (Professional): Pat LoBrutto
Special Award (Non-Professional): Douglas E. Winter
Best Artist: Jeff Jones and Thomas Canty
Special Award: Donald A. Wollheim
Life Achievement Award: Avram Davidson

1987

Best Novel: *Perfume* by Patrick Suskind (translated by John Woods)
Best Novella: "Hatrack River" by Orson Scott Card
Best Short Story: "Red Light" by David J. Schow
Best Anthology/Collection: *Tales of the Quintana Roo* by James Tiptree, Jr.
Best Artist: Robert Gould
Special Award (Professional): Jane Yolen
Special Award (Non-Professional): Jeff Conner and W. Paul Ganley
Special Award: Andre Norton
Life Achievement Award: Jack Finney

COLLECTIONS OF THE BEST

Hugo Award-winning short fiction—up to novella length—has been collected in a series of anthologies edited by Isaac Asimov, to wit:

1962   *The Hugo Winners* (covers 1955–1961)
1971   *The Hugo Winners Volume Two* (covers 1962–1970)
1977   *The Hugo Winners Volume Three* (covers 1970–1975; the overlap with the second volume is because one of the 1970 winners, Fritz Leiber's "Ship of Shadows," was accidentally omitted from *Volume Two*)
1985   *The Hugo Winners Volume 4: 1976–1979*
1986   *The Hugo Winners Volume 5: 1980–1982*

All of these have had hardcover, book club, and paperback editions, so they should be relatively easy to find. Only the first hardcover editions are likely to be at all costly.

Nebula Award-winning short fiction—up to novella length—has been collected in a series of anthologies with a variety of editors and publishers. Most of the following have had both a hardcover and a paperback edition; the later ones have had simultaneous hardcover and trade paperback volumes.

1966   *Nebula Award Stories 1965* edited by Damon Knight
1967   *Nebula Award Stories Two* edited by Brian W. Aldiss and Harry Harrison
1968   *Nebula Award Stories Three* edited by Roger Zelazny
1969   *Nebula Award Stories Four* edited by Poul Anderson

1970 *Nebula Award Stories Five* edited by James Blish
1971 *Nebula Award Stories Six* edited by Clifford D. Simak
1972 *Nebula Award Stories Seven* edited by Lloyd Biggle, Jr.
1973 *Nebula Award Stories Eight* edited by Isaac Asimov
1974 *Nebula Award Stories Nine* edited by Kate Wilhelm
1975 *Nebula Award Stories Ten* edited by James Gunn
1977 *Nebula Award Stories Eleven* edited by Ursula K. LeGuin
1978 *Nebula Award Stories Twelve* edited by Gordon R. Dickson
1979 *Nebula Award Stories Thirteen* edited by Samuel R. Delany
1980 *Nebula Award Stories Fourteen* edited by Frederik Pohl
1981 *Nebula Award Stories Fifteen* edited by Frank Herbert
1982 *Nebula Award Stories Sixteen* edited by Jerry Pournelle
1983 *Nebula Award Stories Seventeen* edited by Joe Haldeman
1983 *Nebula Award Stories Eighteen* edited by Robert Silverberg
1984 *Nebula Award Stories Nineteen* edited by Marta Randall
1985 *Nebula Award Stories 20* edited by George Zebrowski
1986 *Nebula Award Stories 21* edited by George Zebroski

The Science Fiction Writers of America have also produced three books of stories published before the Nebulas were established which SFWA members felt deserved recognition. The Silverberg and Bova volumes had both hardcover and paperback editions; the Clarke and Carr books had only paperback publication.

1970 *The Science Fiction Hall of Fame* edited by Robert Silverberg (short stories)
1973 *The Science Fiction Hall of Fame Volume Two A* edited by Ben Bova (novellas)
1973 *The Science Fiction Hall of Fame Volume Two B* edited by Ben Bova (novellas)
1982 *The Science Fiction Hall of Fame Volume III* edited by Arthur C. Clarke and George Proctor (Nebula winners 1965–1969)
1986 *The Science Fiction Hall of Fame Volume IV* edited by Terry Carr (Nebula winners 1970–1974)

World Fantasy Award winners have been collected in two volumes, published erratically. Neither has had a paperback edition.

1977 *The First World Fantasy Awards* edited by Gahan Wilson
1980 *The World Fantasy Awards Volume Two* edited by Stuart David Schiff and Fritz Leiber

There have been a number of ''best-of-the-year'' anthologies over the years. This list is arranged roughly in chronological order by the starting date of each series. A collection of stories calling itself the best of 1980 would actually contain stories from 1979.

Edited by Everett F. Bleiler and T. E. Dikty (these anthologies had only hardcover publication):

The Best Science Fiction Stories 1949
The Best Science Fiction Stories 1950
The Best Science Fiction Stories 1951
The Best Science Fiction Stories 1952
The Best Science Fiction Stories 1953
The Best Science Fiction Stories 1954

Edited by T. E. Dikty:

The Best Science Fiction Stories and Novels 1955
The Best Science Fiction Stories and Novels 1956
The Best Science Fiction Stories and Novels Ninth Series (1958)

Edited by Everett F. Bleiler and T. E. Dikty (hardcover only):

Year's Best Science Fiction Novels 1952
Year's Best Science Fiction Novels 1953
Year's Best Science Fiction Novels 1954

Edited by Judith Merril (most volumes had hardcover and paperback editions):

SF: The Year's Greatest Science Fiction and Fantasy (1956)
SF: 57 The Year's Greatest Science Fiction and Fantasy
SF: 58 The Year's Greatest Science Fiction and Fantasy
SF: The Year's Greatest Science Fiction and Fantasy, Fourth Annual Volume (published only in paperback) (1959)
The Fifth Annual of the Year's Best Science Fiction and Fantasy (1960)
The 6th Annual of the Year's Best S-F (1961)
The 7th Annual of the Year's Best S-F (1963)
The 8th Annual of the Year's Best SF (1963)
The 9th Annual of the Year's Best SF (1964)
10th Annual of the Year's Best SF (1965)

11th Annual of the Year's Best S-F (1966)
SF 12 (1968)

Edited by Donald A. Wollheim and Terry Carr (all Ace Books paperback originals; some were published in book-club hardcovers as well):

World's Best Science Fiction: 1965
World's Best Science Fiction: 1966
World's Best Science Fiction: 1967
World's Best Science Fiction: 1968
World's Best Science Fiction: 1969
World's Best Science Fiction: 1970
World's Best Science Fiction: 1971

Edited by Harry Harrison and Brian W. Aldiss (most of these had both hardcover and paperback editions):

Best SF: 1967
Best SF: 1968
Best SF: 1969
Best SF: 1970
Best SF: 1971
Best SF: 1972
Best SF: 1973
Best SF: 1974
Best SF: 1975

DAW Books ran a series of paperback horror "bests" (no hardcover editions):

Edited by Richard Davis:

1971 *The Year's Best Horror Stories No. 1*
1974 *The Year's Best Horror Stories: Series II*
1975 *The Year's Best Horror Stories: Series III*

Edited by Gerald W. Page:

1976 *The Year's Best Horror Stories: Series IV*
1977 *The Year's Best Horror Stories: Series V*
1978 *The Year's Best Horror Stories: Series VI*
1979 *The Year's Best Horror Stories: Series VII*

Edited by Karl Edward Wagner:

1980 *The Year's Best Horror Stories: Series VIII*
1981 *The Year's Best Horror Stories: Series IX*
1982 *The Year's Best Horror Stories: Series X*
1983 *The Year's Best Horror Stories: Series XI*
1984 *The Year's Best Horror Stories: Series XII*
1985 *The Year's Best Horror Stories: Series XIII*
1986 *The Year's Best Horror Stories: Series XIV*
1987 *The Year's Best Horror Stories: Series XV*

Edited by Frederik Pohl (Ace Books paperback only):

1972 *Best Science Fiction for 1972*

Edited by Forrest J Ackerman (paperback only):

1973 *Best Science Fiction for 1973*

Edited by Donald A. Wollheim (all DAW Books paperback originals; some were also published as book-club hardcovers):

The 1972 Annual World's Best SF
The 1973 Annual World's Best SF
The 1974 Annual World's Best SF
The 1975 Annual World's Best SF
The 1976 Annual World's Best SF
The 1977 Annual World's Best SF
The 1978 Annual World's Best SF
The 1979 Annual World's Best SF
The 1980 Annual World's Best SF
The 1981 Annual World's Best SF
The 1982 Annual World's Best SF
The 1983 Annual World's Best SF
The 1984 Annual World's Best SF
The 1985 Annual World's Best SF
The 1986 Annual World's Best SF
The 1987 Annual World's Best SF

Edited by Terry Carr (most of these were paperback originals; only the last three had hardcover editions):

1972 *The Best Science Fiction of the Year*
1973 *The Best Science Fiction of the Year #2*
1974 *The Best Science Fiction of the Year #3*

1975   *The Best Science Fiction of the Year #4*
1976   *The Best Science Fiction of the Year #5*
1977   *The Best Science Fiction of the Year #6*
1978   *The Best Science Fiction of the Year #7*
1979   *The Best Science Fiction of the Year #8*
1980   *The Best Science Fiction of the Year #9*
1981   *The Best Science Fiction of the Year #10*
1982   *The Best Science Fiction of the Year #11*
1983   *The Best Science Fiction of the Year #12*
1984   *The Best Science Fiction of the Year #13*
1985   *Terry Carr's Best Science Fiction of the Year* (#14)
1986   *Terry Carr's Best Science Fiction of the Year #15*
1987   *Terry Carr's Best Science Fiction of the Year #16*

Edited by Lester del Rey (this series had hardcover and paperback editions):

1972   *Best Science Fiction Stories of the Year First Annual Collection*
1973   *Best Science Fiction Stories of the Year Second Annual Collection*
1974   *Best Science Fiction Stories of the Year Third Annual Collection*
1975   *Best Science Fiction Stories of the Year Fourth Annual Collection*
1976   *Best Science Fiction Stories of the Year Fifth Annual Collection*

Edited by Gardner Dozois:

1977   *Best Science Fiction stories of the Year Sixth Annual Collection*
1978   *Best Science Fiction Stories of the Year Seventh Annual Collection*
1979   *Best Science Fiction Stories of the Year Eighth Annual Collection*
1980   *Best Science Fiction Stories of the Year Ninth Annual Collection*
1981   *Best Science Fiction Stories of the Year Tenth Annual Collection*

Edited by Lin Carter (these are paperbacks only):

1975   *The Year's Best Fantasy Stories*
1976   *The Year's Best Fantasy Stories #2*

1977   *The Year's Best Fantasy Stories #3*
1978   *The Year's Best Fantasy Stories #4*
1980   *The Year's Best Fantasy Stories #5*
1981   *The Year's Best Fantasy Stories #6*

Edited by Arthur W. Saha:

1982   *The Year's Best Fantasy Stories #7*
1983   *The Year's Best Fantasy Stories #8*
1984   *The Year's Best Fantasy Stories #9*
1985   *The Year's Best Fantasy Stories #10*
1986   *The Year's Best Fantasy Stories #11*
1987   *The Year's Best Fantasy Stories #12*

Edited by Terry Carr (the first two had hardcover and paperback editions; the rest were paperback only except for a book-club edition of the third):

1978   *The Year's Finest Fantasy*
1979   *The Year's Finest Fantasy Volume 2*
1981   *Fantasy Annual III*
1981   *Fantasy Annual IV*
1982   *Fantasy Annual V*

Edited by Terry Carr (paperback only):

1979   *The Best Science Fiction Novellas of the Year #1*
1980   *The Best Science Fiction Novellas of the Year #2*

Edited by Gardner Dozois (all of these huge anthologies have simultaneous hardcover and trade paperback editions):

1984   *The Year's Best Science Fiction First Annual Collection*
1985   *The Year's Best Science Fiction Second Annual Collection*
1986   *The Year's Best Science Fiction Third Annual Collection*
1987   *The Year's Best Science Fiction Fourth Annual Collection*

Another source of the best science fiction of the past is in the form of retrospective ''best-of-the-year'' anthologies. The first mentioned here is a hardcover volume with limited distribution; the second is a paperback original series which began in 1979, with early volumes in the series going into reprint editions.

Edited by Forrest J. Ackerman:

1982   *The Gernsback Awards 1926, Volume I*

Edited by Isaac Asimov and Martin Harry Greenberg (the date in parentheses at the end of each title is the year from which the stories are selected):

Isaac Asimov Presents the Great SF Stories 1 (1939)
Isaac Asimov Presents the Great SF Stories 2 (1940)
Isaac Asimov Presents the Great SF Stories 3 (1941)
Isaac Asimov Presents the Great SF Stories 4 (1942)
Isaac Asimov Presents the Great SF Stories 5 (1943)
Isaac Asimov Presents the Great SF Stories 6 (1944)
Isaac Asimov Presents the Great SF Stories 7 (1945)
Isaac Asimov Presents the Great SF Stories 8 (1946)
Isaac Asimov Presents the Great SF Stories 9 (1947)
Isaac Asimov Presents the Great SF Stories 10 (1948)
Isaac Asimov Presents the Great SF Stories 11 (1949)
Isaac Asimov Presents the Great SF Stories 12 (1950)
Isaac Asimov Presents the Great SF Stories 13 (1951)
Isaac Asimov Presents the Great SF Stories 14 (1952)
Isaac Asimov Presents the Great SF Stories 15 (1953)
Isaac Asimov Presents the Great SF Stories 16 (1954)
Isaac Asimov Presents the Great SF Stories 17 (1955)

You Can't Have It All

We've done our best to provide an identification guide to the sort of material collectors can expect to find in the field.

There's another sort of material that collectors can look for—but that only one will find: unique material.

A prime example of this is in the art field. The collecting of original science-fiction and fantasy art has become increasingly active, with a growing number of collectors seeking the work of a rising number of artists.

No matter what the prices we have listed on material by each artist in our "Names" chapter, you may find original paintings or pen-and-ink work at higher or lower prices—possibly higher, because many artists' work appreciate in value. And we are simply listing *typical* prices. When you buy a unique piece—which will, of course, be the case with *any* original drawing or painting—the value to be considered is its value to you. If you like the subject and the execution of a work of art, you will make the purchase based on those factors.

Some artists price work not to sell; if you pay thousands of dollars for an item, that does not necessarily mean that you can sell the item for that amount. It may simply mean that the artist priced his work above the going rate to discourage buyers.

A piece may be judged by its complexity, its subject, the period of work it represents, the artist, and the amount of that artist's work on the market. A color rough of a completed painting will bring about 10%–15% of the price of the completed painting. (These roughs can provide a nice consolation if you miss out on a chance to buy the finished painting.)

It is sometimes possible to commission pieces from artists for private collections—requesting and paying for a specific piece on a specific subject. Purchase of such a piece of art does *not* automatically confer copyright or printing rights of such material.

Auctions and sale lists will reveal more items of a unique nature, not all of them with unusually high prices. Reports on auctions can

provide fascinating details of this sort of material. At a Guernseys auction in December 1987, for example, the Frankenstein model from *The Bride of Frankenstein* in Karloff's costume was sold for $18,000.00, a plaster cast for *The Illustrated Man* was sold for $425.00, and five issues of the amateur magazine *Science Fiction* (which carried Jerry Siegel and Joe Shuster's original version of Superman) sold for a total of $1,900.00. Though the last-mentioned was not unique, it may never have been seen by the bulk of today's collectors.

There are such oddities in the field as Richard Shaver's rocks (he said that they were actually petrified recordings of the lost races he wrote about) and autographed Polaroid photographs (taken at conventions and autographed by celebrities on the spot). There are individual inscriptions which can make an item unique.

Note, for example, this listing from a 1988 sale list from SF West, Box 4148, Mountain View, California 94040 (for information on getting a current sale list, send a self-addressed stamped envelope): A. Merritt's copy of his first edition of his own book *Dwellers in the Mirage* (1932) carries this notation: "To Anybody it May Concern. This God-damn book is the personal property of A. Merritt And Anybody who takes it & doesn't give it back is a God-damn louse & the offspring of Even worse god-damn lice. I'm tired of having my books Swiped. A. Merritt."

There were annotations in pencil and a typescript of about 1,000 words of the intended ending of the book and other personalizing— and the item was priced at $2,000.00. Face it: There's only one such copy. It's up to you to decide what such material is worth to you.

Science-Fiction and Fantasy Glossary

Many retailers with catalogs provide their own glossaries of their own abbreviations and usages. Study these carefully before ordering.

Ace Double. A line of paperback books from Ace, which printed two "books" back-to-back, one of them upside-down to the other. The books had two "front" covers. They are not the only two-books-to-a-book book but they are the best-known in the field. Tor introduced a similar publishing project in 1988.

Android. An artificial life-form which is not human but has chemical, rather than mechanical origins (in contrast with robots, which are mechanical). Frankenstein's monster is an android; the "droids" of *Star Wars* are robots.

BEM. Bug-Eyed Monster. A sterotypical extra-terrestrial life-form, usually menacing a beautiful woman.

Bedsheet. A nickname for the size of some outsize pulp magazines, the earliest format for some of them. It is roughly 8½″ × 11″.

BNF. Big-Name Fan. A term acknowledging the general fame of a science-fiction fan.

Digest. A magazine of roughly the size of *Reader's Digest*—about 5¼″ × 7½″.

dj or *dw.* Dust jacket or dust wrapper—*not* "wraps."

Fan. A devotee, an admirer; in this case, an admirer of fantasy or science fiction. Fans became known to each other—and in these terms—in the letters columns of the earliest science-fiction-only magazines. Active fandom has continued since those days.

Filksong. A folksong concerning matters of interest to those of a science-fictional or fantastic ilk. "Filksingers" increased in

numbers in the 1970s and 1980s and often gather at science-fiction conventions for nights of performances. A number of records and audiocassettes of such material has been produced in recent years.

FMOF. Famous Monsters of Filmland, a magazine devoted primarily to monster movies and edited by Forrest J Ackerman.

GOH or *GoH.* Guest of Honor. This celebrity is a featured star of the convention at which he appears.

hc. Hardcover book.

Hugos. Annual awards for excellence in science fiction voted on by membership of and awarded at each year's world science-fiction convention. They are nominated and voted for before the event. Actually called Science Fiction Achievement Awards, they have been nicknamed for Hugo Gernsback, the first professional science-fiction editor.

juv. Juvenile book.

Nebulas. Annual professional awards for excellence in science fiction awarded by members of Science Fiction Writers of America, professionals in the field, who nominate and vote on them before the Nebula banquet at which they are handed out.

o/p. Out of print.

Paperback book. A book bound in very light cardboard—as opposed to hardcover. They have come in standard sizes over the years and are sometimes differentiated as "mass-market paperbacks" in standard size and "trade paperbacks" in a variety of larger sizes.

pb. Paperback book.

Pros. Professional science-fiction or fantasy writers, artists, and editors. As contrasted with "fans."

Pulp. A magazine printed on cheap, pulpwood paper—as were most science-fiction magazines of the 1930s and 1940s. These ordinarily had larger page dimensions than today's digest magazines, usually about 7″ × 9″, though some were "bedsheet" size.

Robot. A term for machines that operate in many ways like people. Coined by Karl Capek in his play *R.U.R.* (which stood for

Rossum's Universal Robots), it is an agreed-upon word today. Many writers dealing with robots have adopted Isaac Asimov's "Three Laws of Robotics" as basic to the concept.

SCA. Society for Creative Anachronism. An organization devoted to recreation of certain aspects of earlier eras. Many members of the SCA are involved in science-fiction and fantasy fandom and some write and perform filksongs.

Sci-fi. A term coined by BNF Forrest J Ackerman to designate science fiction (with the analogy to the term "hi-fi" to designate high-fidelity audio equipment). Ackerman's editorship of *Famous Monsters of Filmland* brought the term to the attention of moviemakers and of many young readers who continued to use the term when they became adults. Many science-fiction fans and professionals limit their use of the term to connote corny, mass-market, or otherwise inferior material and prefer the term "SF" as an abbreviation when writing.

SFWA. Science Fiction Writers of America—the professional organization for professional science-fiction writers. Its membership annually chooses the Nebula Awards for the best of the year.

sn. Short novel.

ss. Short story collection.

stf. An abbreviation for the word "scientifiction," an early term used for "science fiction." Some older fans still use it, out of habit.

Worldcon. The World Science-Fiction Convention. A site is chosen by fans for this annual event, almost invariably held over Labor Day Weekend. It is *the* convention of the science-fiction world; by the 1980s, attendance is in the thousands and no single hotel can be the site because of its size.

Wraps. The light-cardboard binding of paperback books. Does *not* indicate "dust wrapper."

Non-Fiction/Reference Material

The science-fiction and fantasy fields are self-referenced enough that a sizable collection could be made simply of the reference material in the fields. The list here is not exhaustive; there are university press studies of the field that are not (yet) in hot demand among collectors. There have even been study guides to some science-fiction and fantasy books—*Cliff's Notes to Robert A. Heinlein*—a concept which itself might have seemed like science fiction only a couple of decades earlier.

We offer a lightly annotated list of some of the material that may supplement a collector's library.

William Contento, *Index to Science Fiction Anthologies and Collections*. Boston, Massachusetts: G. K. Hall & Co., 1978. The hardcover, 608-page volume was also published in England by George Prior Publishers.

Bradford M. Day, *An Index on the Weird & Fantastica in Magazines*. New York, 1953. The edition was limited to 400 paperback copies, with cover printed and interior mimeographed. In addition to indexes of publications devoted to science fiction and fantasy, he offered information on such material in Munsey magazines and some others.

Donald B. Day, *Index to the Science-Fiction Magazines 1926–1950*. Portland, Oregon: Perri Press, 1952. Commonly referred to as "the Daydex," the hardcover was *the* index to science-fiction magazines of the time. It includes an "Errata and Addenda" sheet. See also Norm Metcalf.

L. Sprague de Camp, *Science Fiction Handbook* and *Science Fiction Handbook, Revised* (with Catherine Crook de Camp). The first appearance was in 1953 in hardcover; the second edition was

published in hardcover (with dj) by Owlswick Press (Philadelphia, Pennsylvania) in 1975; and a paperback edition was published in 1977 by McGraw-Hill (New York). The guide to writing and selling imaginative fiction is a standard in the field and contains glimpses of history of the field as well as a guide to writing. There is considerable difference in text between the 1950s and the 1970s versions.

Donald Franson and Howard DeVore, *A History of the Hugo, Nebula, and International Fantasy Awards*. Dearborn, Michigan: Misfit Press. Editions were published in 1971, 1975, 1981, and 1983. The printed booklet contains a listing of all nominees and winners of the respective awards given.

H. W. Hall, *Science Fiction Book Review Index, 1923–1973*. Detroit, Michigan: Gale Research Company, 1975. The 438-page hardcover is just what it says.

Harry A. and Mariane S. Hopkins, *Fandom Directory*. The continuing series (9th edition 1987–1988) is almost a telephone book of a number of fandoms. It lists retail outlets, fellow collectors, and the like, and can be a valuable tool to steer you to what you seek. Send a self-addressed, stamped envelope to Fandata Computer Services, 7761 Asterella Court, Springfield, Virginia 22152 for more information; you can be listed in an upcoming edition at no charge.

Barry McGhan, *Sciencefiction and Fantasy Pseudonyms (Revised and Expanded)*. Dearborn, Michigan: Misfit Press, 1976. The printed booklet contains 77 pages of information on its title subject.

Norm Metcalf, *The Index of Science Fiction Magazines 1951–1965*. El Cerrito, California: J. Ben Stark, Publisher, 1968. The paperback volume with cover by Vaughn Bode was designed as a sequel to Donald B. Day's *Index to the Science-Fiction Magazines 1926–1950*. It includes more than a page of errata and addenda.

Peter Nicholls, *The Science Fiction Encyclopedia*. Garden City, New York: Dolphin Books (Doubleday), 1979. This Hugo-winning thick paperback is the American edition of the book published in England in 1979 by Roxby Press Limited. The 672-page volume is heavily illustrated and contains information in alphabetical order and con-

siderable detail, both under proper noun headings and such general categories as "flying saucers."

James A. Rock, *Who Goes There*. Bloomington (Indiana): James A. Rock & Co., 1979. Subtitled "A Bibliographic Dictionary of Pseudonymous Literature in the Fields of Fantasy and Science Fiction," it is just that. Paperback, 202 pages.

Donald H. Tuck, *The Encyclopedia of Science Fiction and Fantasy*. Chicago, Illinois, Advent Publishers, Inc., 1974–1982. Planned as a sequel to Day's and Metcalf's indexes of magazine science fiction, this three-volume hardcover set is a copious compendium of information on printed science-fiction. There are 920 pages larger than $8\frac{1}{2}'' \times 11''$.

Robert Weinberg, *A Biographical Dictionary of Science Fiction and Fantasy Artists*. Westport, Connecticut, Greenwood Press, Inc., 1988. You can order this from retailer Weinberg, Weinberg Books, P.O. Box 423, Oak Forest, Illinois 60452; send a self-addressed, stamped envelope for information. This is the definitive bibliography of artists in the field. Although it is not illustrated, it has what an art collector needs to know.

Additionally, any reference library will be enriched by as complete as possible a collection of *Locus* and *Science Fiction Chronicle*—and, luckily, many back issues are still available from those publications. (Those addresses again are: *Locus*, Locus Publications, P.O. Box 13305, Oakland, California 94661; *Science Fiction Chronicle*, Algol Press, P.O. Box 4175, New York, New York 10163.) Advertisements in each give information on back issues. *Locus* also offers such material as annotated lists of new and reprint science fiction, fantasy, and horror published in America in a particular year.

Now that the field has begun to attract scholars, there are many indexes and the like. The subject guide volume of *Books in Print* may steer you to more material you will want to collect.

Afterword

The book is done—if a book that is such an ongoing process can ever be really finished. Every omission caused a pang. Every blind alley was a blind alley because we thought we'd include more information and then realized there wouldn't be enough time to explore it or enough room to run it, if we did.

We've already begun to look ahead to a possible future edition of the book, mentally comparing Robert M. Overstreet's current price guide of comic books to the first one that appeared more than a decade and a half ago and realizing that reader requests, creator contributions, retailer information, and critical carps will shape any future versions of the book.

We have our own, growing, list of potential future topics. "How could you devote space to *Man From U.N.C.L.E.* books and not give a detailed list of two-in-one series, like those from Ace, Belmont, and Tor?" "Why didn't you run a complete list of Martin Greenberg's anthologies?" "I hoped you'd run a list of every science-fiction and fantasy book with a cover by Frank Frazetta." What would you like to see in a future volume? Can you help to compile a list?

In any case, this is the time to pause briefly before the volume's end, relax, and make a few remarks of a more personal nature.

We entered the world of science fiction and fantasy at relatively tender ages. We've been fortunate enough to have lived in the field both as A Way of Life and as a Gosh-Darned Hobby. (When we entered the field, most people were more careful about their language than many are today.)

Maggie's mother, Betsy Curtis, was active enough in the science-fiction world for enough years to have had us hobnobbing with the greats (or, more properly, sitting in awe at worldcons while at the same table John and Peg Campbell talked to friends—or watching at a party while the trio of Randall Garrett, Isaac Asimov, and Robert A. Heinlein sang Gilbert and Sullivan songs with their arms on each other's shoulders). Mom/Betsy has remained relatively unknown in

the field, though she had one short story in a pre-Hugo best-of-the-year anthology and one short story nominated for a Hugo. (She's also a Master Costumer, having won best of class at three worldcons.)

We spent a golden afternoon with Larry and Noreen Shaw at their house. And had a wonderful time when Higbee's Department Store in Cleveland decided to promote science fiction and invited Judy-Lynn and Lester del Rey and Leigh Brackett and Joe and Gay Haldeman and Chip Delany and. . . . We've had wonderful weeks with John and Bjo Trimble, as we discussed costuming and the SCA and how Bjo saved *Star Trek* for its third season. We drove with Dick and Pat Lupoff in their convertible as they returned home with the Hugo for their fanzine *Xero*—and had customers at another table in the restaurant we stopped at come over to ask whether our centerpiece wasn't a Hugo and what was it for.

Our years spent in association with the science fiction world has, in other words, been crowded with memories of warm, wonderful, brilliant people. One of the delights of the field is the accessibility of its leading figures; the field is based on the worth of the concept, not on personal beauty or physical skills. Science fiction and fantasy fields exist because their admirers know how to think.

We used to laugh at the anecdote that James Thurber was such a perfectionist that a manuscript had to be physically wrested away from him so that a magazine would be able to publish it. Given his penchant for polishing, he'd have continued to polish each item forever.

Now, *we* are fighting the urge to ask for "just one more week" to check more information, insert more authors, contact one more professional. We know—we *know*—that reviews of this volume will shoot darts into it for this topic unplumbed or that item omitted. And we *know* (and this makes us shudder, because we've been careful but we know Murphy's Law—and whatever can go wrong will go wrong) that a typographical error will make some otherwise-perfect listing the target for still more darts.

Let us close by thanking especially those who offered to help—and mention one last time the retailers who supplied special aid:

American Collectibles Exchange, Box 2512, Chattanooga, Tennessee 37409 (615) 821-8121.

Stephen Buhner, Bookseller, 8563 Flagstaff Road, Boulder, Colorado 80302 (303) 443-1096.

Richard Halegua, 2033 Madison Road, Cincinnati, Ohio 45208 (513) 321-4208.

Larry's Comic Book Store, 1219A West Devon Avenue, Chicago, Illinois 60660 (312) 274-1832.

Alan Levine, P.O. Box 1577, Bloomfield, New Jersey 07003 (210) 743-5288.

Robert A. Madle, 4406 Bestor Drive, Rockville, Maryland 20853 (301) 460-4712.

Weinberg Books, P.O. Box 423, Oak Forest, Illinois 60452. (312) 687-5765.

SF West, Box 4148, Mountain View, California 94040 (415) 424-1984.

Soft Books, 89 Marion Street, Toronto, Ontario M6R 1E6, Canada (416) 588-1334.

Thank you! And we beg all our readers to help us make the next edition better. House of Collectibles will forward your letters; we promise to read every one.

Index

Abbott, Edwin A., 49
Aboriginal SF, 276
Ackerman, Forrest James, 50, 458, 461
Adams, Douglas, 50
Aickman, Robert, 50
Air Wonder Stories, 367
Aldiss, Brian Wilson, 51, 457
Alice's Adventure in Wonderland, recording, 429
Alien Worlds, 374
Allman, Sheldon, 419
Amazing Science Fiction, 277
Amazing Stories, 277
Amazing Stories Annual, 282
Amazing Stories Quarterly, 282
Amazing Stories Science Fiction Novel, 283
American Collectibles Exchange, 17
American magazines
  authors related to increased value, 276
  back-issue magazines, 274
  bedsheet magazines, 274
  digest magazines, 275
  grading, 275–276
  leading publications, 275
  paperback magazines, 275
  pulp magazines, 275
  subscriptions, addresses for, 273
  See also individual titles.
American Science Fiction, 374
A. Merritt Fantasy, 283
Analog, 286
Analog Annual, 283
Analog Anthologies, 284
Analog Yearbook, 284
Anderson, Poul, 52
Anthologies
  Hugo Awards, 454
  Nebula Awards, 454–455
  Science Fiction Hall of Fame, 455
  World Fantasy Awards, 455

Anthony, Piers, 55
Anvil, Christopher, 57
Argosy, 284
Ariel, 285
Arkham Sampler, 285
Arnold, Edwin Lester, 58
Artwork, collecting, 17–19
  conventions, 18
  specialists in, 18
Asimov, Isaac, 58, 454, 461
  See also entries under Isaac Asimov.
Asimov's SF Adventure Magazine, 285
Asprin, Robert Lynn, 61, 420
Astonishing Stories, 285
Astounding Science Fiction, 286, 291
Astounding Stories, 286
Astounding Stories Yearbook, 291
Auctions, collecting source, 17
Audio tape, filksongs, 419–425
Austin, Alicia, 62
Authentic Science Fiction Series, 375
Autographed copies, and value, 29–31
Avenydd, 420
Avon Fantasy Reader, 291
Avon Science Fiction & Fantasy Reader, 292
Avon Science Fiction Reader, 292
Awards
  collections of award-winning works, 454–461
  Hugo Awards, 432–444
  Nebula Awards, 445–449
  source of information, 432
  World Fantasy Awards, 450–454

Back-issue magazines, American magazines, 274
Bags, for collectibles, 20–21
Bailey, Robin, 420
Baker, Colin, *Doctor Who*, 403–404
Baker, Tom, *Doctor Who*, 401–403
Ballard, James Graham, 62
Balmer, Edwin, 63

Bangs, John Kendrick, 63
Barker, Clive, 64
Barr, George, 64
Barrie, James Matthew, 65
Barth, John, 65
Baum, Lyman Frank, 65
Beagle, Peter Soyer, 67
Bear, Greg, 67
Beaumont, Charles, 67
Bedsheet magazines, American
    magazines, 274
Bellamy, Edward, 68
Benedict, Martie, 420
Benet, Stephen Vincent, 68
Benford, Gregory, 69
Bester, Alfred, 69
Best of Omni Science Fiction, The, 292
Best Science Fiction, The, 292
Beyond Fantasy Fiction, 293
Beyond Fiction, 293
Beyond Infinity, 293
Bierce, Ambrose, 70
Biggle, Lloyd, Jr., 71
Binder, Eando, 71
Binder, Earl. *See* Binder, Eando
Binder, Otto. *See* Binder, Eando
*Biographical Dictionary of Science
    Fiction and Fantasy Artists, A*
    (Weinberg), 43, 469
Bishop, Michael, 72
Bixby, Drexel Jerome Lewis, 73
Bizarre! Mystery Magazine, 293
Bleiler, Everett F., 456
Blish, James, 73
Bloch, Robert, 74
Bok, Hannes, 76
Book-club editions, cautions about, 49
Book of Weird Tales, A, 375
Books in Print, collecting source, 16
Borges, Jorge Luis, 77
Boucher, Anthony, 77
Bova, Benjamin William, 78, 455
Brackett, Leigh, 79
Bradbury, Ray Douglas, 80
Bradley, Marion Zimmer, 82
Breen, M. Dorothy, 420
Brin, David, 83
British magazines, collecting, 374
British Science Fiction Magazine, The,
    386
British Space Fiction Magazine, The,
    386

Brooks, Terry, 83
Brown, Frederic, 84
Brundage, Margaret, 85
Brunner, John Kilian Houston, 85
Bryant, Edward, 88
Budrys, Algis, 88
Bulmer, H. Kenneth, 89
Burke, Marty, 420
Burroughs, Edgar Rice, 91
Busby, F. M., 94
Butler, Octavia E., 95

Cabell, James Branch, 95
Caltech Stock Company, 419
Campbell, John Woods, Jr., 95
Campbell, Ramsey, 97
Canty, Thomas, 98
Capek, Karel, 98
Captain Future, 293
Card, Orson Scott, 98
Carr, John Dickson, 99
Carroll, Lewis, 100
Carr, Terry, 99, 457–458, 460
Carter, Linwood Vrooman, 100, 459
Cartier, Edd, 103
Chalker, Jack Laurence, 103
Chambers, Robert William, 104
Chandler, Arthur Bertram, 105
Charnas, Suzy McKee, 106
Cherryh, C. J., 106
Chesterton, Gilbert Keith, 107
Childs-Helton, Barry, 420
Childs-Helton, Sally, 420
Chipping, and value, 28
Christopher, John, 108
Claremont, Christopher S., 109
Clarke, Arthur Charles, 109
Clemens, Samuel Langhorne. *See*
    Twain, Mark
Clement, Hal, 110
Cogswell, Theodore Rose, 111
Collectibles bags, 20–21
Collier, John, 111
Comet Stories, 294
Comic books
    book form, 392–393
    Elfquest, 390–391
    Heavy Metal, 391–392
    sources of information, 390
    Unknown Worlds of Science Fiction,
       392
Comics Buyer's Guide, 22, 394

Conklin, Groff, 112
Conventions
  collecting source, 16–18
  recordings of, 425–428
Cosmic Science Fiction, 295
Cosmic Science Stories, 376
Cosmic Stories, 295
Cosmos Science Fiction and Fantasy,
  295
Coulson, Juanita, 421
Coven 13, 296
Cowper, Richard, 112
Coye, Lee Brown, 113
Crosby, Harry C., Jr. *See* Anvil,
  Christopher
Crowley, John, 113

Dahl, Roald, 114
David, Peter Allen, 114
Davidson, Avram, 114
Davis, Meg, 419, 421
Davison, Peter, *Doctor Who*, 403
Davis, Richard, 457
Dean, Roger, 115
de Camp, Lyon Sprague, 115
Dehorn Crew, The, 419, 421
Delany, Samuel Ray, 118
del Rey, Judy-Lynn, 119
del Rey, Lester, 120, 459
Derleth, August William, 121
Destinies, 296
DeWeese, Gene, 122
Dickinson, Peter, 125
Dick, Philip Kendred, 123
Dickson, Gordon Rupert, 125
Di Fate, Vincent, 127
Digest magazines, American magazines,
  275
Dikty, T. E., 456
Dillon, Diane, 128
Dillon, Leo, 128
Disch, Thomas Michael, 128
Doctor Who
  Baker, Colin episodes, 403–404
  Baker, Tom episodes, 401–403
  Davison, Peter episodes, 403
  Doctor Who magazine, 397, 404
  Hartnell, William episodes, 398–399
  McCoy, Sylvester episodes, 404
  missing episodes, 396
  novelization, 396–397
  Pertwee, Jon episodes, 400–401

  related books, 397
  Troughton, Patrick episodes, 399
Dodgson, Charles Lutwidge. *See*
  Carroll, Lewis
Dog-eared pages, and value, 28
Donaldson, Stephen R., 128
Doyle, Sir Arthur Conan, 129
Dozois, Gardner F., 129, 459–460
Drama
  Doctor Who, 395–404
  Man From U.N.C.L.E., The, 414–415
  movies, 394
  Star Trek, 394–395, 404–413
  Star Wars, 413–414
Dream World, 296
Drenkel, Roy Gerald, Jr., 173
Drew, Dennis, 421
Dunsany, Lord, 130
Dust jackets, 25–26
Dynamic Science Fiction, 297
Dynamic Science Stories, 297

Ecklar, Julia, 421
Eddison, Eric Rucker, 131
Edmondson, G. C., 131
Effinger, George Alec, 132
Eklund, Gordon, 132
Elfquest, 394–395
Elgin, Suzette Haden, 418, 421
Ellison, Harlan, 133, 392
Elwood, Roger, 136
Emshwiller, Edmund Alexander, 136
*Encyclopedia of Science Fiction and
  Fantasy, The* (Tuck), 469
Endore, Guy, 136
Etchison, Dennis, 137

Fading, and value, 28
Fair condition, 24–25
Famous Fantastic Mysteries, 297
Famous Science Fiction, 299
Fandom Directory (Hopkins and
  Hopkins), 468
Fantastic, 299
Fantastic Adventures, 302
Fantastic Adventures Yearbook, 303
Fantastic Novels, 304
Fantastic Science Fiction, 304
Fantastic Science Fiction Stories, 299
Fantastic Story Magazine, 304
Fantastic Story Quarterly, 304
Fantastic Universe, 305

Fantasy, 376
Fantasy and Science Fiction, 306
Fantasy Book, 306
Fantasy Fiction, 307
Fantasy Magazine, 307
Fantasy Quarterly #1, 395
Fantasy Stories, 307
Fantasy Tales, 376
Fanzines, 37
  tapes, 428
Farmer, Philip Jose, 137
Farran, Randy, 422
Ferman, Edward L., 140
Filksongs, 417–418
  audio tape, 419–425
  records, 419
  videotapes, 418
  See also specific artists.
Fine condition, 24, 49, 276
Finlay, Virgil, 140
Finney, Charles Grandison, 140
Finney, Jack, 143
Fish, Leslie, 419, 422
*Flash Gordon Strange Adventure
    Magazine*, 308
Flying Saucers from Other Worlds, 308
Flynt, Clif, 422
Forgotten Fantasy, 308
Foster, Alan Dean, 143
Foundation, recording, 429
Foxing, and value, 28
Frankenstein Unbound, recording, 429
Frazetta, Frank, 144
Freas, Frank Kelly, 145
From the Hells Beneath the Hells,
    recording, 430
From Unknown Worlds, 356
Future Combined with Science Fiction,
    308
*Future Combined with Science Fiction
    Stories*, 309
Future Fantasy and Science Fiction,
    308–309
Future Fiction, 308
Future Science Fiction, 376
Futuristic Science Stories, 376
Futuristic Stories, 377

Galaxy Science Fiction, 310
Galaxy Science Fiction Novels, 313
Galileo, 314
Gallagher, Diana, 422

Gamma, 315
Garrett, Randall, 146
Gaughan, Jack, 146
Gernsback, Hugo, 147
Gervais, Steve, 148
Ghost Stories, 315
Gibbons, Dave, 393
Gibson, William, 148
Godwin, Parke, 148
Golden Fleece, 315
Gold, Horace L., 148
Gonna Roll the Bones, recording, 430
Good condition, 24, 48, 275
Gorey, Edward, 149
Goulart, Ronald Joseph, 149
Gould, Robert, 152
Grant, Charles L., 152
Gravely, Robert Bloch, recording, 429
Great Broads of the Galaxy, The, 422
Great Science Fiction, 316
Great Science Fiction Stories, 354
Greenberg, Martin Harry, 153, 461
Green Hills of Earth, The, recording,
    430
Gunn, James Edwin, 153

Haggard, Sir Henry Rider, 154
Haining, Peter, 155
Hake's Americana & Collectibles, 17,
    22
Haldeman, Joe William, 155
Hamilton, Edmond Moore, 156
Harlan!, recording, 430
Harrison, Harry, 157, 457
Hartnell, William, *Doctor Who*, 398–
    399
Haunt of Horror, The, 316
Hayes, Frank, 422
Heavy Metal, 395–396
Heinlein, Robert Anson, 158
Henderson, Zenna, 160
Herbert, Frank, 161
Hildebrandt, Gregory, 162
Hildebrandt, Timothy, 162
*History of the Hugo, Nebula, and
    International Fantasy Awards, A*
    (Franson and De Vore), 432, 468
Hodgson, William Hope, 162
Horror Sex Tales, 317
Howard, Robert E., 162
How Fear Came, recording, 430
Hubbard, Lafayette Ronald, 165

Hugo Awards
   collections of award-winning works,
      454
   listing of winners, 432–444
Huxley, Aldous, 166

If Worlds of Science Fiction, 317
Imagination, 318
Imaginative Tales, 319
Impulse, 377
Index of Science Fiction Magazines, The
      (Metcalf), 468
Index on the Weird & Fantastica in
      Magazines (Day), 467
Index to Science Fiction Anthologies
      and Collections (Contento), 467
Index to the Science-Fiction Magazines
      (Day), 467
Infinity, 320
Infinity Science Fiction, 320
International SF, 320
Interzone, 377
Isaac Asimov Recorded Library, The,
      recording, 429
Isaac Asimov's Science Fiction
      Anthology, 321
Isaac Asimov's Science Fiction
      Magazine, 321

Jackson, Shirley, 166
Jacob, Piers Anthony Dillingham. *See*
      Anthony, Piers
Jakes, John William, 167
Jeff Wayne's Musical Version of The War
      of the Worlds, recording, 431
Jenkins, Will F. *See* Leinster, Murray
Joanna Russ Interpreting Her Stories,
      recording, 430
Johnson, Crockett, 392
Jones, Heather Rose, 422
Jones, Jeffrey, 168

Kaye, Marvin, 168
Keyes, Daniel, 168
Kingslight, Kathleen, 423
King, Stephen, 169
Kirk, Russell, 170
Klover, Kristoph, 423
Knight, Damon, 170
Koontz, Dean Ray, 171
Kornbluth, Cyril M., 172
Kotzwinkle, William, 173

Kress, Nancy, 173
Kurtz, Katherine, 173
Kuttner, Henry, 174
Kyle, David A., 175

Lafferty, Raphael Aloysius, 175
L. A. Filkharmonics, 423
Lanier, Sterling E., 176
Last Wave, 322
Laumer, John Keith, 176
Lee, Tanith, 178
Le Guin, Ursula Kroeber, 179
Leiber, Fritz Reuter, Jr., 180
Leinster, Murray, 182
Lewis, Clive Staples, 184
Library copies, and value, 28
Life and Future Times of Jack the
      Ripper, The, recording, 429
Linebarger, Paul Myron. *See* Smith,
      Cordwainer
Locus, 45, 469
London, Jack, 184
Long, Frank Belknap, 185
Longyear, Barry B., 186
Loose bindings, and value, 28
Lottery and Other Stories, The,
      recording, 430
Lovecraft, Howard Phillips, 186
Lupoff, Richard Allen, 188
Lynn, Elizabeth A., 189

MacAvoy, R. A., 190
McCaffrey, Anne Inez, 190
McCarthy, Shawna, 191
McCoy, Sylvester, *Doctor Who*, 408
MacDonald, John Dann, 191
McIntyre, Vonda N., 191
McKenna, Richard Milton, 193
McKillip, Patricia, 193
MacLean, Katherine Anne, 193
McQuillan, Cynthia, 423
Magabook, 322
Magafiles, 21
Magazine holders, 21
Magazine of Fantasy, 322
Magazine of Fantasy and Science
      Fiction, The, 322
Magazine of Horror, 325
Magic Carpet, 330
Mail-order firms, collecting source,
      17
Maitz, Don, 194

Man From U.N.C.L.E., The
  authors, 414–415
  paperbacks (Ace), 415–416
Maraschiello, Bill, 423
Mar, Kathy, 423
Markings, and value, 28
Martian Chronicles, The, recording, 429
Martin, George R. R., 194
Marvel Science Fiction, 326
Marvel Science Stories, 326
Marvel Stories, 326
Marvel Tales, 326
Mason, Mary, 423
Matheson, Richard Burton, 194
Mayors, The, recording, 429
Merril, Judith, 195, 456
Merritt, Abraham, 196
Middleton, Margaret, 423
Miller, Walter Michael, Jr., 196
Mimsy Were the Borogoves, recording, 430
Mint condition, 23–24, 49, 276
Miracle Science and Fantasy Stories, 327
Moorcock, Michael, 198
Moore, Alan, 393
Moore, Catherine Lucille 201
Moskowitz, Samuel, 202
Most of Winnie-the-Pooh, The, recording, 430
Most Thrilling Science Fiction Ever Told, The, 327
Mundy, Talbot, 202
Munn, Harold Warner, 203
Murry, John Middleton, Jr. *See* Cowper, Richard
Mysterious Traveler Magazine, The, 328
Mysterious Traveler Mystery Reader, The, 328

Nebula Awards
  collections of award-winning works, 454–455
  listing of winners, 445–449
Nebula Science Fiction, 377
New Destinies, 328
New Worlds, 328 378
New Worlds Anthologies, 380
New Worlds Quarterly, 329
New Worlds Science Fiction Magazine, 329

Night Cry, 329
Niven, Larry, 203
Nolan, William Francis, 204
Norman, John, 205
Norton, Andre, 206
Nourse, Alan Edward, 209
Nowlan, Philip Francis, 209

Odyssey, 329
Official Overstreet Comic Book Price Guide (Overstreet), 394
Offutt, Andrew J., 210
Oliver, Symmes Chadwick, 210
Ones Who Walk Away From Omelas, The, recording 430
Orbit Science Fiction, 329
Oriental Stories, 330
Orwell, George, 211
Oscar Wilde Fairy Tales, recording, 431
Other Worlds, 330
Other Worlds Science Fiction, 330
Out of This World Adventures, 333
Outworlds #50, 428

Page, Gerald W., 457
Palmer, Raymond A., 211
Pangborn, Edgar, 211
Panshin, Alexei, 211
Paperback magazines, American magazines, 275
Paul, Frank R., 212
Peake Mervyn, 213
Perry Rhodan, 333
Pertwee, Jon, *Doctor Who*, 400–401
Phantom, 380
Pini, Richard, 213
Pini, Wendy, 213
Piper, Henry Beam, 213
Planet Stories, 334
Poe, Edgar Allan, 214
Pohl, Frederik, 214, 458
Poor condition, 25
Popular Science Fiction, 380
Pournelle, Jerry, 216
Prather, Anne Harlan, 424
Price, E. Hoffman, 217
Pulp magazines, American magazines, 275

Quark, 337
Quinn, Seabury Grandin, 217

Raymond, Alex, 218
Reamy, Tom, 218
Recordings
  convention/anthology recordings,
    429–432
  filksongs, 417–419
  spoken-word tapes, 428–431
Rein, Chuck, 419
Reluctant Dragon, The, recording, 430
Review editions, and value, 31
Review slip, and value, 31
Reynolds, Mack, 219
Rigel Science Fiction, 337
Robert Silverberg Reads, recording, 430
Roberts, Keith, 220
Robinson, Frank Malcolm, 221
Robinson, Jane, 424
Robinson, Kim Stanley, 221
Robinson, Spider, 221
Rocket Stories, 337
*Rod Serling's The Twilight Zone
    Magazine*, 337
Rogow, Roberta, 424
Rohmer, Sax, 222
Roper, Bill, 424
Russell, Eric Frank, 224
Russ, Joanna, 223

Saberhagen, Fred Thomas, 224
Sagan, Carl, 226
Saha, Arthur W., 460
St. Clair, Margaret, 226
Saki, 226
Satellite Science Fiction, 338
Saturn, 338
Schiff, Stuart David, 227
Schmitz, James H., 227
Schoenherr, John, 227
Science Detective Monthly, 343
Science Fantasy, 339, 381
Science-Fantasy, 381
Science Fantasy Yearbook, 339
Science Fiction, 339
Science Fiction Achievement Awards.
    See Hugo Awards
Science Fiction Adventure Classics, 340
Science Fiction Adventures, 339–340,
    382
Science Fiction Adventures Classics,
    340
Sciencefiction and Fantasy Pseudonyms
    (McGhan), 468

Science Fiction Book Review Index
    (Hall), 468
Science Fiction Chronicle, 45, 469
Science Fiction Classics, 340
Science Fiction Digest, 341, 382
Science Fiction Encyclopedia, The
    (Nicholls), 468
Science fiction/fantasy
  history of, 32–39
    best growth period, 37
    fan involvement (fanzines), 37–38
    first publisher, 33–34
    movies/television, 36–37
    serialized stories, 34–35
    specialized publishers, 38
  market, 40–41
    hot items, 41
Science fiction/fantasy collectibles
  artwork, 17–19
    specialists in, 18
  book-club editions, cautions about, 49
  collectors guides, *Locus*, 10–11, 469
  defects, 26–29
    avoiding repairs, 26
    chipping, 28
    dog-eared pages, 28
    fading, 28
    foxing, 28
    library copies, 28
    loose bindings, 28
    markings, 28
    water damage, 29
  dust jackets, 25–26
  enhanced value
    autographed copies, 29–31
    review editions, 31
    review slip, 31
  grading, 23–25
    fair condition, 24–25
    fine condition, 24, 49, 276
    good condition, 24, 48, 275
    mint condition, 23–24, 49, 276
    poor condition, 25
    very good condition, 24, 48, 275–
      276
  identification of editions, guidelines,
    45
  investment factors, 43–44
  methods of collecting
    by artist, 43
    by author, 43
    by magazine, 42

Science fiction/fantasy collectibles (cont.)
  reference material, 467–469
  selling collection, 21–22
  sources for, 15–17
    auctions, 17
    Books in Print, 16
    conventions, 16–17
    mail-order firms, 17
    specialized bookshops, 16
  storage of, 20–21
    collectibles bags, 20–21
    magazine holders, 21
  terms/definitions related to, 464–467
  types of print material, 7–10
    alternate universes, 8
    elves/gnomes/fairies, 8
    holocaust, 8
    invisibility, 8
    lost civilizations, 8–9
    myth, 9
    space exploration, 9
    time travel, 9
    vampires, 10
    werewolves, 10
  unique material, 462–463
  what to collect, 12–15, 19
Science Fiction Greats, 316
Science Fiction Hall of Fame,
    collections of award-winning
    works, 455
Science Fiction Handbook (de Camp),
    467
Science Fiction Handbook, Revised (de
    Camp), 467
Science Fiction Library, 382
Science Fiction Monthly, 383
Science Fiction Plus, 341
Science Fiction Quarterly, 342
Science Fiction Stories, 342
Science Fiction Yearbook, 344
Science Stories, 330
Science Wonder Quarterly, 343
Science Wonder Stories, 367
Scithers, George, 228
Scoops, 383
Selected Science Fiction, 384
Serling, Rod, 228
Sex Tales, 343
SF Digest, 341
S.F. Greats, 316
SF Impulse, 377
SF Yearbook, 344

Shambleau, recording, 430
Shaw, Bob, 229
Shea, Michael, 229
Sheckley, Robert, 230
Sheldon, Alice. *See* Tiptree, James, Jr.
Sheldon, Raccoona. *See* Tiptree, James,
    Jr.
Shelley, Mary Wollstonecraft, 230
Shepard, Lucius, 231
Shock, 344
Short, Linda, 424
Silverberg, Robert, 231, 455
Simak, Clifford Donald, 234
Sky Worlds, 344
Smith, Clark Ashton, 235
Smith, Cordwainer, 236
Smith, Edward Elmer, 236
Smith, George Oliver, 238
Smith, Thorne, 238
Space Adventures, 344
Space Fact and Fiction, 384
Space Science Fiction, 345
Space Science Fiction Magazine, 345
Space Stories, 345
Space Travel, 319
Spaceway, 346
Specialized bookshops, collecting
    source, 16
Spinrad, Norman Richard, 239
Spoken-word tapes, 428–431
Stapledon, Olaf, 240
Stareagle, Valondis, 424
Starlinglathe, Edward, 424
Star Science Fiction Magazine, 346
Startling Mystery, 346
Startling Stories, 347
Star Trek
  animated cartoons, 408
  books
    Alan Dean Foster "Log" numbered
      books, 410
    Bantam and Pocket editions, 411
    fotonovels (Bantam), 410
    James Blish numbered series, 409–
      410
    nonfiction, 413
    timescape, 411–412
  films, 408
  games, 413
  New Generation, The, 408–409
  Seasons I through III, 405–407
  Star Trek Concordance, 405

Star Wars
  books, 413
  films, 413
  nonfiction, 414
Sternbach, Rick, 240
Stevens, Beth, 424
Stevenson, Robert Louis, 241
Stirring Science Stories, 348
Stoker, Bram, 241
Strange Adventures, 384
Strange Fantasy, 348
Strange Stories, 349
Strangest Stories Ever Told, The, 349
Strange Tales, 349, 384
Stubbs, Harry Clement. *See* Clement, Hal
Sturgeon, Theodore, 241
Subscriptions to magazines, addresses, 273
Supernatural Stories, 384
Super-Science Fiction, 349
Super Science Novels Magazine, 350
Super Science Stories, 350
Suspense, 350
Sutton, Bill, 425
Swann, Thomas Burnett, 246
Sword & Sorcery Annual, 353

Tales of Magic & Mystery, 353
Tales of the Frightened, 354
Tales of Tomorrow, 385
Tales of Wonder, 385
Technical Difficulties, 425
10 Story Fantasy, 354
Tenn, William, 247
Theodore Sturgeon Reads His Stories, recording, 430
Thrilling Science Fiction, 327
Thrilling Science Fiction Adventures, 327
Thrilling Wonder Stories, 367
Thrills, Inc., 385
Through the Looking Glass, recording, 429
Tiptree, James, Jr., 247
Tolkien, J. R. R., 248
Tops in Science Fiction, 354
Treasury of Great Science Fiction Stories, 354
Troughton, Patrick, *Doctor Who*, 399
Tucker, Arthur Wilson, 249
Tuttle, Lisa, 249

Twain, Mark, 249
Two Complete Science-Adventure Books, 355
Two Complete Science Adventure Novels, 355

Uncanny Stories, 355
Uncanny Tales, 386
Uncle Albert's Electric Talking Fanzine, 428
Universe Science Fiction, 330, 356
Unknown, 356
Unknown Worlds, 356
Unknown Worlds of Science Fiction, 396

Vance, Jack, 250
Vanguard Science Fiction, 357
van Vogt, Alfred Elton, 252
Vargo Statten British Science Fiction Magazine, 386
Vargo Statten Science Fiction Magazine, 386
Varley, John Herbert, 254
Venture Science Fiction, 357
Verne, Jules, 254
Vertex, 357
Very good condition, 24, 48, 275–276
Videotapes, filksongs, 418
Vinge, Joan D., 255
Vinge, Vernor Steffan, 255
Vision of Tomorrow, 388
Vonnegut, Kurt, Jr., 255
Vortex, 388
Vortex Science Fiction, 358

Wagner, Karl Edward, 256, 458
Waldrop, Howard, 257
Wandrei, Donald, 257
Water damage, and value, 29
Watson, Ian, 257
Watt-Evans, Lawrence, 257
Wayne, Phil, 425
Weber, Chris, 425
Weinbaum, Stanley Grauman, 258
Weird and Occult Library, 388
Weird Heroes, 358
Weird Tales, 360
Weird Terror Tales, 367
Weird World, 388
Wellman, Manly Wade, 258
Wells, Herbert George, 259
Wessels, Mary Ellen, 425

Whelan, Michael, 261
White, James, 262
White, Ted Edward, 263
White, Terence Hanbury, 263
White, William Anthony Parker. *See* Boucher, Anthony
Who Goès There (Rock), 469
Wilhelm, Kate, 264
Williamson, Jack, 264
Willis, Connie, 266
Willson, Karen, 425
Wilson, F. Paul, 266
Wilson, Gahan, 266
Wilson, Janet, 425
Wilson, Richard, 267
Witchcraft & Sorcery, 296
Wolfe, Gene, 267
Wollheim, Donald A., 457–458
Wollheim, Donald Allen, 268

Wonders of the Spaceways, 388
Wonder Stories, 367, 369
Wonder Story Annual, 369
World Fantasy Awards
  collections of award-winning works, 455
  listing of winners, 450–454
World of If, 370
Worlds Beyond, 370
Worlds of Fantasy, 372, 388
Worlds of If Science Fiction, 317
Worlds of the Universe, 389
Worlds of Tomorrow, 372
Wylie, Philip Gordon, 269
Wyndham, John, 269

Yarbro, Chelsea Quinn, 270

Zahn, Timothy, 271
Zelazny, Roger, 271

About the Authors

Don and Maggie Thompson are co-editors of *Comics Buyer's Guide,* the weekly trade journal and collectors' newspaper of the comic-book industry. In addition to being known through their work in the comics field, they are long-time science-fiction writers, fans, and collectors.

Don's first published fanzine work earned a favorable review in the science-fiction magazine *Imagination* in the 1950s, and he has served as a Nebula Trustee for the Science Fiction Writers of America. Maggie's mother is a science-fiction writer, and Maggie attended her first World Science Fiction Convention in Cleveland in 1955. They have co-written stories published in comic-book science-fiction publications.

Don and Maggie met June 8, 1957, at a picnic of science-fiction fans and professionals at the home of writer Basil Wells. They began a correspondence, co-edited fanzines, and were married June 23, 1962. Since that time, they have published fanzines, attended conventions, collected books and magazines, and generally been active in the field. In the jargon of long-time fans, "fanac" is fan activity, which one pundit once defined as "anything two fans do together." By that definition, their lives have been almost nothing but fanac for more than twenty-five years.

They have two children, Valerie (born two years to the day before man set foot on the moon) and Stephen (born three years and 12 days after man set foot on the moon).

COMICS ARE *BIG* BUSINESS!!

Robert Overstreet, the recognized authority on comic book values, has made it *his* business to provide a *new, exciting* edition of the *Comic Book Price Guide Companion!*

Three superheroes bursting out of a brick wall . . . onto the *Companion*'s cover! The artistry of John Romita, a *complete* section on BIG LITTLE BOOKS . . . these are just a few of the special features that make this book the best!

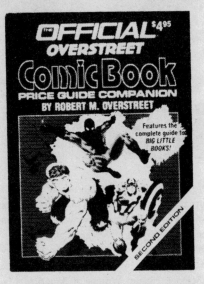